Contextual Theology for Latin America

Liberation Themes in Evangelical Perspective

Commendations

A few years ago two French evangelicals - Sébastien Fath and Jean-Paul Willaine - produced a major study entitled *Une autre manière d'être chrétien en France*. Sharon Heaney is to be commended for her lucid and detailed analysis of 'another way of doing Christian theology in Latin America'. She writes with a sympathetic understanding of the problems and opportunities confronting Latin American evangelicals, including their awareness of the need for a holistic missiology in the face of enormous social and economic needs. Much has been said about the importance of 'contextualization' in theology, not least in the South American scene. Dr. Heaney shows how the historical and cultural context has influenced the shape of Latin American evangelical theology, and also how this theology has sought to address itself to the context. Literature on the subject of Liberation Theology has mushroomed over the past few decades. It is an area in which it is very difficult to make an original contribution and Sharon Heaney has succeeded in doing just that.
Dr Maurice Dowling Lecturer in Church History and Historical Theology, Institute of Theology, Queen's University, Belfast.

This is a book which I will recommend to my students as we try to come to grips with the global context of today's theology and missiology. Sharon Heaney provides a very lucid contribution to our understanding of the developments within the Latin American evangelical Church context today.
Rev. Sonia Jackson Director of Training and Lecturer in Missions, London School of Theology.

Whereas Latin American Liberation Theology is renowned throughout the worldwide Christian community, a fresh expression of evangelical mission theology from the same continent is less well known. In this book, Sharon Heaney redresses the balance. She shows why this latter pattern of theological thought offers a new focus and process for the renewal of theology that successfully combines faithfulness to the full Biblical message with sensitive awareness of the historical and social reality of a turbulent, suffering continent. Her comprehensive, sympathetic and discerning treatment of this theological approach deserves to be read widely, pondered deeply and enacted practically.
J. Andrew Kirk, author of What is Mission? Theological Explorations and Mission under Scrutiny: Confronting Current Challenges.

PATERNOSTER THEOLOGICAL MONOGRAPHS

For over thirty-five years the Latin American Theological Fraternity (now *Fellowship;* FTL, its acronym in Spanish) has been actively engaged in articulating an evangelical and liberating response to a wide variety of socioeconomic, political, cultural, and religious issues that affect the life and mission of the church in Latin America. Without denying the contextual character of the FTL, one is safe in claiming that this theology has very much to say to Christians all over the world. That being the case, many readers will be deeply thankful to Dr. Sharon Heaney for providing a first-class systematic and comprehensive review of the historical background and the main themes of this most significant theological movement in Latin American — and indeed, in the world — today.

C. Rene Padilla, International President of Tearfund, Emeritus President of the Kairos Foundation in Buenos Aires, Argentina.

Latin America is known as the home of Liberation Theology. But prominent among the voices raised at the celebrated Lausanne Congress on World Evangelization were those of Latin American evangelicals. Well-researched, clearly-written, informative and illuminating, Sharon Heaney's study of evangelical theology in Latin America is a significant contribution to our understanding of the contemporary church and its mission.

Stephen N. Williams Professor of Systematic Theology, Union College, Queen's University, Belfast.

PATERNOSTER THEOLOGICAL MONOGRAPHS

A full listing of all titles in this series and Paternoster Biblical Monographs
appears at the close of this book

PATERNOSTER THEOLOGICAL MONOGRAPHS

Contextual Theology for Latin America

Liberation Themes in Evangelical Perspective

Sharon E. Heaney

Foreword by Samuel Escobar

WIPF & STOCK · Eugene, Oregon

Wipf and Stock Publishers
199 W 8th Ave, Suite 3
Eugene, OR 97401

Contextual Theology for Latin America
Liberation Themes in Evangelical Perspective
By Heaney, Sharon E.
Copyright©2008 Paternoster
ISBN 13: 978-1-60608-016-0
Publication date 6/6/2008
Previously published by Paternoster, 2008

PATERNOSTER THEOLOGICAL MONOGRAPHS

Series Preface

In the West the churches may be declining, but theology — serious, academic (mostly doctoral level) and mainstream orthodox in evaluative commitment — shows no sign of withering on the vine. This series of *Paternoster Theological Monographs* extends the expertise of the Press especially to first-time authors whose work stands broadly within the parameters created by fidelity to Scripture and has satisfied the critical scrutiny of respected assessors in the academy. Such theology may come in several distinct intellectual disciplines — historical, dogmatic, pastoral, apologetic, missional, aesthetic and no doubt others also. The series will be particularly hospitable to promising constructive theology within an evangelical frame, for it is of this that the church's need seems to be greatest. Quality writing will be published across the confessions — Anabaptist, Episcopalian, Reformed, Arminian and Orthodox — across the ages — patristic, medieval, reformation, modern and counter-modern — and across the continents. The aim of the series is theology written in the twofold conviction that the church needs theology and theology needs the church — which in reality means theology done for the glory of God.

To
Robert and Sam

Contents

Chapter 5
Contextual Hermeneutics: The Use of Scripture by Liberationists and Evangelicals

Chapter 6
General Themes in Latin American Contextual Theology

Chapter 7
The Search for a Latin American Evangelical Christology

Chapter 8
The Search for a Latin American Evangelical Ecclesiology

Foreword

Doctor Sharon Heaney has honoured me by asking for a foreword to her excellent thesis *Contextual Theology for Latin America: Liberation Themes in Evangelical Perspective*. Though it may appear as a lack of modesty to write a foreword to a work in which one is among the subjects of study, I have agreed to do so because I have come to appreciate her work and I think it should be read by anyone interested in contemporary theological developments.

Latin America is a region of the world in which there has been a continuing and remarkable growth of Evangelical Christianity. As this kind of relatively young form of Protestantism comes of age, in the context of a five centuries old declining Christendom, the search for theological expression within it has faced unique challenges. Colonial Christendom in Latin America did not produce any contextual theological reflection of its own, limiting itself to copy and repeat the patterns of thought of Iberian Roman Catholicism, following the reactionary line of the Council of Trent. Her rapid decline and the acute social crisis of the 1960s imposed a self-critical agenda on the dominant Roman Catholic church, and liberation theologies were the first attempts by Latin American Catholic thinkers to articulate an expression of their faith in a contextual manner. Was the young Evangelical movement going to follow a similar course of four centuries of colonial theology before a contextual effort appeared? That was the dilemma faced by my generation. Theology had been articulated in London, Boston, Texas, Nashville or Edinburgh and good Latin American Evangelicals had to translate it, and pass it on to the new growing number of ministers, leading lay persons and seminary professors. However such imported theological discourse was insufficient and inadequate for our daily pastoral and evangelistic practice. In order to think our faith, rooting our reflection on the Word of God but responding to the demands of our context, a group of us came together and founded the Latin American Theological Fraternity in 1970.

Dr. Heaney thinks that to a certain degree we succeeded in our efforts and she gave herself to the painstaking task of reading an incredible amount of material, selecting some thinkers and trying to detect some lines of thought, some theological patterns. Immersed as we are in the day to day demands of our ministries we ourselves have several times expressed the need to look back and work in that task of collating, gleaning and trying to find a coherent structure, as Dr. Heaney says, in our collective thinking. However none of us have done it. The European or North American reader has to remember that the doing of theology in Latin America does not take place in the universities. It is, as Orlando Costas liked to say, a theology of the road, done in haste, with a sense of urgency and not much time for perfectionism. I hope my Latin American colleagues will agree with me that Dr. Heaney's effort has been successful and will be a point of reference for our own efforts in the future. Her bibliography is most useful and I find very valuable her choice of dominant issues and general themes. Most of all I appreciate in Dr. Heaney's work her effort to grasp our intentions, our perception of our own world, and our effort to articulate a contextual expression of our Evangelical faith. I also hope that her book will be soon translated and published in Spanish.

Samuel Escobar
Valencia, Spain,
August 2006.

Acknowledgments

Professor Stephen Williams, who supervised my PhD research, deserves my sincere thanks for his ability to both encourage and correct my fledgling attempts at grappling with Latin American theology. His integrity in seeking understanding in faith will stay with me as an example of true Christian scholarship.

I am indebted to the staff and students of ISEDET in Buenos Aires for their warm welcome and assistance during my visit in June 2003. In particular, I am thankful for the practical help given to me by the librarian Marisa Strizzi and the student assistant Elizabeth Jones.

I am most thankful to the theologians I have met who clearly demonstrated by their grace, generosity and humour that the gospel can be grounded in the everyday reality of life. I had the privilege of meeting Dr. José Míguez Bonino who graciously agreed to be interviewed. I am deeply appreciative of Dr. René Padilla who generously provided accommodation for me at the *Kairós* Foundation, afforded me use of the *Kairós* library and the Latin American Theological Fraternity archives, and freely gave of his time and insight.

In September 2003 I met with Rev. Dr. John Stott and Rev. Dr. Andrew Kirk. The attitudes of both John Stott and Andrew Kirk, in the past and in the present, bear testimony to the enrichment possible through fellowship with Christian thinkers in Latin America. I am thankful to Dr. Stott for his able recollection of significant events in the recent history of international evangelicalism. I would like to thank Dr. Kirk for his perceptive insight into the early years of the Fraternity. Our meeting deepened my understanding of the evangelical engagement with the theology of liberation and I am most grateful to him.

I am deeply appreciative of Dr. Samuel Escobar and his wife Lilly, who displayed their kindness and hospitality to me during my visit to Valencia in April 2004. Samuel Escobar made his personal library available to me, patiently related the history and development of theology in Latin America, and gave constructive comment on the direction of my work. I was greatly honoured and humbled when he agreed to write the foreword to this book.

My family have been constant in their support and open in their enthusiasm, for which I am most grateful. Finally, I express my deepest thanks to my husband, Rev. Dr. Robert S. Heaney. His enduring patience, steadfast encouragement, and selfless commitment have sustained me to see this project through to fruition. Between the completion of my research and the publication of this book our son Sam was born. Consequently, it is with gratitude that I dedicate this book to Robert and Sam.

Abbreviations

CA	*Acción Católica* Catholic Action
CDP	*Partido Cristiano Demócrato* Christian Democrat Party
CEB	*Comunidades Eclesiales de Base* Base Ecclesial Communities
CELA	*Conferencia Evangélica Latinoamericana* Latin American Evangelical Conference
CELAM	*Consejo Episcopal Latino Americano* Latin American Episcopal Council
CLADE	*Congreso Latinoamericano de Evangelización* Latin American Congress on Evangelism
CLAI	*Consejo Latinoamericano de Iglesias* Latin American Council of Churches
CLASC	*Confederación Latina Americana* *de Sindicatas Cristianas* Latin American Catholic Trade Union Movement
CONELA	*Confraternidad Evangélica Latinoamericana* Latin American Evangelical Confraternity
FTL	*Fraternidad Teológica Latinoamericana* Latin American Theological Fraternity
ISAL	*Iglesia y Sociedad en América Latina* Church and Society in Latin America
ISEDET	*Instituto Superior Evangélico de Estudios Teológicos* Evangelical Institute of Higher Theological Education
UNEC	*Unión Nacional de Estudiantes Católicos* National Union of Catholic Students

UNELAM   *Comisión pro Unidad Evangélica Latinoameriana*
                Commission for Latin American Evangelical Unity

CHAPTER 1

Introductions

1.1 Introduction

The fundamental conviction behind this book is that Latin American evangelical theology remains relatively unknown in the West.[1] This study is an attempt to uncover the vitality of such theology through systematic presentation, while taking cognisance of the Latin American context in which communities of faith live and minister. It seeks to present in a coherent manner the insightful theological reflection evident in the work of evangelical theologians who are members of such communities of faith.

It is my contention that the primary significance of the Latin American contribution is in its identification and application of contextual method. In line with the historical tradition of evangelicalism, the scholars dealt with in this work do not focus on faith seeking understanding alone, but rather are committed to an evangelical understanding of faith which engenders authentic evangelical praxis. This book sets out to systematise the thought of key Latin American evangelical theologians, making it accessible to an English-speaking audience. These theologians are seeking liberation for the whole person, by means of the acceptance and application of the message of the gospel. I have chosen, therefore, to structure their theological reflection under the title of "Contextual Theology for Latin America: Liberation themes in Evangelical Perspective". The term *liberation themes*

---

[1] It is recognised that the definition of the term "Latin America" is a complex one. Latin America is a vast geographical region extending from the southern border of the United States to Patagonia. There are also pockets of Latin American presence in North America for various historical and political reasons. There are some who would prefer the term *Iberoamérica* (Iberian America) which stresses the Hispanic and Portuguese elements. Others prefer to use the term *Indoamérica* (Indian America) to stress the indigenous element. To speak of a distinguishable Latin American identity is similarly complex. This study, therefore, follows the example of Samuel Escobar in his article "Catholicism and National Identity in Latin America", *Transformation* 8, no. 3 (1991): 22-30. The term "Latin America" will be used for the sake of clarity but the diversity and complexity of the contrasts inherent in that term are acknowledged from the outset. It should also be made clear at this juncture that while Brazil lies geographically within Latin America, the theologians dealt with in this book are Spanish speakers. In order to set clear boundaries for this book, therefore, Portuguese texts will not be discussed in detail.

refers to those subjects evident in the works of both Latin American evangelicals and liberationists designed to bring about justice, freedom, transformation and authentic Christian community.[2]

In this introduction, I will briefly outline the *background*, the *motivation*, the *scope* and the *purpose* of this study. Firstly, the *background* of this research project stemmed from an initial interest at undergraduate level in the history, politics, culture and literature of Latin America. Hispanic Studies and Theology was a fascinating combination of degree subjects which inevitably exposed me to the theology of liberation, the internationally renowned voice of Latin American theology. Liberation theologians have placed daunting questions before the Christian church regarding the pertinent issues of poverty, oppression and social injustice. One cannot fail to admire such scholars for their courage and for their willingness to face the dangerous consequences of such a theological approach. However, liberation theologians are not the only Latin Americans to take seriously the need for authentic contextual theology.

Secondly, therefore, this book is *motivated* by the desire to gain an understanding of an alternative approach to liberation themes in contextual Latin American theology. Much Western critique of the theology of liberation, in particular, has been little more than the destruction of one set of ideas without the construction of a viable and working alternative. For such Western theologians would consider a coherent theological approach to be already in place. Latin American evangelical theologians, in contrast, recognise the significance of contextual theology developed, not by those who critique from a distance, but by those who critique from within. The focus of this study, therefore, is the contribution to contextual theology made by such evangelical theologians who have personally experienced the hardship of life in Latin America, and thus are those who can empathise with the desperate longing for liberation. The attitude of indifference and apathy which often prevails in Western society is not an option for evangelicals. For it seems uncontroversial to hold that inherent in the very definition of evangelicalism is active practical ministry entwined with serious theological reflection.

The history of the evangelical movement, which will be dealt with in more detail later, illustrates the serious controversy provoked by issues of social responsibility and political involvement. In 1974, now thirty years ago, the Lausanne Consultation proved to be a watershed for the international evangelical community. Lausanne marked the beginning of the public renewal of the evangelical social conscience and gave opportunity for the exploration of evangelical theology on such matters. It is well documented that the contribution made by Latin American evangelical theologians at Lausanne was memorable, provocative and influential. From their position within the Two Thirds World, they spoke with passion, sensitivity and clarity. Since Lausanne, and during subsequent consultations, Latin American

---

[2] It will become clear as this study progresses that evangelicals and liberationists have developed differing understandings of the concept of liberation and the liberation themes dealt with in this work.

evangelical theologians have consistently challenged the international evangelical community, stimulating discussion and provoking international dialogue. It may seem surprising, therefore, to realise that issues debated at Lausanne remain pertinent topics of discussion, and indeed subjects of disagreement today. For this reason, the Latin American evangelical contribution remains decisive.

Despite much positive interaction with the international evangelical community, Latin American evangelical theologians have also faced severe criticism. Western evangelical critique of liberation thought, and indeed of Latin American evangelical theology has often been reactionary and politically charged. Nevertheless, in spite of such criticism, Latin American evangelicals continue to display a sensitivity of approach towards the theology of liberation, and continue to remain consistent in their commitment to evangelical principles.

Thirdly, it is necessary to clearly define the *scope* of this book. For liberation themes within contextual Latin American theology are varied and far-reaching. The main focus of this study, therefore, will be the work of five evangelical scholars.[3] These theologians have been chosen for two reasons: they were founding members of the Latin American Theological Fraternity and therefore are representative of Latin American evangelical theology, and they are theologians who engaged directly with liberation themes. C. René Padilla was born in Ecuador in 1932. Samuel Escobar was born in Peru in 1934. Emilio Antonio Núñez was born in El Salvador in 1923.[4] Orlando E. Costas was born in Puerto Rico in 1942 and died at the age of 45 in 1987.[5] The British theologian J. Andrew Kirk was born in 1937. He lived and worked in Latin America during the years in which the pursuit of contextual theology began.[6] Not only did these scholars respond to the theology of liberation

---

[3] Biographical details of the life and ministry of these evangelical theologians can be found in C. René Padilla, ed., *Hacia una teología evangélica latinoamericana* (San José: Editorial Caribe, 1984). See Orlando E. Costas, "Teológo en la encrucijada", 13-36; Samuel Escobar, "Heredero de la reforma radical", 51-72; Emilio A. Núñez, "Testigo de un nuevo amanecer", 101-112; C. René Padilla, "Siervo de la Palabra", 113-120. See also Adriana Powell, ed., *La aventura de escribir: testimonio de catorce escritores cristianos* (Lima: Ediciones Puma, 2003), in particular Samuel Escobar, "Aprender a vivir y a escribir", 217-229; Emilio A. Núñez, "Mi afición a las letras", 121-136; C. René Padilla, "Un largo aprendizaje", 139-148. A brief biography of each theologian is also presented in Anthony Christopher Smith, "The Essentials of Missiology from the Evangelical Perspective of the 'Fraternidad Teológica Latinoamericana'" (Ph. D. diss., Southern Baptist Theological Seminary, 1983), 303-331.

[4] See Israel Ortiz, "El quehacer teológico de Emilio A. Núñez" in *Teología y misión: perspectivas desde América Latina*, Emilio A. Núñez (San José: Visión Mundial Internacional, 1996), 11-40.

[5] See Samuel Escobar, "In Memory of Orlando E. Costas (1942-1987)", *Missiology: An International Review* XVII, no. 1 (1989): 85-86 and Raúl Fernández Calienes, "Bibliography of the writings of Orlando E. Costas", *Missiology: An International Review* XVII, no. 1 (1989): 87-105.

[6] It would be fair to say that while Andrew Kirk is a British theologian, no study proposing to deal with liberation themes in Latin American evangelical theology would be

but it is vital to recognise that they were also seeking to develop contextual evangelical theology for Latin America at the same time. For this reason, the liberation themes examined in this book are evident in both the theology of liberation and in Latin American evangelical theology. Not only have these scholars made a significant contribution to the development of evangelical theology within Latin America, but also have contributed at an international level.

While Padilla, Escobar, Núñez, Costas and Kirk were all involved in the early years of the Latin American Theological Fraternity, there is no doubt that others have also made significant contributions to the development of evangelical theology in Latin America.[7] For the purpose of this work, however, the five aforementioned theologians have been selected because of their direct interaction with issues of contextual theology and their inevitable engagement with the theology of liberation as a result. It can be argued that because of this emphasis on contextual theology, these theologians chiefly informed the Latin American evangelical mind and influenced the direction of the Fraternity, which in turn would influence evangelicalism across the world. Each scholar, with the exception of Orlando Costas, continues to write and to make a theological contribution today.

No book proposing to deal with Latin American evangelical theology, and in particular liberation themes within such theology, could ignore the invaluable contribution of José Míguez Bonino, the prominent Protestant liberation theologian. It is no exaggeration to say that the work of Míguez Bonino merits the attention of an entire book and indeed in recent years several important pieces of research have focused on his life and ministry.[8] It was a privilege to meet with Míguez Bonino and discuss his work.[9] The significance of his contribution to the theological development within Latin America is appreciated and his work will be referred to at various points throughout this study. However, in the early years of the Latin American Theological Fraternity, the contribution of Míguez Bonino to that group was limited. In more recent years, his relationship with the Fraternity has grown and he is now a highly respected contributor to evangelical discussion. The distinctly evangelical publishing house, *Ediciones Kairós* (part of the *Kairós* Foundation), has

---

complete without reference to his work. It is important to note that the significance of his contribution was acknowledged during the CLADE IV Consultation held in 2000, when public recognition was given to René Padilla, Samuel Escobar and Andrew Kirk as three of the founding members of the Latin American Theological Fraternity. J. Andrew Kirk, interview by author, 25 September 2003, video recording, Lechlade. For the sake of space, transcripts of these interviews have not been included in this book.

[7] Examples of such contributions will be referred to throughout this study and details can be found in the bibliography. Books which have been published by Ediciones Kairós, in Buenos Aires, represent contemporary contributions to Latin American evangelical theology in particular.

[8] See for example Jorge Daniel Weishein, "La dialéctica de la obediencia. La tematización del cambio social en el discurso teológico protestante de José Míguez Bonino entre 1954-1984" (Ph.D. diss. ISEDET, 2000).

[9] José Míguez Bonino, interview by author, 17 June 2003, video recording, Buenos Aires.

also published several of his recent books.[10] The fact that his work is not dealt with in detail is not a comment on his theological position, for Míguez Bonino has clearly expressed the essence of his evangelical commitment. The scope of this book begins with the early contributions to the Latin American Theological Fraternity. In those formative years, Míguez Bonino was more closely associated with liberation theologians than with this group of evangelical theologians. For this reason, he falls outside the scope of this study.[11]

Finally, the *purpose* of this book is twofold. First, this work seeks to set Latin American evangelical theology in historical and cultural context. A greater understanding of the history and culture of the continent in evangelical perspective is necessary for a fuller appreciation of the task undertaken by evangelical theologians. There is no doubt that the colonisation of the New World by the Old, and the periods of revolution and independence which subsequently ensued, have left indelible marks on Latin American society. Similarly, the significance of the role played by the Roman Catholic Church in Latin America should not be underestimated. The evangelical presence on the continent must be examined in the knowledge of the complex relationship between evangelical communities of faith and the society in which these churches exist.

The foundational developments in Latin American evangelical theology can be traced to the period in which the theology of liberation was also developing and flourishing. The shared historical, cultural and societal context and, in particular, the shared recognition of the imposition of insufficient theology for such a context, led to the exposition of liberation themes in both theological perspectives. It is also clear that Latin American evangelical theologians found it necessary, not only to discuss similar issues, but also to critique the dominant theology of liberation itself. For this reason, there will be chapters of this book (two, four, five, six, seven and eight) in which it is most constructive to discuss Latin American evangelical theology in light of its engagement with the theology of liberation. In other chapters (three and nine), however, it will be more constructive to examine Latin American evangelical theology directly, without reference to the theology of liberation. For it would be a serious underestimation of Latin American evangelical theology if it were portrayed

---

[10] The *Kairós* Foundation is an interdenominational Latin American organisation which strives to promote evangelical theological reflection and active forms of practical ministry. The *Kairós* Foundation represents a variety of ministries including a publishing house, library resources, educational initiatives, and a residential centre in the heart of Buenos Aires. See *Fundación Kairós: una comunidad al servicio del reino de Dios y su justicia* (Buenos Aires: Ediciones Kairós, 2002), 8-9. See also C. René Padilla, "Kairós: Formar al pueblo de Dios para la misión integral", *Orientación Cristiana* (October-December 1996): 1-2.

[11] José Míguez Bonino confirmed the sensitive nature of his relationship with other evangelicals in the formative years of the Latin American Theological Fraternity. He acknowledged that at times he had expressed his theological position in a radical manner which led to some misunderstanding. He is careful to assert, however, that the essence of his evangelical faith was never lost. José Míguez Bonino, interview by author, 17 June 2003, video recording, Buenos Aires.

as simply a reaction to liberation thought. This book, therefore, does not set out to be a study or critique of the theology of liberation. Similarly, this book does not claim to be a complete presentation of the historical development of Latin American evangelical theology. Rather, this study seeks to set Latin American evangelical theology in context, which inevitably will incorporate aspects of the interaction with the theology of liberation. The focus of this book, then, will be liberation themes in evangelical perspective, presented in light of the historical and cultural context of Latin America.

Second, this book seeks to provide a systematic presentation of these liberation themes in Latin American evangelical perspective. One significant disadvantage of Latin American evangelical theology is that it is not systematised, as such. Journal articles, consultation papers, lecture notes, sermon notes, chapters within books and individual books are where this theological development is to be found. The bibliography indicates that I have sought to consult such original sources as widely as possible. I would contend that the absence of a systematised presentation of Latin American evangelical theology is the main reason why much of the theological contribution remains relatively unknown. Yet a study of the contribution made, scattered as the work may be, displays consistency of purpose, development of thought and unswerving commitment to the task. There is much to be learned. The originality of this work, therefore, lies in the collation of Latin American evangelical thought, gleaned from a wide examination of texts in Spanish and English, and also in the coherent, structured presentation of this contribution as liberation themes in evangelical perspective. Any translation in reference to a Spanish text, therefore, is my own unless otherwise indicated.

It could be argued that the Latin American evangelical theology examined in this book is not original. It is openly acknowledged that this contribution displays recognisable patterns of evangelical thought. It is also accepted that, to some, this theological reflection may appear bland. It is my contention, however, that the value of this contribution is in the willingness to reassess and reapply traditional concepts. It is in the clarity of an approach which considers ministry to those in need to be a priority. It is in the consistent pursuit of thoroughly biblical theology which will bring hope to a continent in crisis. This is contextual evangelical theology, carried out within the ambiguity, the uncertainty and the instability of what was, and is, Latin America. Therein lies its potency.

1.2 Conspectus

The twofold purpose of this book will be achieved in eight chapters. The broad contours of Latin American history are, in general, well established. In order to present an accurate understanding of Latin American evangelical theology, however, it is important to consider the evangelical perception of the past.[12] In chapter two,

---

[12] In the main, the evangelical understanding of the context does not differ significantly from the standard accounts, which are footnoted for reference. However, a study of the

therefore, I will draw from Latin American evangelical accounts of the historical context of the continent, the immediate context of the twentieth century, and the rise of the theology of liberation. It is hoped that this brief overview of the colonisation of the New World, the commitment to revolution, and the struggle for independence will set the background to the culture and society of contemporary Latin America. The role of the Catholic Church prior to and during the twentieth century will be discussed in an effort to present the immediate context in which the theology of liberation, and indeed serious evangelical theology developed. In Catholicism and Protestantism alike, it was recognised that the imposed Western theology was insufficient: contextual theology for Latin America was essential. It is only with an appreciation of the historical and cultural context that the motivation for this theological task can be properly understood. While it is obvious that the historical context of the theology of liberation brings understanding of the context for Latin American evangelical theology, it is also important to distinguish between the two movements at this point. For evangelical communities of faith held a minority position within Latin American society which cannot be equated with the position held by those within the Catholic Church itself.

Chapter three, therefore, is a specific examination of the context of Latin American evangelicalism. Firstly, as the term "evangelical" can have various connotations, it will be defined in light of the understanding expressed by Latin American evangelical theologians. Latin American evangelical theologians recognise the importance of establishing fundamental principles of evangelicalism in a manner which will bring interdenominational consensus. Secondly, this breadth of Latin American evangelicalism is discussed in a brief overview of the evangelical presence on the continent. This history demonstrates the various streams within Latin American Protestantism, and the significant changes which took place within Protestantism after the Second World War. An understanding of the growth and diversity of Protestantism is important for this book because the Latin American Theological Fraternity was formed in light of this complex phenomenon. Thirdly, the foundation and influence of the Fraternity is examined. For the Fraternity has provided the arena for evangelical theologians across the spectrum to develop contextual theology. The overview of the historical background and the presentation of the contemporary circumstances of Latin America in chapters one and two, demonstrate that the members of the Fraternity are initiators in Latin American theological reflection. Chapter four, therefore, will deal with the methodology employed in this initiation of contextual Latin American theology.

The theologians of liberation considered the method which they employed to be a "new way to do theology." In chapter four, a brief overview of liberation method

---

evangelical accounts is constructive for the purpose of this book, in order to develop an awareness of the evangelical understanding of the history and context in which their theological reflection is taking place. Evangelicals have been misjudged by others in historical readings of the continent, and for this reason they seek to be accurate and fair in their accounts (see 2.2.1).

will be given in order to examine the propositions made for contextual theology. It has been essential for evangelical theologians to respond to these liberationist proposals and it is insightful to deal with evangelical method in light of this interaction. Three significant aspects of liberation methodology will be identified as: the priority attributed to praxis, the priority attributed to the historical context and the priority attributed to ideology. Evangelical theologians affirm that liberationists have made a crucial contribution to theological method. Despite the shared recognition of the need for a contextual approach, however, Latin American evangelical theologians consider this liberationist method to be insufficient and also to be inconsistent with evangelical principles. While acknowledging the significance of praxis, historical circumstances, and ideology within the Latin American context, evangelical theologians seek to keep the Scriptures foundational. They assert, therefore, that praxis must be built upon the authority of Scripture. They contend that the biblical text, not the historical context, must be the point of departure in theological reflection. They hold that any ideological commitment must be assessed in light of the word of God. In the discussion on contextual method, it becomes clear that the issues of biblical authority and biblical interpretation dominate. The pertinence of the issue of biblical authority and the relevance of biblical interpretation to contextual theology is consistently displayed in subsequent chapters of this work. For this reason, it is appropriate that chapter five deal specifically with contextual hermeneutics.

In chapter five, it will be demonstrated that the nature and use of Scripture is a significant aspect of a contextual theology for Latin America. Firstly, fundamental to the debate on contextual theology is the authority attributed to Scripture. This chapter will begin with a brief overview of the difference in the liberationist and evangelical discussion on the subject. While liberation theologians and evangelical theologians both make reference to the Bible, it will be shown that the emphasis on the authority and sufficiency of Scripture distinguishes the theological reflection of the Fraternity. Evangelicals recognised the need for a reapplication of the doctrine of Scriptural authority which would engender not only understanding but praxis within the evangelical communities of faith. It becomes clear that a position taken on biblical authority will dramatically affect the subsequent interpretation of the Scriptures and the use of biblical material.

Secondly, therefore, the subject of biblical interpretation is foundational. Liberation theologians have proposed a "hermeneutical circle" as the approach they consider to be central to contextual theology. The evangelical critique of this hermeneutic will be discussed and the evangelical proposition of an alternative "hermeneutical spiral" will be considered. For Latin American evangelicals are seeking to develop theology in which there is a real merging between the horizons of the biblical text and the horizons of the historical context. Inherent in contextual theology is relevance to the circumstances in which communities of faith live and minister. Contextual theologians, therefore, seek a fresh reading of Scripture which will convey truth to the Latin American situation.

Thirdly, it will be constructive to examine the evangelical critique of the use of biblical material in the theology of liberation. A brief overview of biblical references and themes in liberation thought, therefore, will be given. For while evangelical theologians concur with liberationists that a fresh reading of the Bible will bring deeper understanding of contextual issues, evangelicals contend that liberation theologians lack thorough biblical exegesis in their approach. Fourthly, in light of this criticism, the search for a contextual evangelical hermeneutic will be examined. Evangelical theologians affirm that contextualisation of the Scripture should take place within the church. For it is the responsibility of the church to function as a "hermeneutical community" which testifies to the living word of God in daily life and expresses its faith in the word of God through works of love. The discussion in this chapter on biblical authority, biblical interpretation and the use of biblical material sets the background for an examination of the relevant biblical themes in contextual Latin American theology.

Individual chapters will deal with the dominant issues evident in contextual Latin American theology: context, method, hermeneutics, Christology, ecclesiology and missiology. Any examination of contextual Latin American theology, however, would be incomplete without reference to what I will call the *general themes*. It is appropriate to deal with these themes in chapter six after an understanding of context, method and hermeneutics has been provided. Similarly, it is appropriate to deal with these themes in chapter six before the presentation of Christology, ecclesiology and missiology. The accepted understanding of each general theme will act as a foundation for later discussion on other aspects of evangelical theology. Firstly, it will be necessary to identify the themes present in the evangelical response to the theology of liberation, comparing and contrasting the differing understanding of each theme. Secondly, it will be helpful then to outline the evangelical exposition and theological development of each theme. The general themes which merit examination are *humanity, sin, liberation, salvation, conversion,* and *the kingdom of God*. It is hoped that the exposition of each theme will demonstrate its significance for contextual theology. Chapter six will not seek to present a complete analysis of these subjects but rather will seek to provide a coherent overview of the evangelical theology which is developing. It will become clear that central to each general theme is the understanding of the person and work of Jesus Christ. For this reason, Christology in Latin American contextual theology will be the subject of the next chapter.

The first aspect of Christology which will be examined in chapter seven is the image of Christ portrayed in popular Latin American culture. These popular images of Christ, and the images of Christ within both Catholic and Protestant faith communities have been deemed as insufficient. They form the backdrop, therefore, against which a more holistic, biblical Christology is being developed. It will then be helpful to provide a brief overview of the evangelical engagement with specific aspects of liberationist Christology. Evangelical theologians concur with liberationists that an urgent reexamination of traditional images of Christ is needed. Similarly, evangelicals affirm the liberationist pursuit to discover the historical

Jesus. Despite this, however, they find it necessary to constructively critique other aspects of liberation Christology. For evangelical theologians consider it imperative to apply the principles of method and hermeneutics detailed in earlier chapters to the Christological search. Also fundamental to the discussion is the understanding of the general themes, as outlined in chapter six. This evangelical Christology is being developed in light of the Old Testament Scriptures and is informed by the New Testament witness to the historical Jesus. It is Christology which is seeking to present a balanced understanding of the humanity and divinity of Jesus Christ. It is Christology which seeks to give hope to communities of faith. As a result of such reflection, evangelical theologians are striving to develop compassionate models of ministry, relevant to the Latin American context. Clearly, holistic and biblical Christology will have serious implications for the communities of faith which seek to bear witness to this understanding of Jesus Christ. The search for a Latin American evangelical ecclesiology, therefore, will be the focus of the following chapter.

In the discussion on the nature, the life and the purpose of the church within Latin American evangelical theology, interaction with three alternative ecclesiological proposals is evident. Chapter eight will seek to present an overview of this engagement in order to set the search for a thoroughly biblical evangelical ecclesiology in context. The evangelical critique of liberationist ecclesiology will be considered. The evangelical response to the "new ecclesiology" proposed and practised within less radical Latin American Catholicism will be discussed. The evangelical understanding of the ecclesiology asserted by the Church Growth movement will be presented. In light of this theological reflection, the search for a Latin American evangelical ecclesiology will be examined. This ecclesiology demonstrates the clear commitment to understand what it means to be the church in a context of oppression, poverty and social injustice. The nature, the purpose and the mission of the church is key to contextual theology. For the community of faith must understand the very reason for its existence if the context in which the church lives and ministers is to be influenced and transformed by the presence of a faithful witness to the gospel.

In chapter nine, therefore, the search for a Latin American evangelical understanding of mission will be presented. It will be most constructive, firstly, to examine Latin American evangelical missiology in light of the international evangelical dialogue on the subject during the last three decades. For it is clear that this interaction has been definitive. Secondly, as a result of international debate and in an effort to develop a biblically based, holistic approach to mission relevant to the Latin American context, evangelical theologians have reflected on three aspects: *mission as discipleship, mission as transformation* and *mission as social responsibility.* Thirdly, this theological and biblical reflection has led to the proposition and ongoing development of the concept known as *misión integral,* which will be focused on in detail. The liberation themes examined in this book are brought together by evangelical theologians as they pursue this understanding of mission. *Misión integral*, therefore, is a primary example of contextual evangelical theology seeking to express the evangelical faith in every sphere of existence.

The conclusion will reflect on the study in two sections. Firstly, in light of the previous nine chapters, a brief synopsis will be given in order to draw together the implications of each liberation theme for Latin American evangelical theology. Secondly, four observations regarding the Latin American contribution in the past and the necessity of future contributions will be made.

CHAPTER 2

The Latin American Context in Evangelical Perspective

2.1 Introduction

The call for liberation by evangelicals and liberationists has arisen from particular historical circumstances in Latin America. An appreciation of both the historical and the contemporary contexts, therefore, is essential in order to understand the development of Latin American contextual theology. In this chapter, a simple outline of the historical background drawn from evangelical accounts will be given in an effort to form an understanding of Latin American history through the eyes of the Latin American evangelical community.

First, a brief history of the Latin American continent will be considered. As will be seen, the significant historical aspects which contributed to the structures of society, the formation of national identities and the practices of religion on the continent are: the colonisation of the New World by the Old World; the epoch of revolution and independence; and the role of the Catholic Church in Latin America prior to the twentieth century.

Second, the immediate historical circumstances in which contextual Latin American theology developed will be examined. In this section, the focus will be placed on the circumstances surrounding post-conciliar Latin American Catholicism, for it was during this period that the most promising Catholic liberationist reflection was carried out. The early thinkers who contributed to the formulation of liberation thought will be identified. The early development of what has become known as the theology of liberation will be considered in the light of the desperate situation of many on the Latin American continent. Inevitably, and particularly for this work, Protestant reflection on the circumstances and the subsequent theological response will also be examined. Therefore the vital contribution and influence of the Protestant movement ISAL, *Iglesia y Sociedad en America Latina* (Church and Society in Latin America), will be considered in the final section of this chapter. It will become clear that an understanding of this period, and an appreciation of the theological reflection which took place, are necessary to accurately place evangelical theology in context.

2.2 A Brief History of Latin America

2.2.1 The Colonisation of the New World by the Old

In seeking to understand the history of the colonisation of Latin America from an evangelical perspective, the work of Samuel Escobar is insightful.[1] Warning his readers of "*la leyenda negra*" (the Black Legend), he is careful to reflect on the history of the continent in a balanced manner.[2] The Iberian conquest and the evangelization of the Americas has been judged with severe hostility, particularly by North American and British historians. Defenders of Spain and Portugal refer to this negative perspective as the "Black Legend," for they consider it to be an exaggerated account. Escobar comments that it is vital to move beyond this "Black Legend" of Latin American history and become acquainted with the facts. He calls for balance and asserts that the Catholic missionary process, in particular, must be understood within the history of conquest and colonial domination. Yet it needs to be acknowledged that not all Catholic mission work was simply a religious cover-up for military conquest and political domination.[3] Escobar writes:

> We Protestants need to reexamine the facile way in which we have used this anti-Catholic and anti-Iberian black legend. The more we study the history of the sixteenth-century missions the better we see how this legend was shaped and learn to distinguish it from the facts…It is very easy to criticize the colonial church for the superficiality of its evangelization and for its defects, but it would be unjust to pass over the sincere believers who struggled against the abuses.[4]

---

[1] Escobar considers history to be a more urgent subject for Latin American evangelical theologians than for theologians who do not live in an atmosphere of such tumultuous social change. He perceives, therefore, that the desire to understand history and the search for God's purpose in historical circumstances constitute a key element of Latin American evangelical theology and indeed are the driving force behind much of the theological reflection. Samuel Escobar, interview by author, 1 April 2004, video recording, Valencia. See Samuel Escobar, "The Need for Historical Awareness" in *Christian Mission and Social Justice*, Samuel Escobar and John Driver (Scottdale: Herald Press, 1978), 11-35; Samuel Escobar, Estuardo McIntosh and Juan Inocencia, *Historia y misión: revisión de perspectivas* (Lima: Ediciones Presencia, 1994), 7-92.

[2] See Samuel Escobar, "The Church in Latin America after Five Hundred Years: An Evangelical Missiological Perspective" in *New Face of the Church in Latin America*, ed. Guillermo Cook (Maryknoll: Orbis Books, 1994), 21-37 at 22-24; Samuel Escobar, "¿Se revisa la nueva leyenda negra?", *Cuadernos Reforma* Suplemento 1992: 1-20 at 3-4; Samuel Escobar, "Católicos y evangélicos en América Latina frente al desafío misionero del siglo veintiuno", *Kairós* 14/15 (January – December 1994): 63-80, at 67; Samuel Escobar, *Changing Tides: Latin America and World Mission Today* (Maryknoll: Orbis Books, 2002), 37-41.

[3] Escobar, "Five Hundred", 22.

[4] Escobar, *Changes*, 37. See also Eddy José Muskus, *The Origins and Early Development of Liberation Theology in Latin America* (Carlisle: Paternoster Press, 2002), 23-30. Muskus discusses examples of sincere Dominican friars such as Pedro de Córdoba and Antonio de

Escobar is not naïve with respect to the difficulties associated with Latin American history, but his caution is a helpful reminder of the complexity of the subject.[5] It would seem no exaggeration to say that "understanding contemporary Latin America comes with the realization that the colonial social structures indelibly marked and shaped" it.[6] It is vital, therefore, that the significance of this history for contextual theology is not underestimated. For the context of Latin American theological reflection cannot simply be limited to the post-Second World War period.

The Latin American continent possesses a powerful and at times disturbing history of vast, ancient civilisations. Astounded by the archaeological evidence of the cultures, the artistry, the architecture, the agricultural and academic achievements of these civilisations, visitors often ask what happened to such people. The answer is simple. Their descendants are present in contemporary Latin America. Yet it remains a continent where poor people inhabit a land rich in resources, a land and people which have been plundered and exploited for centuries.

In 1996, Emilio Núñez and William Taylor published the revised edition of *Crisis and Hope in Latin America*, the standard evangelical account of the Latin American context.[7] They do not claim to be neutral in their work but seek to observe social, cultural and religious transitions from the perspective of the growing evangelical communities. For the purpose of this chapter, it would seem appropriate to draw on

---

Montesinos who became defenders of the Indians and preached against injustice. He comments: "This was the background of the Dominican friar preachers who sought in practical ways, to defend the rights of the colonized people and made evangelization a process that included the protection and advancement of their rights." Muskus also documents the life of Bartolomé de Las Casas and while he recognises the effort Las Casas made to defend the Indians, Muskus raises questions regarding the motives of Las Casas and his understanding of the need for evangelization.

[5] Escobar explains that evangelicals are aware of the need for a balanced perspective on history because they are the subject of a new "Black Legend" developed by some Catholic and Marxist historians who attribute the Protestant missionary work in Latin America during the last two centuries and the Latin American Protestant growth to a CIA-inspired plot against liberation theologians or an attempt by large American corporate industries to manipulate the poor in Latin America. See Escobar, "Five Hundred", 21-37; Escobar, "¿Se revisa?", 4-8.

[6] Emilio Antonio Núñez and William David Taylor, *Crisis and Hope in Latin America: An Evangelical Perspective*, Revised ed. (Pasadena: William Carey Library, 1996), 60.

[7] Aware that Latin America continues to provoke news of global significance, Núñez and Taylor responded to the demand for a revised and updated version of their book, first published in 1989. Drug wars and political crises had attracted international media attention in the decade of the 1980s. The political, economic, social and religious aspects of Latin American life dramatically changed during the 1990s with the collapse of Soviet-style Marxism, fledgling democracies, privatisation and reforms within trade. Yet the future remains unstable as poverty increases and social tension prevails. Writing from the vantage point of two Latin American insiders, Núñez and Taylor provide a panorama of the Latin American world.

the insights shared in Taylor's synopsis of Latin American history in an effort to gain insight into the specifically evangelical understanding of the context.[8] Because the tumultuous history of the continent is well documented from a wide variety of perspectives, a brief summation will suffice here.[9]

It is probable that Mexico has been populated since 20,000 B.C.E. and over the next eight thousand years communities migrated as far south as modern-day Peru. One by one, the great civilisations of the pre-Colombian era rose powerfully to glory and fell violently to destruction. When the Spanish conquistadors explored the New World in 1492, three major civilisations were still in existence: the Mayans of southern Mexico and Guatemala, the Aztecs of central Mexico, and the Incas of the Andes.

From the fourth to the tenth centuries, the classic Maya period, the Maya people lived in Guatemala. They then moved to the Yucatan. Evidence remains today of their agricultural and artistic achievements. Deeply religious, the Maya had a pantheon of gods who were responsible for cosmic and terrestrial affairs.

The Aztec people held power in the central valley of Mexico by the fifteenth century. Taylor notes they had developed a complex and precise calendar,

---

[8] The historical overview provided by Taylor appears to present an agreed evangelical understanding, as far as is possible. In the foreword to the revised edition Escobar writes "the book does not claim neutrality or objectivity. The authors look...at social, cultural and religious transitions from the perspective of the evangelical communities that are now growing in the Latin world...Readers may not always agree with Taylor and Núñez, but because these authors strive to present a fair description and a logical argument, readers will be helped to clarify their own ideas..." Samuel Escobar, "Foreword", in Núñez and Taylor, *Crisis,* ix-xv, at xiv.

[9] Núñez and Taylor, *Crisis,* 48-99. Representative texts suggested by Taylor include George Pendle, *A History of Latin America* (Middlesex: Penguin, 1971); Jacques Lambert, *Latin America: Social Structures and Political Institutions*, trans. Helen Katel (Berkeley: University of California, 1971); Donald Marquand Dozer, *Latin America: An Interpretative History*, Rev.ed. (Tempe: Center for Latin American Studies, Arizona State University, 1979); E. Bradford Burns, *Latin America: A Concise Interpretative History*, 4th ed. (Englewood Cliffs: Prentice-Hall, 1986); Germán Archiniegas, *Latin America: A Cultural History*, trans. Joan MacLean (New York: Alfred A. Knopf, 1972); Esther Arias and Mortimer Arias, *The Cry of My People* (New York: Friendship Press, 1980); Eduardo Galeano, *Open Veins of Latin America*, trans. Cedric Belfrage (New York: Monthly Review Press, 1973). Other texts recommended on the history and culture of Latin America include: Felipe Fernández Armesto, *Columbus* (Oxford: Oxford University Press, 1991); Eugenio Chang-Rodríguez *Latinoamérica: su civilación y su cultura* (Boston: Heinle Publishers, 1991); Simon Collier, Thomas E. Skidmore and Harold Blakemore, eds., *The Cambridge Encyclopedia of Latin America and the Caribbean* (Cambridge: Cambridge University Press, 1992); Benjamin Keen, *A History of Latin America*, 4th ed. (Boston: Houghton Mifflin Company, 1992); Samuel E. Morison, *Admiral of the Ocean Sea – A Life of Christopher Columbus* (Boston: Little, Brown and Company, 1942); Gene S. Stuart and George E. Stuart, *Lost Kingdoms of the Maya* (National Geographic Society, 1993). For other recommended historical accounts see Escobar, "Five Hundred", 22-23.

pictographs, architecture, and an efficient governmental system. Also a religious people, the Aztecs had a plethora of bloodthirsty gods who demanded human sacrifice.

The largest, oldest and perhaps best organised of the Indian civilisations was the Inca, who flourished in the Andes despite the harsh environment. Their society, with the imperial Quechuan language, displayed a unique style of administration and was ruled by a leader who seemed to desire the best for his subjects. They had developed a system of counting based on knotted strings. Their agricultural achievements were evident in the dry highlands. Women played a significant role in society, the home, commerce, agriculture, arts and textiles. The magnificent gold work, art, textiles and ceramics of the Inca can still be seen today.[10]

Other indigenous groups encountered by the conquistadors include the Carib of the Caribbean and Central America, the Chibcha of Colombia, the Araucanian of Chile, the Guaraní of Paraguay, and the Tupi of Brazil. The population of the vast continent numbered over fifty million at a safe estimate. Taylor observes:

> The year 1492 becomes then a double timeline of demarcation, a twin initiation of a new era. The first event was the Spaniards' discovery of the New World...The second event lay in the New World's discovery of the Old. But in the final analysis the Old conquered the New and permanently changed its entire identity.[11]

The conquistadors who arrived on the shores of the so-called Indies, displayed values similar to those which had been evident throughout the Middle Ages on the Iberian Peninsula as the Moors were driven out and all "infidels" expelled. Desire for land, for booty, for valour, for wealth and for honour spurred them on. Their "religious zeal and intolerance, suspicion of non-Spaniards, more prestige for the soldier than the farmer or the family man, and a mentality of exploitation rather than development"[12] shaped every attitude and action.

This conquest and colonization of Latin America, first initiated by Columbus, was a "pacification" of the peoples. Taylor documents:

> It was a matter of "powerful persuasion," the cross and the sword, gunpowder and destruction. Within just fifty years the Spanish decapitated the indigenous societies and thus dominated a landmass that stretched from San Francisco, California, all the way to Tierra del Fuego, north of Antarctica. Armed with royal decrees and blessed by the church, the *conquistadores* marched and subdued.[13]

The colonial social structures established during this period left an enduring mark on the Latin American peoples. It is widely acknowledged that many contemporary

---

[10] Núñez and Taylor, *Crisis*, 53-57.

[11] Núñez and Taylor, *Crisis*, 49.

[12] Núñez and Taylor, *Crisis*, 50.

[13] Núñez and Taylor, *Crisis*, 57. See also John A. Mackay, *The Other Spanish Christ* (London: SCM, 1932; reprint, Eugene: Wipf and Stock Publishers, 2001), 23-42 where the religious epic of the Iberian Conquest is discussed further.

problems on the continent stem from colonial institutions and the manner in which these institutions were imposed.

The monarchy in Spain took counsel regarding colonial affairs from the *Consejo de las Indias* (Council of the Indies), established in 1524.[14] Laws and edicts written in Spain were administered and enforced in the colonies by senior mayors, supported by the judicial court governed by judges. The crown was also awarded effective authority over the church in the Indies by the *Real Patronato* (Royal Patronage system), which contributed greatly to the merging of church and state in the New World.[15] The granting of lands and its people to *encomenderos* led to vast plantations belonging to a chosen few.[16] This *encomienda* system ensured the land was worked by the native inhabitants for the benefit of the colonial powers.[17] The *repartimiento* system enforced the labour of Indians in the fields and mines.[18] Precious metals such as gold and silver were plundered, mined and shipped back to the Old World.

Not only did the conquest and imposition of colonial structures cause tension in the New World but hostility also existed due to the conflict between various strands in the society.[19] Colonial powers and local government favoured those born on the Iberian Peninsula but living in the New World, known as the *peninsulares* (people from mainland Spain). *Indianos* were those who had been born in Spain but came to the New World to make their fortune before returning to their homeland. Children born in the New World of Iberian parents were known as *criollos* (Creoles). A child born of European and Indian parents was called the *mestizo* (mixed blood) or the *ladino* (mixed race). Feelings of superiority, notions of inferiority and the crisis of identity among many people evident in Latin America today can be traced to these times of colonialisation.[20]

---

[14] See Escobar, "Five Hundred", 35.

[15] See Escobar, "Five Hundred", 30.

[16] See Muskus, *Origins*, 25-27. The term *encomenderos* refers to the colonists who were granted control of land and Indians to work for them. The *encomienda* system is the term used to describe this process of awarding land and labourers to the *encomenderos*.

[17] See Samuel Escobar, "El poder y las ideologias en América Latina" in *Los evangélicos y el poder político en América Latina*, ed. Pablo A. Deiros (Buenos Aires: Nueva Creación, 1986), 141-180, at 149.

[18] The *repartimiento* system makes reference to the distribution of the land in the New World.

[19] Escobar, "El poder", 147-148.

[20] Taylor shares from personal experience the problem of racial psychology and the prevailing attitude of "*Es que tenemos mala sangre*" ("It's just that we have bad blood"). He makes reference to Domingo Sarmiento, President of Argentina from 1868-1874, who hoped that the infusion of Saxon blood into the country would improve the race and bring hope for a brighter future. He also mentions the ominous analysis evident in the title chosen by the Bolivian Alcides Arguedas for his book *Pueblo Enfermo* (Sick People) (La Paz: Librería Editorial Juventud, 1982). Núñez and Taylor, *Crisis*, 102-103.

By 1600 the society in cities and towns was structured to maintain Spanish control and to serve Spain's interests.[21] Taylor comments that this focus on urban locations has been a significant factor in the development of Latin America. He writes:

> These baroque cities brought together the major institutions of the colony: the imperial representatives, the regional and local civil government, the church, commerce...and the social and cultural life of the time...This has so favoured the city that the interior is disregarded as inferior and is seen as necessary only in the way that it might supply and strengthen the urban world.[22]

Taylor observes that the Catholic Church dominated not only in these urban areas but also in the rural and remote regions of the New World. As a result of the Royal Patronage system and the authority given to the Church in matters of spiritual significance, the interdependence between the Church and the state was ensured.

> Reliance on political power and alliance with it at the missionary stage also brought the Catholic Church a situation of extreme dependence on civil authorities for her subsistence and continuity...So long as the political situation remained viable and supportive of the formal Church, the territory was considered to be Christian. But in periods of crisis or conflict, the Church was unable to stand on its own as a general source of moral authority or as a carrier of basic values capable of encompassing, yet standing above parties in the dispute.[23]

The Catholic Church gained wealth and power in the cities, owned vast areas of land and exploited the Indians, and later the Africans as slaves. Promoting a message of acceptance and passivity in the face of poverty with the knowledge of a reward after death, it can be argued that the Church manipulated and controlled the masses. "The Church became a major political actor on behalf of the forces that promised to protect it as an institution, rather than a differentiated religious system with roots in the spiritual life of autonomous membership groups."[24] Reflecting the pattern of those who were influential in the new society, it was the aristocracy who were awarded the high-ranking positions among the clergy.

Education was provided by and thus also heavily influenced by the Church. Again, preference was given to those of Spanish parentage and opportunities for Indians or those of mixed blood to take part in education were extremely limited. In 1553 the first Latin American university was founded in Mexico, followed by a new University established in 1571 in Lima. Classic medieval education was undertaken there long before rival universities flourished in North America. Taylor draws attention to the fact that it was evidently a scholastic mindset that monopolized the style and content of education in the New World.

---

[21] See Escobar, "El poder", 149.

[22] Núñez and Taylor, *Crisis*, 62.

[23] Escobar, "Five Hundred", 31. See also Escobar "El poder", 155.

[24] Ivan Vallier, cited by Escobar, *Changing*, 41.

The history of commerce too in the New World is one of exploitation and domination.[25] For mainland Spain benefited from all business and trade in Latin America. Internal development of infrastructure was not permitted and major decisions were taken by several authoritative bureaucrats. "The Counter-Reformation state impugned the religious value of commerce. It banned or restricted enterprise in the private sector. It licensed certain entrepreneurs to develop state monopolies; it favoured state mercantilism over private mercantilism."[26] The suggestion that these early colonial commercial decisions have contributed to economic and social difficulties currently experienced commands widespread consensus. In a succinct assessment of reflections on the contemporary socio-economic situation in Latin America, Taylor considers the problem of racial psychology, previously mentioned, to be a significant contributing factor. The Dependency Theory which is "supported widely by many international experts, members of the intellectual community, Marxists and liberation theologians" is also a critical issue in regard to the socio-economic circumstances.[27] It would appear that Taylor concisely expresses the general prevailing attitude during the colonial era when he observes:

> The colonies were to be exploited, and the state mercantilism assured that the loaded galleons sailed the trade routes solely to Spain. The Iberians were children of the Counter-Reformation, faithful to their Holy Church and suspicious of all potential heresy. The Bible was a closed book; the priests were the intercessors. It was a matter of medieval miracle, mystery and authority, of mass conversion and nominal Christianity. These factors forged the Spanish colonies.[28]

---

[25] Escobar, "El poder", 148-156.

[26] Núñez and Taylor, *Crisis*, 64.

[27] See Núñez and Taylor, Crisis, 102-109. An overview of the opinions of writers who endorse both liberation theology and the Dependency Theory can be found in texts such as Gustavo Gutiérrez, *A Theology of Liberation*, 2nd ed., trans. Sister Caridad Inda and John Eagleson (Maryknoll: Orbis Books, 1988); Enrique Dussel, *A History of the Church in Latin America: Colonialisation to Liberation*, trans. Alan Neely (Grand Rapids: Eerdmans, 1981); José Míguez Bonino, *Doing Theology in a Revolutionary Situation* (Philadelphia: Fortress Press, 1975). Helpful critiques of the Dependence Theory are included in Michael Novak, *The Spirit of Democratic Capitalism* (New York: American Enterprise Institute/Simon and Schuster, 1982); Peter Berger and Michael Novak, *Speaking to the Third World: Essays on Democracy and Development* (Washington DC: American Enterprise Institute for Public Policy Research, 1985); Michael Novak, ed., *Liberation South, Liberation North* (Washington DC: American Enterprise Institute for Public Policy Research, 1981). The contributing factors in the lack of progress in Latin America are recognised but an underlying challenge is made to Latin American intellectuals and leaders to make change through self-analysis and self responsibility throughout the work of Lawrence E. Harrison, *Underdevelopment is a State of Mind: The Latin American Case* (Boston: Harvard University and University Press of America, 1985).

[28] Núñez and Taylor, *Crisis*, 65.

The second critical historical period which is considered to have made a vital contribution to societal structures, national identities and religious practices in Latin America is the era of revolution and independence. This period, therefore, will be dealt with next.

2.2.2 Revolution and Independence

The years from 1810-1824 can be best described as the epoch of revolution and independence in Latin America.[29] In a specific discussion on this period of history, the first Hispanamerican historical congress held in Madrid during 1949, suggested six principal factors that contributed to the struggle for independence. J. Andrew Kirk helpfully documents these factors.[30]

First, the influence of the writings of the French Encyclopedists led to the diffusion of concepts of revolution, independence, liberty, equality and fraternity from Europe to Latin America, and convinced Latin Americans of the possibility of change.[31] The Spanish colonies found inspiration in the American Revolution of 1776, motivation in the French Revolution of 1789, and incentive in the slave rebellion in Haiti in 1791.

Second, the Peninsular Spanish had economic monopoly on the continent and exerted absolute authority in Latin American society as a whole. This resulted in aforementioned agitation between the different strands of the population. A class struggle ensued: the *criollos* resented the privileges given to the *peninsulares,* the *mestizos* wrestled with their issues of identity as they battled for acceptance, and the Indians and the black community were excluded and powerless.

Third, the Peninsular government had made countless serious errors in the colonies and was rapidly declining as a force internationally. Disquiet and crisis dominated Europe. Disputes over political alliances, struggles regarding territory in the New World, and the expansionist plans of the English, French and Dutch pressurised the Iberians.[32] Fourth, the nations rising to power, England in particular, created a political atmosphere for revolution and independence in Latin America. For these other European nations were searching for new international markets, and urged the Latin American Creoles on in their struggle for independence. Fifth, the congress identified the inbred individualism of the Hispanic race as a contributing

---

[29] See Escobar, "El poder", 156-163.

[30] J. Andrew Kirk, *Liberation Theology: An Evangelical View from the Third World* (Basingstoke: Marshall, Morgan and Scott, 1979), 2-3.

[31] For a brief summary of the work of the French Encyclopedists see Colin Brown, *Christianity and Western Thought: A History of Philosophers, Ideas and Movements Vol. 1* (Downers Grove: IVP, 1990), 288. For discussion on their influence in Latin America see John Charles Chasteen, *Born in Blood and Fire* (New York: W.W. Norton & Company, 2001), 92-113; Escobar, "El poder", 159.

[32] Escobar asserts that influential scholars today affirm that this larger framework of the Iberian-Anglo-Saxon confrontation is a key to understanding the religious history of the Americas. See Escobar, "Five Hundred", 23.

factor. Sixth, it observed there had been growing dissension among the Indian population on the continent in the years prior to the revolutionary era and sporadic revolts had already taken place.

These six contributing factors explain the disquiet in Latin America regarding the circumstances at that time. During this period of agitation and civil unrest, generals such as Simón Bolívar and José de San Martín rose to leadership. They became renowned for their command during the battles for independence; Bolívar in the northern region, and de San Martín in the far south of the continent. During these struggles for independence a sense of nationalism germinated, perhaps for the first time. However, notwithstanding the successes on the battlefield, Taylor wisely comments: "The sad story repeated itself – it was easier to win a war than organise a new nation."[33] Despite the fact that Bolívar and de San Martín met for a summit in 1821, they were unable to secure an integrated solution to Latin America. Both men, exhausted and disillusioned, eventually retired from the political struggle. The legacy of mutual distrust, disillusionment and conflict passed on from generation to generation.[34]

By 1830 the modern map of South America was drawn. In the subsequent years until 1880 there was a time of organisation and development in the new countries but history reveals that "freedom had been transformed into a millstone, and the national identity crises cried for relief."[35] Structures within the new societies remained largely unchanged and it became evident that the nations were unprepared for a representative democracy. "The lofty and noble ideals stumbled on the colonial hangovers: ignorance, apathy, poverty, illiteracy, class and racial struggles, clerical domination, land control by a few wealthy families, a closed mentality to new ideas, mercantilism, and an exploitative economy."[36] The opportunity to positively utilise the natural and human resources of the continent was missed by the new Republics. Consequently, while Western Europe and Anglo-America were growing fast, Latin America became an underdeveloped continent.

An era of relative peace and national development can be traced from 1880-1930. At that time, the context of Latin America was changing socially and commercially, greatly influenced by high immigration from Europe. However, the potential for trade between the Latin American nations and the subsequent development of infrastructure were hindered by continuing internal struggles, by wars over land and by the increasing power of the military. It was a period of socio-political experimentation as the new nations sought a model which would bring peace and security.

During these years (1880-1930) the relationship with the United States of America began to become a controversial one. The demand for a greater monopoly

---

[33] Núñez and Taylor, *Crisis*, 70.

[34] See Chasteen, *Born*, 108-112.

[35] Núñez and Taylor, *Crisis*, 75. For further details of the process of organisation and development see Núñez and Taylor, *Crisis*, 72-76.

[36] Núñez and Taylor, *Crisis*, 74.

of Latin American raw materials, the struggle over territory and the desire to establish itself as a major world power with general hegemony over the American continents led to increasing North American intervention. North America sought to have influence in Latin American political, societal and economic decisions. Since 1930 a continuing critical period of instability has been witnessed in Latin America: military conflicts, civil wars, options for change, multiple constitutions, agrarian reform, Marxism, negative self-analysis, and the contentious relationship with the United States of America have caused unrest across the continent.[37]

There is wisdom in the assertion that Latin American issues should not be approached simplistically and it is necessary to heed the warning against making sweeping generalisations. For as Taylor observes, "Latin American history is unique, rich in textures and at the same time tragic in essence and proportion."[38] The essence of the historical era of revolution and independence in Latin America is captured by an appreciation that "as we have seen it is much easier to maintain the present system than to bring about authentic change...The enigma remains: poor people inhabit rich lands."[39]

In this brief history of Latin America, the colonisation of the New World by the Old and the era of revolution and independence have been identified as two significant historical aspects which have marked societal structures, national identities and religious practices on the continent. The third critical feature of Latin American history, which has had serious implications for Latin American theological reflection, is the role of the Catholic Church. A discussion on the position of the Catholic Church is fundamental to an understanding of the context of the development of Latin American theology.

2.2.3 The Role of the Catholic Church in Latin America Prior to the Twentieth Century

As mentioned at the beginning of this chapter, the role of the Catholic Church in Latin America during the colonial era, throughout the years of revolution and independence, and indeed in the present has provoked controversy. However, in the light of Escobar's recommendations to maintain balance, we turn to Kirk who succinctly documents the historical background of the Catholic Church in Latin America from an evangelical perspective.[40]

By 1810 the Catholic Church found itself in a critical position. For although Catholicism had swept across Latin America, and as a continent it appeared to be

---

[37] For further details on 1930 to the present see Núñez and Taylor, *Crisis*, 86-94.

[38] Núñez and Taylor, *Crisis*, 95.

[39] E. Bradford Burns, cited by Núñez and Taylor, *Crisis*, 95.

[40] Kirk, *Liberation*, 3-22. For further discussion on the history of the Church in Latin America see also Dussel, *History*, 37-239; Mackay, *Other*, 23-92. The role of the Catholic Church in Latin America is the subject of H. McKennie Goodpasture, *Cross and Sword* (Maryknoll: Orbis Books, 1989) and Ivan Vallier, *Catolicismo, control social y modernización en América Latina* (Buenos Aires: Amorrortu Editores, 1971).

"Christianised", the prevalent form of Catholicism was nominal and cultural. It would seem no exaggeration to say that Latin American Catholicism was weakly rooted:

> No thorough evangelization had taken place…the Church had been hastily "scattered" rather than "planted." Hence, because it could not count on the enthusiastic loyalty from the population, when moments of crisis came, the institutional church defended itself with political means. That is, the Church as an institution had been set up in colonial society, but people had not been converted to Christianity to the point where their commitment led them to live out their faith in their daily behaviour.[41]

Colonial conditions had resulted in the failure to promote indigenous church leadership which led to a severe shortage of national priests and consequently to a dwindling number of clergy.[42]

In seeking to understand the role of the Catholic Church, the six controlling motivations for revolution, previously mentioned, are considered by Kirk to be "important because they either show irreversible historical tendencies, with which the traditionally conservative Church had to come to terms, or else they directly impinge upon the Church's subsequent attitude to political involvement."[43] In the one hundred years following the complicated struggles for independence, the strained relationship between the Catholic Church and the leaders of the new nations resulted in political conflict and mutual misunderstandings.

The era of independence (1810-1824) had seen significant changes within the Catholic Church on the continent.[44] The Church had always aligned itself with Spain, the colonial government, the military or the wealthy aristocratic landowners and, therefore, was caught unprepared when the revolutionary conflict ensued. It is helpful to bear in mind that while some priests were involved in the struggle for independence, the Catholic Church generally held to a negative attitude regarding their efforts. Any potential changes in society which would impinge on the authority or privileged position of the Church were strongly defied. Despite the fact that new constitutions promoted religious liberty, echoes of the Inquisition resonated throughout Latin America. The reality was that the introduction of tolerance and pluralism would afford the Catholic Church no special privileges.

Kirk explains that the system of Royal Patronage, as previously mentioned, had been critical in the evolution of the relationship between Church and state in Latin America. For Latin America did not have a Catholic Church controlled by Rome but instead a Spanish national Catholic Church controlled from Madrid.[45] The

---

[41] Escobar, *Changing*, 41.

[42] See Escobar, "Five Hundred", 34.

[43] Kirk, *Liberation*, 3.

[44] See Escobar, "Five Hundred", 31.

[45] For a helpful discussion on this aspect of the Catholic Church in Latin America see Emilio A. Núñez, "¡Aquí España!", *Boletín Teológico* 8 (1974): 1-5, at 2-4. Further details on the implications of Royal Patronage for the Church and the state in Latin America and the

implications of such a style of propagation of the faith under the control and influence of the state has affected Latin America until this day.[46] Kirk observes that at the time of independence, the hierarchy of the Church (the majority born and educated in Spain) would not have considered causing any kind of division between the interdependent futures of the Church and the Spanish nation.[47] The principle of the divine right of kings had been the justification used by the Church hierarchy to condemn the revolutionary uprisings. Traditional loyalties to the crown were enforced by adherence to the Vatican encyclicals, through disciplinary measures, and because of the lack of independent reflection in theological preparation of the lower clergy. Despite this, due to the influence of younger clergy who had experience of secular study and had been exposed to Enlightenment thought, by 1820 there was a move towards openness and change, supported by layperson and priest alike.

While the Church denounced the struggles for independence and actively condemned those involved, Kirk suggests that in fact the majority of the new nations simply wanted to convey the privilege of patronage from Madrid to their own governments and then maintain the relationship between the Church and state.[48] Kirk observes that this attitude towards the Church did not prevail for long. For as the Church continued to display intransigence with regard to the struggle for independence and a weak inability to respond effectively, the governments, at times aggressively, sought to implement measures to limit the power held by the Church. Kirk contends that the inability of the Church to face such political challenges in Latin America has been demonstrated up to the present day. He comments that rather than a promotion of creative theological reflection in response to critical circumstances, "there has been a serious shortage of intellectual reserves and a lack of concern to create new ones. This vacuum seriously retarded the development of any indigenous theological thought."[49]

Consequently, during the nineteenth and early twentieth centuries the Catholic Church was mercilessly criticised by Latin American political and intellectual thinkers of the time.[50] Political opposition to the Catholic Church gradually became

---

position and reaction of the Church during the period of independence can be found in Kirk, *Liberation*, 4-14.

[46] See Kirk, *Liberation*, 8-22 for details of the factors contributing to the Church's weakness after independence, where Kirk discusses the attack on the Church during the nineteenth and twentieth centuries, and considers the attempts at renovation during the twentieth century in the light of the new forms of social and political involvement. He gives a concise and thorough outline of the role and position of the Catholic Church on the continent.

[47] Kirk, *Liberation*, 5.

[48] For detailed evidence see Kirk, *Liberation*, 7-8.

[49] Kirk, *Liberation*, 10.

[50] Attacks were launched on the Church by thinkers such as José Victorino Lastarria (1817-1888), Francisco Bilbao (1823-1865), Julio A. Roca (1843-1914), Manuel Gonzalez Prada (1848-1918), Carlos Octavio Bunge (1874-1918) and José Battle y Ordoñez (1865-1929). They challenged the Church on her negative stance, see Kirk, *Liberation*, 12.

deeper, as emerging leaders interested in tangible reform recognised the Church was defending her economic privileges and maintaining a political stance which had become a fundamental principle of its religious convictions.[51] Kirk asserts that the most consistent base for such political philosophy, held by the new leaders, was Positivism.[52]

> A new order was developing in every country; not the colonial order but one which was based on the concepts of progress and science; an order which appeared to be giving thought to the education and material comfort of its citizens. Political liberties were sacrificed for the sake of this order, since they were considered to be superfluous and a source of unrest. In every country, oligarchies came forward to take responsibility for the new order and for its reflection in the field of politics.[53]

Such Positivism, through the elevation of human reason, affirmed the power of science and order to solve problems. It was anticipated that this order would bring progress to Latin America after the years of chaos. It excluded questions of ultimate causes and spiritual values. It allowed individual thinkers to critique their circumstances. Kirk comments: "Positivism was to be used as the great educational weapon to change the mentality of the entire Hispanic people."[54] An enduring struggle ensued between the Church and the state, which in some nations lasted into the middle of the twentieth century. It was observed at the time that "the Catholic religion is searching for its form of government, the Republic form of government is searching for its religion. The policy of the first is monarchy; the religion of the second rationalism."[55]

As the Catholic Church entered the twentieth century, the historical tensions and continental difficulties experienced led to a period of serious self-criticism and serious reflection on ministry in Latin America.[56] The subsequent changes which were implemented, and the critical development of theological reflection, form the

---

[51] Kirk, *Liberation*, 13. It is also interesting to observe the contrasting positive attitude of the emerging leaders towards Protestant churches and missionary work, which was considered to contribute to modernisation and a more open political attitude. See Escobar, "Five Hundred", 32.

[52] The theories of Auguste Comte (1798-1857), John Stuart Mill (1806-1873) and Herbert Spencer (1820-1903) surged to the fore. See Núñez and Taylor, *Crisis*, 79-81. Enrique Dussel also comments "Around 1870 positivism was the dominant ideology...This 'atheistic' materialism was actually an anti-creationist materialism which affirmed the divinity of matter. In short, it was pantheism. It imposed itself on our culture during this period (1870-1890), and our lawyers and doctors are still under its influence." Enrique Dussel, *History and the Theology of Liberation*, trans. John Drury (Maryknoll: Orbis Books, 1976), 104.

[53] Leopoldo Zea, cited by Núñez and Taylor, *Crisis*, 79.

[54] Kirk, *Liberation*, 13.

[55] Francisco Bilbao, cited by Kirk, *Liberation*, 14.

[56] Escobar, "El poder", 163-170; Escobar, *Changing*, 38-41; Muskus, *Origins*, 83-113; Escobar, "¿Se revisa?", 8.

immediate context of the Latin American theology which is central to this study. For this reason, post-conciliar Latin American Catholicism will be examined presently.

2.3 The Immediate Context of Liberation Theology

2.3.1 Post-conciliar Latin American Catholicism

Núñez acknowledges that, from the outset of the twentieth century, some effort had been made within Catholicism to respond to the social and political questions posed by the context of Latin America. The *Rerum Novarum* encyclical of Leo XIII in 1891, the first pontifical social encyclical of the modern period, sought to deal with the problems of the working classes and prompted reflection across the spectrum of Catholicism.[57] There was a subsequent period of attempted renovation within the Church, motivated by the unavoidable challenge to respond to the desperate circumstances of social need, evident throughout the worldwide Catholic Church. The social encyclical *Quadragesimo Anno* of 1931 expressed similar concerns to *Rerum Novarum* and displayed the potential for a new method in dealing with the concrete problems evident in a world where division exists between rich and poor.[58]

The timing of renovation encouraged by the social encyclicals varied across the countries of Latin America. Kirk notes that in Chile, for example, the Church had sought to engage with the worrying circumstances of the working classes before *Rerum Novarum* was even published. In the early decades of the twentieth century, precursors of the movement *Acción Católica* (Catholic Action) were set up in Mexico and Argentina to respond to the difficulties. However, in contrast, little concern regarding social issues was aired until the late 1950s in Peru or Brazil.

José Míguez Bonino asserts that currents of Catholic renewal had influence in the biblical, liturgical, ecumenical and social spheres of the Latin American Church since the early 1950s.[59] Núñez, however, is careful to point out that this happened only among limited groups within Catholicism. The masses remained unaffected.[60]

---

[57] See chapter one in Emilio A. Núñez, *Caminos de renovación* (Grand Rapids: Outreach Publications, 1975) where renewal in Latin American Catholicism is discussed; Muskus, *Origins*, 84; Núñez and Taylor, *Crisis*, 240.

[58] While these encyclicals brought great hope to those who sought to champion the social cause, Muskus notes that many did not consider *Rerum Novarum* a "mandate to be executed by all concerned." Muskus, *Origins*, 85.

[59] See for example Muskus, *Origins*, 100-106 where he discusses the Catholic attempts at renewal through the formation of Youth Social Action and the foundation of Catholic Action in Peru.

[60] Míguez Bonino also recognises the traditional popular Catholic religiosity which has remained basically unaltered in many sectors of Catholicism. José Míguez Bonino, "The Condition and Prospects of Christianity in Latin America" in *New Face of the Church in Latin America*, ed. Guillermo Cook (Maryknoll: Orbis Books, 1994), 259-267, at 262. See also Núñez and Taylor, *Crisis*, 241, and the discussion on the charismatic renewal movement during this period within the Catholic Church in Emilio A. Núñez, *Conciencia e identidad evangélica y la renovación católica* (Guatemala: Grupo Evangélico Universitario, n.d.), 6-7;

However, it would appear that during 1955, there was a poignant awakening within the Catholic Church to the obligation for thorough self-criticism and accurate reflection on the reality of the position of the Church in the lives of Latin American people.[61] This was the year in which the Latin American Episcopal Council known as CELAM was formed. CELAM is a permanent council with a consultative, reflective and active role, interpreting particular decisive encyclicals in the light of the Latin American context.

Kirk considers the three most critical movements established in Latin America in an effort to motivate the Catholic Church to actively respond to the challenge of ministry to be Catholic Action (CA), the Catholic Trade Union Movement (CLASC) and the Christian Democrat Parties (CDP).[62] Two other important factors within the actual structure of the Latin American Church were, firstly, the creation of five hundred new dioceses which reflected the increase in population and its upward mobility and, secondly, the formation of CELAM.

The significance of the Second Vatican Council (1962-1965) as a motivating force in the evident process of change within contemporary Catholicism in Latin America should not be underestimated.[63] Núñez remarks:

> Consider, for example, the new interest in the Bible, the liturgical renaissance, the declaration of religious freedom, the ecumenical openness towards other churches and religions, the new approach to the church's responsibility in the modern world, the crisis of authority in the clerical structures, the presence of theologians eager to

Samuel Escobar, "Identidad, misión y futuro del protestantismo latinoamericano", *Boletín Teológico* 3/4 (1977): 1-38, at 18-19.

[61] Samuel Escobar, "Latin America" in *Toward the Twenty-first Century in Christian Mission*, eds. James M. Phillips and Robert T. Coote (Grand Rapids: Eerdmans, 1993, Reprint, Grand Rapids: Eerdmans, 1995), 125-138, at 128-132; Escobar, "Five Hundred", 28-32. Muskus notes that in 1955 the main concerns expressed by the Latin American bishops were the threat of Protestantism and the shortage of priests. However, it was the beginning of reflection specific to the Latin American reality, *Origins*, 88.

[62] For more detailed discussion on the influence, activities and impact of these movements see Kirk, *Liberation*, 15-18. See also Escobar, *Changing*, 29.

[63] Muskus, *Origins*, 126-148; Samuel Escobar, "Religious Transitions and Civil Society in Latin America" in *Local Ownership, Global Change. Will Civil Society Save the World?*, eds., Roland Hoksbergen and Lowell M. Ewert (Monrovia: World Vision International, 2002), 162-182, at 172-174; Núñez, *Conciencia*, 3-6; Escobar, "Católicos", 66; José Míguez Bonino, *Concilio abierto: una interpretación protestante del Concilio Vaticano II* (Buenos Aires: La Aurora, 1967); José Míguez Bonino, "Implicaciones del Segundo Concilio Vaticano para la vida religiosa de nuestros tiempos, particularmente en América Latina" in *Los Protestantes y el Segundo Concilio Vaticano: Consulta sobre las actuales relaciones y actitudes entre evangélicos y católicos romanos*, ed. Federcio J. Huegel (Mexico: Casa Unida de Publicaciones, 1964), 88-95.

reinterpret traditional dogma, and the apparent veering of Medellín toward the left in its analysis of the continent's social and political problems.[64]

There is no doubt that the Second Latin American Episcopal Conference held in 1968 in Medellín, Colombia, was also a defining moment in the history of the Church on the continent. It has been described as "the Vatican II of Latin America."[65] It would seem accurate to say that the very name of Medellín has become a symbol of the transformations that were shaking the dominant church in the region at that time.[66] It was a consultation which gave Latin American bishops the opportunity to consider the Latin American situation and suggest guidelines for the renovation of pastoral activities on the continent. It allowed for a detailed exploration of the actual circumstances of desolation and oppression in Latin America. It encouraged the advance of pastoral thought particular to the context. It pressed for a more just Latin American society. The bishops were presented with potential options for the establishment of a new epoch for Catholicism in Latin America.[67]

One of the possible options submitted was an approach for complete liberation, that is, liberation for the whole person and, as a consequence, for the nations. This option was an opening for commitment to the class struggle, for championing the cause of the weak and for speaking on behalf of the voiceless in society. The participation of key liberation theologians on task forces at Medellín and their influence on the content and conclusions of the conference ensured that the theology of liberation was given a foothold, perhaps for the first time.[68] Núñez observes that even a moderate appraisal of the significance of Medellín would acknowledge that the way was opened for the theology of liberation.[69] Kirk concurs in this observation and comments that "the bringing together of the concerns of Vatican II and a fresh socio-political and economic analysis of Latin America in the documents of Medellín became a significant catalyst for the 'theology of liberation' movement."[70]

---

[64] Núñez and Taylor, *Crisis*, 241. For further discussion on the liturgical and biblical renewal and the ecclesiastical, socio-political and theological implications on the Catholic Church in Latin America see Emilio A. Núñez, "Posición de la iglesia frente al 'aggiornamento'" in *Acción en Cristo para una continente en crisis*, ed. Samuel Escobar (San José: Editorial Caribe, 1970), 39-43.

[65] José Míguez Bonino, cited by Núñez and Taylor, *Crisis*, 241. See also Míguez Bonino, "Condition", 262-263.

[66] Escobar, "Religious", 172. See also Escobar, *Changes*, 65-67.

[67] See Muskus, *Origins*, 148-166; Núñez, *Conciencia*, 5-6; Escobar, *Changing*, 29-32.

[68] Some insightful thoughts on the Medellín conference from the perspective of Latin American theologians can be read for example in Rosino Gibellini, *Frontiers of Theology in Latin America*, trans. John Drury (London: SCM, 1980), ix-xii, 21-32.

[69] See Núñez and Taylor, *Crisis*, 242. For a discussion on the early liberationist reflections see Escobar, "Católicos", 70-73.

[70] Kirk, *Liberation*, 16.

During the post-Vatican II years, the Catholic Church was being forced to consider the issues surrounding social justice. Within the Church itself, the Vatican social encyclicals required active reflection and reaction.[71] Priests were personally witnessing the poverty and oppression of their people first hand and insisted that the traumatic circumstances of the Latin American reality demanded a response. Priests, who had been given the opportunity to study in Europe, were influenced by thinkers outside of Latin America. Within the priesthood, leaders such as the sociologist Camilo Torres, the brilliant scholar and teacher, led by example. Convinced of the futility of peaceful means, Torres joined the communist-led guerrilla National Liberation Army in Colombia and was killed in a clash with counterinsurgency forces in February 1967.[72] Núñez observes that "the name of Father Camilo Torres, along with his message and his complete surrender to the cause of the liberation of the oppressed classes, form without a doubt part of post-conciliar Latin American Catholicism."[73]

Political tensions internationally meant that the Catholic Church was being continually confronted by radical options for change. Communism was presenting challenges and making assertions with which the Church had to engage. The Cuban revolution of 1959 raised pertinent questions which needed to be addressed. The 'Alliance for Progress', established with the United States of America, had proven to be an utter failure. Latin American sociologists and economists were producing statistics which displayed the continental situation of economic subservience.[74] Military governments were holding nations such as Brazil, Argentina, Paraguay and Bolivia in the grip of growing repression. The Protestant group ISAL was also publishing documents relating specifically to the context.[75] These factors, both from within Latin American Catholicism and from outside, contributed significantly to rising concern within the Church.[76]

---

[71] Relevant encyclicals include *Mater et Magistra* published in 1961, *Pacem in terris* published in 1963, *Populorum Progressio* published in 1967 and *Evangelii nuntiandi* published in 1974. See Kirk, *Liberation*, 18-20. See also Núñez and Taylor, *Crisis*, 245.

[72] Keen, *Independence*, 570.

[73] See Núñez and Taylor, *Crisis*, 246-248, at 248. Núñez details the revolutionary stance taken by Camilo Torres and records extracts from speeches justifying revolutionary commitment made before Camilo's death on 15 February, 1967.

[74] For evangelical reflection on the economic subservience of Latin America in the twentieth century, see Jesús Camargo López, "La dependencia económica de América Latina: un enfoque evangélico", *Boletín Teológico* 37 (1990): 7-30; Franklin Canelos, "Las instituciones financieras y comerciales internacionales y el derecho al desarrollo", *Boletín Teológico* 37 (1990): 31-37; Cristobál Kay, "Estructuralismo y teoría de la dependencia en el período neoliberal: una perspectiva latinoamericana", *Nueva Sociedad* 158 (1998): 100-119.

[75] Kirk, *Liberation*, 20.

[76] For an evangelical perspective on the turbulent aspects of those decades see Samuel Escobar, "La situación latinoamericana" in *Fe cristiana y Latinoamérica hoy*, ed. C. René Padilla (Buenos Aires: Ediciones Certeza, 1974), 13-34, at 18-25.

There is no doubt that the Catholic Church sought to respond to the challenges and circumstances. However, "in spite of this unprecedented development in the Church's social concern, other groups within the Church have arrived at a decidedly different interpretation of revolution and its pressing urgency."[77] The decidedly different interpretations of appropriate reaction from within post-conciliar Latin American Catholicism can be identified as the *violent* revolution, the *pacifist* revolution, the *poetic* revolution, the *pedagogical* revolution and the *theological* revolution.[78]

In distinct opposition to the drastic *violent* revolutionary approach taken by Camilo Torres, the *pacifist* option was espoused by the "Bishop of the Poor," Helder Câmara who was archbishop of Recife (Brazil).[79] With the reputation for denouncing oppression, defending the poor, condemning violence, actively pursuing justice and peace, and motivating the young to exert moral pressure in an effort to realise a more humane world, Câmara stood in the tradition of Mahatma Gandhi and Martin Luther King.[80]

Ernesto Cardenal, a Nicaraguan poet-priest, made his contribution in the form of a *poetic* revolution.[81] Amongst his "protest" poems, Cardenal boldly paraphrased biblical passages, for example Psalm 11 entitled "Liberate us." He also compiled *El evangelio de Solentiname* (The Solentiname Gospels), a collection of thoughts expressed by those within his community in response to the reading of the Gospels.[82] Núñez asserts: "Through the alchemy of his poetic gift, Cardenal converts this [revolutionary] spirit into a message that is an angry and choleric cry for the pain of his people; a voice of anguished protest for the tears of the afflicted; a triumphal song anticipating the overthrow of tyranny."[83]

The *pedagogical* revolution within the post-conciliar Church was greatly influenced by the work of Paulo Freire, the Catholic educator from Brazil.[84] While

[77] Kirk, *Liberation*, 19.

[78] See chapter 8 "Revolutionary Ferment: Liberation Theology" in Núñez and Taylor, *Crisis*, 245-293, at 246-261.

[79] For a discussion on the life and ministry of Helder Câmara see Julio de Santa Ana, "Through the Third World Towards One World", *Exchange* 19, no. 3 (1990): 217-235, at 220-228.

[80] Núñez discusses the approach of Helder Câmara further in Núñez and Taylor, *Crisis*, 248-250. See also Keen, *Independence*, 570-571.

[81] See Núñez and Taylor, *Crisis*, 250-252; Keen, *Independence*, 457.

[82] Ernesto Cardenal, *El evangelio de Solentiname* (Salamanca: Sígueme, 1975). For the purpose of this book, an English translation of the Spanish title of a work mentioned within the text will be given in brackets. It should be noted that the translation of the original title may differ from the title given to a book when it is published in English.

[83] Núñez and Taylor, *Crisis*, 253.

[84] For a thorough study of the work of Paulo Freire from a Latin American evangelical perspective see Samuel Escobar, "Paulo Freire: otra pedagogía política" (Ph.D. diss., Universidad Complutense de Madrid, 1990); Samuel Escobar, *Paulo Freire: una pedagogía latinoamericana* (Mexico: Casa Unida de Publicaciones – Editorial Kyrios, 1993).

Freire does not consider himself to be a theologian, it is acknowledged that the ethical, anthropological and philosophical framework within which he structures his studies has been instrumental in the development of Latin American theological thought.[85] The method of education proposed by Freire seeks to educate by the practice of "conscientization," that is, transforming the mentality of the oppressed and making them aware of their situation.[86] This is then followed by "problem-posing" which encourages the oppressed to challenge the "myths" they have always believed regarding their oppressors and their circumstances. The poor are encouraged to free themselves from their "dominated-conditioned mentality and their passive despair."[87] This style of approach, both the message and the method, was in keeping with the hopes and endeavours of revolutionary movements in Latin America. Many in the Catholic Church promoted education and sought to apply Freire's method of "education as the practice of liberty."[88]

The *theological* revolution taking place in the post-conciliar setting is of greatest concern to this book and will be dealt with in more detail later. Suffice it to say at this juncture, the *theological* revolution was taking place not only within Latin American Catholicism but also within the Latin American Protestant tradition.

In his summary of the differing responses within Latin American Catholicism at this time, Núñez observes:

> Revolution is now present in Latin America in theory and in practice, in the sphere of ideas and in the field of action; in passive resistance and in the outburst of violence by those who seek a rapid and complete change in social order. The revolutionary spirit is seen, for example, in the writings and actions of the pacifist bishop Helder Câmara, in the educator Pablo Freire, in the poet and monk Ernesto Cardenal, in the martyr priest Camilo Torres, who opted for violent revolution, in liberation theologians like Gustavo Gutiérrez, in the priests who have adopted a new pastoral model among the Latin American masses, and in the Roman Catholics who belong to the armed groups that fight for a radical change in our social structures.[89]

In February 1979, the Third Latin American Episcopal Conference took place at Puebla, Mexico. By this stage, there were grave questions to be addressed regarding the theology of liberation, the political activities of some clerics, the destitution of the masses on the continent, the Marxist-Capitalist clash, and the church of the poor. The circumstances surrounding the Puebla consultation were very different to the

---

[85] Núñez and Taylor, *Crisis*, 254. Freire proposed a method in adult literacy programmes which centred the teaching around key words, charged with political meaning. Those who learn to read and write by this approach are then also made aware of their political circumstances. See Núñez and Taylor, *Crisis*, 255-256.

[86] See Paulo Freire, "Conscientizing as a Way of Liberating (1970)" in *Liberation Theology: A Documentary History*, ed. Alfred T. Hennelly (Maryknoll: Orbis Books, 1990), 5-13.

[87] Kirk, *Liberation*, 25.

[88] Kirk, *Liberation*, 25.

[89] Núñez and Taylor, *Crisis*, 246.

atmosphere of Medellín. Medellín had meant to some degree "the end of the centuries-old alliance of the Catholic Church with the conservative ruling powers ruling Latin America."[90] Catholics had become seriously involved in the revolutionary struggle, prompted by the assertions of Medellín. They had endured persecution, arrest, torture and in some cases had faced death for the sake of their beliefs. However, Pope John Paul II was now in place and his response to the turbulence and trauma was moderate. He countered clerical political involvement but did not denounce the theology of liberation. Under his direction, the consultation assented neither to Marxism nor Capitalism but sought other historical alternatives for social transformation.[91] "The Puebla documents seem to be a special effort to integrate the new message on social justice and liberation into the theological framework of traditional Catholicism."[92]

A study of the Catholic Church within Latin America during the twentieth century demonstrates the noteworthy changes which took place in respect of the Church's response to the socio-political circumstances of the continent. The *theological* revolution which led to the exposition of a theology of liberation is the most significant aspect of the period for the purpose of this book. As the post-conciliar context of Latin American Catholicism has now been outlined, the early development of the theology of liberation will be discussed in more detail. For liberation theology is the dominant proposal of contextual theology for Latin America with which evangelical theologians engaged.

2.3.2 The Early Development of a "Theology of Liberation"

As previously discussed, priests and lay people in Latin America were personally facing the traumatic circumstances of poverty and injustice mentioned in many of the Church's documents. They were determined to find an appropriate response. Gustavo Gutiérrez is the name widely associated with the systematisation of the response known as the theology of liberation.[93]

Gutiérrez was one of many theologians who left Latin America to study in Europe. He travelled from his homeland of Peru to become a student in the University of Louvain. In Louvain, the poverty of Latin America and the threat of communism were causing much discussion and debate. Students in Europe were engaging with thinkers such as Jürgen Moltmann, Johann Baptist Metz, Karl Barth, Rudolf Bultmann, Harvey Cox, Paul Lehmann, Wolfhart Pannenberg, and Karl Rahner. They were also absorbed in Christian-Marxist dialogue.[94] The influence of

---

[90] Núñez and Taylor, *Crisis*, 243.

[91] See Núñez, *Conciencia*, 7-8 where he discusses the new strategy adopted by the Catholic Church in Latin America.

[92] Núñez and Taylor, *Crisis*, 244.

[93] For a discussion on the importance of the work of Gutiérrez from an evangelical perspective see Muskus, *Origins*, 3-7.

[94] Muskus, *Origins*, 180-242. Further discussion on the contribution made by these thinkers can be found in Alister McGrath, ed., *The Blackwell Encyclopaedia of Modern*

such political theology is evident in liberation thought and Kirk considers the theology of liberation to be "both a continuation of and a rupture from this brand of political theology."[95] As a result of Vatican II, biblical renewal became a new source of theological reflection within Catholic circles. Biblical scholars such as Gerhard von Rad, Joachim Jeremias and Ernst Käsemann also influenced those developing a theology of liberation in their search for a hermeneutical key to relate biblical thought to social and political conditions.

On his return from Europe, during the early 1960s, Gutiérrez became an enthusiastic teacher at the Catholic University of Lima. He was involved in the National Union of Catholic Students (UNEC) and influenced their doctrinal position which became more radical and emphasised the Marxist analysis of life. During these years, Gutiérrez had already begun the formulation of his thoughts on a theology of liberation. Expectation was high in the light of Vatican II and it was hoped that attitudes towards economic, social and political situations in the world would be dramatically changed. The concrete reality of poverty, oppression and injustice, witnessed personally on a daily basis, compelled these theologians to reflect actively and pursue an appropriate response.

During these years, there was a consistent effort to organise meetings, courses and conferences to study the Latin American reality and the theological response to it. Organisations such as the Pastoral Institute of Latin America, the National Office of Social Investigation, "Priests for the Third World" and "Solidarity Church" sought renewal in the Catholic Church and social change across the continent. Priests ministering across the continent had become aware of the social doctrine of the post-conciliar Church and the ideas their colleagues were developing in regard to liberation. They wanted to be a part of the transformation.

At this early stage, two essential attributes of the theology under construction were strong opposition to the thesis of development and openness to Marxism. Early discussion, in 1964 at a meeting in Petropolis in Brazil, centred around love of one's neighbour, identity with the poor, revolutionary struggle, violence, poverty and social vindication. Gutiérrez is considered to be the most representative of the theologians and the gradual evolution of his thought on these subjects is evident. For example, his first work, *Christian Charity and Love*, was published in 1966.[96] He taught a course entitled "The Church and Poverty" in Montreal in 1967. He also sought to respond to the thesis of development with a theology of liberation as

---

Christian Thought (Oxford: Blackwell, 1993), 30-34, 59-63, 385-388, 420-422, 539-542. This engagement with European political theology has caused some controversy when it has been claimed that the theology of liberation is distinctly Latin American. Moltmann, for example, felt that in many cases his thoughts and insights were not clearly acknowledged. See Jürgen Moltmann, "An Open Letter to José Míguez Bonino (March 29, 1976)" in *Liberation Theology: A Documentary History*, ed. Alfred T. Hennelly (Maryknoll: Orbis Books, 1990), 195-204.

[95] Kirk, *Liberation*, 26. For a brief outline of the main criticisms which the theology of liberation launches against European political theology see Kirk, *Liberation*, 25-26.

[96] Cited by Núñez, *Liberation*, 121.

opposed to a theology of revolution. He challenged the assertion that poverty is the will of God, maintained that poverty opposes justice and called on Christians to fight against the scandal of social sin. He challenged the Church to cease being rich in the midst of destitution. In the following years, Gutiérrez presented papers and published works which evidence the further development of thought, the moulding of ideas, the formulation of fundamental intuitions, the systematisation of concepts and the particular use of expressions, which were finally published in 1971 as his well known work *Teología de la liberación, Perspectivas.*[97]

In 1970, Juan Luis Segundo published a collection of articles concentrating on themes from the developing theology of liberation entitled *From Society to Theology*. Also in 1970, Rubem Alves published his book *A Theology of Human Hope* in Spanish as *Religión: ¿opio o instrumento de liberación?* (Religion: Opium or Instrument of Liberation?). In 1971, Hugo Assmann published *Opresión-liberación: desafío a los cristianos* (Oppression-Liberation: Challenge to Christians). These books were the first steps for liberation theologians in the process of discovering their own identity, in their effort to "break free from a past world, without yet having discovered the contours of a new one."[98] As Núñez rightly notes, the theology of liberation had not then arrived at its final destination, and would not be able to do so as long as the liberation of the poor in Latin America remained an unfinished process.

Theologians were not the only scholars questioning the situation in which Latin America found itself at this time. Economists, sociologists and political thinkers were critiquing ideas promoted in North America. For example, they rejected the idea of development as the process to eradicate poverty. Similarly, they recognised that those working to educate the poor, thus making the poor aware of the alternatives, were facing active suppression. In the light of the conclusions reached regarding exploitation, international debt and the impact of multinational companies, theologians began to actively reflect on their faith. They too rejected the international proposition of development as the answer to the needs of the continent and sought a viable alternative. The theology of liberation took into consideration the political situation, the social milieu, the economic circumstances and the Christian faith. Kirk explains that the word liberation "was chosen for two basic reasons: it formed a direct contrast to the concept of dependence, and it had a long historical usage in biblical and Church tradition as a synonym for salvation."[99]

It is beyond dispute that Gutiérrez's *Teología de la Liberación, Perspectivas* was the first exemplary presentation of the theology of liberation, bringing clarity and definition to the movement. His work prompted varying reactions, and further liberationist thought developed across the world over many years. Consequently, contemporary liberation theology is by no means monolithic. Rather, it is

---

[97] First published in English as *A Theology of Liberation: Perspectives.* (Maryknoll: Orbis Books, 1973).

[98] Kirk, *Liberation*, 23.

[99] Kirk, *Liberation*, 26.

thematically rich and diverse. The term "the theology of liberation" originally referred to the contextual theologies which first emerged in Latin America during the 1960s and 1970s. Currently, however, it is employed to describe any form of theological inquiry which regards the emancipation of oppressed peoples from unjust political, economic or social subjection as its first principle and ordering ideal. These contextual or political theologies come from the Two Thirds World or are developed in the First World under Two Thirds World inspiration. The contemporary array of such theologies includes African, North American Black, Asian, Hispanic and Feminist theologies, spanning the globe as each group seeks to articulate the Christian faith from within their own community, and with reference to the struggles of their individual communities to overcome oppression. The Latin American experience, however, remains the definitive one and themes developed in the Latin American context continue to serve as models for other theologies of liberation.

In this section, the focus has been on the early development of the theology of liberation within Latin American Catholicism. However, the contribution made by Protestant theologians, such as Míguez Bonino, to the formation of liberation theology should not be underestimated. It would seem fair to say that the perception of liberation theology as specifically Catholic theology is erroneous. This book seeks to focus on the evangelical engagement with the liberation themes arising in the Latin American context. For this reason, other Protestant reflection on contextual theology, particularly in the early years of liberationist thought, is pertinent.

2.3.3 The Contribution and Influence of ISAL

The historical circumstances surrounding the development of contextual Latin American theology in Catholic and Protestant tradition obviously intertwine. In what follows, therefore, there may be some repetition of facts. However, in terms of analysis, it is vital that the role played by ISAL be dealt with separately for reasons of clarity.

To understand the roots of contextual theology, particularly in respect of the Latin American Protestant theological community, the organisation known as ISAL is of great importance.[100] ISAL was founded following a continental meeting of forty-two participants from sixteen countries, held in Huampaní in Peru during July 1961.[101] Protestant theologians involved with this movement had been reflecting on

---

[100] For a thorough discussion on the foundation, the methodology, and the challenge presented by ISAL to the Latin American evangelical communities during these years, see C. René Padilla, "Iglesia y Sociedad en América Latina" in *Fe cristiana y Latinoamérica hoy*, ed. C. René Padilla (Buenos Aires: Ediciones Certeza, 1974), 119-147.

[101] The second continental conference was held at El Tabo in Chile during January 1966. The third continental consultation took place in Piriápolis, Uruguay in December 1967. The fourth continental conference was conducted in July 1971 at Ñaña, Peru. For further discussion on the content of the consultations and the historical development of ISAL,

the social problems and the Latin American context of suffering many years prior to the Second Vatican Council.[102] This first consultation focused on three specific issues: Christian responsibility in the face of rapid socio-cultural changes, the prophetic role of the Christian in Latin American political life and the Christian concern regarding economic progress and development.[103]

In 1964 Rubem Alves, the Brazilian Protestant theologian, published an article on injustice and rebellion which clarified the revolutionary option assented to by the Isaline movement.[104] Alves made six affirmations which are considered to be the basic tenets of liberationist thought. First, rich nations exploit poorer nations and such enforced economic dependence causes underdeveloped nations to remain so. Second, a hidden "class struggle" between the poor proletariat and the rich capitalists perpetuates suffering on the Latin American continent. Third, Christians and Marxists can unite to reach their goal of humanisation, that is to say, they can unite in their aim to restore true human dignity and acceptable levels of existence to people trapped in sub-human circumstances. Fourth, God is revealed, not in Scriptures alone, but in events of modern history. Fifth, God is at work in the Marxist revolutionary movement to bring his kingdom to Latin America. Sixth, the church should join this Marxist struggle for liberation. The ISAL movement and Isaline publications formulated the significant doctrines of what Alves named "theology of liberation." It is interesting to note that it has been suggested Alves was indeed the first Latin American theologian to present a structured outline of liberationist thought.[105]

Like the Catholic liberation theologians, the Isaline movement drew from a varied range of sources. In the years following the Second World War the writings of Karl Barth, Emil Brünner, Paul Tillich, Reinhold Niebuhr, and Gustaf Aulén were influential. Similarly, ISAL engaged with the theologians of secularisation, Dietrich Bonhoeffer, John A. T. Robinson and Jürgen Moltmann.[106] The esoteric Marxism of

---

detailing the involvement with the World Council of Churches and the ecumenical movement see Núñez, *Liberation*, 61-77.

[102] It is interesting to examine the assertions of Raymond Hundley with regard to the immediate context of liberation theology and indeed his discussion on how liberation theology "was born." Hundley is not alone in his observation of the significant influence of *Isaline* thought in Latin America at this time. Raymond C. Hundley, *Radical Liberation Theology: An Evangelical Response* (Wilmore: Bristol Books, 1987), 4-9. Núñez also affirms that before the Catholic theology of liberation became known across the continent and indeed across the world, South American Protestantism had already begun to demonstrate a liberationist trend. See Núñez, *Liberation*, 53-82.

[103] Padilla, "Iglesia", 119.

[104] Rubem Alves, "Injusticia y rebelión", *Cristianismo y Sociedad* 6 (1964): 40-53.

[105] Hundley, *Radical*, 7. For further discussion on the fundamental themes in Isaline thought see Samuel Escobar, *La fe evangélica y las teologías de la liberación* (El Paso: Casa Bautista de Publicaciones, 1987), 78-81.

[106] Núñez, *Liberation*, 53-55.

Ernst Bloch and Herbert Marcuse is also evident in the social analysis of the Isaline movement.[107]

The Isaline theologians considered dialogue and interaction between the Christian faith and the revolutionary ideologies to be "possible and necessary."[108] Paul Lehmann, who was committed to and participated in the dialogue between Marxism and Christianity, played a noteworthy role in the development of Isaline thought. Roger Garaudy was the Marxist most interested in entering into dialogue with Catholicism at the time. Like Lehmann, he too found converging elements between the two perspectives. An ideological commitment to Marxism is considered indisputable in the document published after the first *Christians for Socialism* conference in April 1972. Indeed C. René Padilla commented of ISAL at the time: "The point of reference taken for theology is the Latin American situation, seen, however, through the lens of Marxist analysis."[109] The negative repercussions of theology from a Marxist perspective will be dealt with in chapter four where contextual methods are discussed.

Paulo Freire, the Brazilian Catholic educator to whom I referred earlier, also influenced the thought and practice of the Isaline movement. Between the years 1967-1971, many of those committed to ISAL were also involved in urban missionary projects and training programmes which applied his educational theory and approach.[110]

The success of the Cuban revolution in 1959 and the influence of Richard Schaull, a Presbyterian missionary, who brought Lehmann on a lecture tour of Brazil and Argentina during that year, were also significant in the formation of Isaline discussion and debate. In the light of these events and influences, Isaline theologians rejected Scripture as containing the solution to the problems of Latin America. Inevitably the weighty debate of continental reform or revolution broke out within the Isaline movement as members differed in their understanding and interpretation of an appropriate response.[111]

At this point, it is helpful to draw attention to three identifiable stages evident in the evolution of Isaline thought. Míguez Bonino, who was president of the

---

[107] Padilla, "Iglesia", 124.

[108] Núñez, *Liberation*, 55.

[109] Padilla, "Iglesia", 125.

[110] Orlando E. Costas, *Theology of the Crossroads in Contemporary Latin America: Missiology in Mainline Protestantism 1969-1974* (Amsterdam: Rodopi, 1976), 200. For further discussion on the method and message of Paul Freire see Núñez, *Liberation*, 57-61. Núñez also explains "the evangelical Christian is concerned when he sees that Freirean anthropology assigns no proper place to the Scriptures and that man does not appear as a sinner. Dehumanisation is, according to Freire, only the result of an unjust social order. In Freire's program, 'the point of departure of theology has to be anthropological' and 'the theologian has to take as a point of departure his reflection on the history of mankind'", 61. See also Escobar, *Freire*, 11-54, 85-124, 153-184.

[111] Padilla, "Iglesia", 122-127.

committee responsible for the Huampaní conference, constructively outlines the stages as follows:

> In the first few years (1960-65) the analysis of the situation, which at the beginning oscillated between a developmentalist and a revolutionary approach, gained greater consistency, adopted the "sociology of dependence" (structured around the notion of neo-colonialism and dependence) and made a clear revolutionary and socialist option. This ideological clarification was followed in the years 1966-68 by a transformation in the theological perspective, veering from a predominantly Barthian theology to a "theology of God's transforming action in history" greatly indebted to Paul Lehmann and Richard Schaull until Rubem Alves gave it a creative expression in critical dialogue with Marcuse on the one hand and Moltmann on the other...The option for a Marxist analysis and interpretation had now been consciously adopted. But it was not a mere stereotype and interpretations varied...Since that time ISAL has been in search of greater political engagement...Since 1970, it has more and more defined its own function as "mobilization of the people."[112]

A review of the continental conferences held by ISAL and the documents published as a result confirm the observations of Míguez Bonino.[113] For during subsequent years, the thoughts and assertions of ISAL became definitively more radical and Isaline theologians sought a progression from *dialogue with* to *direct participation in* the revolutionary struggle.[114] At Naña in 1971, it is evident that the Isaline movement "turned furiously radical in its ideological commitment to the left."[115] Padilla reflected at the time: "ISAL does not recognise any alternative for the Christian other than participation in the struggle for liberation in line with the dictates of an ideology."[116] The most radical members of ISAL, therefore, became isolated from those within both the Catholic and Protestant traditions who were seeking to "react" and "reform" rather than promote revolution.

Political circumstances and governmental changes on the continent contributed to the demise of ISAL in the early seventies. The hopeful period of theological reflection in Latin America was followed by a wave of brutal repression. Brazil had been closed to ISAL for several years. The repression in Uruguay worsened and ISAL was declared illegal. General Juan José Torres had been overthrown in Bolivia and as a result ISAL, considered one of the most progressive ecumenical movements

---

[112] Míguez Bonino, *Doing*, 54-55.

[113] Costas also details the other publications of the Isaline movement, including the bulletin *Pasos*, the series *Cuadernos de Estudios*, the journal *Cristianismo y Sociedad* and the condensed, scholarly bulletin *Fichas de ISAL*. ISAL also entered into joint publication and distribution ventures with two significant European-Latin American companies *Ediciones Sígueme* and *Siglo XXX Editores*. See Costas, *Theology*, 207-208.

[114] See Padilla, "Iglesia", 133-134; Núñez, *Liberation*, 65-77.

[115] Núñez, *Liberation*, 77.

[116] Padilla, "Iglesia", 140.

there, was driven underground.[117] Following the *coup d'etat* in Chile and the murder of Salvador Allende during September 1973, the Isaline movement there had to disband and reorganise. An organisational form of ISAL is no longer in existence anywhere.[118]

This repression of radical groups, such as ISAL, motivated other Christian groups to pursue an alternative yet active response to the radical challenge which the Isaline movement had presented. For fundamental questions remained unanswered. The Isaline movement, which was rooted in Protestant theology and subsequently became an ecumenical group, merits careful study. For evangelicals who had struggled against the radical, revolutionary and violent call of ISAL remained convinced of the need for a relevant and fitting response.[119]

2.4 Conclusion

This chapter has sought to explore the historical background of Latin America and gain a clearer understanding of the continental context in which contextual theology germinated. Evangelical interpretations of Latin American history have been referred to closely in an effort to maintain continuity with the focus of this work.

The brief history of Latin America emphasises three significant aspects which contributed to the structures of society, the evolution of national identities and the practice of religion. It becomes clear that colonialisation has left an enduring legacy in the culture and context. Despite the struggle for independence and the revolutionary commitment to establish new nations, it can be seen that the atmosphere of exploitation and mistrust continued. Attempts to break away from the colonial past were unsuccessful in this respect. The discussion of the role of the Catholic Church during these periods sets the dramatic religious changes of the twentieth century in a clearer context.

In the second section of this chapter, it is argued that it was in these dramatic changes, demonstrated in the renewal sought through post-conciliar Latin American Catholicism, that the theology of liberation took root. The contribution of both Catholic and Protestant theologians during this era has been considered in an effort to examine the early foundations of contextual theology for Latin America.

An understanding of the historical background and the immediate historical context in which the theology of liberation flourished and in which Latin American evangelical theology is grounded, leads to a greater appreciation of the motivation behind their theological task. The focus of this chapter has been the context of the theology of liberation in particular, from an evangelical perspective. The use of

---

[117] Escobar discusses the significance of the ecumenical aspect of ISAL in Escobar, *Fe*, 76-77.

[118] For further details on the dispersion and reorganisation of ISAL see Costas, *Theology*, 210-212.

[119] Costas, *Theology*, 212-223; Escobar, "Identidad", 31-33.

evangelical accounts enables the reader to ascertain what Latin American evangelicals consider to be the most significant events and most influential aspects in their history. In the light of this, the purpose of the following chapter will be to place Latin American evangelicalism more specifically within its context, both as a Protestant minority within the vast continent of Latin America, and as a voice of protest within the international evangelical community.

CHAPTER 3

Latin American Evangelicalism:
A Perspective

3.1 Introduction

It has been established that to appreciate the development of contextual theology within Latin America, it is vital to have a balanced understanding of the historical background and the socio-political environment. In chapter two, the evangelical perspective of Latin American history has been considered. In light of this discussion, chapter three seeks to focus specifically on the background of Latin American evangelicalism. It will become evident as the book progresses that the historical circumstances and influences dealt with in chapter two and chapter three, have marked the Latin American culture and context indelibly. As a consequence, Latin American theology can only be examined thoroughly when this context is taken into account.

The purpose of this chapter then is to examine in detail the historical presence of evangelicalism within Latin America. First, in contemporary times the term "evangelical" can have various connotations. I will therefore define the term "evangelical" within the specific Latin American context. Second, contemporary Latin American evangelicalism will be set within its immediate historical context in order that the motivation behind the theological task is properly understood. Third, the development of Latin American evangelical theology will be traced since the foundation of the Latin American Theological Fraternity. For reasons which will become clear as the chapter progresses, the genesis of the Latin American Theological Fraternity represents a defining moment in Latin American evangelicalism. Therefore, it is a significant indication of the progression of indigenous Latin American evangelical thought.

3.2 A Discussion on the Term "Evangelical"

Across the Christian world the expression "evangelical" is frequently employed with a variety of understandings, implications and significances.[1] In Latin America

---

[1] Discussion on the significance of the term "evangelical" can be found in the following books. For further study of the origins, doctrines and contemporary realities of the evangelical movement see Derek J. Tidball, *Who are the Evangelicals?* (London: Marshall Pickering, 1994). For a discussion on evangelical theological method see John G. Stackhouse,

evangélico is used practically as a synonym for denominational Protestantism.[2] However, in the context of this study, the term *evangelical* is more specific and therefore is, in fact, simpler to define.

The Latin American evangelicalism which is the focus of this study reflects five key principles attributed to evangelicalism in general. Firstly, God's work of salvation in the person of Christ is proclaimed as the gospel message of good news. Secondly, the uniquely authoritative role of the Bible, God's word to humanity, is affirmed. It is the role of the Holy Spirit to illuminate these Scriptures and give understanding. Thirdly, it is asserted that God's work of salvation is evidenced by conversion. Conversion implies not only a moment of new birth but an experience that energises a transformed life of discipleship under the guidance of God the Holy Spirit, in anticipation of eternity in God's presence. Fourthly, those who have experienced this transformation become committed to mission, which seeks to bring others the message of God's salvation and share his love in the world. Fifthly, evangelicalism is transdenominational.[3] Across the evangelical spectrum, it is generally accepted that four features are central to evangelicalism: *conversionism, activism, biblicism* and *crucicentrism*.[4] This would also seem to fairly reflect Latin American evangelicalism.

John Stott, considered internationally as one of the significant spokesmen for evangelicalism, suggests a more concise definition. He distinguishes evangelicals as *Bible people* and *gospel people*. For it is evangelicals who give the Scriptures central place, who emphasise that a personal response to the work of Christ is necessary, and who affirm that this response will lead to sharing the good news with

---

ed., *Evangelical Futures* (Vancouver: Regent College Publishing, 2000), in particular the helpful discussion in chapter 2 John G. Stackhouse "Evangelical Theology should be Evangelical", 39-58. For an exploration into the historical engagement of evangelical Christianity with the issue of truth and the evangelical engagement with cultural and philosophical trends see Peter Hicks, *Evangelicals and Truth* (Leicester: Apollos, 1998). For discussion on topics of fundamental importance within evangelicalism and the need for constructive evangelical reflection and debate see Craig Bartholomew, Robin Parry and Andrew West, eds., *The Futures of Evangelicalism* (Leicester: IVP, 2003). For a study on the redefinition of traditional evangelical principles and future evangelical identity see Millard J. Erickson, *The Evangelical Left: Encountering Postconservative Evangelical Theology* (Grand Rapids: Baker Books, 1997). For examination of an evangelical "Third Way" to engage with the world see Melvin Tinker, *Evangelical Concerns* (Great Britain: Mentor, 2001). For a series of essays on the challenges presented to the evangelical movement by a post-Christian, post-modern generation see David S. Dockery, *The Challenge of Postmodernism: An Evangelical Engagement* (Grand Rapids: Baker Books, 1995). For a discussion on current issues for Anglican evangelicals see Paul Gardner, Chris Wright and Chris Green, eds., *Fanning the Flame: Bible, Cross and Mission* (Grand Rapids: Zondervan, 2003).

[2] Míguez Bonino, "Condition", 264; Escobar, "Identidad", 2.

[3] For further study of these five principles in depth see Stackhouse, "Evangelical", 39-58.

[4] David Bebbington, *Evangelicalism in Modern Britain: A History from the 1730s to the 1980s* (London: Unwin Hyman, 1989), 2-19; Tidball, *Who*, 14; Hicks *Truth*, 14.

society and the world.[5] Stott has been of great influence in Latin American evangelical circles, and he has dialogued closely with the evangelical theologians dealt with in this work.[6] Stott's uncomplicated approach to defining the essence of evangelicalism is also reflected in the clarity of Latin American evangelical commitment.

Latin American evangelical theologians would concur with the general principles of evangelicalism outlined above. However, despite the consistency of their evangelical position, they have often faced suspicion and harsh criticism, both from fellow Latin Americans and from the international evangelical community. Pablo Deiros reflects on the sensitivity involved in holding to an authentic evangelical position in the Latin American context when he comments:

> Conservative evangelicals insist on the ethical and political relevance of the Christian faith, emphasize its intellectual responsibility, and develop their conviction inside and along the lines of the evangelical denominations. They may express their faith in a radical political and ecclesiastical language, but they remain faithful to the core of evangelicalism, namely, its obedience to the authoritative character of the Christian Scriptures...Conservatives are often branded as "liberals" by the extreme right, and "fundamentalists" by the extreme left. Fundamentalists will criticize conservatives because, in their affirmation of the authority of the Bible, conservatives do not share an inerrantist hermeneutic. Liberationists, on the other hand, charge that conservatives are not committed to social justice, or will not take the radical, revolutionary measures to attain it. Accordingly, conservatives are at the centre of the spectrum of evangelical Christianity and in tense dialogue with both extremes.[7]

In such an unstable and uncertain environment, it has been vital for Latin American theologians to define actively what evangelicalism means for their specific context. In their effort to appropriate the expression "evangelical," they have displayed a determination to reflect on theological issues independent of North American or general Western influence.[8] It is significant that even in the definition of their evangelical commitment, Latin Americans have moved away from

[5] Cited by Tidball, *Who*, 12; see also Tidball, *Who*, 11-14.

[6] Stott first met Samuel Escobar in 1959 and has been involved with the Latin American evangelical theologians dealt with in this book for many years through ministry tours in Latin America, through working together at Consultations and also in the editing of papers which they have presented. John Stott, interview by the author, 20 September 2003, video recording, Blackpool.

[7] Pablo A. Deiros, "Protestant Fundamentalism in Latin America" in *Fundamentalism Observed*, eds. Martin E. Marty and R. Scott Appleby (Chicago: The University of Chicago Press, 1991), 142-196, at 166.

[8] Escobar affirms that evangelical communities have been prompted to search for their own identity within their situation in order to face challenges regarding a "foreign" mentality or "foreign" image associated with evangelical approaches and the need for legitimate models of Latin American evangelical ministry. Escobar, "Situación", 24.

"translated" discussions on the subject.[9] Rather, they have approached the issue by studying the evangelical heritage afresh, by reflecting on evangelical faith specifically for the Latin American context and by considering the challenges Latin American evangelicalism will face in the future.[10]

Within the Latin American context, Núñez emphasises firstly that the Latin American evangelical identity does not depend on the Evangelical-Catholic polemic. For to be evangelical means much more than to be in confrontation with the Catholic Church. Secondly, Latin American evangelical identity does not depend on a particular form of liturgy or style of worship.[11] Thirdly, evangelical identity is not inherent in the methods or strategies employed for the purposes of ministry, pastoral care, or evangelism. Fourthly, evangelical identity is not proven by immersion in an evangelical subculture, or adherence to social practices which are considered "acceptable" evangelical behaviour.[12] Rather, Núñez asserts that the essence of evangelical identity is a deep, personal response to Jesus Christ. It is an identity grounded in a commitment to Reformation principles.[13] Núñez contends:

> What in reality distinguishes us as evangelicals in the face of the Catholic renewal is not only the doctrine which we have believed through the grace of God, but the personal commitment we have made to Jesus Christ, the power of the Spirit and the word to renew us day by day, to the glory of God, and for the blessing of those around us.[14]

Concurring with Núñez, Latin American evangelicals trace the genesis of their contemporary evangelical position to the Reformation. The assertions of *grace*

---

[9] Núñez emphasises the need for Latin American evangelicals to "take off the Anglo-Saxon trappings" and contextualise their faith and identity for Latin America. See in particular chapter 1 in Emilio A. Núñez, *El Cristo de Hispanoamérica* (Mexico: Ediciones las Americas, 1979), 41-46.

[10] See José Míguez Bonino, "La teología evangélica y los evangélicos", *Boletín Teológico* 65 (1997): 7-15, at 7. See also Samuel Escobar, "¿Qué significa ser evangélico hoy?", *Misión* 1, no.1 (1982), 15-18, 35-39. For a helpful article on Protestant identity in general within Latin America see Antônio Carlos Barro, "The Identity of Protestantism in Latin America" in *Emerging Voices in Global Theology*, ed. William A. Dyrness (Grand Rapids: Zondervan, 1994), 229-252.

[11] For a discussion on the significance of evangelical church worship see Orlando E. Costas, "El culto como índice de la realidad que vive la iglesia", *Vida y Pensamiento* 1, no. 1 (1973): 13-18; Orlando E. Costas, "La realidad de la iglesia evangélica latinoamericana" in *Fe cristiana y Latinoamérica hoy*, ed. C. René Padilla (Buenos Aires: Ediciones Certeza, 1974), 34-65.

[12] Núñez reflects further on the need for a biblical sense of identity as an evangelical church rather than perpetuating a subculture which is isolated from society in Emilio A. Núñez, *Desafíos Pastorales* (Grand Rapids: Editorial Portavoz, 1998), 22-24. See in particular chapter 1 on the pastor and the social context, 13-30.

[13] Núñez, *Conciencia*, 9-14.

[14] Núñez, *Conciencia*, 14.

alone, *Christ* alone, *faith* alone, and *Scripture* alone are accepted as fundamental characteristics which require reflection and direct application to the Latin American reality.[15] Other aspects of evangelical heritage, identified by Escobar as having an enduring influence on Latin American evangelical faith include: a passion for evangelism; a commitment to pursue personal piety; an Anabaptist stance towards society (in the sense of ecclesial communities centred in the congregation)[16]; a puritan approach to ethics; and an acknowledgement of the social dimension of the gospel.[17] Escobar is clear in his emphasis:

> The new generation (*generaciones*) in particular needs to know that to be evangelical means doctrinal strength, evangelising passion, personal piety, a lifestyle different to the world and also a social conscience...We have a cloud of witnesses around us and to be evangelical means to be faithful to the inheritance which precedes us...[18]

The "new generation" referred to by Escobar has indeed inherited a contextual, indigenous approach to evangelicalism which has developed as a result of, and in

---

[15] Emilio A. Núñez, "Herederos de la Reforma" in Congreso Latinoamericano de Evangelización (CLADE), II, noviembre de 1979, Quito: *América Latina y la evangelización en los años 80*, eds. Pedro Savage and Rolando Gutiérrez, (Mexico: Fraternidad Teológica Latinoamericana, 1980), 163-170. See also Escobar, "Evangélico", 16. Escobar expounds the historical heritage of evangelicals and the implications for life and doctrine further in *El estudiante evangélico* (Lima: Ediciones Certeza, 1983), see in particular "Nuestra herencia evangélica", 7-45; Samuel Escobar, *Evangelio y realidad social* (El Paso: Casa Bautista de Publicaciones, 1988), 195-205, at 199; Núñez and Taylor, *Crisis*, 232-235; Núñez, *Conciencia*, 11. For a helpful example of the direct application of one of these principles to the Latin American reality see Samuel Escobar, *Sola Escritura: la Biblia en la misión de la iglesia* (Madrid: Sociedad Bíblica, 1997) where Escobar presents a series of Bible studies on the theme of "Scripture Alone."

[16] For a helpful article on the influence of Anabaptist theology in Latin American evangelical circles see Samuel Escobar, "Latin America and Anabaptist Theology" in *Engaging Anabaptism: Conversations with a Radical Tradition*, ed. John D. Roth (Scottdale: Herald Press, 2001), 75-88. See also C. René Padilla, "The New Face of Religion in Latin America and the Caribbean", TMs (photocopy), The Latin American Theological Fraternity Archives, Buenos Aires, (n.d.), 1-10, at 3-8; Luis Scott and Titus Guenther, *Del sur al norte: aportes teológicos desde la periferia* (Buenos Aires: Ediciones Kairós, 2003), 61-67.

[17] Escobar, "Evangélico", 16-18. Escobar also notes with regards to his discussion on the Anabaptist stance that while there are differences in regard to the practice of baptism and personal lifestyle, the Anabaptist position implies that evangelicals in Latin America take up a position which contrasts with the official church, they are a critical minority group with a strong sense of mission not a sense of inferiority, who seek to impact society as faithful followers of Christ. Kirk also confirmed this understanding noting that the understanding of Anabaptism was not so much an issue of church practice but of attitude towards the dominance of the Catholic Church. J. Andrew Kirk, interview with author, 25 September 2003, video recording, Lechlade.

[18] Escobar, "Evangélico", 18. See also Orlando E. Costas, "La teología evangélica en el mundo de los dos tercios", *Boletín Teológico* 28 (1987): 201-229, at 202-205.

response to, the historical context and circumstances within the Latin American continent. It will be unnecessary to repeat the historical and cultural discussion examined in chapter two. Rather, this chapter will seek to place the evangelical presence in Latin America more specifically within that context, in an effort to appreciate the difficulties and challenges faced by the Latin American evangelical community.

3.3 The History of the Evangelical Presence in Latin America

The discussion of the history of Latin America since colonial times in the previous chapter shows the dominant force of the Catholic Church on the continent. Such dominance continues to be evident in the contemporary social and political context. It would seem no exaggeration to say then that Catholicism has inevitably shaped evangelicalism in Latin America. As present day Catholicism develops and seeks to be more open and creative, it is putting into practice many aspects of ministry formerly considered to be "Protestant." Escobar comments therefore that "the changes in Catholicism oblige us to define the distinctives of our evangelical faith."[19] Despite the minority position held by evangelical Protestants in Latin American society, there is no doubt that they have made a valuable contribution in the past. The challenge presented to evangelicals by the renewal within the Catholic Church is to assess this Catholic renovation and sustain a distinctive character where the differences cannot be overcome.[20]

John Mackay identifies precursors to the modern evangelical movement in Latin America as far back as 1555 when John Calvin and Admiral Coligny backed several expeditions which attempted, unsuccessfully, to found a Huguenot colony in Brazil. In the early seventeenth century, a group of missionaries accompanied the Dutch who occupied Bahia in Northern Brazil. Some of these missionaries learned the chief local language Guaraní, shared the gospel with the Indians and taught industry and agriculture. Despite this, the new community was forced to leave in 1664. It was almost two hundred years before Protestant Christianity had a presence on the Latin American continent again.

During the nineteenth century, following the demise of Spanish and Portuguese power, foreign colonies were established across Latin America. Anglicans from Great Britain, Lutherans from Germany, and Waldensian immigrants established

---

[19] Samuel Escobar, "Entender a la América Latina en el nuevo milenio", *Apuntes Pastorales* 17, no. 2 (2000): 12-18. Míguez Bonino also recognises the influence that Catholicism has had on the formation of evangelical churches which characteristically play a militant and polemical role as a minority group. Yet he also acknowledges that while there is a rejection of the Catholic Church, it is interesting to note the influence of Catholic religious ideas regarding death and meditation for example, which are evident particularly in some indigenous and peasant evangelical Pentecostal groups. See Míguez Bonino, "Teología", 8-9. See also Escobar, *Fe*, 34-35.

[20] See Samuel Escobar, "Missions and Renewal in Latin American Catholicism", *Missiology: An International Review* 15:2 (1987): 33-46.

their worshipping communities.[21] *The British and Foreign Bible Society* published twenty thousand copies of the New Testament in Portuguese between 1804 and 1807, launching the distribution of Bibles on the continent. Mackay identifies the specific Protestant missionary activity to begin with James Thomson, agent of *The British and Foreign Bible Society* and representative of the *Lancastrian Educational Society*, in the early 1800s. Thomson was made an honorary citizen of both Argentina and Chile, and was also active in Peru, Colombia, Guatemala and Mexico.[22]

Commenting on the missionaries who initiated the work in Latin America from the 1840s, Míguez Bonino writes:

> It is remarkable to note that, despite their confessional diversity (mostly Methodists, Presbyterians, and Baptists) and origin (North Americans and British), all shared the same theological horizon, which can be characterized as *evangelical...*[23]

The influence of the North American evangelical tradition, in particular, cannot be underestimated.[24] Following the end of the American civil war in 1865, optimism flooded the American nation and indeed the evangelical movement. "The religious awakening, social progress, education – all mutually supported each other"[25] and the United States became a model nation, stimulating other nations into action. The European Pietist tradition also contributed to the missionary effort during this period and their particular theology and piety nourished the early converts.[26]

As the Latin American nations became open to American and British capitalism, the Protestants who subsequently came to Latin America carried not only a message of deep spiritual significance for the continent.[27] These Protestants also brought a

---

[21] For a detailed discussion on the meeting of cultures and religious traditions in the Latin American context see Sidney Rooy, *Misión y encuentro de culturas* (Buenos Aires: Ediciones Kairós, 2001).

[22] Mackay, *Other*, 231-237. For a helpful outline of the history of evangelicals in Latin American and the development of the diverse streams within Latin American evangelicalism, see Tomás J. Gutiérrez, "De Panamá a Quito: los congresos evangélicos en América Latina. Iglesia, misión e identidad (1916 – 1992)", *Boletín Teológico* 59-60 (1995), 34-64, at 35.

[23] José Míguez Bonino, *Faces of Latin American Protestantism*, trans. Eugene L. Stockwell (Grand Rapids: Eerdmans, 1997), 27.

[24] For a thorough discussion on the influence of North American missionary and religious organisations within Latin America, see David Stoll, *Is Latin America Turning Protestant? The Politics of Evangelical Growth* (Oxford: University of California Press, 1990), 135-179. It is also important to recognise the criticism directed against the North American imperialist attitude, mentioned in chapter two, which also influenced the evangelical movement in Latin America, see Escobar, "El poder", 166-167; John A. Mackay, *That Other America* (New York: Friendship Press, 1935), 28-29, 76-116.

[25] Míguez Bonino, *Faces*, 29. See also Míguez Bonino, "Teología", 9.

[26] Escobar, "Católicos", 72-73.

[27] Escobar is careful to explain the necessity of setting the history of Protestant growth in Latin America within the context of the Iberian-Anglo Saxon confrontation. See Escobar,

distinct social and political attitude, promoting change and modernisation through rationalism, individualism, opposition to authoritarianism, and freedom of religion.[28] Escobar observes:

> In the face of modernization, a tentative...generalization is possible, especially in observing developments at the base of the social pyramid. Catholic religion at the grass roots has in many cases provided an ethical discourse to oppose modernization and also forms of solidarity to resist it. Catholics have been more open to resisting systems and using violent means to do so. On the other hand, religious commitment along Protestant lines has been a means to understand modernization and a source of empowerment of persons through a change in values, in order to function better within modernization. In this case, religious dissidence has not been the source of political criticism. Protestants have been more open to accommodate and try to function within new systems.[29]

The first missionaries and the first converts were nurtured in this environment of change and modernisation: churches were established, Bibles and literature were distributed, the gospel was preached, occasional medical work was developed and perhaps, most influentially, significant contributions were made in the realm of education.[30]

There were several distinguishing characteristics of the Latin American "mission field" during this era and these peculiarities notably shaped the evangelical message. First, priority was given to anti-Catholic polemic. New converts were taught Protestant doctrine and encouraged to study the Bible to enable them to debate on such issues effectively.[31] Second, the Bible was given particular prominence. It was "exalted both as a 'weapon' in the 'struggle against error' and as an indispensable tool for evangelism. In both senses, Scripture was conceived as having a 'power', a

---

"Five Hundred", 21-37. David Martin too, in his study of the explosion of Protestant growth on the continent also places this growth in the context of four centuries of struggle between the nations of the Iberian Peninsula, and the British Empire which was then succeeded by the United States of America. See David Martin, *Tongues of Fire: The Explosion of Protestantism in Latin America* (Oxford: Basil and Blackwell, 1989), 9.

[28] Escobar, "Religious", 168-169; Escobar, "El poder", 167; Escobar, *Fe*, 44. Also for a discussion on the theological changes at this time, indebted to the Great Awakening and the Second Great Awakening see Míguez Bonino, *Faces*, 28-29.

[29] Samuel Escobar, "Religious and Social Change at the Grass Roots in Latin America", *The Annals of the American Academy of Political and Social Science* 554 (1997): 81-103, at 103.

[30] Mackay describes such landmarks of the modern missionary movement in depth. He also discusses several indigenous movements such as the Pentecostal movement, evangelical youth initiatives, the World Sunday School Convention, and the impact of the YMCA and the YWCA. See Mackay, *Other*, 241-256.

[31] Escobar makes a brief but helpful comparative study of the evangelical mission strategy and the position and approach of the Catholic Church in Escobar, "Five Hundred", 6.

certain intrinsic efficacy that reproves, convinces and converts."[32] Third, believers were challenged with the responsibility, both at a personal and a community level, to actively engage with society. Latin American evangelicals of this generation were not politically conservative, neither by social extraction nor through political conviction. Total abstinence from political activities was not part of their evangelical tradition.[33] In contrast, they were motivated to confront political conditions in order to secure religious freedom. Padilla reflects that "the struggle for religious freedom is part of the heritage of evangelical churches in this region. In various countries, this struggle was the only matter that could awaken interest in politics among evangelicals."[34] They pursued the secularisation of services such as education, marriage and cemeteries.[35] They struggled for non-discrimination in the spheres of work and education. They sought to be attentive to the welfare of the poor.[36] The early believers in such evangelical churches were intensely loyal to their faith and to their faith community. Faith was lived out through a disciplined and sacrificial lifestyle in a hostile environment where personal conduct made social transformation a possibility.[37] However, it is significant to note that evangelicals abandoned these positions of commitment to non-discrimination, religious liberty and the welfare of the poor when the social circumstances no longer demanded that they take such a stand.

In 1910, the Missionary Conference held in Edinburgh was a controversial event in regards to the debate over whether Latin America should or should not be considered a "mission field."[38] In opposition to the opinion asserted by the Anglo-

---

[32] Míguez Bonino, *Faces*, 31. Escobar also comments "...the distribution of Scripture in many cases preceded the presence of the missionary and prepared the way for it. The reading of Scripture as a requirement of entrance and continuity in the church, as well as the popular forms of Bible instruction developed as part of congregational life gave to lay people the possibility of leadership in the local congregation and participation in mission. This was not possible at the same pace for Catholicism where the centrality of the eucharist in the life of the church demands always the presence of a priest." Escobar, "Five Hundred", 17.

[33] Escobar, "El poder", 168. For a chronology on reflections regarding Latin American evangelical involvement in politics see also Elsa Romanenghi de Powell, "Participación de los evangélicos en la política latinoamericana: una crónica", *Boletín Teológico* 40 (1991): 233-248.

[34] C. René Padilla, "New Actors on the Political Scene" in *New Face of the Church in Latin America*, ed. Guillermo Cook (Maryknoll: Orbis Books, 1994), 82-95, at 90.

[35] It is interesting to consider the use of the term "secularisation" here. Escobar confirms that this is the term he intended to use, as evangelicals joined with other sectors of society who wanted these aspects of society to be free from control of the Catholic Church. Evangelicals were committed to the movement which sought to de-Catholicise education, marriage and regulations regarding cemeteries. Samuel Escobar, discussion with author, 2 April 2004, Valencia.

[36] Míguez Bonino, *Faces*, 31.

[37] Escobar, "Religious", 169-172; Escobar, "Entender", 18.

[38] Escobar identifies Bishop Thomas S. Neely, Samuel Guy Inman, John Mott and Robert Speer as representative of a type of missionary leaders who had a theological background, a

Catholics, the Committee of Co-operation in Latin America was formed to promote mission on the continent.[39] In February 1916, the *Congress for Christian Action in Latin America* was held in Panama and is considered to mark the first acknowledgment of the continental reality of Latin American Protestantism. It was a decisive moment for the future of Protestantism on the continent because it was after the success of the Congress that two further important events were organised, namely the Montevideo Conference in 1925 and the Habana Conference in 1929.[40] These early conferences encouraged evangelical thought in Latin America. The group of evangelicals responsible for these congresses had significant influence on the formation of evangelicalism: they promoted theological education, established publishing houses, published evangelical journals and dedicated themselves to the support of initiatives among young people.[41]

The atmosphere of the time stimulated the earliest attempts at Latin American evangelical theological reflection. Latin American preachers, teachers and thinkers were encouraged in their endeavours by missionaries such as Mackay, Stanley Rycroft and John Ritchie. For the first time, many Latin American intellectuals found a sphere for their theological expression in the journal *La Nueva Democracia* (The New Democracy).[42] While their dialogue reflects the Protestant European theology of the time, they sought to respond critically. Latin American theological expression should no longer be subservient to European or North American thought.

---

degree of awareness of socio-political conditions and a great missionary passion. These men stressed the spiritual needs of Latin America. Escobar is adamant in his assertion that Marxist and Catholic critics along with particular "revisionist" Protestants fail to place these men in the framework of their time and for this reason pursue theories of conspiracy between such evangelical missionaries and imperialists. See Escobar, "Identidad", 6-9; Escobar, "Interpretación", 243-246; Escobar, "Conflict", 117-119; Gutiérrez, "Panamá", 36-37. It is insightful to consult the contemporary discussion on the same issue in Samuel Escobar, *Latin America: Mission Field and Mission Base*, Livingston Memorial Lecture 1998, Belfast Bible College, Belfast.

[39] For further discussion on the circumstances and debate surrounding the Missionary Conference in Edinburgh in 1910, see Escobar, *Fe*, 50.

[40] Escobar, "Five Hundred", 8. For detailed information on the three congresses see also Gutiérrez, "Panamá", 37-44.

[41] "United Seminaries" for theological education were established in Mexico, Matanzas, Puerto Rico and Buenos Aires. Publishing houses such as La Aurora and The United House of Publications were set up and *La Nueva Democracia* journal was published. They also were influential in the evangelical youth initiatives such as the Christian Student Movement (MEC), YMCA and YWCA and the Latin American Union of Evangelical Youth (ULAJE). Escobar, *Fe*, 51.

[42] Gonzalo Baez Camargo and Alberto Rembao from Mexico, the Brazilian Erasmo Braga, Jorge Prando Howard and Juan C. Varetto from Argentina and the Puerto Rican Angel M. Mergal, are amongst those first leading evangelicals who dealt with themes of mission, the manifestation of official religion, hunger for God, ecclesiology, alternative culture and the legitimacy of the evangelical presence in Latin America. See Escobar, *Fe*, 51-52; Gutiérrez, "Panamá", 39.

It would seem fair to say that despite the fact Protestants were in a distinct minority, they took the theological initiative on the Latin American continent. The circumstances created by the Second World War also led to the association of Protestantism with democracy and openness to the future.[43] Míguez Bonino comments:

> All the Protestant congresses from Panama (1916) to Buenos Aires (1949) sound this note. Catholicism is considered the ideology and religious structure of a total system, that of the outworn seigniorial Hispanic order that was forced on Latin America and now must disappear in order to make way for a new democratic order of freedom. Protestantism, which has historically inspired such order, offers itself as a religious alternative for the new world.[44]

The first Latin American Evangelical Conference (CELA I) was held in Buenos Aires in 1949.[45] The consultation affirmed the reality of evangelical Protestantism and defended the right to be an integral part of Latin America. Speaking strongly against curtailments of their liberty, evangelicalism was presented as a viable alternative to a Catholicism, which many considered to be formal and stagnant.[46] Indeed it can be assumed that it was this vibrant, articulate attitude which led to the concerns aired by Catholic bishops in Rio de Janeiro in 1955.[47]

Escobar identifies three movements within Latin America which motivated change in post-Second World War Latin America: the renewal of mass evangelism which displayed some aspects of revivalist Protestantism combined with the mass media; a revival of serious evangelical scholarship in biblical studies and theological reflection; and the emergence of strong evangelical churches connected to the post-World War stream of missionary fervour from North America and Europe.[48]

---

[43] For a discussion on this notion of Protestantism as a form of democratisation and modernisation see Samuel Escobar, "La presencia protestante en América Latina" in *Historia y misión: revisión de perspectivas*, Samuel Escobar, Estuardo McIntosh, and Juan Inocencio (Lima: Ediciones Presencia, 1994), 7-56, at 29-31.

[44] José Míguez Bonino, *Toward a Christian Political Ethics* (London: SCM Press, 1983), 62.

[45] Papers and resolutions are published in *El cristianismo evangélico en la América Latina: informes y resoluciones de la Primera Conferencia Evangélica Latinoamericana* (Buenos Aires: La Aurora, 1949).

[46] Escobar, *Fe*, 52. Gutiérrez, "Panamá", 46-47.

[47] The first General Council of Latin American bishops (CELAM), was called by Pius XII and was held from 25 July – 4 August, 1955 in Rio de Janeiro. The emphasis of the discussions was on the defence of the Catholic faith and clerical problems. In the light of these issues, the Bishops also expressed concern regarding the growth of Protestantism, or as they referred to it "the Protestant danger" on the continent. See Escobar, *Fe*, 34-35; Núñez, *Liberation*, 97.

[48] Samuel Escobar, "Missionary Dynamism in Search of Missiological Discernment", *Evangelical Review of Theology* XXIII, no. 1 (1999): 69-91, at 70. For a reflection on missionary enterprise at this time, see also Samuel Escobar, "The Two-Party System and the

During these years, there were two significant shifts within Latin American Protestantism. First, the Second World War and the Cuban Revolution had a significant impact on the political and ideological development of Latin America. Nazism, communism and capitalism came into conflict. Evangelicals, like democratic groups, had been persecuted by totalitarian regimes promoting Catholicism and nationalism in the past. Their attitude towards the political situation was therefore one of suspicion. During the Cold War years, many independent North American missionaries adopted strict anti-communist attitudes. Participation in politics or social involvement came to be viewed with suspicion and indeed proved to be a sensitive issue.[49] Compounded by a definitive eschatological position, evangelical churches were influenced to support conservative, anti-communist ideology rather than maintain a position of neutrality in the face of political controversy.[50]

The second significant shift came in the relationship between Catholicism and Protestantism on the continent. During the Second World War, Catholics and Protestants alike experienced horror and tragedy to which they sought to develop a Christian response. This ecumenism found expression in the World Council of Churches. The influence of such ecumenism spread to Latin America, particularly among the "transplanted" churches.[51] Some evangelicals, however, were dismayed as they felt that those involved in the ecumenical movement had lost the missionary zeal, were failing to acknowledge the historical difficulties between Latin American Protestantism and Catholicism, and were very much under the influence of European ecumenism.[52]

As a result of these two significant shifts within Latin American Protestantism, enthusiasm for mission in Latin America transferred to the independent evangelical

---

Missionary Enterprise" in *Re-forming the Center: American Protestantism, 1900 to the Present*, eds. Douglas Jacobsen and William Vance Trollinger, Jr., (Grand Rapids: Eerdmans, 1998), 341-360.

[49] This subject of political and social involvement will be addressed specifically in chapter 9. A helpful article discussing the controversial relationship with the United States and the influence of North American missionary attitudes on politics can be found in Enrique Domínguez, "The Great Commission", *NACLA Report on the Americas* 18, no.1 (1984): 12-22. See also Deborah Huntington, "God's Saving Plan", *NACLA Report on the Americas* 18, no.1 (1984): 23-33.

[50] For further elaboration on the political and ideological setting see Escobar, "El poder", 169-177; Escobar, "Situación", 18-34; Escobar, *Fe*, 52-57.

[51] Transplanted churches would include the Anglican Church established across the countries for British immigrants or those involved in business and industry; the Lutheran Church established by German communities in Brazil, Chile and Argentina; and the Mennonite communities in Paraguay and Mexico, for example. See Escobar, *Fe*, 45; C. René Padilla, "Misión integral y evangelization", *Iglesia y Misión* 71/72 (2000): 34-39.

[52] For further discussion on the ecumenical issue within Latin America and the difficulties it raises, see Samuel Escobar, "El problema ecuménico en América Latina", *Misión* 14 (1985): 78-81. For consideration of the phenomena of Catholicism across Latin America see Samuel Escobar, "Catholicism", 22-30.

groups. Escobar comments: "Independent 'faith missions'...played an important role...representing a new generation that threw itself with great vigour into the task of planting churches, translating Scripture and reaching the restless masses."[53] An open door policy and "good neighbour politics," in response to the promotion of Pan-Americanism, encouraged an influx of North American missionaries.[54] These independent evangelical communities and the Pentecostal movement (both of which had previously distanced themselves from Protestant evangelicals represented by CELA) began to structure a parallel group for evangelical co-operation. By the time CELA celebrated its second conference in 1961,[55] this new interdenominational group had already met in 1948 to discuss evangelism, in 1956 to consult on literature and in 1958 to examine communications and the media.[56]

The views held by this independent, interdenominational group on the inspiration of the Scriptures and the atonement, defined them as theologically "conservative" evangelicals. As has already been seen, however, to be conservative did not equate with being fundamentalist.[57] Indeed, Escobar helpfully points out that the conservative evangelical publications were often publicly attacked by those of an extreme right theological position.[58]

As the years passed, the phenomenon of Protestantism in Latin America was understandably becoming more complex.[59] Three streams of Protestant churches can

---

[53] Escobar, "Dynamism", 70.

[54] Gutiérrez, "Panamá", 45-46. It is also important to note that such positive attitudes towards Protestantism are contrasted with the new "Black Legend" regarding the Protestantism referred to in chapter two. For further discussion on this theory see Escobar, "Presencia", 22-29.

[55] Papers published as *Cristo, la esperanza para América Latina: Confederación Evangélica Latinoamericana (CELA II, Lima, 1961)* (Buenos Aires: Conferencia Evangélica Latinamericana del Rio de la Plata, 1962).

[56] Escobar notes that the difference in the theology and approach of the two groups is evident in a helpful comparison of the content of their two magazines, the ecumenical group published *Cuadernos Teológicos* and the new independent Protestants published *Pensamiento Cristiano*. For further observations see Escobar, *Fe*, 55-56.

[57] Míguez Bonino explains that in the beginning fundamentalism was more a defence of the faith in the face of its destruction by modern science and liberal theology which did not recognise the authority of the Scriptures. In Latin America, the centrality of the Scriptures and the centrality of the experience of conversion were the indivisible nucleus of evangelisation and the anti-Catholic polemic. At this early stage it was not necessarily reactionary in a political or social sense. However, in the years following the Second World War, as a result of the influence of reactionary fundamentalism from the United States, a more political and radically conservative wing developed among the evangelical churches. See Míguez Bonino, "Teología", 11. For a detailed discussion on Protestant Fundamentalism in Latin America see also Deiros, "Protestant", 142-195.

[58] Escobar, *Fe*, 56.

[59] See Samuel Escobar, "Conflict of Interpretations of Popular Protestantism" in *New Face of the Church in Latin America*, ed. Guillermo Cook (Maryknoll: Orbis Books, 1994), 112-134. See also the introduction in David Stoll and Virginia Garrard-Burnett, eds.

be identified.[60] The first strand of Protestantism is the "transplanted churches," that is to say those churches established by Europeans to serve the needs of their communities when they emigrated to Latin America. This group can also be considered to represent "historical Protestantism."[61] The second stream of evangelical churches is the fruit of missionary work. Two groups are represented in this category, namely, those who came as missionaries during the nineteenth century and those later arrivals who established independent, interdenominational "faith missions."[62] The third identifiable group are the large Pentecostal churches which extend more widely across the continent than the two previous groups.[63] Míguez Bonino, however, recognises the limitations of such definitions of Latin American Protestantism. He comments:

> The difficulty of characterizing in absolute and unequivocal terms the different groups and churches in Latin America results from an important phenomenon that we must take into account. Some of the more acute tensions and conflicts on the Latin American religious scene have to do with theological interpretations, social commitments, and visions of the mission of Christianity which do not correspond to confessional or

Rethinking Protestantism in Latin America (Philadelphia: Temple University Press, 1993), 1-19; Escobar, "Identidad", 2.

[60] Míguez Bonino, "Condition", 264-266; Escobar, "Conflict", 114-116; Escobar, *Fe*, 44-47; Escobar, "Presencia", 7-56; Costas, "Realidad", 41-44. It is interesting to note the difficulties expressed with regards to writing accurately about the strands of Latin American Protestantism in the preface to Míguez Bonino, *Faces*, vii-x, at ix.

[61] For a helpful discussion on the term "historical churches", see Samuel Escobar, "La misión en América Latina: interpretación sociopolítica desde una perspectiva evangélica" in *La misión de la iglesia, una vision panorámica*, ed. Valdir R. Steuernagel (San José: Visión Mundial, 1992), 237-264, at 239-241; Padilla, "Evangelización", 34.

[62] The Presbyterian, Methodist and Baptist churches in particular sent missionaries to Latin America at that time. The "faith missions" would include the Church of the Central Americas, the Christian and Missionary Alliance, the Peruvian Evangelical Church and the assemblies of the Free Brethren. Escobar, *Fe*, 45.

[63] This Pentecostal grouping would include the Pentecostal Methodist Church in Chile, the *Brazil for Christ* movement, and those Pentecostal churches established as fruit of missionary work, such as the Assemblies of God. Escobar, *Fe*, 46. The significant growth of the Pentecostal movement in Latin America has been the subject of much study and debate. The Pentecostal churches are not the focus of this work and for this reason the subject will not be dealt with in detail. For further discussion see Escobar, "Conflict", 120-122; Escobar, "Interpretación", 241-243; Escobar, "El poder", 174-181; Escobar, "Presencia", 32-36, 48-56; Martin, *Tongues*, 290-295; Stoll, *Turning*, 314-321; Juan Sepúlveda, "Pentecostal Theology in the Context of the Struggle for Life" in *Faith Born in the Struggle for Life*, ed. Dow Kirkpatrick (Grand Rapids: Eerdmans, 1988), 298-318; C. René Padilla, "Pentecostés y la iglesia", *Encuentro y Fe* 35 (1995): 10-13; Costas, "Realidad", 50-64; David Martin, "Iglesia Popular: El resurgimiento evangélico global y sus consecuencias políticas", *Textos para la acción* 8, no. 13 (2000): 23-38; David Dixon and Richard Dixon, "Culturas e identidades populares y el surgimiento de los evangélicos en América Latina", *Cristianismo y Sociedad* XXX/4, no. 114 (n.d.): 61-71.

denominational divisions but cut across them. The result is that we have – and I think we will increasingly have – forms of association which will bring Christians from different churches for common tasks and witness without, in many cases, breaking the ties with their own communities. But this, no doubt, will be potentially conflictive. Or it may introduce a ferment for change, even as it opens up the possibility of new unities.[64]

The various faces of Latin American Protestantism became more distinctive in subsequent decades. At the second CELA conference in Lima during 1961, the theological emphasis was that of the ecumenical Protestant group, reflecting Protestant liberalism or Protestant neo-orthodoxy.[65] In contrast, evangelical Protestantism was definitively expressed at another consultation held in Lima in 1962.[66] Further motivated by participation in the Conference of Evangelisation held in Berlin in 1966, the evangelical wing sought to hold a regional consultation. Consequently, in the year 1969, two very different events took place, reflecting the division in Latin American Protestantism. CELA III was held in Buenos Aires in July and the Latin American Congress of Evangelisation, known as CLADE I, took place in Bogotá during November.[67]

CELA III and CLADE I demonstrate the growing awareness regarding the social and political reality of Latin America, and the realisation among Protestants for the need to respond to it. As previously discussed in chapter two, a branch within the ecumenical Protestant movement responded radically and found expression in the ISAL movement.[68] It is necessary to point out, however, that not all ecumenical Protestants followed the aggressively radical path of ISAL. Likewise, evangelical Protestants were also concerned about the need for the development of theological thought and expression appropriate to their context. They recognised the lack of articulate evangelical theological thinking forged in Latin America.[69] Subsequently, in 1970 *La Fraternidad Teológica Latinoamericana* (The Latin American Theological Fraternity), known as FTL was founded.

The various expressions of theological development in these organisations are clear. In ecumenical Protestantism, Christian social responsibility was clearly placed

---

[64] Míguez Bonino, "Condition", 266.

[65] See Escobar, "Conflict", 115.

[66] The evangelical Protestantism referred to here would be definable in the light of the discussion on Latin American evangelicalism at the beginning of this chapter, see section 3.2.

[67] The Evangelical Declaration of Bogotá is pertinent to this work and can be found in Escobar, *Evangelio*, 208-214. See also Samuel Escobar, "La fundación de la Fraternidad Teológica Latinoamericana: breve ensayo histórico", *Boletín Teológico* 59-60 (1995): 7-33, at 13-17 for a detailed discussion on the historical circumstances surrounding the Bogotá Congress.

[68] Gutiérrez, "Panamá", 51-52. See also chapter 2, section 2.3.3.

[69] In regard to the flourishing Pentecostal movement Escobar comments "We are also limited by the fact that those groups which would seem to be the most dynamic, due to their rapid growth and popular appeal, are not the most given to articulate theological visions of the future." Samuel Escobar, "Identity, Mission and Future of Latin American Protestantism", *Theological Fraternity Bulletin* 1 and 2 (1978): 1-28, at 3.

within the sphere of the churches which were already established. Concern for evangelism, therefore, was minimal. In contrast, concern for social responsibility within the evangelical Protestant tradition went hand in hand with evangelistic activity and a distinct missionary focus.[70] The ecumenical group also found much in common with Catholicism which led to a deeper involvement with the theology of liberation. In contrast, the evangelical group considered there to be impassable barriers between Catholicism and the evangelical Protestant faith, both in terms of the historical interpretation of the social and political reality in Latin America and the interpretation of the contemporary social reality in which they found themselves.[71]

The 1970s mark the beginning of a period of theological development and formation of thought which had been identified as lacking during the previous decade. Protestant theologians across the theological spectrum recognised the need to produce Protestant Latin American theological insight.[72] Such Latin American theological reflection had impact not only on a continental scale but across the world. Works were published not only in Spanish and Portuguese but also in English, provoking reaction from Europe and North America.[73] At the Lausanne conference in 1974, Latin Americans contributed decisively to the worldwide evangelical strategy for mission.[74]

---

[70] Escobar, *Fe*, 59.

[71] Escobar, *Fe*, 60. Escobar is also careful to assert that while those involved with the FTL could not describe themselves as fundamentalist, neither could they hold the position asserted by ISAL. They did not believe it was necessary to adopt Marxist method to interpret reality and yet they did not share the anti-communist naivety of the conservative missionaries. FTL represented a group striving to find a biblical, contextual evangelical theology. See Escobar, "Fundación", 11-12.

[72] As mentioned in chapter two, within ecumenical Protestantism the Brazilian Rubem Alves had begun to deal with issues such as a new reading of biblical texts such as the Exodus, seeking an interpretation of the Latin American reality with reference to Marxism and also making a personal critique of Marxism by 1968. Evangelical Protestants concentrated firstly on the issues surrounding the authority of the Bible in theological reflection. Escobar, *Fe*, 61.

[73] Padilla commented that he was personally most surprised by the varying reactions to his paper at Lausanne. He experienced emotional expressions of gratitude from Two Thirds World theologians and at the same time there were North Americans who told him that he disgusted them with his betrayal of evangelical convictions. C. René Padilla, interview by author, 13 June 2003, video recording, Buenos Aires. Kirk recalls that at Lausanne only three speakers were given a standing ovation, among the three was René Padilla. J. Andrew Kirk, interview by author, 25 September 2003, video recording, Lechlade.

[74] See Tidball, *Who?*, 190; Timothy Yates, *Christian Misson in the Twentieth Century* (Cambridge: Cambridge University Press, 1994), 200-203. Papers submitted by C. René Padilla and Samuel Escobar were fundamental to the Lausanne Covenant and other Latin American evangelical contributions were also presented. See Orlando E. Costas, "In-depth evangelism in Latin America", 211-212; Orlando E. Costas "Depth in Evangelism – An Interpretation of 'In-Depth Evangelism' Around the World", 675-694; Samuel Escobar,

The force of ecumenical strength, represented by CELA and later by UNELAM (Commission for Latin American Evangelical Unity), culminated in 1982 when CLAI, the Latin American Council of Churches, was established.[75] In contrast to the ecumenical movement, the evangelical group continued to maintain a separate identity and remained committed to the formulation of a coherent theological response, in line with evangelical principles. In 1979, the second Latin American Congress of Evangelisation, CLADE II, took place in Lima.[76] A new initiative called the Latin American Evangelical Confraternity, promoting aspects of the Lausanne Consultation, took place in 1982.[77]

The purpose of this section has been to place the evangelical presence within Latin America in its historical context. Not only does such evangelical theology stand in contrast to prominent Catholic theology, but it also presents a challenge to other forms of Latin American Protestant theology. As will be seen in the next section, the Latin American Theological Fraternity has provided and continues to provide a crucial, coherent and cogent presentation of evangelical theology. For this reason, it is important to examine the foundation and influence of the Fraternity in some detail.

3.4 The Foundation and Influence of the Latin American Theological Fraternity

The growth and diversity of Protestantism in Latin America makes it a complex phenomenon.[78] There were many positive aspects to this growth and diversity,

---

"Evangelization and Man's Search for Freedom, Justice and Fulfilment", 319-326; J. Andrew Kirk, "The Kingdom of God and the Church in Contemporary Protestantism and Catholicism", 1071-1080; Emilio A. Núñez, "Personal and Eternal Salvation and Human Redemption", 1060-1070 in *Let the Earth Hear His Voice*, ed. J.D. Douglas (Minneapolis: World Wide Publications, 1975). The paper delivered by Padilla is published as "Evangelism and the World" in C. René Padilla, *Mission Between the Times* (Grand Rapids: Eerdmans, 1985), 1-44. The doctoral thesis of Valdir Raul Steuernagel also traces the important international dialogue following Lausanne, in which the Latin Americans played a significant role. See Valdir Raul Steuernagel, "The Theology of Mission in its Relation to Social Responsibility Within the Lausanne Movement" (Ph.D. diss., The Faculty of the Lutheran School of Theology at Chicago, 1988). See also Samuel Escobar, "El espíritu de Lausana 1974 en América Latina", *Misión* 29 (1989): 110-113.

[75] For an interesting overview of Latin American Protestantism from the perspective of CLAI: Protestantism and culture, Protestantism and liberalism, models of Protestant evangelisation, Latin American ecumenism and projections for the future, see Tomás J Gutiérrez, ed., *Protestantismo y cultura* (Quito: Consejo Latinoamericano de Iglesias, 1994).

[76] CLADE II was held from 31 October – 7 November, 1979. The papers were published in Savage y Gutiérrez, *América*.

[77] For a helpful outline of the polarization among evangelicals during this period, see Gutiérrez, "Panamá", 56-57.

[78] See Escobar, "¿Se revisa?", 8-12; Stoll, *Turning*, 128-134, 305-314; Martin, *Tongues*, 242-289. Martin highlights the difficulties involved in assessing the complex phenomenon of

particularly in the post-Second World War period. Inevitably, however, difficulties and complications also arose. The evangelical message had the potential to be excessively individualistic which affected the witness of communities of faith.[79] Independent leadership could often be divisive and dictatorial, refusing to allow for a plurality of opinion on secondary issues or denying new generations of believers the freedom to employ different approaches. Churches growing numerically were admired and a certain sense of competition was evident. The danger of numerical growth becoming the only criteria in mission or ministry crept in. The Latin American evangelical voice was divided on societal and political issues. A sectarian attitude developed between different evangelical groups, some of whom considered themselves to be the only true guardians of the truth.[80] These words, written in 1957, contained a somewhat prophetic message with regard to the future of the evangelical movement in Latin America:

> For better or worse, the non-historical groups constitute a major factor in the determination of Latin America's Protestant future. The movement can spearhead the aggressive stepped-up program of evangelism that is so urgently needed to meet the challenge of an exploding population in the valley of revolutionary change. The movement can be used of God to infuse new life and vigour into older bodies that may have lost their vitality and momentum. But it can also be instrumental in side-tracking the evangelical church down sterile by-paths of doctrinal extremes and religious oddities and tragically remove it from effective contact with the main stream of Latin American life. And it can so intensify and magnify its divisions as to make it hopelessly unable to resist and overcome the anti-Christian pressures that are building up in the world today.[81]

The Latin American Theological Fraternity was established on 17 December, 1970 in Cochabamba, Bolivia.[82] This was a period of tension between ecumenical Protestant and evangelical Protestant groups, as discussed in the previous section. It

---

Latin American Protestantism in David Martin, "Evangelicals and Economic Culture in Latin America: An Interim Comment on Research in Progress", *Social Compass* 39, no. 1 (1992): 9-14.

[79] Escobar, "Católicos", 74.

[80] Escobar comments on these negative aspects of the evangelical movement in retrospect as he seeks to consider Latin American evangelicalism in a self critical light. See Escobar, "Entender", 18. See also Charles F. Denton, "La mentalidad Protestante: un enfoque sociológico" in *Fe cristiana y Latinoamérica hoy*, ed. C. René Padilla (Buenos Aires: Ediciones Certeza, 1975), 67-79, at 73.

[81] Missiologist Kenneth Strachan, cited by Escobar, "Five Hundred", 9.

[82] "Declaración Evangélica de Cochabamba" in Pedro Savage, ed., *El debate contemporáneo sobre la Biblia* (Barcelona: Ediciones Evangélicos Europeas, 1972), 226-227. See also Pedro Arana Quiroz, ed., *Teología en el camino: documentos presentados en los últimos veinte años por diferentes comunidades cristianas de América Latina* (Lima: Ediciones Presencia, 1987), 27-30. For details on the preparations and programme of the conference see Escobar, "Fundación", 17-22.

was also a period of internal struggles within Latin American conservative evangelicalism itself.[83] Amidst this internal strife, the foundation of the Fraternity would have been almost impossible without the sensitive negotiations carried out by Pedro Savage. Savage counselled two separate groups of evangelicals. For while these groups were united in their desire to develop contextual Latin American evangelical thought, they were divided on the approach which should be taken. According to Escobar, the FTL has survived despite confrontations and tensions both inside and outside the Fraternity, by resolutely committing itself to three principles. First, the FTL has clearly expressed and defined a common evangelical base. Second, the FTL has consistently pursued contextual relevance. Third, the FTL has resisted polarization which could potentially result from debate surrounding "extra-theological" factors.[84] During the last three decades, the Theological Fraternity has played a pivotal role in the development of evangelical responses and theological development at a regional, continental and international level.[85] Míguez Bonino comments:

> It goes without saying that the theological renovation represented by the Latin American Theological Fraternity has become a referential subject for Latin American Protestantism…as was clearly proven at CLADE III, the FTL has come to be a fertile meeting place without it being a "neutral" place…[86]

---

[83] Samuel Escobar explained that there was tension between the more conservative evangelcial theologians and several influential North American missionaries, and other Latin American evangelical theologians who were committed to developing Latin American theology without the influence or direction of such missionaries. Escobar and others were keen to establish a Fraternity which was founded on evangelical principles, but which did not define these principles so narrowly that only one group of evangelicals could adhere to them. Samuel Escobar, discussion with the author, 31 March, 2004, Valencia.

[84] For a historical overview which Escobar describes as a commentary on the formation and development of the FTL and the context in which it was established see Escobar, "Fundación", 7-25. For detailed reflection on the founding of the Fraternity see 13-17, for information on tensions within the Fraternity see Escobar, "Fundación", 21.

[85] For a detailed chronology of the activities of the Latin American Theological Fraternity from 1970 to 1995 see "Cronología de actividades de la Fraternidad Teológica Latinoamericana", *Boletín Teológico* 59-60 (1995): 26-33. This chronology is attributed to information from the fraternity archives in Lima, the personal archives of Samuel Escobar and C. René Padilla, the *Boletín Teológico* and the work of A. Christopher Smith. The following doctoral studies are also helpful in establishing the context in which the FTL was founded and the influence the FTL had on the development of Latin American evangelical theology: see Smith, "Essentials"; see also Daniel C. Elliot, "Theology and Mission from Latin America: The Latin American Theological Fraternity" (Masters diss., Wheaton Graduate School, 1992).

[86] Míguez Bonino, "Teología", 14.

An accurate understanding of the thought, work and ministry of the Latin American Theological Fraternity is of vital significance to this work. For there is little doubt that this group is the voice of evangelical theology on the continent.[87]

As previously mentioned, the first Latin American Congress of Evangelisation, CLADE I, was held in Bogotá, Colombia from 21 to 30 November, 1969.[88] The following year, the first foundational FTL consultation was held in Cochabamba, Bolivia from 12 to 18 December, 1970.[89] During the next decade the Fraternity promoted much theological activity in evangelical circles on the continent.[90] Consultations were held on pertinent subjects such as: evangelical responsibility in contemporary theology, biblical theology, hermeneutics, ecclesiology, social ethics, the kingdom of God, humanity and human structures in Latin America, the family in biblical perspective, abortion in Christian perspective, the evangelical commitment to mission, Church Growth theories and evangelical literature.[91]

---

[87] It is also helpful to reflect on the Fraternity's response to criticisms regarding their work. For example, two articles were written in response to Smith's dissertation. These articles demonstrate the willingness to respond to criticism in a gracious and constructive manner. See C. René Padilla, "La Fraternidad Teológica Latinoamericana: una evaluación crítica", *Misión* 7 (1983): 28-30; C. René Padilla, "La Fraternidad Teológica Latinoamericana en tela de juicio", *Misión* 9 (1984): 62-64.

[88] Conference papers and Bible studies of this consultation are published as Samuel Escobar, ed. *Acción en Cristo para un continente en crisis* (San José: Editorial Caribe, 1970). Samuel Escobar presented his paper "Responsabilidad social de la iglesia", 32-39. See C. René Padilla, "Evangelism and Social Responsibility; From Wheaton '66 to Wheaton '83", *Transformation* 2, no. 3 (1985): 27-33, at 28 (footnote 17) where Padilla records that Escobar's paper was received with a standing ovation, reflecting the consensus among Latin American evangelicals of the desperate need for evangelical theology which would respond to the injustice and harshness of the Latin American reality.

[89] Papers from this conference and the declaration subsequently published are available in Savage, *Debate*. The declaration published can also be found in Escobar, *Evangelio*, 215-219; Quiroz, *Teología*, 27-30.

[90] Escobar describes the ethical, theological, and pastoral reflection which the Fraternity sought to promote in Samuel Escobar, "Elementos para la evaluación de la experiencia política de evangélicos", *Textos para la Acción* 8, no. 13 (2000): 9-22.

[91] The papers from the social ethics conference held in Lima from 5-8 July, 1972 are the contents of Padilla, *Fe*. In Lima from 11-17 December, 1972 a consultation entitled "The Kingdom of God" was held and papers subsequently published as C. René Padilla, ed., *El reino de Dios y América Latina* (El Paso: Casa Bautista de Publicaciones, 1975.) FTL participated in the *Biblical Theology Commission* in San José, Costa Rica from 10-14 December 1973, the papers of which are published in Mervin Breneman. ed. *Liberación, Éxodo y Biblia* (Miami: Editorial Caribe, 1975). From 9-15 March, 1974 the FTL contributed to the Commission of the Life and Mission of the Church consultation on "Man and the structures in Latin America." FTL members took part in the consultation on "The Family in Biblical Perspective" organised by EIRENE International in Quito, Ecuador, from 1-6 December, 1974. In 1975, from 23-27 June, Pinebrook, Pennsylvania was the location for the FTL consultation on Evangelical Literature. See Samuel Escobar, "Fostering Indigenous Authorship", TMs (photocopy), paper presented at Evangelical Literature in the Latin World

During this first decade of the Fraternity (1970-1980), members made valuable contributions to international consultations,[92] not only the previously mentioned Lausanne International Congress of Evangelisation (1974), but also dialogue between the World Evangelical Fellowship and the World Council of Churches in Switzerland (1976); the Willowbank World Consultation on Gospel and Culture (1978); the High Leigh Conference on the Evangelical Commitment to a Simple Lifestyle (1980); and the World Evangelisation Consultation held in Pattaya, Thailand (1980).[93] The FTL also hosted colloquia across the continent with international evangelical scholars such as Carl Henry, Leon Morris, John Stott and Michael Green.[94] Escobar makes four observations regarding this period. First, there

---

Consultation, Pinebrook, Pennsylvania, June 23-27, 1975, Latin American Theological Fraternity Archives, Buenos Aires, 1-30. FTL supported the Consultation on "Abortion in the Christian Perspective" organised by the Ethics and Pastoral Ministries Commission. In Buenos Aires from 13-20 March 1976, the Commission for the life and mission of the Church held a conference on "Our Mission in Latin America today." From 4-7 November 1976, FTL contributed to the first *Kairós* Community Conference on Hermeneutics and also to the second *Kairós* Community Conference on Hermeneutics in Buenos Aires from 19-21 May, 1977. Papers are available as C. René Padilla, Mervin Breneman, Sidney H. Rooy, B. Melano Couch, Eugene Nida, Elsa R. Powell and Samuel Escobar, *Hacia una hermenéutica evangélica Tomo II* (Buenos Aires: Ediciones Kairós, 1977); J. Andrew Kirk, Samuel Escobar, Toribio Martínez, and Mervin Breneman, *Hacia una hermenéutica evangélica Tomo III* (Buenos Aires: Ediciones Kairós, 1977). FTL members took part in the Pasadena consultation on "The Principle of Homogeneous Units" from 31 May – 2 June, 1977.

[92] For a reflection on the challenge of Lausanne I and the subsequent theological reflection in subsequent years see Samuel Escobar, "Lausana II y el peregrinaje de la misiología evangélica", *Boletín Teológico* 36 (1989): 321-333. For a helpful article on the development of Latin American evangelical social ethics and the interaction with the international evangelical community at various consultations see C. René Padilla, "La Fraternidad Teológica Latinoamericana y la responsabilidad social de la iglesia", *Boletín Teológico* 59-60 (1995): 98-111. Escobar also reflects on the internal tensions regarding the issue of mission and social responsibility within the international evangelical community in Samuel Escobar, "A Movement Divided: Three Approaches to World Evangelisation Stand in Tension with One Another", *Transformation* 8, no. 4 (1991): 7-13.

[93] See Douglas, ed., *Earth*; John R. W. Stott and Robert , eds. "The Willowbank Report" in *Down to Earth: Studies in Christianity and Culture* (Grand Rapids: Eerdmans, 1980), 308-339; Ronald J. Sider ed., *Lifestyle in the Eighties: An Evangelical Commitment to Simple Lifestyle* (Philadelphia: The Westminster Press, 1982). For the declaration "The Statement of Concerns from Pattaya" amongst others see C. René Padilla and Chris Sugden, eds., *Texts on Evangelical Social Ethics 1974-1983* (Nottingham: Grove Books Limited, 1985), 22-25.

[94] Carl F. Henry visited Mexico, Guatemala, Costa Rica, Peru, Chile, Argentina, Brazil and Venezuela under the auspices of FTL in the summer of 1973 and led pastoral institutes on "The Evangelical Responsibility in Contemporary Theology." In January 1974, C. René Padilla led pastoral courses with John Stott in association with IFES on the topic "Towards a Holistic Christianity." From 22 June to 19 August, 1976, FTL hosted a series of pastoral institutes in Mexico, Guatemala, Costa Rica, Ecuador, Peru, Chile, Argentina, Brazil and Venezuela with Leon Morris. Themes discussed included hermeneutics, the cross in the New

was a recognised obligation to reflect theologically on *holistic* mission. Second, there was a call for *co-operation* in the mission task between the church and para-church organisations, and also between the varying denominations. Third, there was an awareness of the *global* dimension of theological and missiological developments which identified that Christianity in the Two Thirds World was thriving in comparison to the declining Christianity in the West. Fourth, there was an authentic commitment made to seriously consider the *context* of mission. Reflecting on these years following Lausanne, Escobar writes:

> Lausanne was not the missiological and theological monologue of European or North American Evangelicals, but a brotherly global dialogue of a community that had grown beyond expectations all over the world: a dialogue in search of ways of obedience to the missionary imperatives of Jesus…[95]

The second decade (1980-1990) saw an increase in the publishing capability of the Fraternity. The FTL journal *Boletín Teológico* (Theological Bulletin) had been first published in May, 1972. In 1981, the journal was given a new format and a new director, Rolando Gutiérrez. In March 1982, the first edition of the journal *Misión* (originally entitled *Iglesia y Misión*) was published. In 1984, eleven members of the Fraternity contributed to the seminal book *Hacia una teología evangélica latinoamericana* (Towards a Latin American Evangelical Theology).[96] In 1986, under the direction of René Padilla, the publishing house *Editorial Nueva Creación* (New Creation Publishing Company) was established in association with Eerdmans in Grand Rapids. The first titles published were products of FTL reflection.

Members of the Fraternity continued to support and contribute to theological consultations at a national and international level. In the early years of the 1980s in particular, there was much interaction across the world.[97] Another decisive moment

---

Testament and the Epistles to the Corinthians. John Stott was invited to visit and teach again by FTL in Mexico, Guatemala, Ecuador and Argentina from 6 June to 9 July 1977. From 2 to 27 July, 1979, Michael Green visited Puerto Rico, Santo Domingo, Ecuador and Peru under the auspices of FTL to teach on the subject of "Evangelisation in the Early Church".

[95] Escobar, "Dynamism", 72.

[96] Padilla, *Hacia*. This book is a compilation of personal testimonies of a search for an evangelical theology which would be faithful to the word of God and pertinent to the Latin American situation, as previously mentioned in chapter 1, footnote 3.

[97] Forth Worth, Texas saw the first national Theological and Pastoral Conference of the north American nucleus of the FTL take place from 20-24 June, 1981. Papers from this meeting were published in Orlando E. Costas, ed. *Predicación evangélica y teología hispana* (Miami: Editorial Caribe, 1982). Members also contributed to the Congress of evangelical theologians of mission in the Two Thirds World, from 20 to 25 March, 1982 in Bangkok, Thailand. For consultation papers see Vinay Samuel and Chris Sugden, eds. *Sharing Jesus in the Two Thirds World* (Grand Rapids: Eerdmans, 1984). In Grand Rapids, Michigan, from 19 to 25 June, members of the FTL contributed to the Consultation on the Relationship between Evangelisation and Social Responsibility. From 27 August to 5 September, the same year, Seoul, Korea was the location of a Conference of Third World Theologians, co-sponsored by

in 1982 was the foundation of CONELA, the Latin American Evangelical Fraternity.[98] It is also interesting to note that the FTL organised fewer teaching tours for international evangelical scholars during this period. It would be fair to assume, therefore, that more theologically astute Latin American evangelicals were becoming available.[99] In celebration of twenty years of the Latin American Theological Fraternity during 1990, special preparatory consultations were held in anticipation of the twentieth anniversary conference entitled "Theology and Life," which would take place in Quito, Ecuador, from 4 to 12 December. These preparatory consultations addressed the following issues: Christians in the face of political totalitarianism,[100] Christians in the face of economic dependency and Latin

---

the FTL. The final document was published as "Hacia una cristología misionológica en los Terceros Mundos", *Boletín Teológico* 8 (1982): 17-20. From 24 to 28 May, 1983 a consultation on evangelicals and political power was held in Jarabacoa, in the Dominican Republic. The declaration was published as "Christians and political action." See Pablo A. Deiros, ed. *Los evangélicos y el poder político en América Latina* (Buenos Aires: Nueva Creación, 1986). See also Escobar, "Elementos", 17-20. Tlayacapan, Mexico saw the conference entitled "Hermeneutics in the Americas" take place from 24 to 29 November, 1983. Papers were published in C. René Padilla and Mark Branson, eds., *Conflict and Context: Hermeneutics in the Americas* (Grand Rapids: Eerdmans, 1986). Tlayacapan was also the location of the Second World Congress of Evangelical Theologians on Mission in the Two Thirds World. "Life in the Spirit" was the theme and several papers and final documents can be found in *Boletín Teológico* 21-22 (1986). From 19 to 25 August, 1985 the subject "New Alternatives in Theological Education" was dealt with by those attending the Congress in Quito, Ecuador. See C. René Padilla, ed., *Nuevas alternativas de educación teológica* (Buenos Aires: Nueva Creación, 1986). FTL sponsored the Consultation entitled "Towards a Holistic Transformation" held in Huampaní, Lima from 1 to 6 December, 1987. See Washington Padilla, ed., *Hacia una transformación integral* (Buenos Aires: Fraternidad Teológica Latinoamericana, 1988). "The Christian Faith and Social Sciences" was the subject of the consultation held in Santiago, Chile from 7 to 10 September, 1988. Papers are published in the *Boletín Teológico* 31 (1988). A Consultation "In Search of the Peace of the City" dealing with the subject of urban mission took place at Valle de Bravo, Mexico, from 5-11 December, 1988. See *Boletín Teológico* 33. Lausanne II, International Congress of Evangelisation took place in Manila from 11 to 20 July, 1989. Material contributed by members of the FTL and some commentaries on the event can be found in *Boletín Teológico* 34, 35 and 36 (1989).

[98] This founding conference took place in Panama, from 19 to 25 April, 1982.

[99] The only international visitor on record as invited by the FTL to undertake a teaching tour during this period was John Perkins, who travelled to Mexico, Peru, Chile and Argentina from 18 July to 8 August.

[100] Buenos Aires, 18-22 April, 1990. Final document and papers published in *Boletín Teológico* 38 (1990).

American external debt,[101] Christians in the face of violence in Latin America[102] and the relationship between the gospel and the question of poverty.[103]

In the years following the twentieth anniversary of the foundation of the Fraternity, members have continued to contribute nationally and internationally to evangelical theological scholarship. Issues of freedom, justice, the relationship between the Church and the state, evangelical participation in politics, mission and economics remain on the Latin American theological agenda.[104] The Third Latin American Congress of Evangelisation, CLADE III, was held in Quito, Ecuador from 24 August to 4 September, 1992 under the title "The Whole Gospel for the Whole World from Latin America."[105] Such consultations enabled Latin American evangelical theologians to develop their theology on a regional level and then contribute to the continental and international discussion. For example, the subject of "Economics and the Christian Faith" was addressed during 1993 in regional seminar groups which then met for a continental consultation in Buenos Aires from 1-5 November.[106] In Agra, India from 1 to 5 March 1995, the FTL contributed the results from their preparatory consultations at the Third World Conference in Oxford where the focus was: "The Impact of the Market Economy on Poverty."

In more recent years, it is interesting to observe the increasing influence of the FTL in the area of publication. Conferences on pertinent issues continue to be held and the documents are currently made more widely available. FTL continues to promote evangelical reflection in the areas of family life in contemporary society,

---

[101] Santiago, Chile, 17-19 August, 1990. The Documents can be found in *Boletín Teológico* 39 (1990).

[102] Lima, Peru, 2-4 September, 1990. See *Boletín Teológico* 39 (1990).

[103] Sao Paulo, Brazil, 14-16 September, 1990. See *Boletín Teológico* 40 (1990).

[104] The fourth International Mission Consultation of Evangelical Theologians met in Osijek, Yugoslavia from 10 to 16 April, 1991 to discuss "Freedom and Justice in the Relationship between Church and State." The conference declaration is available in *Misión* 34. The second consultation on "Evangelical Participation in Latin American Politics" was held in Buenos Aires from 24 to 28 October, 1991. See *Boletín Teológico* 44 (1991). In Huampaní, Peru from 26 to 30 April, 1993 a consultation entitled "The Future Path and Projections of the FTL" was held. Conference details can be found in *Boletín Teológico* 50 (1993). "Indigenous Theology" was the theme of the consultation which met at Villa la Paz, Peru from 22 to 25 June, 1994. See *Hacia una teología indígena* (Lima: Fraternidad Teológica Latinoamericana, n.d.) Regional consultations on "The Family" were held during 1994 from 8 to 10 July in Misión Mazaua, Mexico, 24 to 28 October in Villa La Paz, Peru and from 26 to 29 October in Tegucigalpa, Honduras.

[105] See Congreso Latinoamericano de Evangelización (CLADE), III, 24 de agosto a 4 de septiembre de 1992, Quito. *Todo el Evangelio para todos los pueblos desde América Latina* (Quito: Fraternidad Teológica Latinoamericana, 1993). See also Samuel Escobar, "The Whole Gospel for the Whole World from Latin America," *Transformation* 10, no. 1 (1993): 30-32; Gutiérrez, "Panamá", 58-59.

[106] Regional conferences were held at Santiago, Chile, 28-30 May; Lima, Peru, 26-28 August; Antigua, Guatemala, 26-28 August.

holistic mission, holistic ministry, ethics, power, poverty, social justice, human rights, post-modern spirituality (*religiosidad*), and ecclesiology.[107]

Perhaps the most significant event in the recent history of evangelical theology within Latin America would be the fourth Latin American Congress of Evangelisation, CLADE IV, held from 2 to 9 September, 2000 in Quito, under the auspices of the Latin American Theological Fraternity.[108] Guided by the title: "The Evangelical Witness in the Third Millennium: Word, Spirit and Mission" various conference groups examined issues surrounding holistic mission, poverty, the consumer society, stewardship of creation and the Christian presence in the academic world.[109]

---

[107] For example, FTL published an evangelical approach to marriage, see C. René Padilla and Carmen de Perez *Hacer el amor en todo lo que hace: como se cultivan relaciones conyugales permanentes* (Colombia: Fraternidad Teológica Latinoamericana: 1996). See Gregorio Rake, C. René Padilla and Tetsunao Yamamori, eds., *Servir con los pobres en América Latina: modelos de ministerio integral* (Buenos Aires: Ediciones Kairós, 1997). This book is the result of the Latin American Consultation of Holistic Ministry held in Quito, Ecuador in November 1996. The FTL also began to publish a collection of books reflecting the discussion evident in the *Boletín Teológico*. For example, see Samuel Escobar *De la misión a la teología* (Buenos Aires: Ediciones Kairós, 1998); John H. Yoder, Lilia Solano and C. René Padilla, *Iglesia, ética y poder* (Buenos Aires: Ediciones Kairós, 1998); Tito Paredes, *El evangelio: un tesoro en vasijas de barro* (Buenos Aires: Ediciones Kairós, 2000). See also C. René Padilla and Tetsunao Yamamori, eds. *El proyecto de Dios y las necesidades humanas* (Buenos Aires: Ediciones Kairós, 2000). For papers from the FTL consultation in Buenos Aires on "Ethics and Religiosity in Post-modern times" see Sik Hong, Edgardo Moffatt, Daniel Tomasini and Nancy Bedford, *Etica y religiosidad en tiempos posmodernos* (Buenos Aires; Ediciones Kairós, 2001). For a recent publication on an ecclesiology for holistic mission see C. René Padilla and Tetsunao Yamamori, eds. *La iglesia local como agente de transformación: una eclesiología para la misión integral* (Buenos Aires: Ediciones Kairós, 2003). For a discussion on the Trinity and holistic mission see Pedro Arana Quiroz, Samuel Escobar and C. René Padilla, *El Trino Dios y la misión integral* (Buenos Aires: Ediciones Kairós, 2003).

[108] The Consultation Statement is available as "Testimonio evangélico hacia el tercer milenio: palabra, espíritu y misión." *Iglesia y Misión* 74 (November - December 2000): 16-18.

[109] For CLADE IV consultation papers see C. René Padilla and Tetsunao Yamamori, eds., Congreso Latinoamericano de Evangelización (CLADE), IV, Quito, Ecuador, 2 a 9 de septiembre de 2000: *Misión integral y pobreza: el testimonio evangélico hacia el tercer milenio: palabra, espíritu y misión* (Buenos Aires: Ediciones Kairós, 2001); H. Fernando Bullón, Juliana Morillo and Sergio Membreño, eds., Congreso Latinoamericano de Evangelización (CLADE), IV, Quito, 2 a 9 de septiembre de 2000: *Sociedad de consumo y mayordomía de la creación: el testimonio evangélico hacia el tercer milenio: palabra, espíritu y misión* (Buenos Aires: Ediciones Kairós, 2002); Sidney H. Rooy, ed., Congreso Latinoamericano de Evangelización (CLADE), IV, Quito, Ecuador, 2 a 9 de septiembre de 2000: *Presencia cristiana en el mundo académico: el testimonio evangélico hacia el tercer milenio: palabra, espíritu y misión* (Buenos Aires: Ediciones Kairós, 2001).

CLADE IV was a vibrant, active consultation demonstrating the development in Latin American evangelical theology since the foundation of the FTL thirty years previous.[110] The Fraternity has given Latin American evangelical theologians across the spectrum the opportunity to develop contextual evangelical theology. There is no doubt as to the evangelical principles held by the Latin American Theological Fraternity. Yet it has provided, and continues to provide, an arena in which there is freedom for Latin American evangelicals to engage theologically with one another. CLADE IV represents the development possible in an open, motivating environment.

3.5 Conclusion

In this chapter a definition of the term "evangelical" has been considered by examining the Latin American exposition of foundational evangelical convictions. The history of the evangelical presence within Latin America has been traced. Clear distinctions have been drawn between the streams of Protestantism on the continent in an effort to accurately depict Latin American evangelical Protestantism. The circumstances surrounding the foundation of the Latin American Theological Fraternity have been outlined. The subsequent discussion of the activities of the Fraternity evidences its influence and the contribution it has made to the development of evangelical theology in Latin America and on an international level. It is true to say that *evangelicalism* in the Latin American Theological Fraternity means a life of personal discipleship, dedication to contextual biblical theology, and commitment to sharing the good news of Jesus Christ. Such evangelical conviction should be evident in every facet of a person's existence. The Latin American Theological Fraternity continues to influence and promote evangelical theology on a continental level. New generations of Latin American evangelicals are encouraged and motivated to continue the pursuit of contextual evangelical theology.[111]

This book does not set out to be a complete exposition of the theology of the Fraternity. Rather, the purpose of this study is to examine the evangelical perspective on liberation themes evident in contextual Latin American theology. It should be made clear, however, that the theology of the Fraternity is not limited to a reactionary theological response to interlocutors such as the theology of liberation. On the contrary, in the light of both the historical background and the contemporary situation which have been presented, it is fair to say that the Fraternity is an initiator

---

[110] For a reflection on the thirty years of theological development and documentation of the consultation statements see C. René Padilla, "Itinerio de la misión integral: de CLADE I a CLADE IV", *Iglesia y Misión* 74 (2000): 4-15.

[111] More recent publications by members of the Latin American Theological Fraternity include Paredes, *Evangelio*; Escobar, *Changing*; C. René Padilla, *Economía humana y economía del reino de Dios* (Buenos Aires: Ediciones Kairós, 2002); Quiroz, Escobar and Padilla, *El Trino*; Arturo Piedra, Sidney Rooy and H. Fernando Bullón, *¿Hacia dónde va el protestantismo? Herencia y prospectivas en América Latina* (Buenos Aires: Ediciones Kairós, 2003).

in Latin American theological reflection. It would seem appropriate, therefore, to deal with the subject of method in contextual Latin American theology in the following chapter. For the methodology employed is foundational to the Fraternity's commitment to originate active, contextual theology. An examination of contextual method will bring a fuller understanding of the exposition of liberation themes in evangelical perspective.

CHAPTER 4

Contextual Methods:
Liberationists and Evangelicals

4.1 Introduction

It is constructive to examine contextual evangelical method in light of the evangelical critique regarding liberationist method. For, evidently, liberationist methodology was the most dominant contextual approach in Latin America during the years in which serious evangelical reflection was established. It is widely acknowledged that one of the most distinguishing features of the theology of liberation is the method which it proposed. The purpose of this chapter, then, is to examine the Latin American evangelical engagement with this "new way to do theology," and consequently to gain a greater understanding of the search for a contextual evangelical method.

While it is recognised that the "theology of liberation" represents a diverse movement, there are general principles of theological method which are applied, irrespective of the location or the community in which the theological reflection is taking place. This chapter sets out to identify the distinctive aspects of such an approach. For this reason, I will briefly focus first on the work of Gustavo Gutiérrez, as he is the liberation theologian who has presented the most structured outline of accepted liberation method. Second, in light of the overview given of liberationist methodology, the Latin American evangelical critique will be considered. Third, building on this critique, the Latin American evangelical search for an appropriate evangelical theological method will be examined.

4.2 "A New Way to Do Theology": A Brief Overview of Liberationist Method

We are celebrating the "coming of age" of liberation theology. This theology is no longer uniform. It is pluralistic and in process; more and more liberation theologies are being born among the diverse oppressed peoples of this earth. Feminist and black theologies; Jewish and Palestinian theologies of liberation; Minjung theology, "water buffalo" theology, "barefoot" theology...these are only some of the rich variety of theologies which owe debt of origin to what was born...in Latin America.[1]

It is evident that the theology of liberation is not monolithic. Liberation theologians do not seek to present a monochrome position. Despite mutual stimulation, liberation thought does not form a homogeneous "school" of theology in the European sense. For liberationists deal with different subjects, write with a variety of foci in mind and specialise in diverse theological fields.[2] Padilla comments:

> The task of defining and evaluating liberation theology is an impossible one...The term is useful in referring briefly to a wide variety of theologies sharing common characteristics, but the heterogeneity of the theological positions associated with the term should not be overlooked.[3]

As circumstances in the world have changed and continue to change, liberationist reflection and liberationist ideas continue to evolve and develop. The theology of liberation is open-ended reflection within dynamic and volatile situations. Despite this, however, within liberation thought similar areas of concern are addressed and a common basic theological methodology is evident.[4]

In the early years of liberationist reflection, theologians of liberation considered the approach to demonstrate a "new way to do theology." There is no doubt that the methodology employed broke with familiar theological patterns of the past, and set the theology of liberation apart. Núñez observes:

---

[1] Otto Maduro, "Introduction" in *The Future of Liberation Theology: Essays in Honor of Gustavo Gutiérrez*, eds. Marc H Ellis and Otto Maduro (Maryknoll: Orbis Books, 1989), xv-xviii, at xvi. Stephen Bevans also comments "If a theology is able to contribute positively to a dialogue among various contextual theologians, such vitality is a sign that it is a genuine expression of faith. One of the signs of the truth of the theology of liberation is how radically it has challenged not only other Latin American theologies, but also theologies from various parts of the world." Stephen Bevans, *Models of Contextual Theology* (Maryknoll: Orbis Books, 1992), 19.

[2] For a discussion on the multifaceted nature of the schools of thought within the movement referred to as the theology of liberation see José Míguez Bonino, "El nuevo catolicismo" in *Fe cristiana y Latinoamérica hoy*, ed. C. René Padilla (Buenos Aires: Ediciones Certeza, 1974), 83-118, at 98-113. See also Kirk, *Liberation*, 45; Samuel Escobar, "Beyond Liberation Theology: A Review Article", *Themelios* 19, no. 3 (1994): 15-17, at 15; C. René Padilla, "Liberation Theology: An Appraisal" in *Freedom and Discipleship*, ed. Daniel S. Schipani (Maryknoll: Orbis Books, 1989), 34-51, at 34; Muskus, *Origins*, 1-7; C. René Padilla, "Una nueva manera de hacer teología", *Misión* 1, no.1 (1982): 20- 23, at 20; Miroslav Volf, "Doing and Interpreting: an Examination of the Relationship between Theory and Practice in the Latin American Theology of Liberation", *Themelios* 8, no. 3 (1983): 11-18, at 12. It is also helpful to note the plurality used in reference to the theologies of liberation in the title of the previously mentioned evangelical response written by Samuel Escobar, namely *La fe evangélica y las teologías de la liberación*.

[3] Padilla, "Liberation", 34.

[4] Kirk, *Liberation*, 45.

In reality we Latin Americans find ourselves facing a new way of doing theology, in answer to economic, social, and political problems of the Latin American people. That new approach represents an effort to radically change the traditional concept of what it means to be the church of Jesus Christ, or to be Christians, in a society marked by conflict, such as ours. It is much more than a theology of revolution; it is nothing less than a revolution of theology itself.[5]

For an insightful discussion on liberation method we turn to the work and writings of Gutiérrez.[6] Accepted as "the most creative representative and systematic expositor of Latin American liberation theology,"[7] Gutiérrez presents the factors he considers to have made a significant contribution to the methodology applied by the theology of liberation.[8] These seven aspects of the Latin American context, identified by Gutiérrez in the early 1970s, influenced the development of liberation method in its earliest stages.

First, Gutiérrez asserts that *charity* has become central to the life of Christians once more. Second, he explains that the view of Christian *spirituality* has changed dramatically and is being sustained by the desire to find a lay spirituality. Third, Gutiérrez maintains that the *anthropological aspects* of revelation are treated with more sensitivity. Fourth, he highlights the *life of the church* as a vital source for theological analysis. Fifth, Gutiérrez identifies *philosophical issues* which reinforce the significance of the actions of humanity as the point of departure for theological reflection. To these significant factors, Gutiérrez adds sixthly the *influence of Marxism*. For he considers the confrontation between Marxism and theology to be a fruitful debate. Finally, Gutiérrez contends that the rediscovery of the *eschatological dimension* of theology has placed historical *praxis* in a central position. Reflecting on the purpose of liberation method, he contends:

> The goal is to balance and even to reject the primacy and almost exclusiveness which Christian doctrine has enjoyed in Christian life and above all to modify the emphasis, often obsessive, upon the attainment of an orthodoxy which is often nothing more than fidelity to an obsolete tradition or a debatable interpretation. In a more positive vein, the intention is to recognize the work and importance of concrete behaviour, of deeds, of action, of praxis in the Christian life.[9]

---

[5] Núñez, *Liberation*, 35.

[6] For further discussion and in order to understand the new method employed by the theology of liberation from the liberationist perspective see for example Gutiérrez, *Theology*; Juan Luis Segundo, *The Liberation of Theology*, 6th ed. (Maryknoll: Orbis Books, 1976, Maryknoll: Orbis Books, 1991); Leonardo Boff, *Jesus Christ, Liberator*, trans. Patrick Hughes (Maryknoll: Orbis Books, 1979); Jon Sobrino, *Christology at the Crossroads: A Latin American Approach*, trans. John Drury (London: SCM, 1978).

[7] Muskus, *Origins*, 3-6, at 3.

[8] See Gutiérrez, *Theology*, 5-13, 29-33, 54-57; James B. Nickoloff, ed., *Gustavo Gutiérrez: Essential Writings* (London: SCM, 1996), 23-74.

[9] Gutiérrez, *Theology*, 8.

These seven factors motivated theologians of liberation to respond specifically to the Latin American reality and the desperate needs which were evident there. In light of the circumstances, the fundamental starting point of liberation theology and the first crucial element in their approach was, and is, a *preferential option for the poor*. While it is evident that active concern for the poor and marginalized is historical within the Christian tradition, this liberationist emphasis implies both a pastoral commitment and a political realignment for the church. For the defining characteristic of the method employed by liberation theologians is the privileged role given to the experience and the perspective of the poor. Liberation thinkers insist that the central tenets of the Christian faith should be tested "from below," that is against the experience of the powerless and oppressed. The poor are considered to be a collective prophetic voice, denouncing the injustice of humanity through their suffering. This idea constitutes an important hermeneutical key. All communion with God, Gutiérrez argues, is testified to by opting for the poor and exploited, identifying with their plight and sharing their fate. Liberation theologians maintain that the poor person, who is treated and regarded as "other" in the world, reveals the totally "Other" to humanity. In short, the poor reveal the divine. Consequently, it is argued that Christians should understand God from within history, mediated through the lives of oppressed human beings. To experience history from this perspective, it is asserted that one must also become like the poor. Significantly, it is this first necessary act of personal identification with the poor which preludes the more theoretical act of reflection.[10]

Gutiérrez asserts that a true Christian life evidences such identification in "concrete and creative commitment of service to others."[11] He emphasises that such pastoral activity is the first duty of the church. Theology then is reflection upon this pastoral activity. Theology does not produce the activity. In this sense, for liberation theologians theology is secondary, and praxis is primary. Gutiérrez describes theology then as "the second step."[12]

Such *praxis* is the second crucial element in liberation methodology.[13] It does not refer simply to the action or the practice of the church. Rather it is critical reflection

---

[10] See for example José Comblin, *Called for Freedom: The Changing Context of Liberation Theology*, trans Philip Berryman (Maryknoll: Orbis Books, 1998), 7-9, 72-78; Maduro, "Introduction", xvii; Leonardo Boff, "The Originality of the Theology of Liberation" in *The Future of Liberation Theology: Essays in Honor of Gustavo Gutiérrez*, eds. Marc H Ellis and Otto Maduro (Maryknoll: Orbis Books, 1989), 38-48, at 42-43; Gregory Baum, "Community and Identity" in *The Future of Liberation Theology: Essays in Honor of Gustavo Gutiérrez*, eds. Marc H Ellis and Otto Maduro (Maryknoll: Orbis Books, 1989), 102-112; Justo L. González, *Mañana: Christian Theology from a Hispanic Perspective* (Nashville: Abingdon Press, 1990); Muskus, *Origins*, 17-19.

[11] Gutiérrez, *Theology*, 9.

[12] Gutiérrez, *Theology*, 9-10. See also Míguez Bonino, *Doing*, 86-105; Núñez, *Liberation*, 140; Padilla, "Liberation", 35.

[13] Volf notes that one rarely finds a precise definition of "praxis" given by liberation theologians. He observes that it has a wide range of meanings from contrasting activity with

on the intersection of theory and practice in the light of faith. The significance of praxis underscores the importance of "doing" as well as "seeing" the truth. Liberationists assert that orthodoxy, or right belief, stems from orthopraxis, that is right action. "The understanding of the faith appears as the understanding not of the simple affirmation...of truths, but of a commitment, an overall attitude, a particular posture towards life."[14]

The implication of reflecting upon the presence and action of the church in the world, for Gutiérrez means going beyond the visible boundaries of the church. Classical theology has generally used revelation and tradition as starting points. The theology of liberation in contrast begins with facts, questions and issues emanating from the world and from history. Gutiérrez insists that theologians then will be "personally and vitally engaged in historical realities with specific times and places." [15] The true interpretation of the meaning revealed by theology is achieved only through this historical praxis.

When the preferential option for the poor has been elected and the primary priority of historical praxis has been established, the third element in liberation method is an *analysis of the socio-economic and political situation*. Such analysis is designed to discover the roots of oppression in an effort to gain an understanding of the *realidad* and context. Literally translated as "reality" and sometimes meaning "truth," the concept of *realidad* reunites the past and the present. It is not only a reflection upon actual circumstances but also an analysis of the historical causes of those circumstances. This rereading of history has contributed significantly to the liberationist understanding of the contemporary situation. It becomes clear that in liberation method, Marxism is the ideological framework within which this historical analysis is made.

For Gutiérrez, the application of these three elements and the practice of "critical reflection on Christian praxis in the light of the word"[16] represents, not simply a new focus for consideration but rather, a totally new approach. Gutiérrez argues:

> It is for all these reasons that the theology of liberation offers us not so much a new theme for reflection as a *new way* to do theology. Theology as critical reflection on historical praxis is a liberating theology, a theology of the liberating transformation of the history of humankind and also therefore that part of humankind – gathered into *ecclesia* – which openly confess Christ. This is a theology which does not stop with reflecting on the world, but rather tries to be part of the process through which the world is transformed. It is a theology which is open – in the protest against trampled

---

passivity, to the more technical Marxist sense as "...human activity which reshapes the person himself and the world", see Volf, "Doing", 15. Míguez Bonino simply explains "praxis does not mean merely doing, but doing that is related to understanding." José Míguez Bonino, interview by author, 17 June 2003, video recording, Buenos Aires.

[14] Gutiérrez, *Theology*, 6. For further explanation on praxis in liberation thought, see Gutiérrez, *Theology*, xxx.

[15] Gutiérrez, *Theology*, 10.

[16] Gutiérrez, *Theology*, 11.

human dignity, in the struggle against the plunder of the vast majority of humankind, in liberating love, and in the building of a new, just and comradely society – to the gift of the kingdom of God.[17]

It is clear, then, that the theology of liberation strives to liberate theology from the constraints of methodological assumptions which ignore the culture of the oppressed and the historical experience of their suffering. For liberationists, theology should be an energetic, active process which incorporates the contemporary understanding of epistemology, anthropology and history. Through personal participation in the struggle for a new Latin American society, theological truth is discerned and formulated. This praxis is much more than a simple application of theological truth. It is committed action. It is engagement with a new way of living. It is a fresh understanding of the Christian presence in the world.

Drawing together the methodological assertions made by Gutiérrez in this brief overview, it is possible to summarise with three specific characteristics of liberation method in general. The first distinctive feature is the *priority of praxis*. Liberation method is evident in the practical, for action rather than reflection is primary. The second distinctive feature is the *priority of context*. The theology of liberation begins with the reality of poverty, oppression and social injustice. It is historical, for God speaks through concrete circumstances. The third distinctive feature is the *priority of ideology*. Liberation theologians contend that faith without ideological insight is ineffectual because it is historically irrelevant. In the next section, these distinctive aspects of liberation method will be examined in more detail, as the evangelical critique of each is taken into account. It is hoped that this evangelical critique will demonstrate principles of the contextual method which Latin American evangelical theologians are developing from within the same context.

4.3 The Latin American Evangelical Critique of Liberationist Method

Padilla describes the theology of liberation not as "an academic dissertation but a prophetic message."[18] Liberation theology is not an invitation to consider a new and interesting theological theory. It is a call to repentance. It is a challenge to Christians that they must demonstrate the historical efficacy of their faith.[19] Latin American

---

[17] Gutiérrez, *Theology*, 12.

[18] Padilla, "Liberation", 39. See also C. René Padilla, "Por qué Leonardo Boff ha sido silenciado", *Cuadernos de Teología* VI, no. 4 (1985): 107-112 for a discussion on the controversial debate surrounding the liberationist message to not only the world but also the church. A similar article is available as C. René Padilla, "Cuatro tesis de Leonardo Boff sobre la iglesia", *Misión* 14 (1985): 94-96.

[19] C. René Padilla, "La teología de la liberación: una evaluación crítica", *Misión* 1, no. 2 (1982), 16-21, at 16. It is interesting to note that many years before the emergence of the theology of liberation, John A. Mackay had challenged evangelicals within Latin America to live out their theology and their faith "on the road" so to speak, rather than theologising "on the balcony" at a distance from reality. Cited by Samuel Escobar, *Fe*, 86.

evangelicals have approached liberationist method in a thoughtful and constructive manner. From the outset evangelicals affirm:

> It is indispensable to remember that in liberation theology we are confronted with a new theological method having its own point of departure, its own special relationship to the theology of the church, its own hermeneutic norm, and, of course, its own philosophical framework.[20]

I shall begin by discussing the evangelical understanding of the methodological approach employed by liberation theologians. Secondly, I will consider the critical evaluation of that method in evangelical perspective. Thirdly, I will examine the search for an evangelical theological method which inevitably will contrast with the liberationist approach. For it is in this engagement with the dominant contextual theology in Latin America that the strength of the evangelical commitment is most evident. Similarly, evangelical contextual method continues to sustain contemporary evangelical reflection and therefore, in the passage of time, has proven to be a viable alternative.

In his discussion on method, Gutiérrez stresses that the notion of theology as *wisdom* and the notion of theology as *rational knowledge* have both been superseded by the understanding of theology as critical reflection on praxis. Evangelical theologians identify the following implications of such an understanding. First, a "historical praxis" is a *conditio sine qua non* for doing theology. Second, the "historical situation" is the starting point for theological reflection. Third, the present historical reality is understood through application of the social sciences. Fourth, theological reflection inevitably takes on ideological forms.[21] These implications will be dealt with more specifically in the following sections.

4.3.1 Praxis Under the Authority of Scripture

The emphasis on the priority of "historical praxis" in liberationist method is the driving force behind the theology of liberation. Indeed, Kirk comments that this "interaction between social praxis and theology is the most decisive methodological factor for actual and future Latin American theology."[22] It is widely acknowledged that in their insistence on praxis, liberation theologians have done a great service to theology in general.[23] Escobar comments:

---

[20] Núñez, *Liberation*, 131.

[21] Padilla, "Liberation", 35.

[22] Kirk, *Liberation*, 37.

[23] See Bevans, *Models*, 71. As a contemporary missiologist, Bevans comments on the significance of the liberationist contribution when he writes, "In some way this model takes the concrete situation more seriously than any other model, since it regards theology not as a generally applicable, finished product that is valid at all times and in all places, but as an understanding of God's presence in very particular situations – a movement of fairer housing laws, a campaign for voter registration, an earthquake in a particular part of the world, a

There is a way in which these theologians almost glory in the fact that theirs is not just a new academic fashion, but that its novelty comes from its rootedness in a new praxis, in a new way of living and understanding the Christian presence and action in the world... Maybe the captivity of theology in the academic world, where professional theologians teach, write and discuss it, needs this disturbing wind of liberation.[24]

This call to make praxis a priority has stimulated theology to move from being a discussion about faith to being the obedience of faith.[25] Theology then, which can be described as critical reflection on historical praxis, becomes the "handmaid of pastoral action."[26]

While there is no doubt that evangelical theologians applaud the emphasis laid on the practical outworking of faith, the first question raised in response to the theology of liberation is the root of the motivation for such knowing obedience to God.[27] Escobar is careful to point out that without the proclamation of the word of God, there can be no spiritual rebirth. Without spiritual rebirth, there can be no new people. Without new people who have responded to God's call and who are seeking to live in obedience to Him, there can be no new authentic praxis.[28] Costas concurs with Escobar, asserting that to fully participate in the transformation of the world, one must have experienced the grace and forgiveness of God in order to experience restitution and freedom for service.[29]

The basic assumption of the liberationist approach is that the true knowledge of God is equivalent to the doing of God's will. Escobar maintains, however, that praxis does not generate the word of God and knowledge of God. Rather, it is the word of God which generates new life and in consequence, it is the word of God which generates new praxis. Escobar voices concern regarding the imbalance towards so-called orthopraxis in the theology of liberation and he warns against making praxis the reference point. Naturally, as an evangelical theologian, Escobar seeks to make Scripture the reference point of theology and obedience. He insists, therefore, that praxis should not be given a superior position.[30]

Núñez summarises liberationist method succinctly as "we must *do* in order to *know*, and hope that orthodoxy will arise from orthopraxis."[31] He recognises that the method is undergirded by an understanding of the Christian faith as commitment to

---

moment of transition in a particular parish. There is a certain permanence and even generality needed in the theological enterprise, of course, but the praxis model offers a corrective to a theology that is too general and pretends to be universally relevant."

[24] Samuel Escobar, *Liberation Themes in Reformational Perspective* (Sioux Center: Dordt College Press, 1989), 38.

[25] Kirk, *Liberation*, 198.

[26] Padilla, "Liberation", 35.

[27] See Escobar, *Themes*, 38-40.

[28] Escobar, *Fe*, 84-105, 179-200.

[29] Orlando E. Costas, *Evangelización contextual: fundamentos teológicos y pastorales* (San José: Editorial Sebila, 1986), 24.

[30] Escobar, *Themes*, 40-43.

[31] Núñez, *Liberation*, 67.

liberating praxis and of theology as a product of pastoral activity. Núñez too concludes that liberation theologians are very far from taking the Scriptures as central to the theological task. While he affirms the need for the practice of faith and love in the Christian life, he asserts, however, "that is very different from suggesting that there is a hierarchical order according to which praxis is supreme...in any case our responsibility is to submit praxis to the word, instead of giving supremacy to praxis."[32]

In agreement with the other evangelical theologians, Padilla also acknowledges that the theology of liberation rightly emphasises the importance of obedience or praxis for the understanding of truth. Padilla affirms with liberation theologians that the purpose of theology should be practical. "Gospel truth is always truth to be lived out, not merely truth to be intellectually known."[33] Theology should be set free from a rationalistic framework and made obedient to the word of God. However, Padilla warns of the pitfalls of pragmatism. Liberation theology claims to reflect on praxis "in the light of faith." Padilla points out that if faith is "historical liberating praxis," as Hugo Assmann the prominent liberationist declares, then theology becomes reflection on praxis, in the light of praxis. It is not, in fact, reflection on praxis in the light of faith. Juan Luis Segundo, another significant figure in liberation thought, also recognises this methodological concern. With regard to this difficulty, Segundo observes:

> If the Christian contribution is hung, as it were, from a prior revolutionary commitment, this latter appears hung, as it were, from a correct, non-deviationary, evaluation of socio-political praxis. One preunderstanding presupposes another. Do they not, then, enter into a circle?[34]

In the liberationist attempt to reflect on praxis, Padilla identifies what he refers to as the *objectivistic concept of science* at work. He also observes what he describes as a *subjectivistic concept of revelation*. Padilla contends that correction of this inconsistency is needed. He asserts that the two following facts should be taken into account by liberation theologians. First, there is no science without presuppositions (and, therefore, no omnipotent self-authenticating analysis of reality). Second, the knowledge of God has a belief-content, although it cannot be identified with believing certain things. If these facts are ignored, one's evaluation of praxis will lead to a vicious circle, as noted by Segundo. Consequently, there will be no possibility of practising theology as reflection on praxis "in the light of faith."[35] In a similar vein, Míguez Bonino observes:

> Christian obedience, certainly understood as historical praxis and therefore incarnate in a historical mediation (rational, concrete) embodies, however, a dimension which, to

---

[32] Núñez, *Liberation,* 150.

[33] Padilla, "Liberation", 40. See also Escobar, *Themes,* 40.

[34] Cited by Padilla, "Liberation", 41.

[35] Padilla, "Liberation", 41.

use Christological language, cannot be separated or confused with it. In other words, how is the historical praxis of a Christian affected by the original (or, better said, "germinal") events of the faith, namely, God's acts in Israel, the birth, life, death and resurrection of Jesus Christ, the hope of the kingdom? If on this point we are condemned to remain silent, we are really resigning any attempt to speak of such a praxis as *Christian* obedience.[36]

With Escobar and Núñez, Padilla subsequently concludes that reflection on Scripture is essential to the theological reflection on praxis. Padilla further argues that the purpose of reflection is not merely intellectual knowledge of revealed truth. Rather, the purpose of reflection is the obedience of faith which is not possible without entering into the context of a personal relationship with God.

For Padilla, God's *logos* is not simply an incarnate *logos*, but a *logos* who has spoken. The message exists to be understood and obeyed. "*Doing* the truth is not equivalent to *making* the truth through praxis, but to *practising* the truth, which has been given [to] us through revelation."[37] Praxis therefore takes place in dialogue with the concrete historicity of the biblical texts. Simultaneously there must be critical reflection on praxis and critical reflection on the word of God. "Faith seeks results from the convergence between the knowledge of God's truth inscripturated in the Bible and the knowledge of God's truth incarnate in history."[38]

If theology is to be a critical reflection on praxis in the light of faith then the hermeneutical circle between the past and the present, between Scripture and the historical situation is unavoidable. Padilla explains that the answer to both a rationalistic theology concerned with orthodoxy and a pragmatic theology concerned with orthopraxis, is a contextual theology concerned with faithfulness to the word of God and relevance to the historical situation at the same time. He contends:

> If the gospel is to be not just intellectually accepted but also lived, it must necessarily take shape within our cultural context. The role of theology is to interpret and clarify God's word for the sake of obedience to Christ in the concrete historical situation. In other words, theology is an instrument for the contextualization of the gospel. And for it to fulfil its purpose it must be based on biblical revelation, in the context of real life and for obedience to Christ today.[39]

There is no doubt that the significance of praxis in liberation method has far reaching implications. For Latin American evangelicals, in particular, a method which gives priority to praxis is intricately interwoven with debates surrounding issues of biblical authority, revelation, and hermeneutics. These subjects will be the focus of the following chapter. Suffice it to say at this point that "the practice of Christians, the life of the church in her mission, is what revitalizes theological

---

[36] Cited by Padilla, "Liberation", 42. See Míguez Bonino, *Doing*, 98.

[37] Padilla, "Liberation", 42.

[38] Padilla, "Liberation", 42. See also Padilla, *Mission*, 106-107.

[39] Padilla, *Mission*, 106.

inquiry; but in the evangelical conviction there must be a word, outside of praxis itself, that is the norm to evaluate praxis."[40]

In summary, Latin American evangelicals affirm the liberationist unequivocal call to authentic praxis. However, Kirk suggests that the definition of concrete praxis laid down by liberation theology is often "vague, unreal and tending towards romanticism."[41] Latin American evangelicals, therefore, recognise the importance of being specific and definitive in their search for authentic evangelical praxis. Together with liberation theologians, however, Latin American evangelicals affirm:

> To understand God's word is not only an intellectual process of grasping some propositions; it is submission to the Spirit of God. It touches the will; it is openness to correction. There are many humble Christians who practise the two commandments. They are expressing their love to God and their love to the neighbour, and they *know* better than theologians who discuss academically the intricacies of the text and the methodology of inspiration.[42]

4.3.2 The Point of Departure: Historical Context or Biblical Text

The second distinctive aspect of liberation method, which is also open to evangelical critique, is the priority of context. Assmann displays this liberationist understanding when he comments:

> Perhaps the greatest merit of the theology of liberation is its insistence on the starting-point of its reflections: the situation of "dominated (Latin) America"...One thing virtually all the documents so far published agree on is that the starting-point of the theology of liberation is the present historical situation of domination and dependence in which the countries of the Third World find themselves.[43]

---

[40] Escobar, *Themes*, 43.

[41] Kirk, *Liberation*, 200. Bevans also comments "...the language of liberation does not necessarily mean that the full method of liberation theology – critical reflection on praxis – is operative in various theologies in which liberation is the theme. A case in point is one of the most important liberation theologians, Leonard Boff. Boff is certainly aware of the importance of praxis in the theological enterprise, but several of his books do not immediately reflect the method of praxis at the heart of their construction...Boff is certainly among those who employ the praxis model, but even he does not use it all the time..." Bevans, *Models*, 72.

[42] Samuel Escobar, Pedro Arana, Valdir Steuernagel and Rodrigo Zapata, "A Latin American Critique of a Latin American Theology", *Evangelical Review of Theology* 7, no. 1 (1983): 48-62, at 59.

[43] Cited by Núñez, *Liberation*, 132. See Hugo Assmann, *Theology of a Nomad Church* (Maryknoll: Orbis, 1975), 38, 53.

The point of departure, then, for the theology of liberation is the *realidad*.[44] "The 'text' is our situation" Assmann asserts.[45] Liberation theologians maintain that most European and North American theology has remained insulated from socio-political reality and has "taken flight into a conceptual world where the cry of the people is never heard."[46] Both liberation theologians and Latin American evangelical theologians argue that European and North American theology is largely dualistic and abstract. Padilla comments that "if God is relegated to the 'spiritual' aspect of human life, and salvation is totally outside the historical realm, it is virtually the salvation of a spiritual nomad."[47] In contrast to an acontextual method, Padilla argues that Scripture sees the person as a unitary human being in whom body and soul are inseparable. Thus, the historical situation of that person is central. Such contextual methodology can be applied to any historical circumstances, for those specific circumstances are where the method begins.[48]

To use the Latin American historical situation as the starting point means "reading" the social, political, economic and cultural dimensions of the context, and the Bible from the perspective of solidarity with the poor. In the theology of liberation, a theologian is encouraged to take the worldview of those who are oppressed and make it his or her own worldview. Theology, then, should be "a call to adopt the vision from the underside of history and to read God's word from that perspective."[49] Consequently, the primary "text" is not the written witness to Jesus of the prophets and apostles, but the global reality of history. This reality is analysed

---

[44] Goldsmith observes "Liberation theologians deliberately attack traditional theology for its non-situational objectivity, affirming that all true salvation theology should spring from existential historical realities. We are forced to face the question today of the relationship of theology to historical situations..." Martin Goldsmith, "Contextualization of Theology", *Themelios* 9, no.1 (1983): 18-23, at 21.

[45] Cited by Núñez, *Liberation*, 134. See Assmann, *Nomad*, 104.

[46] Padilla, "Liberation", 43.

[47] Padilla, "Liberation", 43.

[48] The subject of the contextualization of theology has been a controversial one within traditional evangelicalism. Goldsmith comments, "Evangelicals in particular have been slower to see the need of contexualization than more liberal Christians. Evangelicals have such a strong emphasis on the unchanging nature of revelation and such a healthy fear of heresy that they sometimes hesitate to adventure boldly in their understanding of Scripture and in their theological expression. Their fears have been compounded by the fact that many of the pioneers of contextualization have not held firmly to the absolute authority of the word of God. A result of this has been that evangelicals who have often criticised Catholics for their adherence to tradition have themselves in many cases become tradition-bound in their biblical and theological interpretations." Goldsmith, "Contextualization", 18.

[49] Escobar, *Themes*, 25. In chapter four of this book, "The Vision from the Underside", Escobar discusses the definition of the term "poor", and the evangelical theological position regarding the poor in the light of the Latin American context and the liberationist option for the poor.

and understood through the application of the human sciences.[50] This "hermeneutical circulation" between the two "texts," that is the historical situation and the biblical text, can be accurately referred to as the *hermeneutic of liberation*.[51]

While Padilla affirms the liberationist emphasis on the importance of the historical situation, he voices concern that the theology of liberation is in danger of historical reductionism. Padilla insightfully notes that there is the potential for the subordination of the word of God to the human context. He explains that concepts and attributes of the kingdom of God are reduced in order to fit within the confines of history. Such an approach can also lead to a selective reading of the Bible. As a consequence of this selectivity in liberation thought, the theological focus becomes limited to the ethical and political realms alone. This results in an imbalanced theology which does injustice to the totality of the biblical revelation. For "instead of showing the relevance of revelation to revolution, it makes revolution its source of revelation. The result is a secular gospel whose dominant emphases parallel those of Marxism."[52] In the theology of liberation, anything unrelated to ethical and political praxis is set aside. Latin American evangelicals stress, therefore, that the theology of liberation must face the criticism that it fails to deal with many serious theological issues. Padilla writes:

> The point here is not to advocate an ahistorical, individualistic approach to the Christian faith. Such an approach is not only politically irrelevant but also unbiblical...There must be, however, a better way to relate the public and the private, the social and the personal, life shared with others and the inner life of the individual person than the way suggested either by an ahistorical theology or by a theology bent towards historical reductionism.[53]

Padilla proposes that a hermeneutical circle between Scripture and the historical situation is the answer. He suggests that if theology is to be a reflection on praxis in the light of faith, such theology will have to read the situation in the light of Scripture and in turn read Scripture in the light of the situation.[54]

In summary, it is evident that Latin American evangelicals appreciate the importance of contextual theology which seeks to be relevant to the local situation and circumstances. Costas is representative of Latin American evangelicals when he

---

[50] Escobar comments "Liberation theologians may not agree as to the degree to which the social sciences are determinative of their practice and their reflection, but they do agree about the need to use social sciences in order to understand the nature of Christian commitment today." Escobar, *Themes*, 30. See also *Volf*, "Doing", 16.

[51] Padilla, "Liberation", 36. See also J. Andrew Kirk, *Theology Encounters Revolution* (Leicester: IVP, 1980), 118-120.

[52] C. René Padilla, "Revolution and Revelation" in *Is Revolution Change?*, ed. Brian Griffiths, (London: IVP, 1972), 70-83, at 80.

[53] Padilla, "Liberation", 44.

[54] Padilla, "Liberation", 44. Goldsmith also comments "We need...to understand the word *in* its context and then interpret it and reapply it *in* our context today. This is contextualization of theology and interpretation of the word." Goldsmith, "Contextualization", 20.

asserts: "An agent of the gospel can be neither neutral nor passive in the face of reality. Christians live under the captivation of the Spirit. They must demonstrate this with a new style of life, one of liberty and service, justice and peace."[55] Once more, Latin American evangelicals are in agreement with the liberation theologians regarding the necessity to respond to the specific Latin American reality. However, the liberationist point of departure, which takes the Latin American situation as the "text" over and above Scripture, causes evangelical theologians difficulty. As evangelical theologians, they naturally seek to live by the Spirit and discern the leading of the Spirit of God through the word of God. Once more, the method employed by the theology of liberation raises issues of biblical authority, revelation and hermeneutics.

Latin American evangelicals agree that the liberationist critique of theology is justifiable. Similarly, they concur with the liberationist assertion that theological reflection should be evident in active, compassionate praxis. As has been seen in this section, evangelical theologians also remain committed to appropriate contextual theology. Yet, once again, liberationists and evangelicals are divided on the use of Scripture. For, despite the insufficiency of theological reflection in the past for the Latin American context, evangelicals strive to maintain the evangelical principle of the primacy of God's word in their pursuit of contextual method.

> In good Evangelical theology the church bows before the authority of the word. Human traditions and systems, the praxis of the Christian and non-Christian, every historical moment, all are to be illuminated by the word of God and judged by it. At every point of their pilgrimage on earth God's people have to subject their praxis to the light and judgement of God through his word. Here is where we have found the weakness of traditional Evangelical theology as we received it in Latin America. It has not dealt adequately with our own situation.[56]

4.3.3 Ideology in the Light of Scripture

Liberation method is distinctive in the emphatic importance attributed to praxis and in taking the present historical reality as the point of departure for theological reflection. The third distinguishing aspect of liberationist methodology, in particular, has left the theology of liberation open to wide and severe criticism.[57] Western theologians have pronounced:

---

[55] Costas, *Evangelización*, 25.

[56] Escobar, Arana, Steuernagel and Zapata, "Critique", 58.

[57] See for example Arthur F. McGovern, *Liberation Theology and Its Critics* (Maryknoll: Orbis Books, 1989); Ronald H. Nash, ed., *On Liberation Theology* (Michigan: Mott Media, 1984); Carl E. Armerding, ed., *Evangelicals and Liberation* (USA: Presbyterian and Reformed Publishing Company, 1977); Muskus, *Origins*, 232-242; Padilla, "Teología", 16; Hundley, *Radical*, 11-76; Kirk, "The Gospel and Ideology" in *Liberation*, 45-54.

It has Marxist leanings;...it espouses violence;...it reduces the gospel to sociology, economics or politics;...its use of the Bible is too selective;...it is partisan and therefore destroys the universality of the gospel;...it is too contextually conditioned...[58]

It is clear that an understanding of the present historical reality, contributed to by the social sciences, is an essential aspect of the theological task in liberation thought. As a consequence, in an effort to employ social sciences, the theological reflection of liberation theologians has inevitably taken on ideological forms. For in their effort to change the world, not simply explain it, liberationists have opted for the social sciences, sociology and economics in particular, as partners for dialogue. Consequently, engagement with other disciplines has become an essential aspect of the theological and hermeneutical task.[59]

It is evident that the ideological assertions of Marxism have significantly influenced the formation of liberation thought.[60] Writing in 1971, Gutiérrez displayed this influence in his comments during the early development of a theology of liberation:

Many agree with Sartre that "Marxism, as the formal framework of all contemporary philosophical thought, cannot be superseded." Be that as it may, contemporary theology does in fact find itself in direct and fruitful confrontation with Marxism, and it is to a large extent due to Marxism's influence that theological thought, searching for its own resources, has begun to reflect on the meaning of the transformation of the world and human action in history.[61]

Marxist sociology provides a global diagnosis of historical reality which sets out to discover not only the phenomenon of poverty but the causes of the phenomenon. Marxism clarifies that the existence of the poor is due to injustice. Thus, it is a completely new social order which is demanded, not simply economic development. In an effort to understand the economic situation in Latin America, the "theory of dependence" has become identifiable as an essential key in liberation theology for understanding the Latin American reality.[62] Liberation theology would affirm that in today's world we cannot simply set out to reproduce biblical models. Rather,

---

[58] Padilla, "Liberation", 40.

[59] Padilla, "Liberation", 46.

[60] For an early discussion on the Latin American evangelical response to Marxism see Samuel Escobar, *Diálogo entre Cristo y Marx* (Lima: Publicaciones AGEUP, 1967). See also Samuel Escobar and Kwame Bediako, *The Gospel and Contemporary Ideologies and Cultures* (n.p.: NFES Publication, 1979).

[61] Gutiérrez, *Liberation*, 8.

[62] For further discussion on the theories of development and dependence see Míguez Bonino, *Doing*, chapter 2 entitled "Understanding our World", 21-37; Gutiérrez, *Liberation*, xxiv; Kay, "Estructuralismo", 100-119; López, "Dependencia", 7-37; Escobar, "Situación", 19-20.

contemporary sociological insights should be employed to enable Christians to articulate love historically.[63]

While Kirk recognises that "theology is a necessary mediator between faith and political commitment,"[64] he contends that ideology has its limitations as a tool for doing theology. In reference to the use of Marxism made in liberation theology Kirk concludes: "the claim of Marxism to be an objective socio-political tool of analysis is valid within a limited field of competence; as a contribution towards a more faithful understanding of the biblical message about God, man and history it is ambiguous."[65]

In his assessment of the ideological content of liberation method, Padilla also seeks to judge fairly the alleged dependence liberationists have on Marxist thought. He is careful to contend that the acceptance of the validity of Marxist insights does not necessarily imply that one has become a Marxist.[66] Indeed, Padilla recognises that there are attractive aspects of Marxist thought and comments that "no honest Christian can deny the biblical overtones present in Marx's invectives against injustice."[67] Latin American evangelical theologians concur with Padilla when they comment:

> We cannot deny that it [Marxism] has brought to light the economic realities behind every social and political process and that it has uncovered the fact of oppression in economics inside capitalism. However, by making economics the base of every aspect of reality it gives us a unilateral and distorted view of the world…A critical task is open then for evangelical theology in the Third World. The word of God has much to say about justice, a desirable social order, real peace. We have discovered in Latin America the biblical teaching about the kingdom of God as a key to understanding God's work and our mission. The theological poverty of extreme dispensationalism and pop-eschatology is completely unable to answer the all-encompassing challenge of Marxist ideology.[68]

Padilla questions then, whether the theology of liberation has gone beyond an acceptance of Marxist insights warranted by biblical revelation. He poses several key questions in regard to the liberationist use of Marxist analysis. Firstly he asks what kind of precaution is taken so that the theory of Marxism is kept under control

---

[63] Padilla, "Liberation", 38; Escobar, *Themes*, 45-54.

[64] Kirk, *Liberation*, 39.

[65] Kirk, *Liberation*, 165. See also Kirk, *Revolution*, in particular chapter 8 "Latin America: the Rich Man's Table is the Poor Man's Grave", 114-130.

[66] Míguez Bonino emphasises that while liberation theologians employed Marxism as a tool for social analysis, they were never concerned with Marxist philosophy. For this reason, he asserts that liberationists have often been misjudged in the past. José Míguez Bonino, interview by author, 17 June 2003, video recording, Buenos Aires.

[67] Padilla, "Liberation", 45.

[68] Escobar, Arana, Steuernagel and Zapata, "Critique", 60. For further discussion see J. Andrew Kirk, *A New World Coming* (Basingstoke: Marshall, Morgan and Scott, 1983), in particular chapter 2, "The Glories and Follies of a Passing Age", 24-31.

by the belief content of an authentic Christian commitment. Secondly, he raises the issue: if Marxism is to be seen as a strictly scientific theory, on what basis is it then to be regarded *also* as the historical project in which the Christian faith ought to be embodied in order to become historically relevant? Padilla, it seems, is correct when he criticises liberation thought for employing Marxist political strategy in order to build up the kingdom of God. He alleges that liberation theologians "have fallen prey to a humanist illusion that is not in agreement with either the historical facts or biblical revelation."[69]

Liberationists recognise that they leave themselves open to accusation regarding ideology but they maintain that a faith without an ideological meditation is dead because it is historically irrelevant. If theology does not consciously accept its partiality, liberation theologians add, it should be "unmasked" as an ideological expression of the self-interest of the bourgeoisie.[70] In the light of this challenge to "unmask," Padilla observes that the theology of liberation rightly emphasises the importance of recognising the ideological condition of theology but is still in danger of reducing the gospel to an ideology.[71] Padilla does not deny that Western theological tradition is also under "ideological captivity." Indeed, it would be fair to say that Latin American evangelical theologians affirm that evangelical hermeneutics too must be purified constantly from ideological presuppositions.[72] Active biblical faith expressed through theology should not be used to cover up an ideology of the *status quo*. Padilla recognises that no theology is free from ideological entanglements.[73] Escobar is in agreement:

> Protestantism has been so closely linked to modernity and the modernization processes, even in its missionary history, that it has not adequately distinguished between the biblical message and the Enlightenment ideas. The question about justice in national and international relationships, for instance, can take us to a critical assessment of capitalism and the international order created by market economies. Are they fruit of the Reformation or are they in many ways fruit of the Enlightenment? In the contemporary debates it is interesting to observe how easily defenders of capitalism use Enlightenment categories rather than those of the Reformation of biblical revelation.[74]

Núñez too, is careful to draw attention to the fact that it is not valid to approve the method of liberation theology by using the excuse that conservative evangelicals also come to the Scriptures under the influence of ideology. He writes that the solution is not found in exchanging one ideology for another. Observing that liberation theology appears to criticise everything except its own method, Núñez challenges evangelical Christians to respond by weighing both the method employed

---

[69] Padilla, "Liberation", 45.
[70] Padilla, "Liberation", 39.
[71] Padilla, "Revolution", 80-83.
[72] Escobar, *Themes*, 43; Padilla, *Mission*, 104; Escobar and Bediako, *Gospel*, 17.
[73] Padilla, "Revolution", 74.
[74] Escobar, *Themes*, 50.

by liberation theology and their own methodology in the balance of the word of God.

Padilla thirdly raises the question of whether there is a way out of the vicious circle in which ideology determines the historical praxis which in turn determines theology. He recognises that liberation theology asserts that the Bible ought to be read in light of Marxist socio-political analysis in order to release the revolutionary power of the Scriptures. Liberationists acknowledge their hermeneutical partiality but respond that all hermeneutics display a conscious or unconscious bias. Padilla also asks why, if liberation theologians maintain an historical situation can be read objectively, do they reject the possibility of an objective reading of Scripture. Padilla asks whether faith can remain authentically biblical if Scripture is not allowed to judge freely one's ideological commitments. He proposes that a superior alternative would be a theological approach which reads the Bible on its own terms and refuses to force it into an ideological straitjacket.[75]

Padilla considers it possible to construct a theology which continually seeks integration between Scripture and present obedience through a "synthetic act" in which past and present, word and Spirit, are brought together. This implies that past events, such as the death and resurrection of Jesus, are not limited to being past events only but are present events in the sense that they are living and powerful. Padilla proposes this alternative to be a theology engaged in dialogue with both Scripture and the concrete situation.[76] He suggests that this would be a theological approach concerned with the historical manifestation of the kingdom of God.

In light of liberationist method, Kirk reflects on the four principal challenges which he considers that Marxism presented to Latin American communities of faith. Evangelical theologians have sought to engage with these challenges and consequently develop a more biblical understanding of the implications of individual salvation and personal integrity. First, the challenge to defend the dignity of human beings is presented. Second, the need to analyse the causes of inequality and oppression among humans is identified. Third, a strong element of hope is demonstrated. Fourth, open hostility to the practice of religion and to belief in God is a disturbing reminder to evangelicals of the need to engage directly with ideological presuppositions.[77] Challenges such as these motivated and continue to motivate evangelical theologians in the search for an appropriate contextual method.

As has been seen, historically speaking, the theology of liberation has been ideologically committed. Obviously, in a contemporary context, this ideological commitment is being questioned. For events during the last decades in Eastern Europe and China have ensured that the liberation hope inspired by the Marxist faith

---

[75] Padilla, "Liberation", 47. See also Samuel Escobar, "Vivir el evangelio", *Certeza* 65 (1977): 11-13 in which Escobar challenges the use of biblical material to promote Marxist utopian ideals and the manipulation of the biblical text for ideological reasons.

[76] See also Escobar, *Themes*, 55-57.

[77] Kirk, *World*, 44-46. For a more contemporary evangelical engagement with different ideological positions see J. Andrew Kirk, *The Meaning of Freedom: A Study of Secular, Muslim and Christian Views* (Carlisle: Paternoster Press, 1998).

that history was moving towards socialism, has been denied. However, it is impossible to examine the evangelical engagement with liberationist method without recognising the influential role which Marxism played. Escobar asserts emphatically that the questions raised by the Marxist social criticism employed by liberation theology in regard to inequality, corruption, racism, and the abuse of human rights remain unanswered in Latin America. Consequently, he writes that "evangelical theologians who did not share that [Marxist] hope will continue to work in their own agenda of relating their hope in the Lordship of Christ and his final victory to the struggle of a growing number of poor people for survival."[78]

4.3.4 The Search for a Latin American Evangelical Theological Method

Evangelical theologians recognise that the purpose of the prophetic voice of the theology of liberation is not to simply convey information or propound theories. Rather, liberationists seek to shake the Christian world out of complacency and call the world to repentance. Liberationists believe that the Christian should stand in a prophetic tradition which desires a better world where justice and liberty reign.[79] The evangelical engagement with the theology of liberation clearly demonstrates that Latin American evangelical theologians are standing in such a tradition. The constructive evangelical critique of liberation methodology displays the evangelical recognition of the need for contextual method but also displays the determination to hold to evangelical principles in the pursuit of such method.

Escobar similarly affirms the importance of the evangelical commitment to a combination of theology, ethics and action.[80] He stresses that evangelical theological method should be distinctive in the significance which it attributes to the divine initiative; to human and ethical responsibility; to the need to respond to the call of God; and to the commitment to walk in practical obedience to God's word. Escobar writes:

> The global economic and political order demands the courageous presence of advocates of justice and compassion within the powerful nations of the world. It is easy to forget that though many of the Reformers were not revolutionaries, they and their followers have left us a rich heritage of prophetic ministry to the powerful of their day...What evangelical theologies from the Third World...are proposing is a new sense of history in which the church refuses to be a passive subculture dominated by salesmen of a truncated gospel. Protestantism needs to regain a dynamic view of the church as the history-making body of believers through whom God sends His gospel of salvation. We

---

[78] Escobar, "Beyond", 17.

[79] Padilla, "Revolution", 80.

[80] Escobar, "Vivir", 11. See also Orlando E. Costas, "La vida en el Espíritu", *Boletín Teológico* 21-22 (1986): 105-112 where Costas comments that such a commitment to theology, ethics and action is evident when Christians make responsible decisions in respect of social, economic, political, biological, ecological, and cultural issues in order to build community, struggle for a just society and enable people to live in freedom.

are not denying the urgency of the evangelistic task, but we are asking about the kind of presence that the messengers of the gospel are to be in our world today.[81]

Escobar appreciates that the Utopian ideals held by liberation theologians have intermittent flickers of truth. In reality, however, he asserts that truth is to be found first in the word of God.

Building upon their critique of liberationist method, Latin American evangelicals recognise the need to dedicate themselves to serious biblical exegesis and commit themselves to correct biblical reflection in response to the challenge of the historical context of Latin America. Evangelical theologians realise the importance of thorough training in biblical and theological sciences. Similarly, they realise the importance of being capable to instruct, motivate and enable future pastors and teachers. However, in line with liberation theologians, they are aware of the temptation which exists to be so immersed in the pursuit of academic excellence that the surrounding social situation remains unchanged. It is vital, therefore, that a biblically based response is structured in respect of what it means to be the church in countries troubled by volatile processes of social change.

Núñez argues that in the search for method which is contextual and historically relevant, centuries of theological thought and development should not be discarded. For he acknowledges the arrogant assumption present in some evangelical communities that the Holy Spirit has remained silent until now. Just as theology is indebted to the past, evangelical theology must also take advantage of current theological contributions.[82] Núñez emphasises that evangelical theology in Latin America must not simply be a "Latin American theology" for the sake of it. Rather, they must strive to structure a theology which is "pre-eminently biblical, expressed by Latin Americans for Latin Americans."[83] Núñez maintains, therefore, that Latin American evangelical method must strive to produce theology which is:

> *Biblical* in its foundations, *ecclesiastical* in its close relationship to the community of faith, *pastoral* in its attempt to be an orientating voice for the people of God, *contextualized* with regard to that which is social and cultural, and *missionary* in its purpose to reach with the gospel those who are not Christians.[84]

4.4 Conclusion

There is no doubt that Latin American evangelical theologians remain committed to the development of a thoroughly evangelical methodology. If theology is to be contextual, it must not only engage with the context for which it is being structured but must also seek to function within that context to motivate and enable local

---

[81] Escobar, *Themes*, 53.
[82] Núñez, *Liberation*, 282.
[83] Núñez, *Cristo*, 46.
[84] Núñez, *Liberation*, 280.

believers. Consequently, as will be seen in the final conclusion, Latin American evangelical theologians will continue to face the challenge of communicating their contextual approach to local communities of faith. In their insistence on the combination of theology, ethics and action it will be imperative to convey to local believers the essence of such commitment. In order to promote serious biblical exegesis and biblical reflection in Latin America, creative forms of dissemination will need to be sought.

The theology which is developing within Latin American evangelicalism is active, biblical, contextual, and practical. It is theology which faces historical realities, taking cognisance of the struggles of the poor and oppressed. It is theology which engages in dialogue, both with Scripture and the concrete contemporary situation. It is theology which focuses on the historical manifestation of the kingdom of God, seeking to engender the active outworking of faith in the present, in anticipation of the kingdom which is to come.

In this chapter, a brief overview of the methodology proposed by the theology of liberation has been provided in order to present the dominant Latin American contextual method. In light of this overview, the evangelical engagement with liberationist method has been discussed and the evangelical critique of the "new way to do theology" has been considered. Despite their objections to specific aspects of liberationist methodology, Latin American evangelicals are not reticent in acknowledging what they consider to be the crucial contribution made to contextual method by liberationist proposals. The discussion in this chapter has demonstrated that Latin American evangelical method differs most from liberation methodology in respect to its attitude towards the Scriptures. Consequently, issues of biblical authority, revelation and biblical interpretation are central in the pursuit of contextual Latin American theology and in the exposition of liberation themes. For this reason, the use of Scripture by evangelicals and liberationists will be dealt with in the following chapter.

CHAPTER 5

Contextual Hermeneutics: The Use of Scripture by Liberationists and Evangelicals

5.1 Introduction

As is seen in earlier chapters of this study, the nature and use of Scripture is central to a contextual theology for Latin America. In chapter two, it was established that biblical renewal within post-conciliar Catholicism led to a fresh approach to the Scriptures (see section 2.3.1). This notable change in attitude was influential in the early development of liberation thought (see section 2.3.2). In chapter three, it was demonstrated that the emphasis on the authority of Scripture is a definitive principle of evangelicalism in general, and Latin American evangelicalism specifically (see section 3.2). It was also acknowledged that the new openness to the Scriptures within Latin American Catholicism motivated Latin American evangelicals to study the Scriptures in a contextually appropriate manner (see section 3.3). In the previous chapter (see section 4.3), the discussion on contextual methods clearly established that the use of Scripture is a significant point of debate in the development of contextual Latin American theology.[1] Escobar expresses the evangelical commitment to Scripture and the evangelical conviction of the importance of engaging with the alternative contextual approaches on this subject when he writes:

> Though Luther and Calvin would still have debates with contemporary Catholic theologians about the authority of God's word as the *sola fidei regula*, they would have to accept the tremendous influence that Protestantism has had among Catholics in the work of Bible translation, biblical scholarship, and theological method. Without this development of the most recent decades in Latin America, evangelical Protestantism would have had no ground to dialogue with "theologies of liberation." But because of this development liberation themes come to us now as biblical themes to which we are obliged to pay attention…it is our conviction that in every moment of renewal for the church there has been a return to God's word. If the challenges posed by liberation theologies are an indication that another critical moment is upon us, demanding

---

[1] For details on definitions, principles and trends in evangelical biblical interpretation at this time see I. Howard Marshall, "How do we interpret the Bible today?", *Themelios* 5, no. 2 (1980): 4-12; D.A. Carson, "Hermeneutics: A brief assessment of some recent trends", *Themelios* 5, no. 2 (1980): 12-20; David Baker, "Interpreting texts in the context of the whole Bible", *Themelios* 5, no. 2 (1980): 21-25; James Packer, "Hermeneutics and Biblical Authority", *Themelios* 1, no. 1 (1978): 3-12.

renewal for the Protestant churches, it would be important to have an idea of the kind of return to God's word that this hour demands.[2]

The purpose of this chapter is to examine the search for a contextual Latin American evangelical hermeneutic. This study will incorporate the evangelical critique of the hermeneutics employed by the theology of liberation, thus helping to establish clear evangelical principles in contextual interpretation and application of Scripture. For in this engagement with liberation hermeneutics, the consistency and coherence of evangelical hermeneutics are demonstrated. The contemporary Latin American evangelical theology, which has been developing over the past three decades, is founded on this distinctly evangelical understanding of the use of Scripture. Arising from the previous chapters, the subject of contextual hermeneutics will be dealt with in four sections. First, the foundational issue of biblical authority will be discussed. Second, the "hermeneutical circle," which is central to the interpretative process applied by liberation theologians, will be briefly outlined. The evangelical engagement with this interpretative approach will then be considered. Third, the evangelical critique of liberationist exegesis will be examined in light of the key biblical texts used in the theology of liberation. Fourth, the effort to develop a contextual hermeneutic, which is distinctively evangelical, will be presented. It is anticipated that dealing with contextual hermeneutics in these four sections will provide a coherent overview of both the context and the content of biblical interpretation in Latin American evangelical theology.

It will become apparent that the contribution made to contextual hermeneutics by Latin American evangelical theologians is not an original one, as such. It is fair to say that Latin American evangelical theology presents a rehearsal of familiar evangelical convictions regarding Scripture. Nonetheless, it is in this willingness to reassess and reapply familiar evangelical principles that Latin American evangelical theology demonstrates its vitality. Similarly, it is in this determination to hold to evangelical conviction regarding Scripture, in the face of contradictory approaches employed by alternative contextual theologians, that Latin American evangelical theology demonstrates its strength and consistency.

5.2 The Foundational Issue of Biblical Authority

In chapter three, it was established that the commitment to *Sola Scriptura* is a foundational principle of the world-wide evangelical community.[3] There is no doubt that such emphasis on the authority and sufficiency of Scripture is an evangelical distinctive. The general consensus across evangelicalism can be summarised in the words of chapter one, paragraph six of the Westminster Confession of Faith (1647).

The whole counsel of God concerning all things necessary for his own glory, man's salvation, faith and life, is either expressly set down in Scripture, or by good and

---

[2] Escobar, *Themes*, 7-9. See also Núñez, *Conciencia*, 4.
[3] Escobar, *Sola*, 11.

necessary consequence may be deduced from Scripture: unto which nothing at any time is to be added, whether by new revelations of the Spirit, or traditions of men.[4]

The theological and spiritual continuity with the Reformation of the sixteenth century is evident in evangelicalism in the following: first, in the commitment to make Scripture the basis for the life and thought of the Christian community, and second, in the constant assessment of the life and thought of the Christian community in the light of Scripture.[5] Escobar comments:

> In the first place the Reformers developed a theology of the word of God and its authority in the church. The conviction about the Sola Scriptura brought a revitalization of preaching, liturgy, pastoral care, and many other areas of church life. That renewal of vitality among the people of God is a key element in understanding the powerful growth of the Reformation movement in Europe.[6]

There is no doubt that within evangelical circles, different opinions exist in regard to the issue of Scriptural authority.[7] However, for the purpose of this thesis, the focus will be placed on the fact that "there is nevertheless a shared emphasis on the total reliability and trustworthiness of Scripture as the ultimate foundation and criterion of …[a] saving knowledge of God."[8]

In Latin America, the evangelical commitment to the authority of Scripture has been evident from the genesis of the Latin American Theological Fraternity.[9] The

---

[4] See the Westminster Confession of Faith in Wayne Grudem, *Systematic Theology: An Introduction to Biblical Doctrine* (Leicester: IVP, 1994), 1180.

[5] Escobar, *Themes*, 9-10; Samuel Escobar, "Hacia una hermenéutica evangélica" in *Hacia una hermenéutica evangélica Tomo II*, C. René Padilla et al, (Buenos Aires: Ediciones Kairós, 1977), 1-7, at 7; J Andrew Kirk, "Algunas pautas para una definición de la perspectiva evangélica" in *Hacia una hermenéutica evangélica Tomo III*, J. Andrew Kirk et al (Buenos Aires: Ediciones Kairós, 1977), 1-11; Orlando E. Costas, "Evangelical Theology in the Two Thirds World" in *Conflict and Context: Hermeneutics in the Americas*, eds. Mark Lau Branson and C. René Padilla (Grand Rapids: Eerdmans, 1986), 311- 323, at 314.

[6] Escobar, *Themes*, 1.

[7] In respect of Latin America, see for example C. René Padilla, "La autoridad de la Biblia en la teología latinoamericana" in *El debate contemporáneo sobre la Biblia*, ed. Pedro Savage (Barcelona: Ediciones Evangelicas Europeas, 1972), 121-154, at 128-129. For a thorough discussion on the evangelical view of Scripture, see John Perry, "Dissolving the Inerrancy Debate: How Modern Philosophy Shaped the Evangelical View of Scripture", *Journal for Christian Theological Research* [http://apu.edu/ctrf…] 6:3 (2001): 1-17.

[8] Alister McGrath, "Evangelical Theological Method: The State of the Art" in *Evangelical Futures*, ed. John G. Stackhouse (Grand Rapids: Baker Books, 2000), 15-37, at 29. McGrath also details other helpful material available which discusses the various interpretations of the *Sola Scriptura* principle and different understandings of Scripture evident in recent evangelical writing.

[9] As early as 1962, C. René Padilla published an article entitled "The Purpose of the Bible" for evangelical students, demonstrating his awareness then of the need to discuss

focus of the first Fraternity Consultation in 1970 was "The Contemporary Debate about the Bible." Latin American evangelicals from diverse traditions examined the subjects of the revelation of God, the authority and inspiration of the Bible, and hermeneutical interpretation.[10] Míguez Bonino makes this observation about the Fraternity:

> The movement began with an affirmation of the centrality of Scripture, in the twofold critique of crass literalism and the arbitrary interpretation of fundamentalism, and of a liberalism which seemed to reduce the Bible to a collection of documents from the past or a repository of religious truths and general and universal ethics.[11]

The Cochabamba Declaration, drawn up at this first consultation, clearly expresses the reaffirmation of the significance of Scripture and the recommitment to develop sound Latin American evangelical biblical interpretation.[12]

> Assent to the authority of the Bible could be considered as one of the most general features of the evangelical movement in Latin America...However, it can be admitted that the actual use of the Bible by most Latin American evangelical people does not always coincide with the assent [to Scriptural authority] that distinguishes...[the evangelical movement]. The Bible is revered, but the voice of the Lord who speaks through it is not always obeyed; and the disobedience is rationalised in different ways. We need a hermeneutic which in every case will do justice to the biblical text...The biblical message has indisputable relevance for the Latin American person, but its proclamation does not have the place in our midst that it should...[13]

It has been established that by 1970, Latin American evangelicals had already identified the responsibility to develop contextual theology which demonstrated active dedication to the authority of the Scriptures. At this time, liberation theologians and evangelical theologians alike, were seeking to respond appropriately

---

issues of Scriptural authority and revelation. See C. René Padilla, " El propósito de la Biblia", *Certeza* 10 (1962): 95.

[10] Papers presented at this consultation were published in Savage, *Debate*. See Padilla, "Autoridad", 121-154; Pedro Aran Quiroz, "La revelación de Dios y la teología en latinoamérica", 37-78; J. Andrew Kirk, "La Biblia y su hermenéutica en relación con la teología protestante en América Latina", 115-214; Samuel Escobar, "Una teología evangélica para Iberoamérica", 17-36. For further discussion on the consultation and the pertinent issues discussed see Escobar, *Fe*, 132-157.

[11] Míguez Bonino, *Faces*, 49.

[12] For a discussion on the influence of the Cochabamba consultation on the development of Latin American evangelical hermeneutics see Escobar, "Hermenéutica", 1-2.

[13] "Cochabamba" in Savage, *Debate*, 226-227; Escobar, *Fe*, 212-214; Quiroz, *Teología*, 27-30. In later reflection, Escobar discusses "The Bible and the social revolution in Latin America" in *Evangelio*, 43-73. He draws helpful distinctions between churches which have taken Bible teaching, interpretation and application seriously and those which have not. See also Padilla, "Autoridad", 138.

to the desperation of the Latin American situation.[14] The Cochabamba declaration also recognised the biblical movement evident in less radical Catholic circles in Latin America at that time.[15] Indeed, as has already been seen, the presence of biblical material in Catholic liturgy, preaching, study groups and theology awakened Latin American evangelicals to the necessity of renewal within the evangelical biblical movement also.[16] They needed to be stirred out of the "...apathy into which many evangelicals [had] fallen, with a closed Bible in their hands."[17]

In the argument of the previous chapter, it was demonstrated that the Latin American evangelical method differs most from liberation methodology in respect of its attitude towards the Scriptures.[18] It would not be an overstatement to say, therefore, that the issue of biblical authority permeates the entire evangelical engagement with the theology of liberation. An overview of the evangelical interaction with the theology of liberation indicates that the issues of biblical authority and biblical interpretation are consistently addressed, regardless of the aspect of contextual theology under debate. Evangelical dialogue on the understanding of history, context, method, hermeneutics, biblical themes, Christology, ecclesiology, and missiology returns to the subject of Scripture time and again.[19]

It is also important to acknowledge at this point that attitudes towards Scripture vary greatly among liberation theologians. Assmann, for example, conveys his concept of Scripture when he writes that he "is not directly interested in the concrete content of the Bible, or exegetical method, or the challenge of the biblical method to

---

[14] Padilla, "Autoridad", 124. See also Kirk, "Biblia", 115-214; Escobar, "Iberoamérica", 32-36.

[15] "According to Vatican II 'all preaching of the church must be nourished and ruled by Sacred Scripture'; the Bible is the chief source of theology and the training of priests should be built around a Bible centred theology rather than polemically oriented theology; not only preaching but catechetics and 'all other Christian instruction' should be nourished by the 'primary and perpetual' source of the Bible." Escobar, *Themes*, 7.

[16] For a further historical and theological discussion on the Catholic Church and the Scriptures see Emilio A. Núñez, "La Iglesia Católica Romana y las Escrituras", TMs (photocopy), Latin American Theological Fraternity Archives, Buenos Aires, 1-40.

[17] Cited by Escobar, *Fe*, 136.

[18] To gain helpful insights on the liberationist hermeneutical approach and for some recent liberationist readings of the Scriptures see the selection of papers in Leif E. Vaage, ed. *Subversive Scriptures: Revolutionary Readings of the Christian Bible in Latin America* (Valley Forge: Trinity Press International, 1997); Pieter G. R. de Villiers, ed. *Liberation Theology and the Bible* (Pretoria: University of South Africa Press, 1987); for a Protestant approach see Ely Eser Barreto César, "A Reading of the Bible, Beginning with the Poor of Latin America" in *Faith born in the Struggle for Life*, ed. Dow Kirkpatrick (Grand Rapids: Eerdmans, 1988), 38-51.

[19] See for example Kirk, *Liberation*, 95-203; Núñez, *Liberation*, 131-274; Escobar, *Fe*, 132-178; Hundley, *Radical*, 23-34 where discussion on Scripture is evident throughout the works in response to the theology of liberation.

today's reality."[20] In contrast liberationists such as Gutiérrez, Segundo, Severino Croatto and José Porfirio Miranda consider the contribution which biblical revelation can make to be critical.[21] Their works evidence a more thoughtful approach towards biblical material.[22]

Bearing in mind the significance of the Scriptures in evangelical thought, it is understandable therefore that evangelicals have reacted strongly to the perception that liberationists give the Bible a secondary place in their methodology. Identifying the authority given to praxis, to the community and its context, and to Marxist ideology, together with a particularly Catholic concept of revelation, it appears the Latin American evangelical contention that the Bible is secondary in liberation method can be sustained.

The first area of concern for evangelical theologians, previously mentioned in regard to liberation method, is the authority ascribed to praxis. As this aspect has been dealt with in detail in the previous chapter, it will be examined here only in specific relation to hermeneutics.[23] Núñez recognises that all theologians approach Scripture with personal, theological, ecclesiastical and political prejudices. He writes that it is impossible to come to the biblical text "chemically pure."[24] Nevertheless, it is natural that as an evangelical theologian Núñez cannot abandon the conviction that God has spoken and is speaking in the sacred Scriptures. For Núñez, this written revelation is the supreme authority in every issue of faith and practice. In his critique of liberationist hermeneutics, he contends: "We recognise the seriousness of hermeneutic problems, but we do not believe that the solution to them is found in exalting Christian praxis above what God has revealed to us."[25] As a result of their method, liberation theologians believe that in the midst of historical praxis it is possible to understand the word of God in a new way. This fresh understanding has deeper dimensions and progressive implications for the church, as it moves towards the total fulfilment of eschatological promises. Núñez fears that sooner or later meaningful theology may evaporate in liberationist thought, as sociological and political issues are given precedence.

In his evaluation of the liberationist approach to the Scriptures, Escobar acknowledges the amount of biblical material interpreted by liberationists. In

---

[20] Kirk, *Liberation*, 53.

[21] Escobar, *Fe*, 137-138.

[22] See for example Gutiérrez, *Theology*; Segundo, *Liberation*; Severino Croatto, *Liberación y libertad. Pautas hermenéuticas* (Buenos Aires: Mundo Nuevo, 1973); Severino Croatto, *Exodus: A Hermeneutic of Freedom* trans. Salvator Attanasio (Maryknoll: Orbis Books, 1981); Severino Croatto, *Hermenéutica bíblica* (Buenos Aires: La Aurora, 1984); José Porfirio Miranda, *Marx and the Bible: A Critique of the Philosophy of Oppression* trans. by John Eagleson (Maryknoll: Orbis Books, 1974).

[23] See Padilla, "Iglesia", 125.

[24] Núñez, *Liberation*, 152; Padilla, "Iglesia", 127; C. René Padilla, "El círculo hermenéutico" in *Hacia una hermenéutica evangélica Tomo II*, C. René Padilla et al (Buenos Aires: Ediciones Kairós, 1977): 1-4, at 1.

[25] Núñez, *Liberation*, 152.

particular, Escobar highlights the biblical work of those previously mentioned, that is Gutiérrez, Segundo, Croatto and Miranda. The manner in which these liberation theologians approach the biblical material, however, demonstrates to Escobar, once again, that the theology of liberation attributes authority not primarily to the Scriptures themselves but to reflection on praxis.[26] Escobar argues that this emphasis on praxis inevitably leads to a selective reading of the Scriptures.

Kirk too insists that the Bible should occupy a different place in a hermeneutic of liberation than that generally allowed it by liberationists. He maintains that the theology of liberation would, in fact, benefit from a more biblical, and in his opinion a subsequently more radical, hermeneutic of liberation in relation to the demands of praxis. This firmer foundation in biblical hermeneutics would facilitate future reflection on liberation issues in a powerful way. Kirk critiques the lack of a satisfactory hermeneutical procedure to interpret Scripture in liberation theology and asserts that despite the priority given to praxis, there is a need to relate the call to obedience and action to a relevant use of Scripture. Kirk describes the hermeneutical procedure employed in the theology of liberation to be "questionable."[27] For he explains that while liberation theology seeks to be a theological reflection on political praxis in the light of God's word, it cannot escape the hermeneutical questions which any systematic theological position must answer. Kirk finds himself questioning the actual significance liberationists give to the phrase "in the light of God's word." For the selectivity and emphasis of the liberationist approach leaves many issues unanswered. Concurring with Kirk, in respect of the selectivity of the liberationist hermeneutical approach, Padilla questions why the Exodus is the hermeneutical key, yet the Exile is not. Similarly, he asks why the prophetic line is acceptable but the priestly line is not.[28] It is clear evangelicals are convinced that an approach which attributes appropriate authority to Scripture and which is not limited by such a selective attitude should, in fact, illuminate more brightly the implications of Christian praxis.

The second aspect of the liberationist approach to hermeneutics which concerns evangelical theologians, in particular, is the authority attributed to the historical context of a community. In this regard, Núñez questions whether liberationists are actually advocating a theology or simply a sociology. He maintains that authority is given to human beings and their context in the liberationist assertion that "the word of God gathers and is incarnated in the community of faith."[29] Núñez comments:

> The Christian community in its activity of reflection is, according to Gutiérrez, a point of departure and much more: "it is the soil into which theological reflection stubbornly and permanently sinks its roots and from which it derives its strength"...Already at the opening words of Gutierrez's theology the conservative evangelical begins to have serious questions as he becomes aware that the point of departure and the foundation

---

[26] Escobar, *Fe*, 137.
[27] Kirk, *Liberation*, 207.
[28] Padilla, "Iglesia", 126.
[29] Gutiérrez, *Theology*, 7.

for the theological task is not Holy Scripture but the theological reflection of the
Christian community.[30]

Escobar adjudges that Scriptural authority is further undermined in the
liberationist approach to biblical material by the questions which they choose to
address to the text. These questions demonstrate clearly that the community context
has authority over the biblical text itself. For liberationists ask: Who is reading the
Bible? Where is the reader situated? What is the context of the reader?[31] It is
apparent, once more, that the consequence of such emphasis leads liberation
theologians to consider some biblical texts to be more relevant to the context of the
community. These "relevant" Scriptures, therefore, hold supremacy over other
biblical texts. Escobar criticises such a rejection of the unity of the Bible, asserting
that in evangelical theology the whole of the Bible is accepted as vital to the
Christian message and the Christian life.[32] It becomes clear that this selective choice
of biblical material, evident in liberation theology, is consistently confronted by
evangelical theologians.[33] Concurring with Escobar, Padilla argues:

> When you understand the historical situation as "the text," "the first theological
> reference point," you pave the way for the subordination of the word to the human
> context...the result is a selective reading of the Bible...The concentration of
> hermeneutics on ethics and politics results in a theology which does not do justice to
> the totality of the biblical revelation.[34]

In response to such criticism, liberation theologians consistently defend their
hermeneutical approach which takes the historical context as the point of departure.
Segundo would be representative of the liberationist view when he writes:

---

[30] Núñez, *Liberation*, 135.

[31] Escobar, *Fe*, 139.

[32] Escobar emphasises the danger of displacing the Bible from an authoritative position
and elaborates on the transforming message found throughout the Scriptures, not only in
limited passages. For a discussion on the biblical content of the transforming Scriptural
message see *Evangelio*, 59-66.

[33] The limitations of the selective liberationist approach are also discussed in Luis N.
Rivera Pagán, "Toward a Theology of Peace: Critical Notes on the Biblical Hermeneutic of
Latin American Theology of Liberation" in *Faith born in the Struggle for Life*, ed. Dow
Kirkpatrick (Grand Rapids: Eerdmans, 1988), 52-75. Pagán comments "The historical and
prophetic books, as well as a sizeable number of the hymns and confessions, grow out of the
experience of the exile and not the Exodus. Latin American theology, in its anxiety to
emphasize popular liberation as a central biblical event, has exaggerated the role the Exodus
played in the genesis of the Judeo-Christian Scriptures. It has also failed to perceive the
significance of the captivity and exile in the formation of the Old Testament canon." Pagán,
"Toward", 64.

[34] Padilla, "Teología", 19; Padilla, "Iglesia", 126; see also Kirk, "Biblia",115-214.

I hope that it is quite clear that the Bible is not a discourse of a universal God to a universal man…Partiality is justified because we must find, and designate as the word of God, that part of divine revelation which today, in the light of our concrete historical situation, is most useful for the liberation to which God summons us…[35]

Segundo argues that those who attack the hermeneutical procedure of liberation theology are even more partisan, although they may not realise it.[36] He observes that they try to make one particular portion of Scripture apply to all situations and all moments in history. He is critical of the fact that the word of God is not applied more specifically to particular situations and particular moments in time.[37] Segundo openly acknowledges that the liberationist approach to the relationship between the community and the Scriptures "always presupposes a profound human commitment, a partiality that is consciously accepted…We must realise that there is no such thing as an autonomous, impartial, academic theology floating free above the realm of human options and biases…"[38]

The theology of liberation faces evangelical criticism, not only for the selective use of Scripture, but also for its attitude regarding the relationship between the Old Testament and the New Testament. Kirk identifies three weaknesses in liberation thought on this subject. Firstly, he criticises the liberationist "injustice" towards the continuity of the Old and New Testaments. Liberation theologians, in general, do not emphasise the historical fulfilment of the Old Testament in Christ and thus envisage a continuous relationship between the Testaments. Kirk argues that the liberationist approach "emphasises the 'added' elements in the New Testament's interpretation of the Old, and tends to transpose the Old Testament themes onto a new plane."[39] Secondly, Kirk contends that as a consequence of this approach, the theology of liberation underestimates the significance of the Christ event. Thirdly, he maintains that liberation theologians display a lack of critical awareness of ideological determination in their exegesis. Kirk, in opposition, affirms the centrality of the New Testament and seeks to show the decisive manner in which the New Testament authors used the Old Testament to interpret the Christ-event. He traces the ideas of fulfilment and reinterpretation in this development. With regards to the ongoing tradition of interpretation, Kirk critiques the use of terms such as "reinterpretation," "reserve of meaning," "donation of meaning," "word significance," and "word in suspense" in liberationist thought. He observes that liberation theologians creatively seek to translate prophecy spoken within the

---

[35] Segundo, *Liberation*, 33.

[36] Escobar warns evangelicals of approaching the Scriptures with such ideological commitment, which subtly manipulates the text for its own benefit, not in an effort to interpret the Scriptures accurately. See Escobar, *Evangelio*, 69.

[37] Segundo, *Liberation*, 34.

[38] Segundo, *Liberation*, 13.

[39] Kirk, *Liberation*, 153; Samuel Escobar, "Our Hermeneutic Task Today" in *Conflict and Context: Hermeneutics in the Americas*, eds. C. René Padilla and Mark Lau Branson (Grand Rapids: Eerdmans, 1986): 3-8, at 5.

"history of salvation" and make it applicable to the current movement towards the "salvation of history."[40] Yet Kirk maintains that this is a hermeneutical task based on a false deduction. For the Scriptures themselves know nothing of a general "salvation history" as this term is employed by liberation theology. He asserts:

> No amount of hermeneutical juggling can ever remove this basic understanding of liberation from the Old and New Testaments. In other words, modern man's unaided attempt to transcend a structural fault in present being, however he may clothe this in contemporary ideological language, only contributes further testimony to the biblical evidence of his ontological alienation.[41]

Latin American evangelical theologians recognise the pertinence of the contemporary Latin American situation for theological reflection. They also acknowledge the desperate need for biblical theology which is appropriate and actively relevant to the context of the community. However, in contrast to the theology of liberation, evangelical theologians are striving to develop an evangelical hermeneutic which attributes superior authority to Scripture, over and above the authority attributed to praxis or to the context. Evangelicals seek to bring a biblical message to the Latin American context, and for the Latin American communities that is vital, powerful and transformational.[42] This biblical message should influence the Christian praxis which takes place, and consequently should have a dramatic effect on the historical context of each community.

The third concern which evangelical theologians have in respect of the hermeneutical approach evident in the theology of liberation, is the apparent authority attributed to Marxist ideology, over and above the authority attributed to Scripture. This criticism was also dealt with in detail in the previous chapter. In respect of liberationist hermeneutics, Escobar expresses concern that ideological presuppositions suppress the biblical text. He critiques liberation theologians on the fact that authority is given to the Marxist ideological interpretation of the Scriptures rather than to the Scriptures themselves.[43] Míguez Bonino too warns of the danger of the Marxist influence in hermeneutical procedure when he argues:

> The text of Scripture and tradition is forced into the Procrustean bed of ideology, and the theologian who has fallen prey of this procedure is forever condemned to listen only

---

[40] Kirk, *Liberation*, 157.

[41] Kirk, *Liberation*, 173.

[42] See the discussion on the message of the gospel in Núñez, *Desafíos*, 49-57; Escobar, *Evangelio*, 60-68.

[43] Escobar is also careful to acknowledge the challenge presented by Marxism to deal with the person as a complete human being, to react against the individualistic notion of life often promoted in European and Anglo-Saxon theology and the need to rediscover the sense of Christian hope. See *Evangelio*, 72-73. See also Padilla, "Iglesia", 126.

to the echo of his own ideology. There is no redemption for this theology, because it has muzzled the word of God in its transcendence and freedom.[44]

Readings of Scripture, influenced by Marxist ideology and echoing with ideological terminology can be found throughout liberationist writings. For example, in response to the Exodus, Gutiérrez remarks that "the liberation of Israel is a political action. It is the breaking away from a situation of despoliation and misery and the beginning of the construction of a just and comradely society."[45] A more recent example of a liberationist approach to Scripture which clearly demonstrates a presupposed ideological reading of the text is the interpretation of Revelation 18 as the judgement of God on the multinationals.[46]

In his assessment of the liberationist use of Scripture, Escobar is forced to ask whether liberation thinkers actually believe the Bible is the revealed and inspired fruit of divine initiative. If they do not believe in the true significance of the Bible, and its subsequent authority, then Escobar makes the suggestion that the theology of liberation should concentrate on Marxist texts instead.[47] While Escobar voices these criticisms of the ideological influence in liberation hermeneutics, however, he also acknowledges that Latin American evangelical theologians must face the challenges which such ideology presents. For example, Marxist anthropology reveals the need for evangelicals to structure a coherent biblical anthropology. Likewise, the futuristic hope given by Marxism should motivate Latin American evangelicals to form a contextual theology based on thoroughly Christian eschatology. Escobar considers the rise and fall of Marxist ideology to present a timely reminder to evangelical theologians. Evangelicals, too, must strive to be self-aware and self-critical in order to recognise the religious, philosophical and ideological influences at work in the evangelical attempt to formulate contextual Latin American theology.[48]

Padilla similarly expresses concern regarding the influence of a politically determined position on liberationist hermeneutics. He asserts theologians must realise there is a danger that "instead of showing the pertinence of revelation to revolution, revolution is made into the source of revelation."[49] The consequence, in Padilla's opinion, is the inevitable metamorphosis of faith into ideology. Núñez succinctly summarises the essence of the Latin American evangelical determination to bring ideology under the authority of Scripture:

---

[44] Míguez Bonino, *Doing*, 87.

[45] Gutiérrez, *Theology*, 88.

[46] See Dagoberto Ramírez Fernández, "The Judgement of God on the Mulitnationals: Revelation 18" in *Subversive Scriptures: Revolutionary Readings of the Christian Bible in Latin America*, ed. Leif E. Vaage (Valley Forge: Trinity Press International, 1997), 75-100.

[47] Escobar, *Fe*, 154.

[48] Escobar, *Evangelio*, 70-73.

[49] C. René Padilla, "Mensaje bíblico y revolución", *Certeza* 39 (1970): 200; Padilla, "Iglesia", 135. See also the section on the myth of revolution in C. René Padilla, "God's Word and Man's Myths", *Themelios* 3, no.1 (1977): 3-9, at 7.

I have the profound conviction that the written revelation of God is far above all
political ideologies as the final word of authority for the faith and conduct of the
Christian, and that every political system, far from being absolute, is relative,
imperfect, and temporary, and therefore is always subject to change, whereas the word
of the Lord abides forever...without pretending to have a false political neutrality, the
Christian should always reserve the right to criticize any political system, whether of
the left or of the right, in the light of the word of God.[50]

It is evident that the evangelical critique of liberation hermeneutics centres on the
issue of the authority of Scripture. In this section, it has been highlighted that
evangelicals consider the biblical interpretation presented by the theology of
liberation to ascribe authority first and foremost to praxis, to context and to
ideology. It would appear that foundational to this approach, is a particular
understanding of revelation which also differs significantly from the Latin American
evangelical understanding of the concept.

An overview of the issue of biblical authority demonstrates that the whole notion
of revelation is much broader in Catholicism than in Protestantism.[51] Indeed this
difference in the understanding of the very concept of revelation is the root of a
serious problem for dialogue between evangelical theologians and liberation
theologians. For liberationists, revelation is evident through history. Revelation is
the action of God present in the struggle for a new society. This action, or revelation
of God, is manifest in history through the committed actions of human beings who
pursue the creation of a renewed future.[52]

Padilla expresses the core of the Latin American evangelical understanding of
revelation in three assertions. First, the revelation of God consists of historical
events interpreted by the prophets and the apostles as evident in the Scriptures.
Second, the revelation of God is inseparable from the redemption of God.[53] Third,
the historical person of Jesus Christ is the centre of the revelation of God.[54] Núñez
displays the significance of the evangelical belief in the biblical witness to this
revelation when he maintains:

It is not easy to recognize our own personal, theological, ecclesiastical, and political
prejudices; it is even more difficult to abandon them in the face of the majesty of the
revelation of God. But that fact, which is so human and overwhelming, is not a valid

---

[50] Núñez, *Liberation*, 12-13.

[51] Escobar helpfully compares the significance of Scripture and the significance of
tradition within the Catholic Church, see Escobar, "Hermeneutic", 7-8. See also Núñez,
"Iglesia", 7-23.

[52] Padilla, "Iglesia", 129.

[53] Padilla, "Autoridad", 127.

[54] C. René Padilla, "El lugar de la revelación en la epistemología" in *Hacia una
hermenéutica evangélica Tomo II*, C. René Padilla et al (Buenos Aires: Ediciones Kairós,
1977), 1-2. See also Pedro Arana Quiroz, "La revelación de Dios y la teología en
Latinoamérica" in *El debate contemporáneo sobre la Biblia*, ed. Perdo Savage (Barcelona:
Ediciones Evangélicas Europeas, 1972), 37-78.

excuse for abandoning the conviction that God has spoken and is speaking to us by means of the sacred Scriptures, and that written revelation is the supreme authority in every issue of faith and practice. The principle of *sola Scriptura* has not lost its relevance to us.[55]

Kirk too acknowledges that the issue of revelation is a serious one for contextual theology.[56] He argues that the subject of revelation needs to be based upon a core biblical message, comprehensible within its own terms of reference, if it is to be coherent. However, Kirk also recognises that there is much to be learned from the liberationist approach to the text:

Clearly, liberation theology's contribution to the discussion of synthesising the horizons is the challenge to hear what the text communicates when studied from a praxis of solidarity with the oppressed, the despised and the heavy laden.[57]

Escobar also devotes attention to the theology of biblical revelation.[58] Working in very familiar patterns of evangelical thought, he focuses on the presuppositions of biblical theology and affirms three aspects which clearly reflect evangelical convictions. Naturally, Escobar asserts that God has spoken, that God has spoken in Christ and that God has spoken in Christ to save humanity.[59] In the search for an evangelical hermeneutic, Escobar asserts that practicalities of faith and theological reflection are revitalised, are given a new dimension, and in fact are made more dynamic by the whole word of God. It is the word of God which produces fruit. Escobar emphasises that the renewal of evangelical theology has to begin with a revitalisation of the biblical hermeneutic and a return to the biblical sources. He maintains that the Spirit of God renews the church by his word and that it is only the Spirit of God who can renew the truth of theology. Such a renewal through the Scriptures is only possible, Escobar would contend, when two principles are held in relationship between ancient scholar and modern exegete. Firstly, the interpreter should believe in God, who has spoken through the prophets, and calls different people to different tasks. Secondly, the interpreter should also be one who belongs to a community which has been called by this same God.[60]

Escobar rightly recognises the issue of revelation as a key dispute in the engagement with liberation theology. For while evangelicals assert the supremacy of the Scriptural revelation, and remain committed to the faithful interpretation of that revelation, they must also be prepared to ask: how can we articulate our faith in this context of poverty, repression, and injustice? Concurring with the liberation theologians, Escobar identifies the theological, pastoral and missionary task of

---

[55] Núñez, *Liberation*, 152.
[56] Kirk, *Liberation*, 169-184.
[57] Kirk, *Liberation*, 182.
[58] Escobar, *Fe*, 158-178.
[59] See also Padilla, "Autoridad", 130-149.
[60] Escobar, "Hermeneutic ", 3-8.

developing contextual theology which is indigenous and appropriate. However, he maintains that in this theological development and in biblical interpretation, it is critical to do justice to the authority of the word of God. Authentic and relevant Latin American theology must be thoroughly biblical, must be thoroughly contextual and must seek to place obedience to the Lordship of Christ at its centre. Escobar contends that the pursuit of such evangelical theology, which seeks to read the Bible with new eyes from within the Two Thirds World, must be founded on "the presupposition of the revelatory nature of Scripture and its authority."[61]

The Latin American evangelical theologians who are the focus of the present work demonstrate this commitment to the revelatory nature of Scripture. As has been discussed, they also consider the liberationist priority of praxis, context, and ideology, to undermine the authority of Scripture. For evangelical theologians then, there is a serious question regarding the hermeneutical procedure employed by the theology of liberation. An interpretation of biblical material which can be authoritatively applied is fundamental to contextual theology for Latin America. For this reason, the interpretation of Scripture will constitute the focus of the next section.

5.3 The Hermeneutical Circle

The hermeneutical circle, proposed and elaborated by Segundo, constitutes a significant contribution to the hermeneutical discussion. In liberationist thought, this hermeneutical circle is central to the interpretation of Scripture. Segundo emphasises two preconditions to the functioning of such a hermeneutical circle.[62] First, the theologian must exhibit suspicion of his or her contemporary circumstances and consequently ask profound and enriching questions about that situation. Second, the theologian must seek a new equally profound and enriching interpretation of the Bible, relevant to those circumstances. Segundo explains that "each new reality obliges us to interpret the word of God afresh, to change reality accordingly, and then go back and reinterpret the word of God again and so on."[63] He proposes four decisive factors in the hermeneutical circle. The first factor is a personal way of experiencing reality which leads to ideological suspicion. The second element is the application of this ideological suspicion to the whole ideological superstructure in general and to theology in particular. The third aspect is a new way of experiencing the theological reality which leads to exegetical suspicion that the prevailing interpretation of the Bible has not taken important pieces of data into account. The fourth factor contributing to the hermeneutical circle, then, is the recognition of a new way to interpret Scripture, making use of new elements gained through the process which are now at the disposal of the theologian. In other words, the fourth

---

[61] Escobar, *Themes*, 20. See also Padilla, "Círculo", 2.

[62] Padilla, "Nueva", 23.

[63] Segundo, *Liberation*, 8.

element is a *new* hermeneutic.[64] Gutiérrez describes the significant aspects of the hermeneutical circle employed by the theology of liberation:

> This then, is the fundamental hermeneutical circle: from the human being to God and from God to the human being, from history to faith and from faith to history, from the human word to the word of the Lord and from the word of the Lord to the human word, from the love of one's brothers and sisters to the love of the Father and from the love of the Father to the love of the brothers and sisters, from human justice to God's holiness and from God's holiness to human justice...[65]

Evangelical theologians have engaged directly with this proposition and have seriously reflected on the challenges such a hermeneutic presents. While they concur with the liberationist assertion of the need to look objectively at the Bible, they also affirm that the church, as a historical community, has inherited a rich heritage of faith regarding the Scriptures which cannot be ignored. Neither can this heritage be accepted uncritically. Escobar writes that in the dynamic activity of theology, the role of the Holy Spirit is vital and input from "all the saints" must be considered. Escobar affirms that the word of God is a central and decisive reality. He reaffirms the supremacy of the word of God. However, in regard to interpretation of the word of God, he recognises subjectivity as a problem and suggests that subjectivity without orthodox doctrine is a danger.[66]

It would appear that Padilla is the Latin American evangelical theologian who has reflected most specifically on biblical interpretation and contextual hermeneutics. He comments:

> The word of God was given to bring the lives of God's people into conformity with the will of God. Between the written word and its appropriation by believers lies the process of interpretation, or hermeneutics. For each of us, the process of arriving at the meaning of Scripture is not only highly shaped by who we are as individuals but also by various social forces, patterns and ideals of our particular culture and our particular historical situation.[67]

In a helpful discussion, Padilla reflects on the most common forms of biblical interpretation.[68] Firstly, he identifies the "intuitive" approach to be the most popular

---

[64] Segundo, *Liberation*, 9. See also Padilla, "Nueva", 23.

[65] Nickoloff, *Gutiérrez*, 60.

[66] Escobar, *Fe*, 132-137.

[67] C. René Padilla, "Hermeneutics and Culture – a Theological Perspective" in *Down to Earth: Studies in Christianity and Culture*, eds. John R. W. Stott and Robert Coote (Grand Rapids: Eerdmans, 1980), 63-87, at 63. See also Padilla, "Autoridad", 147.

[68] See Padilla, "Hermeneutics", 63-65; C. René Padilla, "The Interpreted Word: Reflections on Contextual Hermeneutics", *Themelios* 7, no. 1 (1981): 18-23; Kirk, "Biblia", 163-168. See also Sidney Rooy, "Un modelo histórico hermenéutico" in *Hacia una hermenéutica evangélica Tomo II*, C. René Padilla et al (Buenos Aires: Ediciones Kairós, 1977), 1-17; J. Andrew Kirk, "Exégesis técnica y anuncio de la fe" in *Hacia una*

in Latin America. This method, emphasising personal application, is to be found in older commentaries, contemporary popular preaching and devotional literature. However, Padilla warns that the intuitive approach can lead to allegory which causes the meaning of the text to be lost.[69] Secondly, Padilla discusses the "scientific" approach, which employs tools of literary criticism, historical analysis, anthropological studies, and linguistics. While Padilla acknowledges that this approach appreciates the need for an understanding of the original context, he observes that it may not encourage sensitivity to contemporary social, economic and political factors or cultural forces. Padilla also recognises the merits and defects in the scientific approach. He considers the scientific approach to concentrate on the definition of the original meaning of the text while avoiding the responsibility of making it relevant to the contemporary reader. He argues that the scientific approach assumes the interpreter can achieve an "objectivity" which Padilla writes is neither possible nor desirable.[70] No interpreter comes to the text without bias of any kind, and it is this very context and culture of the interpreter to which the text should speak. For "ultimately, if the text written in the past does not strike home in the present it has not been understood."[71] Padilla observes: "A serious problem of both methods is that they tend to be naïve about the way contemporary social, economic, and political factors and other cultural forces affect the interpretive process."[72] For one method assumes the meaning of the text is immediate, the other assumes the meaning of the text is acontextual.

Padilla describes the raw material of theology as "a message embedded in historical events and the linguistic and cultural backgrounds of the biblical authors."[73] He is convinced that "unless modern interpreters allow the text to speak out of its original situation, they have no basis for claiming that their message is continuous with the message recorded in Scripture."[74] Padilla proposes an alternative:

> A third approach is the "contextual" approach. Combining the strengths of the intuitive and scientific methods, it recognises both the role of the ancient world in shaping the original text and the role of today's world in conditioning the way contemporary readers are likely to "hear" and understand the text.[75]

---

hermenéutica evangélica Tomo III, J. Andrew Kirk et al (Buenos Aires: Ediciones Kairós, 1977), 1-19.

[69] For other problems associated with this style of approach see C. René Padilla, "El uso de la Bibla en el púlpito", *Misión* 7 (1983): 21-23.

[70] Padilla, "Círculo", 1.

[71] Padilla, "Interpreted", 19.

[72] Padilla, "Hermeneutics", 64.

[73] Padilla, "Interpreted", 19.

[74] Padilla, "Interpreted", 19.

[75] Padilla, "Interpreted", 18. See also Padilla, "Teología", 18.

Padilla identifies three elements essential to sound hermeneutics when the contextual approach is employed. Firstly, the assumption is made that Scripture is not the sole domain of academic theologians but is meant for ordinary people. Secondly, the role of the Holy Spirit is highlighted as the person who illuminates the meaning of the Scripture for a believer. Thirdly, the purpose of Scripture is not simply to bring readers to a point where they intellectually understand truth but to evoke a conscious submission to the word of God speaking in Scripture.[76]

Padilla seeks to find a method which will bridge the past and the present. He sets out to combine insights from classical hermeneutics with insights from the modern hermeneutical debate. He explains that in the *contextual* approach both the ancient and the modern context are given importance. Padilla considers hermeneutical interpretation to be a complex, dynamic two-way interpretative process. This dynamic interplay is also depicted by Padilla as a hermeneutical circle. However, a study of the development of a Latin American evangelical hermeneutic will demonstrate that while the aspects which constitute the evangelical hermeneutical circle are similar up to a point with those constituting the hermeneutical circle applied by the theology of liberation, the circle is distinct.

Padilla suggests the following four elements of the hermeneutical circle in which interpreters and text are mutually engaged. These elements are consistent with a commitment to evangelical principles. The first element is the interpreter's historical situation. Humans live in concrete historical situations and in particular cultures which influence not only language but also thought patterns, behaviour, styles of learning, emotional responses, personal and community values, interests and ambitions. In Christ, God became man and lived among humanity in such a concrete human situation in order to reveal himself. In the light of the incarnation, Padilla urges evangelical theologians to consider the significance of an incarnational approach to communicate the message of Christ. Padilla recognises that in every culture there are aspects favourable to the understanding of the gospel and similarly in all cultures there are elements which conspire against the understanding of God's word. Padilla emphasises that "no transposition of the biblical message is possible unless the interpreters are familiar with the frame of reference within which the message is to become meaningful."[77] Padilla comments on the communication of this message when he writes:

> The real problem...is how to be faithful to the word of God and relevant to human life *now* — both at the same time...Whenever preaching attempts to be relevant by conforming to the world, it has no more relevance than a mere rhetorical exercise. On the other hand, whenever preaching attempts to be faithful to the word of God by simply repeating seemingly biblical concepts, it is a far cry from the word that became

---

[76] Padilla, "Interpreted", 19.
[77] Padilla, "Hermeneutics", 69.

flesh. The only way for preaching to be relevant is by being faithful to the word of God; and the only way for it to be faithful is by being relevant to life in the world today.[78]

The second element of the hermeneutical circle is the interpreter's "world-and-life view," as Padilla refers to it. The world-and-life view reflects the particular perspective of the interpreter and the particular manner in which the interpreter understands reality. Padilla observes that "whether or not they are conscious of it, this world-and-life view, which is religiously determined, lies behind all their activities and colours their understanding of reality in a definite way."[79]

The third element of the hermeneutical circle is Scripture. The dialogue between Scripture and the contemporary context is central to hermeneutics. Letting an ancient text speak requires an understanding of the text in its original situation:

> The effort to let Scripture speak without imposing on it a ready-made interpretation is a hermeneutical task binding upon all interpreters, whatever their culture. Unless objectivity is set as a goal, the whole interpretive process is condemned to failure from the start.[80]

However, such a commitment to objectivity should not be confused with neutrality. Padilla recognises that such a reading of the Scriptures is not simply taking the literary and historical aspects seriously but is also a reading from the perspective of faith. This faith perspective is open to God's word, believes that God has spoken through the Scriptures and recognises that this demands a response.

The fourth element of the hermeneutical circle is theology. Padilla expresses his understanding of theology:

> Theology cannot be reduced to the repetition of doctrinal formulations borrowed from other latitudes. To be valid and appropriate, it must reflect the merging of the horizons of the historical situation and the horizons of the text. It will be relevant to the extent that it is expressed in symbols and thought forms which are part of the culture to which it is addressed, and to the extent that it responds to the questions and concerns which are raised in that context. It will be faithful to the word of God to the extent that it is based on Scripture and demonstrates the Spirit-given power to accomplish God's purpose. The same Spirit who inspired Scripture in the past is active today to make it God's personal word in a concrete historical situation.[81]

[78] Padilla, "Myths", 4.

[79] Padilla, "Interpreted", 20.

[80] Padilla, "Interpreted", 21.

[81] Padilla, "Interpreted", 21. Padilla discusses the suggestion that this approach is witnessed to in the New Testament text, as early Christians evangelised and dialogued with the Greeks. They were faithful in their contextualization of the Gospel message in pagan environments. He comments: "The way in which Christianity was communicated in the first century sets the pattern for producing contextualized theology today." Padilla clearly

The objective of the four aspects of the hermeneutical circle is to bring transformation of the people of God within their concrete, historical, and human situation.[82] Given this goal, it seems that in fact a Latin American evangelical hermeneutic is not a hermeneutical circle but a hermeneutical spiral – for it is progressive and continually seeks transformation. Each new historical context demands new dialogue between Scripture and that context under the guidance of the Holy Spirit.[83] When the gospel and the situation are mutually engaged, then the gospel takes shape within history as the people of God evidence the word of God at work in their lives. Padilla remarks:

> It is only as the word of God becomes "flesh" in the people of God that the gospel takes shape within history. According to God's purpose the gospel is never to be merely a message of words but a message incarnate in his church, and through it, in history. The contextualization of the gospel demands the contextualization of the church, which is God's hermeneutical community for the manifestation of Christ's presence among the nations of the earth.[84]

In response to the liberationist proposal that theology is reflection on praxis in the light of faith, evangelicals emphasise the need for obedience of the whole counsel of God. Neither an understanding of Scripture nor an understanding of the concrete situation is adequate unless both constantly interact and are mutually corrected. Consequently, the alternative to both the "theology of the word" and the "theology of praxis" is a "hermeneutical circulation," as Padilla describes it, in which a richer and deeper understanding of historical context, and a deeper and richer understanding of the context leads to a greater comprehension of Scripture from within the concrete situation and under the leading of the Holy Spirit.[85]

> For the biblical text, approached from a more congenial world-and-life view, and addressed with deeper and richer questions, will be found to speak more plainly and fully. Our theology, in turn, will be more relevant and responsive to the burning issues which we have to face in our concrete situation.[86]

Escobar contributes to the discussion on the problem of hermeneutics and draws the following constructive conclusions. Firstly, evangelicals must come to the Scriptures aware of their personal ideological commitment. He warns that such ideological commitment is evident when certain aspects of biblical theology are

---

expresses that proclamation and worship are not possible without "a living theology." See Padilla, "Interpreted", 21-22.

[82] Padilla, "Interpreted", 22; Padilla, "Círculo", 3-4.

[83] Padilla, "Autoridad", 149-153; Padilla, "Púlpito", 22.

[84] Padilla, "Interpreted", 23.

[85] Padilla, "Liberation", 47; see also Mervin Breneman, "El uso del Antiguo Testamento en el Nuevo Testamento" in *Hacia una hermenéutica evangélica Tomo II*, C. René Padilla et al (Buenos Aires: Ediciones Kairós, 1977), 1-5, at 5.

[86] Padilla, "Interpreted", 23.

emphasised and other aspects are ignored. Secondly, he reminds evangelicals to be aware of their social conditioning and social environment. He challenges evangelicals to be conscious of the influence this has and the temptation to manipulate hermeneutics to suit a particular political persuasion. Thirdly, Escobar clearly identifies the need for constructive self-criticism throughout the hermeneutical task.[87] He remarks:

> The life of the church is the ground of every authentic theology. The church in mission is the source of the new questions to God's word that are at the very beginning of theology. This being the case, the existence today of thriving churches in what today is called the Third World confronts Old European or North American churches with a new set of questions, a new way of looking at God's word, through the eyes of the new Christians.[88]

It is clear in this section that both liberation theologians and evangelical theologians in Latin America are committed to looking at God's word through new eyes, and also that both groups recognise the importance of addressing a new set of questions to Scripture, seeking relevance for the Latin American context. It has been demonstrated that while there is dialogue regarding biblical material between evangelical theology and the theology of liberation, consensus has not been reached in respect of the authority given to the Scriptures or the hermeneutical approach used in interpreting Scripture for contextual theology.

Latin American evangelical theologians have not only contributed to the hermeneutical discussion within Latin America, but have also engaged with evangelical theologians internationally. Stott comments on the importance of this contribution from evangelical theologians in the Two Thirds World:

> As with the authors of the Scripture, so with its readers, the Holy Spirit does not bypass our personality and teach us in a vacuum. He used the cultural background of the biblical writers in order to convey through it a message appropriate to them as real people in real situations. In the same way he uses the cultural inheritance of Bible readers to convey out of the Scriptures living and appropriate truth. To allow and even encourage other Christians to perceive the truth of the gospel "freshly through their own eyes" is a mark of respect both for human beings and of confidence in the Holy Spirit.[89]

The issue of biblical authority has been discussed and the implications of alternative hermeneutical circles employed in Latin American biblical interpretation have been considered. In the following section, the discussion will move on to briefly overview the textual details of this fresh reading of the Scriptures, and the search for an appropriate message to convey living and appropriate truth to the Latin American situation.

---

[87] Escobar, *Evangelio*, 69-71.

[88] Escobar, *Themes*, 17.

[89] Cited by Escobar, *Themes*, 19.

5.4 A Brief Overview of the Bibilical Material Used in the Theology of Liberation

As has already been stated, it is fair to say that Gutiérrez's *A Theology of Liberation* is a representative presentation of liberation thought. In his work, Gutiérrez demonstrates that the theology of liberation certainly makes use of biblical material. Biblical themes such as creation, salvation, liberation, the Exodus, eschatological promises, the kingdom of God, Christ as liberator, conversion to one's neighbour and Christian hope are evident throughout his systematisation of liberation thought.[90] A brief overview of the manner in which Gutiérrez deals with these biblical themes will give the reader a sense of the liberationist approach.

The two biblical themes of creation and salvation are used by Gutiérrez to trace the history of Israel through the books of Isaiah, the Psalms, Amos, Jeremiah and Malachi.[91] The political liberation of Israel through the Exodus is considered as it is presented in Deuteronomy, and is also discussed in light of the Psalms and the reflections on the event through the testimony of the prophets.[92] The work of Christ bringing salvation to complete fulfilment is considered in reference to the epistle to the Colossians, the first letter to the Corinthians, the book of Hebrews and the letter to the Ephesians.[93] The work of Christ as a new form of creation draws on references from the letters to the Romans, to the Galatians and the Corinthians.[94] Eschatological promises are traced throughout the Scriptures from Abraham, to the Covenant with Israel, to the New Covenant, to the hope of the kingdom of God in the "last days."[95] Images of the kingdom of God are taken from the Old and New Testament, where the establishment of peace, justice, love and freedom are signs of the kingdom.[96]

Latin American evangelical theologians acknowledge the abundance of biblical study and work in the theology of liberation. They also recognise that the technique employed in respect of biblical work is clearly set within the boundaries of the methodology discussed in the previous chapter.[97] In later chapters of this thesis, biblical themes evident in the theology of liberation will be dealt with in more depth. In examining these biblical themes, attention will be given to the hermeneutical weaknesses perceived by evangelicals with regard to the understanding of these

---

[90] Gutiérrez, *Theology*, x-xi, 257-260.

[91] See for example, Isaiah 43:1, 42:5-6; Psalm 74, 89, 93, 95, 135, 136; Amos 4:12, 5:8; Jeremiah 33:25, 10:16, 27:5, 32:17; Malachi 2:10.

[92] See for example, Exodus 1:1-10, 13,14, 15-22, 3:7-10, 5:6-14; Deuteronomy 32:6, 5:6; Psalm 74, 87, 89; Isaiah 43:1, 15, 41:20, 43:7, 45:8, 48:7.

[93] See for example, Colossians 1:15-20; 1 Corinthians 8:6; Hebrews 1:2; Ephesians 1:1-22.

[94] See for example, Romans 8; Galatians 6:15; 2 Corinthians 5:17.

[95] See for example, Genesis 12:1-3, 15:1-16; Acts 13:23; Romans 4:13; Galatians 3:22-29.

[96] See for example, Leviticus 25:10; Isaiah 29:18-19, 32:17; Psalm 85; Matthew 11:5; Luke 4:16-21.

[97] Escobar, *Fe*, 137.

themes.[98] At this point, therefore, the purpose of this section is simply to draw attention to the implications of the liberation hermeneutic for the principal theme of the Exodus and the key subject of Christology. For the exegetical approach of liberation theologians in relation to these subjects has formed a substantial part of the evangelical critique.

The practice of thorough and skilled biblical study is considered to be of utmost importance in evangelical theology. Escobar, citing Bernard Ramm, emphasises and illustrates the significance of biblical exegesis for sound evangelical theology:

> The historic Protestant position is to ground theology in biblical exegesis. A theological system is to be built up exegetically brick by brick. Hence the theology is no better than the exegesis that underlies it. The task of the systematic theologian is to commence with these bricks ascertained through exegesis, and build the temple of his theological system. But only when he is sure of his individual bricks is he able to make the necessary generalizations, and to carry on the synthetic and creative activity that is necessary for the construction of a theological system.[99]

In light of this evangelical commitment to biblical exegesis, Kirk is critical of the fact that liberation theologians have not undertaken what he would consider to be an acceptable exegetical study of the biblical text. Kirk claims that liberationists depend on contemporary exegetical studies carried out by others, from which they then draw their interpretations. He observes that they do not make a conscious attempt to employ these studies as a tool but, in his opinion, use them as an "interpretative launching pad."[100] As a result, Kirk argues that the liberationist method and the liberationist use of the text both lack critical awareness and exegetical verification. Kirk rightly identifies the controlling factor in their interpretation of a text to be the requirements of the circumstances to which the text must be addressed, rather than a thorough exegetical method which then applies or contextualises Scripture to situations. It would appear that the liberationist approach to the Exodus event evidently reflects the priority given to praxis, to context and to ideology which evangelical theologians have expressed concerns about.

In the theology of liberation, the event of the Exodus is central to the interpretation of the Scriptures.[101] It is no exaggeration, therefore, to refer to the Exodus account as "a privileged text."[102] Gutiérrez states:

> The Exodus experience is paradigmatic. It remains vital and contemporary due to similar experiences which the People of God undergo. As Neher writes, it is

---

[98] In later chapters, the principal themes of sin, salvation, liberation, Christology, ecclesiology, missiology and social responsibility will be discussed in light of the liberationist interpretation of these themes, and the evangelical engagement with those themes within the Latin American context.

[99] Bernard Ramm, cited by Escobar, *Themes*, 6.

[100] Kirk, *Liberation*, 96.

[101] Padilla, "Iglesia", 126; Kirk, "Biblia", 173-180.

[102] Kirk, *Liberation*, 95.

characterized "by the twofold sign of the overriding will of God and the free and conscious consent of humans." And it structures our faith in the gift of the Father's love. In Christ and through the Spirit, persons are becoming one in the very heart of history, as they confront and struggle against all that divides and opposes them.[103]

Kirk seeks to illustrate his criticisms of the liberation hermeneutic by a thorough systematic exposition of the interpretation of the Exodus in liberation theology. He observes that little historical justification is given for the two basic assumptions made with regard to the Exodus narrative by liberationists.[104] First, it is assumed that previous to the dramatic deliverance from Egypt, the Israelites did not possess a "consciousness of people-hood."[105] Second, the actual Exodus narrative is assumed to be "the result of elaborate theological reflection, *ex eventu*, which has obscured an original, non – 'mythical' account of an escape to freedom."[106] Kirk is critical that liberation theologians draw hermeneutical lessons for present day liberation from these inaccurate presuppositions.

Núñez considers the liberationist treatment of the Exodus to be a clear example of imposing a particular ideology onto the text. It is this ideology that leads to serious problems in the interpretation of the event. He observes:

> The truth is that there was no popular uprising to dethrone Pharaoh by means of a violent struggle. Neither did the Israelites devise a political project to change the structures of Egyptian society. They were not supposed to stay in Egypt to transform it, but to serve Yahweh in another place...Clearly such reasoning pertains to a purely speculative realm. The only objective biblical basis we have for our theological reflection concerning the victorious exit of Israel from Egypt is the narrative in the book of Exodus and the interpretation of that narrative in the rest of the Scriptures.[107]

Núñez concludes that while the text demonstrates that there was economic, social and political oppression in Egypt, strict exegesis of the biblical text does not allow for a reading which proposes the Exodus as a paradigm for political and revolutionary struggle.[108] Rather, Núñez considers the covenantal promises of Yahweh to be the key to the interpretation of the Exodus. The theological significance of the event is that the intervention of Yahweh to liberate his people is in faithfulness to the commitment made to Abraham, that his people would be blessed and would be a blessing to the world.

For Latin American evangelicals, the Exodus narrative, though clearly a text referring to political emancipation, also has deeper resonances. The people were enslaved ultimately because of the sin of Joseph's brothers. The great Exodus event foreshadowed an even greater Exodus inaugurated by the one whom Matthew

---

[103] Gutiérrez, *Theology*, 91.
[104] Kirk, *Liberation*, 95-104, 147-152.
[105] Kirk, *Liberation*, 148.
[106] Kirk, *Liberation*, 148.
[107] Núñez, *Liberation*, 191.
[108] Núñez, *Liberation*, 192; see also Escobar, *Fe*, 146-148.

depicts as the second Moses.[109] It is important, therefore, to consider briefly the hermeneutical approach to the person of Jesus Christ taken by the liberationists.

The liberationist search for the historical Jesus has led to a portrayal of Christ as a zealot who can be considered a model for revolutionary figures in contemporary times. The liberationist approach to the Gospels has also led to interpretations of the death of Christ as part of a political, nationalistic strategy. For the Latin American evangelical, such interpretations ignore the interpretations of Christ's death made within the Gospel texts and indeed the rest of the New Testament.[110]

Núñez turns his attention more specifically to the evidence that in approaching the biblical text, liberation theologians question the authenticity of various portions of the New Testament. Núñez observes the liberationist preference to interpret biblical Christology in terms of "theological evolution." That is to say, as time passed the Christian community came to regard Jesus of Nazareth as divine. Thus, liberationist Christology is founded primarily on human reflection rather than divine revelation. Núñez contends, therefore, that he has yet to find in liberation theology a clear cut, unambiguous confession that Jesus is God grounded on the fact that Scripture affirms it by the inspiration of the Holy Spirit. Núñez maintains that this liberationist approach raises serious doctrinal issues for evangelicals. "The discrepancy goes far beyond the political and ecclesial; it transcends the conflict between capitalism and socialism and touches the very foundations of our faith."[111]

Núñez acknowledges, however, that liberation theology has forced evangelical Christians to reawaken and face Christological challenges. He concedes that Christology today can no longer have the same emphasis as Christology which was a product of evangelical reaction to Protestant liberalism in the nineteenth century. He asserts:

> Without isolating ourselves from our life context, we must continue to study the sacred Scriptures diligently, because they are what give the fundamental and authentic testimony concerning the person and the work of the Son of God.[112]

Authentic testimony regarding the community of Jesus is also to be found in the Scriptures. As liberationist Christology is influenced by a critical approach to the New Testament, so too Núñez highlights the fact that liberation ecclesiology is informed by sociological and theological reflection rather than thorough biblical exegesis. He asserts that liberation theologians have failed to take advantage of the abundant ecclesiological material in the New Testament.[113] Again, this reflects that

---

[109] Scott McKnight, "Matthew, Gospel of" in *Dictionary of Jesus and the Gospels*, eds. Joel B. Green and Scott McKnight (Downers Grove and Leicester: IVP, 1992), 526-541, at 533.

[110] Escobar, *Fe*, 148-152.

[111] Núñez, *Liberation*, 235.

[112] Núñez, *Liberation*, 239.

[113] See for example John 17 and Matthew 5:13-16 where the gospels teach that the church is in the world, but does not belong to the world. The church is sent to be the salt of the earth

liberationists do not hold a high view of Scripture but depend on their "new way of doing theology" for inspiration. Núñez concludes that fundamental biblical truths are a missing feature in the ecclesiology of liberation.

The key theme of the Exodus permeates liberation hermeneutics. It has become clear that the interpretation of the event has implications for liberation Christology, for liberation ecclesiology and also for the general themes such as sin, salvation and liberation.[114] These subjects will be discussed in more detail in later chapters. Suffice it to say here, that the issue of biblical interpretation and the discussion surrounding the manner in which biblical material should be approached are recurring features in the development of contextual Latin American theology. For while liberation theologians and Latin American evangelical theologians disagree on the authority which Scripture is to be given, both seek societal transformation. Against the backdrop of the liberationist readings of Scripture, Latin American evangelicals seek to present a thoroughly biblical message of transformation.

When Escobar maintains that the biblical message is powerful and transformational, it is in contrast to the dead orthodoxy critiqued by the theology of liberation. It is also an obvious point for evangelicals that detailed biblical study and thorough exegesis reveal that the word of God addresses issues pertinent to the Latin American reality. Concurring with the assertions of the theology of liberation, Escobar emphasises that indifference to social and political issues is a contradiction of biblical teaching.[115]

Firstly, Escobar deals with the social implications of the Old Testament. The Law reveals not only the will and intention of God for humanity and society but also reveals the character and nature of God. The Law clearly transmits the notion of social justice. The regulations in respect of property, usury, the social conditions of citizens, and economic exploitation demonstrate that the sanctity of life should be reflected in the health and well-being of humanity.[116] The message of the Old Testament prophets also asserts principles of social ethics, explicitly condemning social injustice, abuse and disobedience of the law. In contrast to the reality of the human society around them, the prophets shared a vision of the kingdom of God, where peace, abundance, justice and harmony reign.[117] Contrary to the individualistic message often propagated by Protestant churches, Escobar draws attention to the biblical anthropology which communicates the notion of humans in community. Individuals within the community are responsible for their own needs

---

and the light of the world. In 1 Peter 2:9-10 the New Testament teaches that the church must retain its identity in the world. The New Testament draws a dividing line between the "church" who have received Christ and those who have rejected Christ, see John 3:36, 14:6; Acts 4:12; 2 Thessalonians. 1:3-10. Núñez, *Liberation*, 248.

[114] See Kirk, "Biblia", 180-188.

[115] Escobar, *Evangelio*, 61-67.

[116] See for example, Genesis 9:6; Leviticus 25:8-32, 25:35-38, 19:9,10,13.

[117] See in particular the books of Isaiah, Jeremiah and Amos.

and the needs of others. Individuals in the community will protect one another from danger.[118]

Secondly, Escobar discusses the social implications of New Testament teaching, which can be properly understood in light of the Old Testament. The example of Christ in the New Testament is an active demonstration of Christian ethics. Those believers who identified themselves with Christ and who followed his example became the early community of Christians whose lifestyles, attitudes, and practices were distinct from those around them.[119] The early Christian community lived in expectation of the imminent return of Christ which influenced their existence. It is imperative, argues Escobar, that Christians live in the light of this hope and communicate this hope to the world with a message of transformation.[120]

In this brief overview of the evangelical critique of the liberationist approach to the Bible, it is evident that evangelical theologians are seeking to develop a Latin American evangelical approach to hermeneutics which is distinct yet faithfully evangelical. The following section will consider this search for a contextual evangelical hermeneutical approach.

5.5 The Search for a Contextual Evangelical Hermeneutic

It is natural for Latin American evangelicals to assert that contextual theology must dialogue with the surrounding social and cultural context. Evangelical theology should represent an attempt to answer the specific questions troubling Latin Americans.[121] It is obvious too that they consider the whole counsel of God necessary to convey the message of the Scriptures. Despite the developments in biblical theology, the need to communicate this message from the word of God remains vital.[122] In the past, Núñez admits that evangelicals have been guilty of giving prominence to the New Testament and emphasising the individualistic

---

[118] See for example Exodus 22:19,27.

[119] See Acts 17:6.

[120] See for example 1 Corinthians 7:29-31; Philippians 4:5, 12, 13.

[121] Several helpful examples of the Latin American evangelical attempt to find an appropriate hermeneutical response to their specific context can be found in Padilla, "Myths", 3-9; J. Andrew Kirk, "Race, Class, Caste and the Bible", *Themelios* 10, no. 2 (1985): 4-14; C. René Padilla, "Towards a Contextual Christology from Latin America" in *Conflict and Context: Hermeneutics in the Americas*, eds. Mark Lau Branson and C. René Padilla (Grand Rapids: Eerdmans, 1986), 81-91; C. René Padilla, "El estado desde una perspectiva bíblica" in *Los evangélicos y el poder político en América Latina*, ed. Pablo A. Deiros (Buenos Aires: Nueva Creación, 1986), 23-40; Samuel Escobar, "The Hermeneutical Task in Global Economics", *Transformation* 4, 3/4 (1987): 7-11; C. René Padilla, *Los derechos humanos y el reino de Dios* (Lima: Concilio Nacional Evangelico de Peru – PROMIES, 1992). See in particular chapter one entitled "The Bible and Human Rights", 12-23, and chapter two "The Bible and the Kingdom of God", 42-51.

[122] Emilio A. Núñez, "Que prediques la Palabra", *Apuntes Pastorales* 10, no. 4 (1993): 30-32.

aspects of salvation. Consequently, the evangelical focus concentrated on the spiritual life of the believer, it promoted commitment to the local church but not the local society, and it stressed the significance of trivial aspects of salvation. Such attitudes worked to the detriment of Old Testament teaching which abounds with relevant teaching on issues raised in the Latin American context. Núñez is convinced that the Scriptures contain great ethical principles which the Christian community should follow. He calls for a holistic restoration of the teachings of the Bible and recognises the need to recover those biblical elements which have been forgotten.[123] Escobar concurs with Núñez when he writes:

> This fresh reading of Bible material has called our attention to some aspects of the biblical message that had remained obscure, unknown, or even purposefully forgotten. We will have to acknowledge that subjects like justice, poverty, and oppression are not accidental departures, here and there, from the great lines of biblical teaching. To our surprise they may be inseparable from the great themes of revelation, relationship with God, repentance and the essence of Christian life.[124]

Padilla reflects on the evangelical commitment to the Bible in the search for contextual theology when he affirms:

> Evangelical theology is by definition one that recognizes the normativity of the Scriptures in which the Evangel has been recorded. In practical terms, it is a theology which constantly takes into account the classical principles of biblical hermeneutics related to the literary context, the language, history and culture.[125]

Padilla maintains that theology includes but is far more than exegesis. It is the result of a process of transposing the word of God from its original Hebrew or Graeco-Roman milieu into a contemporary situation, for the purpose of producing in the modern readers or hearers the same kind of impact that the original message was meant to produce in its original historical context.[126]

Padilla asserts that an evangelical biblical foundation presupposes communal, pneumatic, contextual and missiological hermeneutics. He also identifies four presuppositions of such an evangelical biblical foundation. Firstly, it is presupposed

---

[123] See also Escobar, *Evangelio*, 69.

[124] Escobar, "Global", 8. It is also insightful to read the papers presented by the Bible study groups at the Context and Hermeneutics in the Americas Conference held in Tlayacapan, Mexico in November 1983. The discussions which follow each presentation illustrate clearly the fresh reading of the Scriptures brought by Latin American evangelicals in comparison with the understanding conveyed by the North American representatives. See the interpretations brought by the study groups on Exodus, Isaiah, The Magnificat, 1 Corinthians and Galatians 3 in *Conflict and Context: Hermeneutics in the Americas*, eds. Mark Lau Branson and C. René Padilla (Grand Rapids: Eerdmans, 1986), 155-280.

[125] C. René Padilla, "Biblical Foundations: A Latin American Study", *Evangelical Review of Theology* 7, no. 1 (1983): 79-88, at 79.

[126] Padilla, "Biblical", 79.

that the purpose of the word of God is to create a people who are distinctively God's own. Secondly, it is acknowledged that the Holy Spirit is necessary for comprehension of the word of God. Thirdly, it is recognised that the interpretation of the word of God involves a hermeneutical circulation between the horizons of the biblical text and the horizons of the contemporary situation. The purpose of such interpretation is to motivate obedience which comes from faith. Fourthly, it is affirmed that faith is expressed through works of love which evidence the power of the word of God.[127]

Padilla contends that "the gathered community of believers is meant to be the organ through which the word of God takes up fresh meaning in relation to a concrete situation."[128] It is interesting to draw comparisons between the style of biblical study also undertaken in the ecclesial base communities and this concept of communal hermeneutics proposed by the evangelical churches.[129] Concurring with the theologians of liberation, Padilla is critical of the Western attitude which has consigned Bible study and interpretation to the academy, resulting in theology which is unrelated and irrelevant to believers in their daily lives as they seek to live out the mission of the church.[130] Padilla argues:

> The church in the Third World needs a theology that answers to its own needs. From Western missions it has received the gospel reduced and wrapped in cultural clothing that robs it of much of its transforming power. This is its greatest tragedy and its greatest challenge.[131]

He comments that the knowledge of the truth has been separated from the practice of the truth. Revelation has been reduced to the communication of abstract truths and faith has been intellectualised.[132] "As a result, theology is divorced from the church and the Bible is assumed to be a book closed to ordinary people."[133] Padilla asserts that Latin American evangelicals cannot afford the luxury of theology as a predominantly academic discipline. It becomes clear that, like the liberation

---

[127] Padilla, "Biblical", 80; Padilla, "Círculo", 3.

[128] Padilla, "Biblical", 81; Padilla, "Círculo", 1.

[129] The approach of base ecclesial communities will be discussed further in chapter eight. Escobar helpfully pointed out that while the style of Bible Study is comparative in base ecclesial communities and evangelical churches, the presuppositions with which the text is approached are distinct. Samuel Escobar, discussion with the author, 2 April 2004, Valencia.

[130] Escobar discusses the influence of Western theological interpretation on Latin American theology in "Iberoamérica", 26-32.

[131] Padilla, *Mission*, 99.

[132] Padilla, "Teología", 17.

[133] Padilla, "Biblical", 81. Padilla seems to imply here that Western theologians are concerned with the interpretation and explanation of a religious tradition, not of application of faith to daily life. It appears they assume that it is professionals who should study the biblical text. Ordinary people, therefore, are not given the opportunity to interpret it. In this sense, both theologians and ordinary people assume the Bible to be a closed book for those who are not professionals in the field of theology.

theologians, the context and situation of evangelical theologians demands a theology which will grow out of and respond to the needs of the Christian community. This theology must be based on communal hermeneutics.[134]

> If the gospel is to become visible in the life of the church, the whole church has to be recognised as the "hermeneutical community," the place where the interpretation of Scripture is an ongoing process. God's purpose in speaking through Scripture is not to provide a basis for theological systems, but to shape a new humanity created in the image of Jesus Christ. Biblical hermeneutics is a concern of the whole church for it has to do with God's creation of a community called to manifest his kingdom in every area of life.[135]

Padilla affirms that the biblical foundation for theology in the Two Thirds World presupposes a church that functions as the "hermeneutical community"- the place where the gospel is received not as a human word, but as it actually is, the living word of God.[136]

Padilla is further critical of the Western approach which emphasises scientific techniques in an effort to respond to the hermeneutical questions. As a result, ordinary people are left to depend on scholars to tell them what a scriptural passage meant in its original context and indeed what to believe.

> The fact remains, however, that the comprehension of God's truth contained in Scripture is not merely a matter of Bible-study techniques. Biblical scholarship is a necessary but not a sufficient recourse for that purpose...knowing God's message is far more than mastering the biblical text. It involves a personal relationship – a relationship with the God who is behind the text.[137]

Padilla asserts that no true evangelical theology is possible without illumination from and guidance by the Holy Spirit. "The same Spirit who inspired Scripture in the past is the Spirit who enlightens the heart and enables it to comprehend God's truth in the present."[138]

Padilla affirms the need to take "seriously the cultural context of the contemporary reader as well as of the biblical text."[139] The effort to contextualise the gospel is evident in the life and practice of the early church. Padilla recognises that the task of contextualising the gospel today is as vital as it was in the New Testament times. The church in the Two Thirds World must choose to either import a Western theology and attempt to adapt it, or search for an alternative contextual approach. Padilla recognises that this will be a struggle:

---

[134] Padilla, "Autoridad", 124; Escobar, "Hermenéutica", 2-4.

[135] Padilla, "Biblical", 82.

[136] Padilla, "Biblical", 82; Padilla, "Círculo", 1.

[137] Padilla, "Biblical", 83.

[138] Padilla, "Biblical", 83; Escobar, "Hermenéutica", 3.

[139] Padilla, "Biblical", 84.

> A struggle for a theology with a biblical foundation in the wider sense – a theology resulting from the merging of the horizons of their own situation and the horizons of the biblical text...It can only be the result of a new, open-ended reading of Scripture with a hermeneutic in which the biblical text and the historical situation become mutually engaged in a dialogue whose purpose is to place the church under the lordship of Jesus Christ in its particular context.[140]

Contextualisation of the word of God in the early church took place in an effort to communicate the gospel to people living in a different situation. Such a mission perspective will ensure a balanced commitment to faithfulness and a desire for that faith to be relevant to the concrete historical context. Padilla warns against the dangers of an unbalanced perspective. It can lead, on the one hand to more interest in conserving the theological tradition with little relevance to daily life or, on the other hand, to greater concern with social respectability than with the proclamation of the word of God. Padilla contends that relevance and faithfulness are characteristics of a church which expresses its faith through works of love. Such an active witness to the word of God communicates more to the Latin American situation than attributes of academic theology.[141]

Padilla summarises that to speak of a biblical theology is to acknowledge the church as a hermeneutical community, the witness of the Holy Spirit as the key to understanding, contextualisation as the New Testament pattern for sharing the gospel and Christian mission as the manner in which God calls all people to himself.

Escobar recognises that such evangelical biblical theology will communicate a message which can not only transform lives, but which subsequently can transform society. Escobar affirms that in the field of Latin American evangelical theology the issues surrounding biblical hermeneutics are a constant source of discussion and the development of an evangelical hermeneutic continues to be closely pursued.[142] Costas emphasizes the importance of hermeneutical developments for contextual theology in Latin America when he writes:

> The Scriptures are normative in the understanding of faith, the lifestyle of God's people, and the way Christians go about their theological reflection. Yet the Scriptures are not to be heard and obeyed unhistorically. Indeed, the normative and formative roles of Scripture are mediated by our contexts - contexts that are, generally speaking, characterized...as a reality of poverty, powerlessness, and oppression on the one hand, and religious and ideological pluralism on the other. Thus a contextual hermeneutic appears a *sine qua non* of evangelical theology in the Two Thirds World.[143]

The commitment of Latin American evangelical theologians to the Scriptures is evident, not only in their pursuit of a contextual hermeneutical approach, but also in

---

[140] Padilla, "Biblical", 85.

[141] Padilla, "Biblical", 87.

[142] For further discussion on the Bible and social transformation see Escobar, *Evangelio*, 43-73; Escobar, "Hermeneutic", 6-7.

[143] Costas, "Evangelical", 316.

their dedication to Bible translation work.[144] Escobar notes that the distinctive aspect of pioneer missionary work in Latin America was the clear emphasis on Bible translation.[145] "The concern to put the Bible in the hands of the people, in their own language, was related to the conviction that God speaks through his word and by His Spirit in a way that the average Christian can understand."[146] Latin American evangelical theologians have demonstrated their continuing conviction of the power of the Bible and the importance of an accurate, accessible translation. It is interesting to note that in conjunction with other Latin American evangelical theologians, Padilla, Escobar and Núñez were involved in the production of the new edition of the *Nueva Versión Internacional.* Unlike the previous editions which had been direct translations from the English *New International Version,* the committee for this edition worked from the original biblical languages. All but one of the members of the translation committee speaks Spanish as their first language, indicating the significant development in indigenous evangelical scholarship.[147] Latin American evangelicals also recognise the necessity of further development of Bible study materials which are accessible to the Latin American people.[148] Escobar reflects on the importance of such a continual commitment to the communication of the Scriptures:

> The Bible in the language of the people has played a decisive role in the rise of thousands of Evangelical communities among the poor and the native peoples across Latin America. In our times, the promise of indigenous theologies is again the promise of what can happen when such theologies are a way of giving back to the people the leaven of the gospel, when the way in which these people think their faith and their life is shaped by the word of Jesus Christ who said: "the truth will set you free."[149]

5.6 Conclusion

In this chapter, the search for a contextual Latin American hermeneutic has been discussed, in light of the Latin American evangelical engagement with liberation

---

[144] In 1971, Padilla emphasized the need for modern Latin American translations of the Scriptures, see C. René Padilla, "La Biblia hoy", *Certeza* 42 (1971): 56-59.

[145] For a discussion on the significance of the Bible and Bible translation in Latin American evangelical missionary practise see Samuel Escobar, "Formación bíblico-teológica del misionero transcultural", *Kairós* 24 (January - June 1999): 61-70, at 62-64.

[146] Escobar, *Themes,* 3.

[147] See "El comité de traducción bíblica de la Nueva Versión Internacional", *Iglesia y Misión* 65 (July - September 1998): no page numbers given.

[148] See for example Jorge Atiencia, Samuel Escobar and John Stott, *Así leo la Biblia: cómo se forman maestros de la palabra* (Barcelona, Buenos Aires and La Paz: Certeza Unida, 1999); Escobar, *Sola.*

[149] Samuel Escobar, "The Role of Translation in Developing Indigenous Theologies – a Latin American View" in *Bible Translation and the Spread of the Church: the Last Two Hundred Years,* ed. Philip C. Stine (Leiden, The Netherlands: E. J. Brill, 1990), 81-94, at 94.

hermeneutics. It becomes clear that the foundational issue is the subject of biblical authority. In contrast to the theology of liberation, Latin American evangelical theology considers Scripture to be the point of departure for all theological discussion.

As Latin American evangelical theologians continue to develop contextual hermeneutics, it will be necessary to anticipate criticism which may arise regarding what some may perceive as the dominance given to context in their approach. It will be vital that they demonstrate thorough interpretation in which the significance of context is held firmly in balance with the biblical authority which they espouse. It will be important to evidence such interpretation of Scripture, not only in regard to the themes discussed within this thesis but also in the application of evangelical hermeneutics to contemporary issues as they arise in Latin America. The final conclusion of this study will seek to reflect on the apparent need for a structured systematisation of Latin American evangelical theology undergirded by the evangelical hermeneutics discussed here.

Evangelical theologians argue that praxis, historical circumstances and ideological commitment should all be brought under the authority of Scripture. Evangelicals assert that God has been revealed in Scripture and Scripture bears witness to the revelation of God in Christ. Such an understanding of revelation is central to a Latin American evangelical theological method. As a consequence, the hermeneutical circle proposed by Latin American evangelical theologians evidences a difference in emphasis from the hermeneutical circle proposed by the theology of liberation. Such an understanding of revelation also results in the affirmation of the unity of the Old and New Testament, and a commitment to strive to read the whole of the biblical text in a less selective manner. For evangelicals recognise that, in the past, evangelical scholarship has demonstrated its own particular selectivity to the detriment of significant biblical themes. Latin American evangelical theologians seek contextual hermeneutics which evidence submission to the authority of Scripture; competence in biblical scholarship; sensitivity to the reality of historical circumstances, and commitment to the communication of the transformational gospel message.

This chapter has demonstrated that the subject of hermeneutics is a central issue in the development of contextual theology for Latin America. As mentioned in the introduction to this chapter, the biblical renewal movement within post-conciliar Catholicism (see chapter two) significantly influenced the liberationist attitude to the Scriptures. The evangelical response to the liberationist challenge and the evangelical critique of that approach has been presented here. In chapter three, submission to the authority of Scripture was stated to be an essential characteristic of evangelical theology. It is apparent that Latin American evangelical theologians adhere to this principle. In chapter four, the methodology employed by the theology of liberation was discussed and the evangelical concerns regarding liberation method were considered. This chapter has dealt specifically with the evangelical concern regarding the use of Scripture in theology of liberation, and the search for an appropriate evangelical contextual hermeneutic. In the light of this discussion on the authority and the interpretation of Scripture, the following chapter will deal with the general biblical themes pertinent to the development of contextual theology for Latin America.

CHAPTER 6

General Themes in Latin American Contextual Theology

6.1 Introduction

The dominant liberation themes evident in the development of contextual theology for Latin America are dealt with in the individual chapters of this thesis. The subjects of history, contemporary context, method and hermeneutics have already been discussed. The topics of Christology, ecclesiology and missiology will be examined in chapters seven, eight and nine. While individual chapters deal with these issues in depth, there are also what I will refer to as *general themes* present within the search for contextual Latin American theology. These themes are dealt with at this juncture because they arise from the historical context, illustrate the method and hermeneutical approach, and will act as the foundation for further discussion on the remaining dominant themes.

The purpose of this chapter is first to identify the general themes, which are present in Latin American contextual theology. Second, the evangelical exposition and theological development of these general themes will be outlined. While these themes are not prolifically debated in Latin American evangelical theology, it is important that an outline of each issue is presented. For it would seem fair to say that there is an accepted evangelical understanding of each general theme which permeates all other aspects of Latin American evangelical theology. Writing in 1975, Núñez reveals the pertinence of these subjects when he expresses the contemporary questions facing evangelical theologians in Latin America at that time:

> We are asked today if the gospel is extramundane or intramundane; if Christianity is only "vertical," turned towards heaven, or if it is "horizontal," at the service of the "total man" within the context of human society; if our proclamation is fundamentally futuristic or focused on the present; if the message is for here and now, or only a promise for the beyond; if our attitude is one of escapism or absenteeism or one of social compromise; if it is true that it is our intention to divide the being of man into two or three constitutive parts and only preach the "salvation of the soul" taking no

interest in his temporal needs; if the Christian message is liberation in the broadest sense of the term, or if the Christian message is the "opium of the people"?[1]

I adjudge the general themes which merit examination to be *humanity, sin, liberation, salvation, conversion,* and *the kingdom of God.* This chapter does not set out to present a complete analysis of these subjects in Latin American contextual theology. Rather, the focus of this chapter is to compare and contrast the evangelical understanding of these issues with the widely accepted understanding presented in liberation thought. For it is in this interaction that the evangelical perspective on liberation themes is most constructively defined. In light of this engagement, I will examine the subsequent development and expression of these themes in contemporary Latin American evangelical studies.[2]

In this chapter, each theme will be dealt with in turn. The presentation of each in this manner will give a coherent overview of the contextual evangelical theology which is being developed. While it is evident that these subjects support and strengthen the dominant themes discussed in the individual chapters of this thesis, the amount of material written specifically on the general themes is less extensive. For this reason, a brief outline of the discussion surrounding each theme should be sufficient to gain an understanding of the underlying theological principles implied generally in Latin American evangelical theology. Inherent in the development of contextual theology is the desire to respond to the needs of people in their historical circumstances. The first subject to be dealt with, therefore, is the understanding of humanity.

6.2 Humanity

Across the theological spectrum, theologians have been motivated to present a coherent understanding of the doctrine of *humanity* in order to structure effective contextual theology. The observation made that the theology of liberation does not contain a systematic developed doctrine of humanity would seem to be a fair one.[3] However, there is no doubt that a concern for the welfare of humanity is central to liberation thought and consequently the theology of liberation has prompted others to consider the subject in a more systematic manner.

Christian theological tradition affirms that humanity was created by God, in the image of God. It is significant that all of humanity is considered to reflect the likeness of God. Such an understanding of creation and humanity affects theological

---

[1] Emilio A. Núñez, "Salvación personal y eternal y liberación humana" in Núñez, Cristo, 47-61, at 48. I have sought to translate this more clearly than the English version found in Núñez, "Personal", 1060. The Spanish version is also available as Emilio A. Núñez, "Salvación personal y eterna y liberación humana", *Boletín Teológico* 10 (1974): 7-18.

[2] For a brief overview of the foundational themes identified by a Latin American evangelical theologian see the short study by Roberto Compton, *La teología de la liberación: una guía introductoria* (El Paso: Casa Bautista de Publicaciones, 1984).

[3] Compton, *Teología*, 66.

thinking and practical implications of theology.[4] Humanity was created to govern the world with wisdom and in a responsible manner. Humanity was not given the right to act in an individualistic or egoistic manner, but rather humanity was called to cultivate and to work in mutual harmony with one another. Gutiérrez summarises the concept well when he notes the purpose of humanity: "To dominate the earth as Genesis prescribed, to continue creation, is worth nothing if it is not done for the good of humanity, if it does not contribute to human liberation, in solidarity with all, in history."[5]

Latin American evangelical theologians are seeking to apply an orthodox anthropology which takes into account the needs of their situation.[6] It would seem fair to say that Núñez has contributed the clearest systematic approach to the subject in his article "Dios y el ser humano" (God and the human being).[7] Firstly, Núñez considers the understanding of human dignity. Created in the image and likeness of God,[8] humanity was the culmination of God's creative activity, the "crown of creation."[9] Núñez emphasises that this fundamental principle applies to all of humanity and consequently, all humanity are "neighbours" in origin, in nature and in dignity. In contrast to the liberationist approach which separates humanity into two groups, namely the oppressed and the oppressor, evangelical theologians search for an understanding of humanity which is not limited by such boundaries. Diversity of race, culture and class should not diminish the unity of the human race in these aspects of origin, nature and dignity.[10] However, the significant implication of an understanding which affirms the dignity of human nature, is an awareness that human beings should not offend or ignore such dignity in other people. Respect, love and service to others should be the response of the Christian who recognises the image of God in fellow human beings; just as respect, love and service are offered to

---

[4] See for example, Keith Ward, *Religion and Human Nature* (Oxford: Clarendon Press, 1998), 153; Grudem, *Systematic*, 442-450; Stackhouse, *Futures*, 48-49; Charles Sherlock, *The Doctrine of Humanity* (Leicester: IVP, 1996).

[5] Gutiérrez, Theology, 90.

[6] For a helpful discussion on the debate surrounding the subject of humanity at that time, see J. Andrew Kirk, "The Meaning of Man in the Debate between Christianity and Marxism", *Themelios* 1, no. 2 (1976): 41-49; J. Andrew Kirk, "The Meaning of Man in the Debate between Christianity and Marxism Part 2", *Themelios* 1, no. 3 (1976): 85-93. While these articles are not direct responses to the theology of liberation, the questions which are raised and discussed give an understanding of the context and are illustrative of the evangelical response to liberation thought.

[7] Emilio A. Núñez, "Dios y el ser humano", *Boletín Teológico* 16 (1984): 15-27. See also the section entitled "La Biblia y los derechos humanos" in Padilla, *Derechos*, 12-23.

[8] Genesis 1:26-27.

[9] Núñez, "Dios", 15; Padilla, *Derechos*, 15.

[10] Acts 17:26. See also C. René Padilla, *Discipulado y misión: compromiso con el reino de Dios* (Buenos Aires: Ediciones Kairós, 1997), in particular "Misión y derechos humanos", 178-180; "Responsabilidad cristiana frente al racismo", 184-186; "Hombre y mujer, coherederos del reino", 196-198.

God.[11] Kirk too reflects on this concept of mutual respect between human beings. While his exposition of the biblical text is a familiar one, in the context of the oppressive and domineering regimes in Latin America his observations provide an authentic reminder of the biblical presentation of human relationships which counters the experience of many Latin America people. He notes:

> In the first chapter of Genesis we find the command given to man to subdue and have dominion over the earth. The earth includes every animate and inanimate creature; these are the rightful object of his sovereignty. *But man is excluded.* Man has no right whatsoever to subjugate his fellow man. Only God is man's legitimate sovereign. Thus man when he refuses to live in God's world according to God's will makes himself, by this act, into a pseudo-god with the right to dominate and manipulate man, to be his sovereign.[12]

Secondly, Núñez addresses the subject of the nature of humanity. He draws attention to the fact that, in the Old Testament, there is no dichotomy between the spiritual and physical aspects of the human being.[13] Likewise, Núñez asserts that the New Testament does not fall into dualism either. The body is not presented in the New Testament merely as the "prison of the soul" but as the instrument used in the practice of justice and of good works, which will be glorified at Christ's return.[14] Núñez also affirms the biblical principle that a human being is not created to be alone, but to exist in family, in community, and in society.[15] He summarises his thoughts on the nature of humanity and the responsibilities of the human race when he asserts:

> A human being is physical and spiritual, individual and social, with needs and responsibilities in these three orders of his or her existence. He or she has to watch over the well-being of his or her family, contribute for the good of society, wisely administer the resources of the planet, as God's steward. With this host of needs and responsibilities, humanity needs to be saved, not in solitude, but in solidarity with other human beings, not apart from the world, but in the world, in order to bless the world.[16]

Evangelical theologians recognise that there are, in fact, similarities between biblical anthropology and Marxist anthropology.[17] According to the Bible, as previously mentioned, humanity was created to work and to rule over the whole of

---

[11] Núñez, "Dios", 18.
[12] Kirk, "Meaning", 88.
[13] Padilla, "Misión", 37.
[14] Núñez, "Dios", 19.
[15] Padilla, "Misión", 38.
[16] Núñez, "Dios", 19.
[17] See Kirk, "Meaning", 85.

creation.[18] Human beings are not only creatures, but also are creators, artists and labourers as they live and work on earth. The Bible affirms that the alienation of humanity is evident when human beings dominate one another through work. Old Testament examples of such oppression include the slavery of the Hebrew people in Egypt and the clear prophetic denunciation of the manner in which wage labour was being bought and sold.[19] In the New Testament, James condemns the exploitation of fellow human beings and rebukes those who do not pay fair wages.[20] Paul affirms that work is a form of service towards fellow human beings not an opportunity to acquire power and influence over others.[21] The Bible also portrays humans as historical beings. Kirk observes:

> Abraham, for example, when he obeyed God, believing his promises, made history. He was responsible for a fundamental shift in world history. The biblical faith is also responsible for eradicating every kind of historical fatalism and determinism. Man, in collaboration with God, is the subject and not only the object of history.[22]

Over the last thirty years, Latin American evangelical theologians and theologians of liberation alike have drawn attention again to the importance of biblical anthropology. Theology founded on an appreciation of the origin, the nature, the dignity and the creativity of all humanity should influence and challenge every Christian, whatever their context.

Humanity, irrespective of race or culture, exhibits not only the positive aspects discussed in this section, but also displays an ability to offend, to cause pain and to destroy. Sin, therefore, is evident in the alienation of humanity and in the brokenness of relationships. As Kirk writes,

> Man, therefore, becomes alienated from his Creator when he attempts to overturn the true relationship which he was meant to enjoy with God. He also becomes alienated from his fellow man when he tries to be god to him...and [becomes alienated] from himself when he rejects his true humanity.[23]

All human beings and human communities reflect the consequences of such a rejection of true humanity. It would appear necessary, then, to briefly examine the Latin American evangelical understanding of the subject of sin. For it would be no

---

[18] For a presentation of the Latin American evangelical understanding of a biblical concept of work, see Emilio A. Núñez, "Apuntes sobre el concepto bíblico de trabajo" in Núñez, *Cristo*, 69-88.

[19] Exodus 1:11-14, 5:4-19; Isaiah 10:1,2, 58:3,4; Jeremiah 8:10, 22:13-17; Amos 2:6,7, 5:11,12; Micah 2:1,2.

[20] James 5:1-6.

[21] Romans 12:6-8; 1 Corinthians 9:12-15; Philippians 4:14-18; 2 Thessalonians 3: 11-13; Titus 3:14.

[22] Kirk, "Meaning", 85.

[23] Kirk, "Meaning", 89.

exaggeration to say that in regard to this topic in contextual Latin American theology evangelical theologians and liberation theologians differ significantly.

6.3 Sin

The structures of oppression evident in Latin American society raise serious questions for the theologian attempting to develop an effective contextual theology. The subject of *sin* cannot be avoided. That the church, as an institution, may be responsible for sustaining and maintaining such structures of oppression, is a sobering concern for all theologians. Aldo Etchegoyen, an Argentine Methodist, reflects:

> As far as the church is concerned, in the face of these structures of oppression its fidelity to the liberating gospel of Jesus Christ is at risk. We find in the church, on the one hand, martyrs of the faith and prophets of the truth. On the other hand are those who hide reality through silence or use the word of God to support the dominating power.[24]

The historical context of Latin America, discussed in chapters two and three, reveals that the structures of oppression and injustice established centuries ago continue to influence contemporary Latin American society.[25] During the conference held in Huampaní, Peru, during November 1982, the Assembly of Latin American Council of Churches (CLAI) reflected on the realities of the Latin American context at that time. Such reflections remain relevant today:

> The structures of power are, in the final instance, the causes of the great problems which our continent faces today. These problems include: serious levels of malnutrition, infant mortality, unemployment, lack of housing, limited access to health, educational and social security services, etc. It is not minorities but large majorities of our Latin American compatriots who suffer these disgraces in their own flesh. With regard to this, the socio-economic organization dominant among our people, rather than contributing to the improvement of the situation, causes it to become increasingly worse, turning it into a determining factor in the violation of the rights of the working class and of those who defend democratic liberties…The economic system predominant in Latin America means the strengthening of the so-called developed countries and the growing deterioration of the countries of the Third World. International capitalism subordinates these latter countries to their interests for profit and accumulation of

[24] Aldo Etchegoyen, "Theology of Sin and Structures of Oppression" in *Faith born in the Struggle for Life*, ed. Dow Kirkpatrick (Grand Rapids: Eerdmans, 1988), 156-166, at 158.

[25] See Orlando E. Costas, "Pecado y salvación en América Latina" in Congreso Latinoamericano de Evangelización (CLADE), II, noviembre de 1979, Quito: *América Latina y la evangelización en los años 80*, eds. Pedro Savage and Rolando Gutiérrez (Mexico: Fraternidad Teológica Latinoamericana, 1980), 271-287, at 282-285. A similar article is available in English as "Sin and Salvation in an Oppressed Continent" in Orlando E. Costas, *Christ Outside the Gate* (Maryknoll: Orbis Books, 1982), 21-42.

capital, leading to the weakening of the conditions of interchange, to technological dependence, to political-military control, to the strengthening of internal domination and the increase of the external debt which reaches astronomical figures. The doctrine of National Security becomes the justification for power, exercised both by the centres of world capitalism, and by the dominating classes in the countries in the Third World.[26]

Núñez acknowledges it cannot be said that the theology of liberation denies the reality of sin or diminishes the seriousness of its existence.[27] For Gutiérrez is clear when he writes:

> Sin is not only an impediment to salvation in the afterlife. Insofar as it constitutes a break with God, sin is a historical reality, it is a breach of the communion of men with each other, it is a turning in of man on himself which manifests itself in a multifaceted withdrawal from others. And because sin is a personal and social intrahistorical reality, a part of the daily events of human life, it is also, and above all, an obstacle to life's reaching the fullness we call salvation.[28]

However, it is not unexpected that in the theology of liberation, the subject of social sin is given priority. Núñez is critical, therefore, that liberationists assert "above all, it is society which must change."[29] He critiques the lack of liberationist thought regarding sinning individuals who contribute to the existence of such unjust societal structures. Gutiérrez demonstrates this liberationist emphasis when he comments:

> But in the liberation approach sin is not considered as an individual, private, or merely interior reality – asserted just enough to necessitate a "spiritual" redemption which does not challenge the order in which we live. Sin is regarded as a social, historical fact, the absence of brotherhood and love in relationships among men, the breach of friendship with God and with other men, and, therefore, an interior, personal fracture. When it is considered in this way, the collective dimensions of sin are rediscovered...Sin is evident in oppressive structures, in the exploitation of man by man, in the domination and slavery of peoples, races and social classes. Sin appears, therefore, as the fundamental alienation, the root of a situation of injustice and exploitation...[sin] demands a radical liberation, which in turn necessarily implies a political liberation. Only by participating in the historical process of liberation will it be possible to show fundamental alienation which is present in every partial alienation.[30]

While Núñez does not deny the reality of the existence of sinful societal structures, he expresses his concern that the theology of liberation accentuates this understanding of sin. He notes:

---

[26] Cited by Etchegoyen, "Theology", 157.

[27] See Núñez, *Liberation*, 176.

[28] Cited by Núñez, *Liberation*, 176.

[29] Núñez, "Personal", 1062.

[30] Gutiérrez cited by Núñez, *Liberation*, 176-177.

The injustices of the dominant classes are denounced, but not that of the oppressed classes. The latter must free themselves from their slavery, freeing at the same time their oppressors, by whose agency the devil is acting in the world. However, they [liberation theologians] do not underline personal or social culpability of which the oppressed must free themselves.[31]

Latin American evangelical theologians have reflected on the manifestation of sin on the Latin American continent and are committed to the search for a biblical understanding of the concept.[32] Evangelical theologians, in general, often face the criticism that their understanding of sin is too individualistic. Latin American evangelical theologians, however, reflect an appreciation for the reality of the sin of individuals, yet they do not diminish the repercussions of such individual sin for the whole of society:

In the Bible, sin is not a topic for speculation; it is a question of relationships. Sin manifests itself in the relationships between humanity and God, in the relationships between one human being and another, and in the relationship between humanity and the environment. One cannot speak of sin without reference to its consequences. That is why sin is presented as a destructive force which thwarts and deforms human life. Therefore the problem of sin cannot be understood and explained; it is possible only to register its presence and its consequences.[33]

For Costas, a biblical understanding of sin begins first with the recognition of sin as disobedience towards God and defiance of his reign. Sin is rebellion against God. Sin is the rejection of his love.[34] Second, Costas considers sin as injustice and alienation.[35] He comments: "If disobedience implies the rejection of the rule of God on the part of humanity, injustice means hatred and repudiation of fellow human beings. Sin then is every unjust act..."[36] Costas regards sin as alienation which affects every aspect of a person's existence. A human being is alienated not only from God the creator,[37] but is also alienated from creation, from fellow human

---

[31] Núñez, "Personal", 1062.

[32] See the Bible study entitled "La condición humana" in Samuel Escobar, *Cristianismo Esencial* (Lima: Sociedad Bíblica Peruana, n.d.), 6-8. It is also interesting to note that Míguez Bonino considers the radical conception of human sin in the Protestant tradition to have been a significant distinction between Catholic and Protestant liberation theologians. He explains that, as a Protestant, he felt less optimistic regarding the potential for change in humanity than Catholic liberationists and therefore less disillusioned when dramatic progress was not always achieved. José Míguez Bonino, interview by author, 17 June 2003, video recording, Buenos Aires.

[33] Costas, "Pecado", 271.

[34] Genesis 3:1, 4:3, 11:1-9, 18:16, 37:2; Acts 17:16-32; Ephesians 1:21-22, 3:10-22, 6:12, Colossians 1:16, 2:15.

[35] Romans 1:29; Jeremiah 23:3, 13-17, 22:16; Micah 6:8.

[36] Costas, "Pecado", 272.

[37] Genesis 3:19, 23-24.

beings and from him or herself. Third, Costas asserts that sin is presented in the Bible as disbelief and idolatry. He remarks that "faith is not an intellectual question but an ethical one. It is commitment verified in daily life. To believe in God is to do his will. To disbelieve is to refuse to follow his precepts."[38] Costas maintains that such disbelief is the logical conclusion of disobedience and injustice. Idolatry then, is the culmination of corruption, alienation and disbelief. Kirk describes such idolatry as "much more than honouring or reverencing external objects: idolatry is the choice to abandon, in whole or in part, the order of things created by God, and to seek to live in a world of one's own construction."[39]

Costas develops his discussion of a biblical understanding of sin as he reflects on both the outworking of sin in the life of the individual, and also the collective blame for sin. Disobedience, injustice and disbelief are not generic concepts for Costas. Rather they are personal actions which demonstrate that sin is a reality in the life of every human being.[40] The consequences of personal sin are not limited to the person who committed the sin. For the Bible presents each person as part of a society. All personal action, then, affects that community. In this respect, personal sin carries with it collective guilt.[41] Similarly, action taken within the structures and institutions of society call for personal responsibility. Costas considers sin not only to be personal but also to be structural. The Latin American reality vividly demonstrates that structural sin affects people.[42] Costas asserts:

> It is not sufficient to speak of human sin in universal terms, because then we fall into useless abstractionism. Sin must be understood specifically in order for the gospel to have a positive impact. In the same way, salvation is not an idea but an experience; it is not a simple future promise but a dynamic and present reality. What the gospel declares is a salvation of the past, the present and the future.[43]

Latin American evangelical theologians recognise that to place emphasis on the subject of human sinfulness is not popular in certain Christian spheres, particularly in reference to oppressed peoples in underdeveloped countries. It is more acceptable to identify Christ as present in these people and in their religions. It is acknowledged, therefore, that there is a need for a balanced understanding of human sinfulness. Sin applies to the whole of humanity and there can be no attitude of superiority from any particular society towards another in this regard. Neither can one sphere of society claim less inherent sinfulness than another.

It becomes clear that a structured doctrine of humanity and a coherent understanding of the doctrine of sin are essential foundations of a contextual Latin

---

[38] Costas, "Pecado", 273.

[39] Kirk, *Meaning*, 20.

[40] Costas illustrates this from Romans 3:10b-18.

[41] Costas cites the Old Testament example of Achan found in Joshua 7. He refers also to the argument presented by Paul in Romans 5.

[42] Isaiah 6:5; Romans 9:3; Galatians 6:7.

[43] Costas, "Pecado", 287.

American evangelical theology. An overview of the biblical understanding of humanity leads to a realisation of the lack of true humanity in human societies. With this realisation, questions are raised regarding the sin evident in humanity, which has been discussed in this section. The destruction and oppression portrayed in society should motivate theologians to present a doctrine of liberation which functions with an appropriate doctrine of sin. Kirk contends:

> The Christian understanding of sin is thus at the centre of a Christian understanding of freedom. But this is true only in so far as it supplies the necessary context in which freedom may, or may not be exercised. For the Christian, freedom ultimately means being wholly available for the purposes for which God created human beings: creativity, scientific endeavour, right human relationships, self-giving for others, enjoyment of God's presence and the natural world. As sin destroys in some measure all these ventures, we cannot claim to be truly free until we have been freed from the corrosive power of sin. If our analysis of the human condition at its most fundamental and influential level is correct – and the case rests not only on the message given by the Hebrew prophets and the Christian apostles, but on the observable, intractable nature of human conduct – then freedom becomes a reality more as a gift received than as something that can be created and sustained by human imagination and power. That is why Christians speak about salvation in terms of *liberation into freedom*...Freedom is achieved ultimately by freely serving the liberating purposes of the One who is both the source, the goal and the *meaning of freedom*.[44]

Contextual evangelical theology strives to present a coherent doctrine of sin and also to present a structured biblical theology of liberation which conveys the true meaning of freedom.

6.4 Liberation

In contextual Latin American theology, liberation and salvation cannot be understood apart from one another.[45] On the one hand, the concept of liberation focuses on, but is not limited to, the transformative process in the world. On the other hand, salvation (while not excluding the process of liberation) is God's redeeming action towards the world, in the past, in the present and in eschatological consummation in the future.

For a continent in crisis such as Latin America, the hope of *liberation* sustains communities and motivates people to survive.[46] The theology of liberation seeks

---

[44] Kirk, *Meaning*, 245.

[45] See for example, 6.5 and 6.7.

[46] See Samuel Escobar, "Esperanza y desesperanza en la crisis continental" in Congreso Latinoamericano de Evangelización (CLADE), II, noviembre de 1979, Quito: *América Latina y la evangelización en los años 80*, eds. Pedro Savage and Rolando Gutiérrez (Mexico: Fraternidad Teológica Latinoamericana, 1980), 318-335. Costas also identifies such hope within Hispanic communities in North America. See Orlando E. Costas, "Sobrevivencia,

more than the hope of liberation; it is committed to the actualisation of liberation.[47] Gutiérrez, representing the theology of liberation in general, identifies three levels of meaning in the concept of liberation. Reflecting on the work of Gutiérrez, Núñez describes these three liberationist levels of meaning in the following manner:

> "Economic, social and political liberation" corresponds to the level of "scientific rationality which supports real and effective transforming political action." "Liberation which leads to the creation of a new man in a new society of solidarity" corresponds to the level of "utopia, of historical projections." "Liberation from sin and entrance into communion with God and with all men" corresponds to the level of "faith." The first level is political, and the third level is that of faith. Utopia is between the two, tying them both together.[48]

It becomes clear that in liberation thought, the concept of liberation is closely entwined with the understanding of creation and salvation. Again, Núñez makes this summary:

> According to Gutiérrez, creation is tied to the Exodus, and that event is a political liberation. Man continues the work of creation through his work and builds a new society by means of liberating praxis. In that way the history of salvation and the process of man's liberation are united. There is no natural order of creation and supernatural order of redemption; the perspective of political liberation allows for only one, in which salvation as the self-creation of man takes place. It is man who, by means of his work and his liberating praxis in history, ties together creation with redemption, salvation with the liberation process.[49]

It is interesting to note that while liberationists claim that the traditional understanding of "liberation" for Latin American is too limited, the concept of liberation actually espoused by the theology of liberation is, in fact, too narrow for Latin American evangelical theologians. The Methodist Church in Latin America expresses a more holistic understanding of liberation, with which evangelical theologians would concur:

> When we consider our goals and priorities we must keep visible the total reach of the term *liberation*. This expression embraces two inseparable concepts, indissoluble and interdependent: personal salvation and the redemption of society. A strategy which does not include in it, in integral form and with solidarity, both dimensions will be incorrect and vacillating. An adequate and relevant strategy must do away with the disjunction between the material and the spiritual, the individual and the social, the

---

esperanza y liberación en la iglesia hispana de Estados Unidos: estudio de un caso", *Vida y Pensamiento* 17, no. 1/2 (1987): 101-109.

[47] For a discussion on the rediscovery of the term *liberation* see Orlando E. Costas, *The Integrity of Mission: the Inner Life and Outreach of the Church* (New York: Harper and Row, 1979), 62-69.

[48] See Núñez, *Liberation*, 196.

[49] Núñez, *Liberation*, 196-197.

present life and the after life. Such disjunctions are unfaithful to the gospel just as the individual cannot be separated from the community of which he/she is a part, or the spiritual life from the material or the kingdom from its present significance.[50]

Escobar exemplifies this holistic and far-reaching understanding of liberation. For unlike some conservative evangelical theologians in the West, Latin American evangelicals do not appear to be limited to a spiritual notion of liberation. Escobar simultaneously challenges the narrow notion of "earthly" liberation in the theology of liberation, and the bias of emphasis on "heavenly" liberation in evangelical fundamentalism:

> Please notice that the simple liberation from human masters is not the freedom of which the gospel speaks. Freedom in Christian terms means subjection to Jesus Christ as Lord, deliverance from bondage to sin and Satan (John 8:1-38) and consequently the beginning of a new life under the Law of Christ (1 Corinthians 9:19), life in the family of faith where the old human master becomes also the new brother in Christ. However, the heart which has been made free with the freedom of Christ cannot be indifferent to the human longings for deliverance from economic, political or social oppression. And this is what many expect from the one who evangelises. Not that he says: "I come to announce to you a spiritual freedom and because of that I do not care about your social, economic or political oppression." But rather that he says: "I care about your oppression. I am with you in your search for a way out, and I can show you a deeper and most decisive deliverance that may help you to find a better way out of your social and political oppression."[51]

In seeking to develop an appropriate and effective Latin American evangelical understanding of liberation, Núñez draws on the Old Testament roots of redemption, ransom and deliverance. He considers these ideas to be closely entwined in biblical theology.[52] Núñez draws the conclusion that there can be no freedom (liberation) without the means to freedom (liberation).[53] This leads Núñez to focus on the significance of the cross:

> This is, therefore, the divine message for man today that Christ died for our sin, that he was resurrected, and that he will return to establish throughout the world his reign of justice and peace. All authentically Christian liberation bases itself on that proclamation. Every actual liberation in Christ confirms to us the promise of the cosmic liberation which is to come, the regeneration which the Son of Man will bring (Matt 19:28), and the restoration of all things which God has revealed through his prophets

---

[50] From the document entitled "The Strategy of the Methodist Church of Argentina" cited by Etchegoyen, "Theology", 163.

[51] Escobar, "Evangelization", 322. See also Escobar, "Esclavitud y libertad" in *Cristianismo*, 12-13.

[52] Exodus 6:6; Psalm 74:2; Matthew 20:26.

[53] Núñez, "Personal", 1065.

(Acts 3:21). Meanwhile we are called upon to live and serve in the dynamics of this new and glorious hope.[54]

Costas concurs with Núñez that "the communication of God's liberating news is centred on the cross of Jesus Christ and leads to a call to conversion."[55]

The evangelical understanding of the biblical message of liberation, however, is not limited to the Old Testament or the witness of the Gospels.[56] For Núñez considers liberation to be a prominent theme in Pauline theology. Paul expounds the possibility of liberation in the present and the hope of a future liberation when Christ returns. Núñez maintains that "liberty is the promise for the remote future and reality for today."[57] In agreement with Escobar, Núñez also emphasises the wholeness of liberation presented in the Scriptures when he notes:

> The believer is redeemed in all dimensions; spiritual, mental, and physical. In the salvation plan of God there is no antithesis between the soul and the body such as we generally apply and which has conveyed the impression that our Christianity is, in this respect, docetic, or without body...Paul highly esteems the body of the believer; he sees it in its present glory (temple of the Spirit, instrument of justice), and in its future glory.[58]

Kirk too, examines the biblical concept of liberation into true freedom. He emphasises the breadth of the understanding of liberation in his assertion that "the nature of freedom depends on the nature of the slavery, or other constraint, from which one seeks to be liberated."[59] Kirk is careful to recognise the external forms of captivity from which human beings should be set free: exploitation, starvation, and physical restraint, for example.[60] He balances this with the identification of the need for internal, spiritual liberation which will enlighten human beings with a new way of perceiving human existence.[61] Kirk demonstrates the close relationship between the fundamental principles of conversion and liberation in evangelicalism when he maintains:

> Freedom is the fruit of conversion – a radical transformation of the way one is oriented as a person, either towards the truth as it is revealed in Christ or towards the false assumptions of a world unconscious of any need to be accountable to its Creator. The change is made possible by God himself who, in the death and the conquest of death by Jesus Christ, has taken upon himself all the consequences of our moral futilities,

---

[54] Núñez, "Personal", 1065.

[55] Orlando E. Costas, *Liberating News* (Grand Rapids: Eerdmans, 1989), 112.

[56] See Costas, *Integrity*, 69-75.

[57] Núñez, "Personal", 1067. See also Romans 8:23, 11:26; 1 Thessalonians 1:10.

[58] Núñez, "Personal", 1065. See also 1 Corinthians 15:35-38; Philippians 3:20, 21.

[59] Kirk, *Meaning*, 206.

[60] Psalm 146:7; Isaiah 61:1.

[61] Kirk, *Meaning*, 210. See also John 8:31-8; Galatians 5:1; Colossians 1:12-14; Acts 26:18; 1 Corinthians 6:9-11; Ephesians 5:5, 8-11.

existential confusions and moral blindnesses and broken their power to keep us enslaved to an unreal world.[62]

In the Latin American context it appears that it is Latin American evangelical theologians who have developed an understanding of the concept of liberation with wide-reaching implications. Costas asserts that "because the liberation that Jesus brings is not just a future hope, but a present possibility, therefore, it is given as a charge to the church."[63] The implications of this liberation are not only for the individual or for the church, but also for the society in which that person lives and in which the church exists. Kirk succinctly summarises the Latin American evangelical stance:

> The Christian concern for freedom is expressed in searching for and discovering the right balance between liberty *from* arbitrary authority and liberty *for* non-oppressive structures. The authenticity of such structures is measured by their ability to enable people to become what God, as revealed in Jesus Christ, created them to be.[64]

An overview of the general themes in Latin American evangelical theology reveals the close relationship between the notion of liberation and the idea of salvation. It is appropriate, therefore, to deal with the subject of salvation in the following section.

6.5 Salvation

Gutiérrez explains the liberationist understanding of *salvation* when he states:

> Man is saved if he opens himself to God and to others, even if he is not clearly aware that he is doing so. This is valid for Christians and non-Christians alike – for all people. To speak about the presence of grace – whether accepted or rejected – in all people implies, on the other hand, to value from a Christian standpoint the very roots of human activity. We can no longer speak properly of a profane world.[65]

The differences between the concept of salvation in liberationist thought and the concept in Latin American evangelical theology are critical. Núñez summarises the liberationist understanding of salvation in these terms:

> (1) Salvation is intrahistoric and this-worldly, not ahistorical or otherworldly. It is the action of God here and now, transforming the whole of human reality and carrying it towards its fullness in Christ. (2) Salvation is for the total man and goes beyond that which is merely individual. It also has social and cosmic dimensions. (3) Salvation's

---

[62] Kirk, *Meaning*, 210.
[63] Costas, *Integrity*, 73.
[64] Kirk, *Meaning*, 221.
[65] Gutiérrez, cited by Núñez, *Liberation*, 179-180.

centre is Christ. In the words of Gutiérrez, salvation is "a concept central to the Christian mystery."[66]

While there is no doubt that evangelical theologians would concur with the assertion that salvation is indeed central to the "Christian mystery," they would clearly differ on the understanding of the concept. Latin American evangelicals share the liberationist concern regarding an understanding of salvation which is too "otherworldly." Núñez succinctly expresses his understanding that salvation is not simply a salvation of the soul, if the soul is understood as the spiritual aspect of the human being. Núñez remarks:

> In Christ a human being is saved in all the dimensions of their personality and in all the relationships of his or her existence. Christ saves for today and for eternity, for earth and for heaven, for oneself and for others, in the family, in church and in society. This is the gospel, this is the good news...[67]

Núñez affirms the completeness of salvation and also the divine initiative for salvation. Salvation did not originate with humanity. The human responsibility, however, is the decision of whether to believe or reject the good news. Núñez also identifies three fundamental aspects of the salvific work of God. First, he describes salvation as a new position and a new possession in Christ. Second, he considers salvation as a progressive and practical reality, achieved by the power of the Holy Spirit. Third, he affirms the final consummation of salvation will occur when Christ returns in glory.[68]

Latin American evangelical theologians are convinced that the implications of salvation are not only for the individual, but also for the community of which that individual is a member.[69] Evangelicals, in general, have often been criticised for an individualised approach to salvation which stresses the benefits in life after death. Kirk confronts this emphasis directly:

> Contrary to the belief of many in the West, it is not possible to be a Christian on one's own. The idea of faith as an internal, personal matter which one may exercise if one is so inclined without any necessary relationship to the faith of others is a contradiction of Christianity. It drives to one extreme the Protestant emphasis on personal response as a necessary part of genuine faith in God. It is reinforced by the cultural insistence that the individual is the locus of belief and action and by the notion that faith has more to do with the territory into which one was born than with a voluntary community to which one chooses to belong. For the Christian faith, however, God's purpose is not so much the salvation of isolated individuals as the reconstitution of authentic human

---

[66] Núñez, *Liberation*, 178.

[67] Núñez, "Dios", 20.

[68] Núñez, *Caminos*, 31.

[69] See Samuel Escobar, "La naturaleza comunitaria de la iglesia" in *La iglesia local como agente de transformación*, eds. C. René Padilla and Tetsunao Yamamori (Buenos Aires: Ediciones Kairós, 2003), 75-102.

community, broken by the abuse of freedom. The church is intended to be the first-fruits of a new society, where people use their gifts and talents for the benefit of all.[70]

Latin American evangelicals affirm that a biblical understanding of salvation deals both with the alienation of the individual human being and with the alienation of human society.[71] These characteristics of biblical salvation are not limited to relationships within the community of faith. Kirk is in agreement with Núñez again, when he notes:

> [The Bible] emphasizes that man is 'total' only when his relationships with his neighbour are just and pure (and individualism, in contrast to individuality, cannot be justified by biblical anthropology). Thus, God's plan for mankind's salvation is a new community, man reproducing his new regenerated nature in perfect social relationships. Man is an individual, but his significance as an individual cannot be isolated from his social relationships.[72]

Likewise, Escobar clearly expresses the significant implications of salvation for this world and the mortal life. He maintains:

> "To preach the gospel to the poor; To heal the broken hearted, To preach deliverance to the captives and recovery of sight to the blind, To set at liberty them that are bruised." These are words that cannot be spiritualised in a world like ours, where there are millions of persons who are poor, brokenhearted, captive, blind and bruised.[73]

Latin American evangelical theologians are seeking to develop a contextual theological framework in which sin, salvation and liberation are fundamental doctrines. Just as Costas exhibits an understanding of sin which takes into consideration both the personal and the collective implications, so too does his understanding of salvation:

> One cannot speak of salvation purely in personal terms because one would leave social sin untouched. Neither can one speak exclusively of social salvation because one would leave the personal root of sin untouched. Salvation, to be truly efficacious, has to be salvation of "the soul and the body, the individual and the society, humanity and the whole of creation."[74]

Costas elaborates his understanding of salvation in three points. His understanding of salvation is inextricably linked to his understanding of sin. For he presents salvation antithetically to sin, as discussed previously. Firstly, salvation is understood as submission to the kingdom of God. Costas is careful to assert that

---

[70] Kirk, *Meaning*, 210-211.

[71] Kirk, "Meaning", 89.

[72] Kirk, "Meaning", 88.

[73] Escobar, "Evangelization", 319.

[74] Costas, "Pecado", 276.

obedience is not a condition for salvation but is evidence of faith in action. Obedience is the fruit of grace revealed in Jesus Christ.[75] Secondly, salvation is presented as justification and liberation.[76] Thirdly, Costas develops an understanding of salvation as reconciliation and communion. For just as sin destroys community, societal structures and the environment, salvation can transform them. Justification, liberation, reconciliation and communion are not simply personal experiences but experiences which become a reality in the lives of other human beings as a result of disciples living out such principles.[77] Costas contends:

> Jesus unequivocally shifted the whole concept of salvation – from benefit and privilege to commitment and service. To be saved by faith in Christ is thus to come to Jesus where he died for the world and gave his life for its salvation; it is to commit oneself to those for whom he suffered. Salvation lies outside the gates of the cultural, ideological, political, and socio-economic walls that surround our religious compound and shape the structures of Christendom. It is not a ticket to a privileged spot in God's universe but, rather, freedom for service.[78]

The understanding of sin and salvation developed by Costas leads to a search for an evangelical biblical eschatology. For he comments, "the communion of the believers is not only a fruit of the reconciling work of God in Christ; it is a sign of the future of his reign."[79] Before the subject of eschatology is discussed, however, the theme of conversion should be addressed. For Latin American evangelicalism is typical of evangelicalism in general, in that the experience of conversion is inextricably linked to the understanding of humanity, sin, liberation and salvation.

6.6 Conversion

It would be no exaggeration to say that the understanding of *conversion* varies greatly between the theologians of liberation and evangelical theologians. Núñez comments on the liberationist understanding when he observes:

---

[75] Romans 1:5; 1 John 2:3, 3:7; 1 Thessalonians 1:3; James 2:18.

[76] Romans 1:17. The Spanish, like the English Authorised Version, reads "*mas el justo por la fe vivirá*", that is "the just shall live by faith." In English the translation suggested in contemporary commentaries reads "the one who is righteous will live by faith." See the discussion on the term *dikaios* in James D.G. Dunn, *Word Biblical Commentary: Romans 1-8* (Texas: Word Books, 1988), 44-46; Douglas Moo, *The Epistle to the Romans* (Grand Rapids: Eerdmans, 1996), 76-79, 88. See also Romans 3:21-22, 5:1.

[77] 2 Corinthians 5:19, 21; Ephesians 2:14-16; Colossians 1:21-23; Romans 8:20-21.

[78] Costas, *Christ*, 191. See also Escobar, "Naturaleza", 88; Alberto Guerrero, "Líderes-siervos: facilitadores de la misión integral" in *La iglesia local como agente de transformación*, eds. C. René Padilla and Tetsunao Yamamori (Buenos Aires: Ediciones Kairós, 2003), 179-212.

[79] Costas, "Pecado", 279.

According to the liberational theologians, the mission of the church is to compromise with the political-social liberation. To this end it must denounce every dehumanizing situation, question the *status quo*, and render the masses conscious and political. Gutiérrez believes that becoming converted means embracing the cause of the poor and that "in the present Latin American context it should be said that the church must politicize when evangelising."[80]

There is no doubt that one of the distinctive aspects of evangelical theology, in general, is the call to conversion.[81] This call to conversion marked the arrival and establishment of evangelicalism in Latin America during the nineteenth and twentieth centuries. Míguez Bonino notes that "in comparison with Roman Catholic form and ritual, Protestant preaching stressed the need for personal encounter with Jesus Christ, a vivid experience of forgiveness and a new moral life."[82] Núñez too maintains that the depth of the evangelical concept of conversion is understood through images of a new birth, of a new creation, of a new life. Conversion means a new beginning for a new person.[83] Costas explains that "we should think of conversion as a distinct moment, a new beginning, as well as a continuous transformative process."[84] Escobar emphasises the far-reaching implications of conversion for the individual which affects a human being at the deepest level of his or her being. For it determines decisions, attitudes, and reactions.[85]

Costas argues that conversion is a dynamic, complex experience. He presents a "constructive effort toward the development of a more biblical, theological and socio-historically sound formulation of the Christian doctrine of conversion" in the light of the Latin American context.[86] Costas describes five aspects of conversion when he contends:

> First, conversion means a turning from sin (and self) to God (and his work). Secondly, this act involves a change of mind, which implies the abandonment of an old worldview and the adoption of a new one. Thirdly, it entails a new allegiance, a new

---

[80] Núñez, "Personal", 1062. The use of the term "compromise with" is misleading. The Spanish text uses the verb *comprometerse* which would be more accurately rendered "the mission of the church *to commit to* political-social liberation." See Núñez, "Salvación", 8.

[81] For a discussion on conversion from the Latin American evangelical perspective in response to an article written on the subject, see the round table conversation in Pablo Perez, Emilio A. Núñez, Sidney Rooy, Mervin Breneman and Elsa R. de Powell, "Mesa redonda sobre la conversión", *Misión* 12 (March 1985): 12-18. See also the chapter entitled "The call to conversion" in Costas, *Liberating*, 112-130.

[82] Cited by Escobar, "Transitions", 168.

[83] Núñez, *Caminos*, 35-84; Escobar, "El Hombre Nuevo" in *Cristianismo*, 14-19; Padilla, "Misión", 37.

[84] Costas, *Liberating*, 113.

[85] Escobar, *Evangelio*, 47.

[86] Orlando Costas, "Conversion as a Complex Experience: A Personal Case Study" in *Gospel and Culture*, eds. Robert Coote and John Stott (Pasadena: William Carey Library, 1979), 240-262, at 240.

trust and a new life-commitment. Fourthly, it is but the beginning of a new journey and carries explicitly the seed of new turns. Fifthly, it is surrounded by the redemptive love of God as revealed in Jesus Christ and witnessed to by the Holy Spirit.[87]

Costas asserts that conversion should be understood, then, as both a distinct moment and a continuous process. It is the first in a series of transforming experiences.[88] In the New Testament, Costas observes that conversion is expressed in relation to the kingdom of God.[89] The kingdom represents a future reality which is nonetheless anticipated in the present. It is both a personal experience and an experience in the community of faith. It is a response to what God has done and what God will do, demonstrated by obedience of faith. Costas explains:

> Christian conversion revolves around this future-present, socio-personal, reflection-action reality. In the words of José Míguez Bonino, it is "the process through which God incorporates (women and men), in [their] personal existence, into an active and conscious participation in Jesus Christ…Conversion is, therefore, a passage from a de-humanized and de-humanizing existence to a humanized and humanizing life…it is the passage from death and decay to life and freedom. In conversion, women and men are liberated from the enslavement of the past and given the freedom of the future, they are turned from the god of this age, who passes away, to the God who is always the future of every past."[90]

Costas, in language not usually associated with evangelicals at the time, emphasises firstly that conversion cannot be limited to a single moment. For this limitation implies a static existence.[91] Rather, conversion should signify a distinct moment and a dynamic continuous process in life. Those who believe, live a life in anticipation of God's coming kingdom, focusing their hopes on the city which is to come yet living on earth in the light of that hope.[92] Believers should not withdraw from life, or seek to escape from history but rather they should actively participate in its transformation of that history.[93] Such participation will result in new challenges, new experiences and new "turnings." Secondly, Costas affirms the socio-ecclesial reality of conversion. The believer enters into a dialectical relationship with society because of the historical context of his or her reality. A believer evidences transformation in his or her personal life which should profoundly influence society. Communities of faith, then, are the visible, concrete demonstration of conversion in society. Thirdly, Costas maintains that conversion is a missional commitment, in the sense that women and men are put at the service of the kingdom of God. Míguez Bonino makes similar observations to Costas when he states:

---

[87] Costas, "Conversion", 252.
[88] 2 Corinthians 3:16-18.
[89] Mark 1:15.
[90] Costas, "Conversion", 253.
[91] Costas, *Integrity*, 9.
[92] See Hebrews 13:14.
[93] Costas, "Conversion", 254.

The call to conversion is an invitation to discipleship...whether it takes the direct form of Jesus' call to follow him or the apostolic form of participation through faith in the Messianic community...It revolves around the kingdom. Consequently, it involves a community which is engaged in an active discipleship in the world.[94]

Núñez affirms the understanding of conversion as both an internal and external renewal. Naturally, Núñez assumes that all spheres of a believer's existence will be influenced.[95] As has been mentioned, the believer is a member of the community of faith, called to incarnate the gospel in daily life: in marriage, in the home, in the family, in the place of employment, and in the local community.[96] Familiar as this contention may be, Latin American evangelical theologians continue to reiterate the implications of faith in the mundane practicalities of life. For therein lies the authenticity of contextual theology.

While the concept of "conversion," as understood in Latin American evangelical theology, is not a notion widely discussed in the theology of liberation, the idea of discipleship and living out faith is. The practice of faith and obedience to the reign of God are vividly expressed in terms of the kingdom of God. This obedience has implications for the present and provides eschatological hope for the future.

6.7 The Kingdom of God

The theology of liberation uses the theme of the *kingdom of God* in response to the questions which are raised regarding salvation and the struggle for a just society in ongoing history. For the theologians of liberation, "the kingdom of God is already inaugurated and in process. It is a matter of the 'already' and the 'not yet' of the kingdom."[97] Gutiérrez comments:

> Without liberating historical events, there would be no growth of the kingdom. But the process of liberation will not have conquered the very roots of oppression and the exploitation of man by man without the coming of the kingdom, which is above all a gift. Moreover, we can say that the historical, political liberating event *is* the growth of the kingdom and *is* a salvific event; but it is not *the* coming of the kingdom, not *all* of salvation. It is the historical realization of the kingdom and, therefore, it also proclaims its fullness.[98]

In 1972, the theme of the second Latin American Theological Fraternity Consultation was "The Kingdom of God and Latin America." At this conference the nature of the kingdom of God was discussed in the light of the concepts of the

---

[94] Cited by Costas, "Conversion", 255. See also José Míguez Bonino, "On Discipleship, Justice and Power" in *Freedom and Discipleship*, ed. Daniel Schipani (Maryknoll: Orbis Books, 1989), 131-138.

[95] Núñez, *Caminos*, 99-152.

[96] See also Kirk, *Meaning*, 215-220.

[97] Núñez, *Liberation*, 201.

[98] Cited by Núñez, *Liberation*, 203.

kingdom presented in the Old and New Testaments and in theology. The relationship between the church and the kingdom of God was also debated, and the association between the kingdom of God and history was considered.[99] The implications of the messianic hope of the kingdom of God on contemporary hermeneutics were presented. The influence of a biblical understanding of the kingdom of God on evangelical eschatology and subsequent implications for social and political ethics were also discussed.[100]

Writing in 1972, Escobar recognised the urgent need to recover an understanding of the implications of the kingdom of God for believers and the influence an appreciation of eschatology should have in their lives. He comments:

> The social and political alternatives have changed our continent. The change that interests us most, however, is that which has taken place within the Protestant community itself. It would seem that growth and the longing for a new social role has changed us from a dedicated and disciplined minority to a middle class subculture in which ambitions of status and social prestige have replaced discipleship. Hope and eschatological dynamism have been abandoned.[101]

For the theologians of liberation and Latin American evangelical theologians alike, the theme of the kingdom of God was particularly appropriate for the development of contextual theology.[102] As Escobar notes, the kingdom of God presents a dramatic alternative to Latin American reality:

> We reaffirm our hope that the kingdom may come soon in fullness. But as an evidence of that hope we should also reaffirm our willingness to be a community of disciples of Christ which tries to demonstrate in the context of development or underdevelopment, affluence or poverty, democracy or dictatorship, that *there is a different way* for men to live together dealing with passions, power, relations, inequality, and privilege; that we are not only able to proclaim that "the end is at hand" but also to encourage one another

---

[99] See Padilla, *Reino*. To give an overview of the evangelical theology at that time, see Emilio A. Núñez, "La naturaleza del reino de Dios", 17-36; C. René Padilla, "El reino de Dios y la iglesia", 43-68; José Míguez Bonino, "El reino de Dios y la historia", 75-95; Juan H. Yoder, "La expectativa mesiánica del reino y su carácter central para una adecuada hermenéutica contemporánea", 103-120; Samuel Escobar, "El reino de Dios, la escatología y la ética social y política en América Latina", 127-156.

[100] See Escobar, "Reino", 134-140, 144-150. See also Padilla, "La Biblia y el reino de Dios" in *Derechos*, 43-51. For more specific details on the discussion surrounding the subject of the kingdom of God in Latin American evangelical theology see Terrell Frank Coy, "Incarnation and the Kingdom of God: The Political Theologies of Orlando Costas, C. René Padilla and Samuel Escobar" (Ph.D. diss., Southwestern Baptist Theological Seminary, 1999).

[101] Escobar, "Kingdom", 14.

[102] For an overview of the understanding of the kingdom of God at the beginning of the 1970 period see Kirk, "Kingdom", 1071-1082.

in the search to make this world a bit less unjust and cruel, as an evidence of our expectation of a new creation.[103]

Escobar traces the development in the understanding of the kingdom of God in Latin American evangelical thought.[104] In the early years of the 1970s, Escobar presented the following picture of the reality of the understanding of the kingdom of God and the implications that such thought should have on the evangelical presence in society:

> The fact is that in the present decade the average evangelical church in Latin America does not see itself as an element of challenge to the established order, it denies any identification with revolutionaries, and generally avoids any demonstration that would make it seem to be critical of the current government. For this attitude, an inoffensive eschatology seems very appropriate.[105]

In his discussion on eschatology, Escobar insightfully shares how Latin American evangelical eschatology has been conditioned by history. Separation between church and state is a principle firmly maintained. Eschatological thinking generally holds to dispensationalist and pre-millenialist opinion. Escobar observes that for evangelicals in this context, who are particularly under the influence of North American fundamentalism, the social and political manifestations of the kingdom of God have become the North American way of life: capitalism, "free enterprise" and "liberal democracy."[106] Escobar explains the implications of such thinking, which appear to reflect the evident contradiction within Latin American evangelical thought:

> A dispensationalist and pre-millenial theology presupposes the vision of a fallen world, whose sinfulness is reflected in its structures and way of life. The kingdom of God will come in the future. For that reason no worldly kingdom can be considered "The Kingdom of God." The consequences of such a belief ought to be a critical attitude toward all the kingdoms of this world and their opposition to the kingdom of God. But conservative Protestantism has reduced their concept of worldliness to four or five social taboos – alcohol, tobacco, certain ways of dress, the cinema and dancing. They don't criticize, worse yet, they accept and defend the social practices of capitalism...profit as a determining factor in life, the manipulation of the consciences of people by means of mass media, the political corruption of the existing government...Some isolated voices here and there are beginning to give a sound of alarm. They are fought and silenced by the more powerful conservative ecclesiastical groups, but in spite of that they are symptomatic of a new mentality and a new attitude.

---

[103] Escobar, "Evangelization", 326.
[104] Samuel Escobar, "The Kingdom of God, Eschatology, and Social and Political Ethics in Latin America", *Theological Fraternity Bulletin* 1 (1975): 1-42, at 14. See also Escobar "Reino", 127-156.
[105] Escobar, "Kingdom", 15.
[106] Escobar, "Kingdom", 15.

It is worth mentioning that in all these groups a rediscovery of the dimensions of the kingdom of God is taking place.[107]

Escobar observes that Latin American evangelical eschatology is conditioned by the historical and social situation.[108] He asserts that this renders the eschatological thinking ineffectual in the face of Marxist eschatology.[109] For this evangelical eschatology does not reflect the word of God and consequently has lost its dynamism. The Marxist criticism of Christian hope recognises this weakness, and describes religion as "opium" which renders humanity incapable of an active response.[110]

In light of this accusation, Escobar sets out to discover the implications for the life and ministry of the Latin American evangelical church of an awakening to the reality and the centrality of the kingdom of God. To begin with, he identifies the ethical dimension of the kingdom as "a specific direction for the search for and practice of that which is good."[111] Drawing on biblical examples, Escobar observes that the kingdom values of peace, justice and love are a demonstration of the possibility of different relationships between humanity and God, between fellow humans and between humanity and nature.[112] Such an understanding of the kingdom, once again, may seem familiar. Nevertheless, Latin American evangelicals realise that familiarity with such concepts has not brought effectual transformation. They seek, therefore, to reapply the well-known implications of the reality of the kingdom of God to the Latin American context.

Firstly, then, Escobar outlines the ethical dimension of the kingdom.[113] He contends that the authentic implication of peace "means that men transform their instruments of destruction into instruments for goodness."[114] Naturally, Escobar asserts that justice and truth are inextricably linked with such peace.[115] The ultimate fulfilment of the hope of peace is found in Christ.[116] Escobar considers it important to emphasise that the New Testament does not spiritualise these hopes. Peace is brought between God and humanity through Christ, and this peace is then reflected

---

[107] Escobar, "Kingdom", 16-17. See also Escobar, "Reino", 137.

[108] See Samuel Escobar, "The Return of Christ" in *The New Face of Evangelicalism*, ed. C. René Padilla (Downers Grove: IVP, 1976), 255-264.

[109] See Escobar, "Reino", 140-144.

[110] Escobar, "Kingdom", 19-25. For a helpful discussion on the relation between Christian eschatology and the Marxist vision of the future see "Kingdom of God, Utopia and Historical Engagement" in Míguez Bonino, *Doing*, 132-153.

[111] Escobar, "Kingdom", 27.

[112] See also Costas, *Evangelización*, 13-17; Pagán, "Toward", 52-75.

[113] See Escobar, "Reino", 144-150.

[114] Escobar, "Kingdom", 28. See also C. René Padilla, "La lucha por la paz" in *Discipulado*, 181-183; Isaiah 2:4; Leviticus 26:1-6; Psalm 122:6-9; Jeremiah 29:10-11.

[115] See Psalm 85:10; Isaiah 48:18-22; Isaiah 57:19-21.

[116] See Isaiah 2:2-4, 11:1-9; Haggai 2:7-9.

between humans through the community of faith.[117] Escobar affirms that the New
Testament teaches that this ethic of peace must be demonstrated. Concepts and
attitudes must change.[118] Social prejudice must be transcended.[119] The conduct of
believers must contrast with that which is socially accepted.[120] Escobar affirms:

> The presence of a community with these radically new characteristics affected the
> ancient world, and transformed it. It began by being a new alternative in the social
> realm and that in itself constituted a factor of change. Nowadays, beyond the limits of
> the Christian community, its members, within their possibilities, can contribute to peace
> in the wider community in which they live. It is a logical result of their vocation, their
> practice and their hope. They share with the utopians the desire for world peace. They
> hope for it at some future date, but different from the utopians they do not believe that
> men by themselves will produce a state of world peace.[121]

Escobar identifies that the Latin American context, in particular, displays the
need for a rediscovery of the call for justice.[122] Escobar maintains that a biblical
understanding of justice begins with the concept of a just God who makes specific
commands to his people regarding justice.[123] Again, the New Testament
understanding of justice is not simply a spiritualising of the Old Testament
principles but is concrete action within the Christian community which influences
the wider society.[124] Padilla asserts that communities of faith will demonstrate such
principles in four ways. First, as a consequence of pursuing justice and love,
Christian communities will break down social barriers of race, economics,
nationality and gender. Respect for the rights of each human being will be evident.
Second, Christians will act in a responsible manner, not only as citizens of the
kingdom of God, but also as citizens in their local communities. Third, Christian

---

[117] See Romans 5:1, 14:19, 12:18; Colossians 5:20; Ephesians 2:11-22, 4:3; Hebrews
12:14; Matthew 5:9.
[118] See Galatians 3:26-28; Colossians 3:9-11.
[119] See James 2:1-9.
[120] See the letter to Philemon.
[121] Escobar, "Kingdom", 29-30.
[122] Escobar writes "...in the particular aspect of the relationship between workers and
management, capitalist and proletariat, in Latin America, the simple statistics about the
distribution of income and consumption show a scandalous reality. Are there men of God
who will speak for the poor or will they leave that to the Marxist?...Do we only have a
'hunger and thirst for justice' in the spiritual realm?" Escobar, "Kingdom", 32. See also C.
René Padilla, "Justicia y paz", *Misión* 11 (1984): 140-143, at 143; Lilia Solano, "Iglesia, ética
y poder" in *Iglesia, ética y poder*, John H. Yoder, Lilia Solano and C. René Padilla (Buenos
Aires: Kairós Ediciones, 1998), 49-61, at 58-60; C. René Padilla, "El sueño de un mundo de
justicia" in *Discipulado*, 47-49.
[123] See Deuteronomy 1:16, 16:18-20; Leviticus 19:15, 35,36; Amos 4:1, 5:11, 21-24. See
Escobar, *Evangelio*, 61-63.
[124] Matthew 5:20; Luke 10:7; 2 Corinthians 6:14, 9:14; Ephesians 4:24; Colossians 4:1; 1
Timothy 5;18; James 5:1-4. See Escobar, *Evangelio*, 64-69.

communities will actively work for justice and peace, displaying the hope of the kingdom through practical projects which meet the needs of the local community. Fourth, Christian communities will work for justice and peace as they struggle to defend victims of injustice and demonstrate the compassion of God in such situations.[125]

In light of the biblical presentation of the kingdom principles of peace, justice and love, Escobar maintains secondly, that the community must also reflect an awareness of social reality and an ability to critique this reality.[126] He explains:

> We believe that starting with the teachings of the kingdom, there is no room for a passive attitude nor for inability to state a criticism. For the Christian the double work of understanding the world and of changing it is always present and urgent. The immediate work of theology here is to discover how evangelical theology can articulate a critical vision of the world…The critical dimension is more than just proclaiming the death sentence on false human hopes.[127]

Costas also recognises that "an agent of evangelism cannot be neutral or passive in the face of reality."[128] Padilla too emphasises that it is imperative for the church to critique society with a prophetic denouncement of injustice and the denial of human rights. In contrast to such practices, the church should proclaim the good news of the kingdom of God in a holistic manner and should struggle for justice and for peace. Not only should the church critique the context by speaking out against wrongdoing but the church should also actively demonstrate the biblical alternative.[129]

Thirdly, Escobar asserts that there is an apologetic dimension undergirding the ethical outworking of kingdom principles and the commitment to voice criticism when these principles are refuted.[130] Evangelical theologians need to be apologists as they trace authentic kingdom ministry in the past and defend it against those, within and without Christianity, who critique such work.[131]

Fourthly, Escobar considers the dimension of hope to be central to an effective understanding of the kingdom. For this hope motivates faithfulness to the kingdom principles, even in seemingly inconsequential aspects of life.[132] Padilla too

---

[125] Padilla, *Derechos*, 21-22. For an outline of an evangelical biblical understanding of justice and peace see Padilla, "Justicia", 140-143.

[126] Escobar, "Reino", 150-151.

[127] Escobar, "Kingdom", 35.

[128] Costas, *Evangelización*, 25.

[129] Padilla, *Derechos*, 18-21; Padilla, "Justicia", 141.

[130] Escobar, "Reino", 151-153.

[131] Escobar refers to those who undervalue the kingdom principles demonstrated by Christians who have served in nursing, in education, in the Red Cross, in the fight for literacy, in the practice of rural medicine, and in the protection of Indians in Latin America. He challenges those who only value Christian work that "produces results" and who condemn social projects that overflowed from hearts desiring to serve God and his kingdom. Escobar, "Kingdom", 37.

[132] Escobar, "Kingdom", 38. See also Núñez, *Caminos*, 153-166.

emphasises the hope and the purpose which is given to a community of faith possessing a right appreciation of the kingdom of God.[133] He explains:

> To speak of the kingdom of God is to speak of God's redemptive purpose for the whole creation and of the historical vocation that the church has with regard to that purpose here and now, "between the times." It is also to speak of an eschatological reality that is both the starting point and the goal of the church...The same God who has intervened in history to initiate the drama is still acting and will continue to act in order to bring the drama to its conclusion. The kingdom of God, is, therefore, both a present reality and a promise to be fulfilled in the future: it has come (and is thus present among us), and it is to come (and thus we wait for its advent). This simultaneous affirmation of the present and the future gives rise to the eschatological tension that permeates the entire New Testament...[134]

While Padilla identifies the influence of the kingdom of God on the community of faith, he is careful to distinguish between the church and the kingdom of God itself and comments:

> If the dynamic concept of the kingdom is correct, it is never to be identified with the church...In the biblical idiom, the kingdom is not identified with its subjects. They are the people of God's rule who enter it, live under it, and are governed by it. The church is the community of the kingdom but never the kingdom itself...The kingdom is the rule of God; the church is a society of men.[135]

The implications of Padilla's understanding of the kingdom of God are fourfold. First, evangelism and social responsibility can be appreciated only in the light of the present reality and the future hope of the kingdom of God.[136] The kingdom of God cannot be considered as a movement of the progressive social improvement of humankind. Neither can the kingdom of God be understood as the rule of God in the moral and spiritual aspects of the soul. Instead, for Padilla, it is "God's redemptive power released in history, bringing good news to the poor, freedom to the prisoners, sight to the blind and liberation to the oppressed."[137]

Second, evangelism and social responsibility are inseparable. For the gospel is the good news of the kingdom and good works are the signs of the kingdom. Padilla remarks:

> The kingdom of God is not merely God's rule over the world through creation and providence. Were that the case, we could not regard it as having been inaugurated by Jesus Christ in any significant sense. Rather, the kingdom is an expression of God's

---

[133] Padilla exhibits the four principles mentioned regarding the implications of a biblical understanding of the kingdom of God in Padilla, *Economía*, 9-72.

[134] Padilla, *Mission*, 186-188.

[135] George E. Ladd, cited by Padilla, *Mission*, 190.

[136] See also Padilla, "Reino", 10-11.

[137] Padilla, *Mission*, 197.

ultimate kingship over creation, which, in anticipation of the end, has become present in the person and work of Jesus Christ. Both the proclamation of the kingdom and the visible signs of its presence made through the church are brought about by the power of the Spirit – the agent of eschatology in the process of realization – and point to its present and its future reality.[138]

The third implication of Padilla's understanding of the kingdom is the responsibility which is given to the church to manifest the kingdom and the principles of the kingdom. For the church is both a historical and an eschatological reality. Costas explains:

> Whoever believes in Jesus Christ knows him personally, is in fellowship with the Father and has entered the kingdom. Therefore, the church, which is *not* the kingdom, is nevertheless its most *visible expression* and its most *faithful interpreter* in our age. It is the body of Christ. As the community of believers from all times and places, the church both *embodies* the kingdom in its like and *witnesses* to its presence and future in its mission.[139]

Fourth, then, the church must evidence submission to the Lordship of Christ, acknowledging that the consummation of the kingdom of God is the work of God.[140] Padilla is emphatic that the kingdom of God will not be established by human beings, for it is, as the term indicates, the kingdom of *God*. It is imperative therefore that humanity does not fall under any illusion of power.[141]

Writing in 1985, Padilla observes that the relationship between the kingdom of God and history has been one of the fundamental concerns of contemporary contextual Latin American theology. Theologians have been seeking to discern the manner in which God acts in history and to correlate this with an understanding of the kingdom of God. They are striving to understand the presence of God within the concrete historical process and in relation to that, define the historical role of Christianity. Their thinking on the kingdom of God closely relates to an effort to link faith with political choice.[142] Padilla recognises that the theme of the kingdom of God has been of interest to theologians across the spectrum of churchmanship.[143]

Summing up humanity's relationship to God's kingdom, Padilla notes the dependence of humanity on God to live under the rule of the kingdom:

---

[138] Padilla, *Mission*, 197.

[139] Costas, *Integrity*, 8.

[140] See also Padilla, "Reino", 11.

[141] Padilla, *Mission*, 199.

[142] C. René Padilla, "El reino de Dios y la historia en la teología latinoamericana", *Cuadernos de Teología* 7, no. 1 (1985): 5-12.

[143] For example, in the 1960s the kingdom of God was a theme discussed by ISAL. See *América hoy* (Montevideo: ISAL, 1966). In the 1970s the subject of the kingdom of God was given prominent place in the discussions of theologians in the Latin American Theological Fraternity. See Padilla, *Reino*, 43-126.

It is impossible to exaggerate the importance of the relationship between the Holy Spirit and the church in order to understand the relationship between the kingdom of God and the church. The church depends entirely on the Spirit for its existence. Like the community of the kingdom, the church is called to be, by the power of the Spirit, a new humanity in which love and justice, reconciliation and peace, solidarity and forgiveness, new attitudes and new relationships take on flesh and bone.[144]

The evangelical understanding of the kingdom of God as the reign of God, and the dependence of humanity on God to empower men and women to live life on earth in the light of the kingdom, reflects the evangelical appreciation of eschatology. Humanity lives in the light of the kingdom here and now, but also in anticipation of the coming kingdom.[145] Kirk recognises the tension that exists between the limited change which is possible now and the total change which will take place in the future. He comments that "this eschatological tension between realism and hope is in itself a powerful challenge to be committed to change. What exists today does not conform to what will be."[146] Núñez too reflects on this anticipation when he asserts:

Liberation will not be total until the return of Christ the Lord. The transformation of this world in a reign of justice and peace for all of humanity will not be human work, but a work of God. The gospel is a message of hope – of hope in Christ, not hope in humanity enslaved to evil.[147]

Costas too acknowledges that consummate justice and complete liberation will only be brought about at the eschaton.[148] However, Costas is careful to emphasise that Christians should not withdraw from commitment to social transformation in the present, in anticipation of the second coming of Christ which will bring the fulfilment of justice and liberation. It is the responsibility of Christians to express the liberating power of the gospel message for society on earth, seeking to live out the justice of the kingdom of God in every social and political realm for the good of all humanity and creation. Such commitments will be partial manifestations of the power of the gospel.[149]

These manifestations of the power of the gospel are signs of the future reign of the kingdom of God. Reconciliation between God and humanity; reconciliation between people of different nations, of different gender, and of different generations; and reconciliation between humanity and creation are a necessary

[144] Padilla, "Reino", 11. See also Padilla, *Derechos*, 49-51.

[145] Costas, *Integrity*, 6.

[146] J. Andrew Kirk, *Theology and the Third World Church* (Downers Grove: IVP, 1983), 42.

[147] Núñez, "Personal", 1070. See also Costas, *Evangelización*, 20-24; Escobar, *Evangelio*, 53-58.

[148] See "La renovación cósmica en Cristo" and "La renovación de todas las cosas" in Núñez, *Caminos*, 167-170, 211-214. See also Costas, *Christ*, 30.

[149] Costas, "Pecado", 279.

reflection of the reality of salvation.[150] Such peace and reconciliation is a present challenge for every believing community, and is a poignant expression of their faith affirmed by Costas when he observes:

> Reconciliation is always an experience and a promise. In Christ we are reconciled with God, with our neighbour and with creation, but still we wait for the definitive reconciliation of the whole of creation. This hope moves us to commitment...concern and commitment to a more humane life, to a more just society, to a healthier environment are not alien to the experience and hope of salvation; they are part and parcel of the same.[151]

Kirk emphasises the influence of a biblical understanding of the kingdom on the development of contextual theology when he writes:

> Theology done from within a commitment to change for the sake of the kingdom has an important tactical role to play. In confrontation with arrogant power complexes it may show how, for example, God's word is applicable to particular cases...In any ensuing period of suffering and grief its role will be that of a theodicy...Theology can also aid in the search for a meaningful, positive and lasting change. In each of these three areas it will have some creative and perhaps unusual work to do. If it is true Christian theology, it should be in its element.[152]

6.8 Conclusion

In this study of the general themes in Latin American theology it is important to note the significant differences between evangelical theology and the theology of liberation. There is no doubt that there are similarities in some aspects of thought, and evangelical theologians acknowledge that the theology of liberation has provoked them to clarify their understanding of these themes. However, on these fundamental doctrines, there are distinctions which cannot be overcome.

Firstly, in relation to the subject of sin in liberation thought, the emphasis is placed not on the sin of the individual, but on social sin. An offence against a fellow human being is the characterisation of sin. Evangelical theologians observe that in liberation thought, there is no reference to the eternal consequences of sin. They are also critical of the fact that there is no mention in the theology of liberation of the responsibility of the oppressed in the face of the justice of God. Rather the biblical teaching that no one is righteous before God is overlooked.[153]

Secondly, in contrast to the emphasis on the divine initiative for salvation, "salvation for Gutiérrez is the work of God and the work of man in a synergism of faith and works...Salvation is social, universal, intrahistorical, eschatological and

---

[150] Costas, "Pecado", 281; Costas, *Integrity*, 6.
[151] Costas, "Pecado", 281.
[152] Kirk, *Third*, 44.
[153] Núñez, *Liberation*, 205.

human."[154] Evangelical theologians are critical of the lack of attention given to the redemptive significance of the death of Christ. Likewise, there is little discussion regarding the ministry of the Holy Spirit and the word of God in the salvation process.[155]

Thirdly, evangelical theologians observe that there is no mention of repentance towards God in liberation thought. There is no development of the idea of faith which is necessary for salvation. The doctrine of conversion, or new birth which is central to the evangelical understanding is obviously absent in the theology of liberation.

Kirk demonstrates the manner in which the general themes discussed in this chapter are entwined together when he notes:

> At the centre of Jesus' whole life was the kingdom of God. He was the Messiah-King who not only preached its coming but actually inaugurated it, inviting men and women to join him by entering it. The coming of the kingdom brought with it a crisis...The crisis implied a call to both conversion and a liberating praxis in line with the reality of the kingdom as God's new order breaking into the old one dominated by sin, the law, disease and death. Jesus stressed that there is no access to God apart from access to the kingdom, that is, apart from God's action and call to a new way of living...Commitment to Jesus Christ is commitment to the one who preached, lived, suffered and rose again so that the kingdom might become a tangible reality in the world. Christian theology can only be done by those who, as disciples of this Jesus, are witnesses, agents and evidence of the kingdom – the central theme of God's drama.[156]

Latin American evangelical theologians seek to be such witnesses, agents and evidence of the kingdom of God. They are committed to the search for a contextual theology which will enable Latin American Christians to evidence in their lives the reality of a coherent biblical understanding of the concepts of humanity, sin, liberation, salvation and conversion. It will become clear in the following chapters that the general themes dealt with here form a firm foundation on which to construct contextual evangelical Christology, ecclesiology and missiology for Latin America. It is evident that the person and work of Jesus Christ is central to the exposition of each general theme within contextual theology. Evangelicals seek to bear testimony to the Lordship of Christ, not only in their lives but also in their theological reflection, as will become apparent in the following chapter: the search for a Latin American evangelical Christology.

---

[154] Núñez, *Liberation*, 205.

[155] Núñez, *Liberation*, 205.

[156] Kirk, *Third*, 41.

CHAPTER 7

The Search for a Latin American Evangelical Christology

7.1 Introduction

The person and work of Christ is central to evangelical theology and evangelical mission. It has been established that the principle of *Christ alone* is one of the four fundamental convictions in evangelicalism (see section 3.2). This arises from an evangelical method which considers Scripture to be the point of departure for all theological reflection (see section 4.3.2). The evangelical commitment to the authority of Scripture results in an evangelical hermeneutic that gives Christ prominence (see sections 5.4 and 5.5). For evangelicals would contend that it is the Christ revealed in the Scriptures who has come to bring salvation, to liberate humanity, and to extend the kingdom of God (see section 6.7). As a result of the preceding chapters, therefore, the subject of contextual Christology will be examined presently.

The purpose of this chapter is to examine the search for a contextual Latin American evangelical Christology. This will be achieved in three sections. First, to gain a fuller understanding of the issues surrounding Latin American Christology in general, it is important to set the Christological question in the historical context of the continent. The images of Christ in popular Latin American culture will be identified as the backdrop against which a more authentic and holistic biblical Christology is being developed. The influence of these popular images of Christ prompted both evangelical theologians and theologians of liberation to discover an image of Christ which would enable them to respond effectively to the circumstances in which they found themselves. Second, the liberationist approach to Christology will be briefly discussed in reference to the Latin American evangelical critique of it. This chapter does not set out to expound the Christology developed by the theology of liberation in detail. Rather, this chapter will focus on the Latin American evangelical engagement with the proposals made by liberation Christology. For in this critique, the position of evangelical theologians is clearly defined and established. Third, the search for a Latin American evangelical Christology will be examined.

7.2 The Image of Christ in Latin America

It would appear that the Christian faith and more specifically the person of Christ was unheard of in Latin America until the arrival of Christopher Columbus and his companions in 1492. It is recorded that Columbus considered himself to be, in fact, a true "bearer of Christ," bringing faith and religion to a land of heathen peoples. Núñez describes the "Christ" brought by Columbus to be "one of austere medieval garb, one of the cold and inflexible Scholastics, the Christ of Spain."[1]

> In many cases the spirit of the sword was stronger and more powerful than the spirit of the cross. For many, Christ was not a saviour who had given his life for them, but a celestial tyrant who destroyed lives for his glory, through the conquest of the lands of others.[2]

Missionaries who came in the centuries following Columbus sought to contextualise Christology for Latin America. However, in their efforts to relate to the Indian culture, it was almost inevitable that religious syncretism emerged. The practices of local religion and Spanish Christianity were combined and became difficult to distinguish. Núñez observes:

> Christ, the Virgin, and the saints merely swelled the ranks of the deities of the American pantheon, while countless numbers of Indians continued to worship their former gods in the images brought by Catholicism. Behind these saints with white skin and blue eyes, the magical and powerful presence of regional gods and goddesses arose, unrestrained and unchallenged in the religious experience of their worshippers.[3]

It is clear that the Catholic Christ came to Latin America via the Iberian Peninsula. It would be fair to say that the Protestant Christ came from other countries such as England, Germany, France, the Netherlands and the United States of America. In the tradition of the Reformation, "rather than seeking Christ in the shadow of altars, in ancient parchment of ecclesiastical tradition, or in the philosophical-theological writings of the Scholastics, they [Protestants] turned to the Sacred Text."[4] This biblical approach to Christology caused the person of Christ to be given pre-eminence in Protestant theology, liturgy and service. In Latin American Protestantism the emphasis is placed, not only on the cross, but also on the empty

---

[1] Emilio A. Núñez, "Los 'cristos' de nuestras tierras", *Apuntes Pastorales* 8, no. 6 (1991): 6-13. A similar article is also available in English as the chapter entitled "The Hispano-American Christs" in Núñez and Taylor, *Crisis*, 227-236.

[2] Núñez, "Hispano-American", 228.

[3] Núñez, "Hispano-American", 229. See also Key Yuasa, "The Image of Christ in Latin American Indian Popular Religiosity" in *Sharing Jesus in the Two Thirds World*, eds. Vinay Samuel and Chris Sugden (Grand Rapids: Eerdmans, 1983), 61-85.

[4] Núñez, "Hispano-American", 232.

tomb. Christ is celebrated as the one who is Lord of life, the one who is conqueror of death and the one who lives now and forever.[5]

The origins of evangelical Christology in Latin America can be traced to the significant contribution of John Mackay[6] in his classic work *The Other Spanish Christ*. Mackay adjudges the most striking feature of the historical Creole Christ in Latin America to be what he describes as Christ's lack of humanity.[7] Mackay observes that Christ "appears almost exclusively in two dramatic roles – the role of the infant in his mother's arms, and the role of a suffering and bleeding victim. It is the picture of a Christ who was born and died, but who never lived..."[8]

The image of Christ as the helpless infant in his mother's arms awakens a sense of sympathy within Latin American people. "He is the child that cannot talk; only Mary, who holds and protects him, can at times understand his infant babblings...Deprived of the wonderful gift of speech, he poses no threat to anyone."[9] God portrayed as such a tiny child could not be responsible for the abuse of power, the lust, the greed, and the injustices of the white men. A simple Indian identifies with the helplessness and powerlessness of this image of Christ and seeks refuge in the shelter of Mary's arms. Mackay captures well the impassive Christ of Latin America and his seeming subservience to his mother:

> A Christ known in life as an infant and in death as a corpse, over whose helpless childhood and tragic fate the Virgin Mother presides...a Virgin Mother who by not tasting death, became the Queen of Life, - that is the Christ and that is the Virgin who came to America! He came as Lord of Death and of the life that is to be; she came as Sovereign Lady of the life that now is.[10]

The image of the Spanish Christ, who is the tragic victim, is vividly portrayed by the prominent writer Miguel de Unamuno[11] as he reflects on a masterpiece found in

---

[5] Núñez, "Cristos", 12; Orlando E. Costas, "Proclaiming Christ in the Two Thirds World" in *Sharing Jesus in the Two Thirds World*, eds. Vinay Samuel and Chris Sugden (Grand Rapids: Eerdmans, 1983), 3-15, at 8. An earlier version of this keynote address is available as Orlando E. Costas, "Proclamando a Cristo en los Terceros Mundos", *Boletín Teológico* 8 (1982): 1-15.

[6] See Samuel Escobar, "The Legacy of John Alexander Mackay", *International Bulletin of Missionary Research* 16 (3) (July 1992): 116-122. A similar discussion is available in Escobar, *Misión*, 43-63.

[7] See also Samuel Escobar, "The Search for a Missiological Christology in Latin America" in *Emerging Voices in Global Christian Theology*, ed. William A. Dyrness (Grand Rapids: Zondervan, 1994), 199-227. A revised and updated version is available as "La búsqueda de una cristología misiológica en América Latina" in Escobar, *Misión*, 7-42.

[8] Mackay, *Other*, 110.

[9] Núñez, "Hispano-American", 229.

[10] Mackay, *Other*, 102. See also Escobar, *Fe*, 148.

[11] Miguel de Unamuno was born in Bilbao in 1864. He died in 1936 and during his lifetime became one of the most prominent and influential Spanish writers of his generation, contributing to the arts, philosophy, politics and religious thinking. For information on the

the *Iglesia de la Cruz* (Church of the Cross) in Palencia. In the painting of the *Crucified Christ of Velasquez*, the dying figure of Christ is cradled in the arms of Franciscan nuns. Jesus is dead forever, and indeed has become the incarnation of death itself.[12] Reflecting sentiments which are not unlike the thoughts of Núñez, Unamuno writes:

> This Corpse Christ... is not the Word which became incarnate in liveable flesh...This Spanish Christ who has never lived, black as the mantle of the earth, lies horizontal and stretched out like a plain, without soul and without hope, with closed eyes facing heaven...And the poor Franciscan nuns of the Convent in which the Virgin Mother served – the Virgin of all heaven and life, gone back to heaven without having passed through death – cradle the death of the terrible Christ who will not awake upon earth. For he, the Christ of my land (*tierra*) is only earth (*tierra*), earth, earth, earth...flesh which does not palpitate, earth, earth, earth, earth...clots of blood which do not flow, earth, earth, earth, earth...And Thou, Christ of Heaven, redeem us from the Christ of earth...[13]

This image of the suffering Christ is a principal feature of Hispano-American Catholicism. The symbol of the cross represents a Christ that is dying, a Christ that is powerless. Good Friday, when Christ is portrayed as the prisoner, beaten and flogged, wearing a crown of thorns, nailed to the cross, appears to be the most prominent church festival. It seems that the tragedy of Good Friday overshadows any joy or celebration associated with the resurrection on Easter Sunday. Christ is crucified, dies and is buried; year after year, century upon century.[14] Padilla notes:

> These are the images of Christ that have generally defined Christian thought and action in Latin America for almost five centuries. They can be traced back to the Christ brought by the conquerors in the sixteenth century – a Christ that, as is widely recognised within the Catholic Church today, was at best a weak representation and at worst a caricature of the New Testament Christ.[15]

---

life and the extensive works of Miguel de Unamuno see César Barja, *Libros y autores contemporáneos* (New York: Las Américas, 1964); Howard T. Young, *The Victorious Expression: a Study of Four Contemporary Spanish Poets: Miguel de Unamuno, Antonio Machado, Juan Ramón Juménez, Federico García Lorca* (Madison: University of Wisconsin Press, 1964); www.jaserrano.com/unamuno (15/01/04).

[12] Mackay, *Other*, 97. See also C. René Padilla, "Hacia una cristología evangélica contextual", *Boletín Teológico* 30 (1988): 87-101, at 88. A similar paper is available in English as Padilla, "Towards", 81-91.

[13] Miguel de Unamuno, "El Cristo Yacente de Santa Clara (Iglesia de la Cruz) de Palencia" in *El concepto contemporáneo de España*, eds. Angel del Rio and M.J. Benardete (Buenos Aires: Editorial Losada, 1946), 130.

[14] See Núñez, "Cristos", 8.

[15] Padilla, "Hacia" 88.

Costas is representative of Latin American theologians when he identifies that the central Christological issue in the Two Thirds World is that theology is built upon what can be best described as a "foreign" image of Christ.

> The foreignness of the [Incarnate] Word has as a corollary what we might describe as the disfigured face of Jesus. The Jesus proclaimed in far too many situations of the Two Thirds Worlds has been given faces that are not only removed from the cultural, social, racial, economic and political reality of the people, but also of the very witness of the New Testament Gospels. Indeed Jesus has often appeared in the church's proclamation with every possible face except one that reflects local features. The disfiguration of Jesus has taken place both at the conceptual level and the historically-concrete level.[16]

The infant Christ of Catholicism is too helpless. Similarly, the Catholic image of the suffering Christ is too powerless. Núñez rightly observes that, for Catholics, "he was not the man Christ, powerful in word and deed, who identified Himself fully with the people, who experienced their anguish...as one of them, among them and on their behalf, announcing the kingdom of God and its liberating power."[17]

If the imported Catholic Christology is too weak and too mortal, the imported victorious eschatological Christ of Latin American Protestantism is too "other worldly" to respond to the contemporary circumstances. Núñez maintains that while the Christ presented in evangelical circles was, in theory, a divine-human Christ, he was, in practice, irrelevant for the Latin American reality. "A great number of evangelical Christians hold to a Christ who remained immobile and silent before the painful social panorama of Latin America."[18]

The silence of the traditional images of Christ in the face of Latin American reality became justifiably unacceptable within the theological circles of the political left of Latin America. They sought to present a distinct image. Núñez observes these developments:

> The Christ they proclaim is anthropological and sociological; a capable economist and skilled statistician; mass psychologist; expert in foreign and domestic politics; revolutionary theoretician; and social reformer. He is the nonconformist Christ, the activist, the rebel (even violent) who dresses like the common labourer and speaks the complicated language of the technologists of our time.[19]

In response to what was perceived to be radical "left wing" thought, Catholics and Protestant theologians alike were faced with the challenge of developing a biblically orthodox Christology which would effectively relate to the Latin American reality.

---

[16] Costas, "Proclaiming", 7

[17] Núñez, *Liberation*, 236.

[18] Núñez, *Liberation*, 236-237.

[19] Núñez, "Hispano-American", 235. See also Núñez, *Desafíos*, 31-33. For an overview of such Christological types see Samuel Escobar "El Cristo de Iberoamérica" in *¿Quién es Cristo hoy?* Samuel Escobar, C. René Padilla and Edwin M. Yamauchi (Buenos Aires: Ediciones Certeza, 1970), 9-23.

Catholic theologians turned to the New Testament, to search out a new biblical Christology. Protestants returned to the New Testament, to refresh their approach and seek to develop relevant and appropriate Christology.

In the early years of Latin American evangelical reflection, Mackay had identified the urgent need for a contextual presentation of the Jesus of the Gospels. He recognised that the Latin American images of Christ as a child and Christ as a victim corresponded to the central truths of the Incarnation and the Atonement. Nonetheless, for Mackay, this portrayal of Christ was found lacking. He reflects on such Christology:

> Incarnation is only the prologue of a life, while atonement is its epilogue. The reality of the former is unfolded in life and guaranteed by living; the efficacy of the latter is derived from the quality of the life lived. The Divine Child in His Mother's arms receives His full significance only when we see the man at work in his carpenter's shop, receive the Spirit in the baptismal waters of the Jordan, battle hungry and lonely with the tempter, preach the glad tidings of the kingdom to the poor, heal the sick and raise the dead, call the heavy laden and children to His side, warn the rich and denounce hypocrites, prepare His disciples for life and Himself for death, and then lay down his life not as a mere victim of hate or destiny, but voluntarily, and in dying ask the Father to forgive his slayers. In the same way the Crucified, in mortal anguish on the cross, is transfigured when we think that in life He had experienced the temptations of a strong man and overcame them. It was the Man who died, the true, the second Man, the Lord from heaven as a man, such a man as never has been nor shall be.[20]

Writing over fifty years later, Padilla acknowledges that the task to develop orthodox Christology which provokes orthopraxis remains unfulfilled.[21] Mackay urged evangelicals to proclaim both the historical Jesus and Jesus as the resurrected Lord. For he perceived that such proclamation and witness would subsequently impact every aspect of an active disciple's life.[22]

Within Latin American Catholicism, the revival of interest in Christology came much later than it had done in Latin American evangelical circles. The rediscovery of the Jesus of the Gospels became an important aspect of post-Vatican II Catholicism where there was a clear emphasis on the use of the Scriptures and contextual liturgy, and where worship and song were introduced in the vernacular.[23] The agitated circumstances of the late sixties and early seventies forced many Latin American Catholics to seek a Christology relevant to the times.[24]

---

[20] Mackay, *Other*, 110-11.

[21] Padilla, "Towards", 83.

[22] For a brief discussion on the origins of evangelical Christology in Latin America see Escobar, "Search", 210-213.

[23] Escobar, "Search", 212.

[24] Padilla offers a critical summary of the Catholic search for a contextual Christology, as exemplified by Jon Sobrino, the Jesuit theologian from El Salvador. In the discussion he compares the Latin American search with other parallel developments in the Two Thirds World. See C. René Padilla, "Cristología y misión en los dos-terceros mundos", *Boletín*

It was during this period, when members of the Latin American Theological Fraternity were actively involved in ministry particularly among students and professional people,[25] that the urgent need for a clear evangelical Christology became evident once more.[26] Both the desire to communicate the gospel message with reference to the actions and teachings of Jesus in the Gospels, and the need for apologetics with regard to the historicity of Jesus are displayed by Padilla and Escobar in 1970 when they seek to answer *¿Quién es Cristo hoy?* (Who is Christ Today?):

> Yes, Christ. But, which Christ? "Christ the King" of the traditional right? "Christ the great Teacher" of the eastern mystics (*los esotéricos y orientalistas*)? "Christ the pale Galilean Rabbi" of certain poets? Perhaps "Christ the Guerrilla" of the radical left? At times, it seems that each group…tries to take possession of one of these illustrious figures in order to put it to their service.[27]

During these years, an important self-critical discovery was made. Evangelicals realised that the same docetism which Mackay had criticised in Catholicism was evident in their own community.[28] Such an attitude could be traced to the independent groups of North American missionaries who came to Latin America in the years after World War II. As previously mentioned (see section 3.3), these missionaries were heavily influenced by dispensationalism. They were also products of a Cold War mentality which was suspicious of change. Their attitude and

---

Teológico 8 (1982): 39-60. This article is also available in English published as "Christology and Mission in the Two Thirds World" in *Sharing Jesus in the Two Thirds World*, eds. Vinay Samuel and Chris Sugden (Grand Rapids: Eerdmans, 1983), 17-47.

[25] It is evident that this concern to reach students with the message of the gospel significantly influenced the direction of Latin American evangelical theology. For discussion on the evangelical student movement in Latin American see Samuel Escobar, *La chispa y la llama* (Buenos Aires: Ediciones Certeza, 1978). For an overview of the engagement with contemporary issues at that time, see Samuel Escobar, *Decadencia de la religión* (Buenos Aires: Ediciones Certeza, 1972); Samuel Escobar, *Irrupción juvenil* (Miami: Editorial Caribe, 1977).

[26] The paper presented by Samuel Escobar at CLADE 1 in Bogóta during November 1969 in particular reflects the development of evangelical thought with regards to the social implications of a thorough evangelical Christology. See Samuel Escobar, "Responsabilidad social de la iglesia" in *Acción en Cristo para un continente en crisis*, ed. Samuel Escobar (San José: Editorial Caribe, 1970), 32-39. This paper is available in English as "The Social Impact of the Gospel" in *Is Revolution change?*, ed. Brian Griffiths (London: IVP, 1972), 84-111.

[27] Samuel Escobar, C. René Padilla and Edwin M. Yamauchi, *¿Quién es Cristo hoy?* (Buenos Aires: Certeza, 1970), 7. See also Samuel Escobar, "La revolución de Jesús: dos versiones", *Certeza* 44 (1971): 99-103, at 101.

[28] Samuel Escobar, "La misión cristiana y el poder espiritual: una perspectiva misiológica" in *Poder y Misión. Debate sobre la guerra espiritual en América Latina*, Edward Rommen et al (San José: Asociación Instituto Internacional de Evangelización a Fondo, 1997), 110-137, at 134.

approach to life and ministry was dominated by a focus on the issues previously associated with the debates between liberals and fundamentalists.[29] As a result,

> It must be recognized that the most common images of Christ in evangelical circles in this region very often fail to do justice to New Testament Christology. Despite its theoretical acknowledgement of Christ's full humanity, evangelical Christianity in Latin America, as in the rest of the world, is deeply affected by docetism. It affirms Christ's transforming power in relation to the individual, but is totally unable to relate the gospel to social ethics and social life...[30]

It is evident that Latin American theologians, in general, acknowledge the insufficiency of their traditional images of Christ. For the purpose of this book, we will focus specifically here on the discussion surrounding the Christological quest within Latin American contextual theology, in light of the critique made by evangelicals of liberation Christology.

7.3 The Latin American Evangelical Critique of Liberation Christology

Evangelical theologians recognise the urgency of a reexamination of the traditional images of Christ.[31] They affirm the effort to discover the historical Jesus and allow this Jesus to determine the shape of Christian discipleship and Christian mission in the modern world.[32] The Latin American evangelical response to the Christology proposed by the theology of liberation is not one of complete condemnation, but rather it is an attempt to constructively critique.

Hugo Assmann, writing in 1971, acknowledged the lack of a structured Christology within liberation thought.[33] An examination of the works produced by liberation theologians confirms this. Leonardo Boff made some of the earliest reflections in *Jesuscristo el Liberador* (Jesus Christ Liberator), published in 1972. In the epilogue, he introduces the relevance of socio-political liberation for Christology and the social setting as the point of departure for Christological reflection.[34] In 1973, José Porfirio Miranda also made a contribution to the early christological

---

[29] Escobar, "Search", 215.

[30] Padilla, "Towards", 83.

[31] For a helpful general overview of Latin American Christologies see José Míguez Bonino, ed. *Faces of Jesus: Latin American Christologies* trans. Robert R. Barr (Maryknoll: Orbis Books, 1984).

[32] Padilla, "Cristología", 39. See chapter three entitled "Mission in the way of Christ" in J. Andrew Kirk *What is Mission? Theological Explorations* (London: Darton, Longman and Todd Ltd, 1999), 38-55.

[33] Hugo Assmann, *Theology for a Nomad Church* trans. Paul Byrnes (Maryknoll: Orbis, 1975), 103.

[34] Boff, *Jesuscristo*. In 1975 Boff presented his clear exposition and defence of the theology of liberation in *Teología desde el cautiverio* (Bogotá: Indo-American Press Service, 1975).

discussion in *El Ser y el Mesías* (Being and the Messiah).[35] However, his reflection on the person and work of Christ is limited to the Johannine writings.[36] It would seem, therefore, that the first structured presentation of a liberationist Christology is Jon Sobrino's *Cristología desde América Latina: esbozo a partir del seguimiento del Jesús histórico* (Christology from Latin America: an Outline from the Following of the Historical Jesus) published in 1976.[37] This is an introductory Christology "from below" which draws heavily on the Synoptic Gospels. Kirk is accurate, therefore, in his observation that no exhaustive biblical study has been seriously undertaken by theologians of liberation in their search for a liberation Christology. Despite this, Kirk acknowledges:

> What has been done in the way of elaborating a New Testament Christology, using the hermeneutical key of oppressors/oppressed, although it is very limited, is not...[in]significant. We have been able to discover in the writings of the theology of liberation a certain typology in the use of the symbolic status of the historical Jesus. This typology has at least a three-fold dimension: the concept of grace in Jesus' teaching and attitudes; Jesus' attitude to the political reality of his time; and the Christology inherent in the 'parable' of the Last Judgement (Matt. 25. 31-46).[38]

In comparison to liberal theology, the theology of liberation demonstrates an awareness of biblical eschatology and thus to a certain extent presents a more orthodox Christology as a result. Similarly, theologians of liberation oppose the emphasis on the individualistic and personal interests of humanity conveyed by soteriological Christology. Christology founded on the resurrection of the Son of God is also criticised in liberation thought for giving insufficient importance to the life, words, deeds and death of the historical Jesus.[39] Consequently, the most memorable aspect of the Christology evident in the theology of liberation, is the unequivocal stress on the humanity of Jesus.

> It is the conviction of Boff that a Christology developed in Latin America should give primacy to the anthropological aspect over the ecclesiastical, to the utopian (in the sense of a historical liberating project) over the factual, to the critical over the dogmatic, to the social over the personal, to orthopraxy over orthodoxy. Thus he

---

[35] José Porfirio Miranda, *El Ser y el Mesías* (Salamanca: Sígueme, 1973) is available in English as *Being and the Messiah* trans. John Eagleson (Maryknoll: Orbis Books, 1974).

[36] See Kirk, *Liberation*, 123.

[37] Jon Sobrino, *Cristología desde América Latina: esbozo a partir del seguimiento del Jesús histórico* (Mexico: Centro de Reflexión Teológica, 1976); Jon Sobrino, *Christology at the Crossroads: A Latin American Approach* trans. John Drury (London: SCM. 1978). It is interesting to note that the title in Spanish differs significantly from the English. Núñez considers the Spanish title to emphasize the liberationist assertion that it is in the praxis of following Jesus that he is revealed to us in his divinity. See Núñez, *Liberation*, 223.

[38] Kirk, *Liberation*, 123-124. Kirk discusses each of these aspects of liberation Christology in more depth, see 124-135.

[39] See Núñez, *Liberation*, 210.

chooses to begin with Jesus of Nazareth, the Jesus theologically interpreted by the primitive Christian community of the Gospels. Furthermore, one "cannot simply speak about Jesus as we would speak about other objects. We can only speak with him as a starting point, as people touched by the significance of his reality."[40]

Latin American evangelical theologians, in general, consider the contribution made by Sobrino, the Jesuit priest and professor of philosophy and theology in El Salvador, to be key in the task of developing a Latin American Christology.[41] For Sobrino, the whole task of liberation has Christological issues at its centre. "The course that Jesus took is to be investigated scientifically, not just to aid in the quest for truth but also in the fight for truth that will make people free."[42]

Sobrino begins by affirming that Christ is the Jesus of history. This understanding of the historical Jesus incorporates the person, the teachings, the attitudes, the actions, and the deeds of Jesus of Nazareth which are attainable through historical and exegetical investigation.[43] Sobrino comments that "the history of the church shows, from its very beginning...that any focusing on the Christ of faith will jeopardise the very essence of the Christian faith if it neglects the historical Jesus."[44] Evangelicals have responded with the criticism that in seeking to address an imbalance in Christology, liberation Christology itself becomes imbalanced. Sobrino considers it important to recognise two distinct stages in the life of the historical Jesus. The first stage is exemplified by the proclamation of the kingdom of God as an eschatological reality which was embodied in the life and actions of Jesus.[45] The second stage of the life and ministry of Jesus is set apart by conflict and suffering.

Núñez accepts the importance of the liberationist assertion to take the Christ of the Gospels seriously. He acknowledges the need to develop Christology which corresponds to the cultural and social reality of Latin America. But Núñez also reiterates that the evangelical commitment to the authority of Scripture and evangelical adherence to fundamental Christian doctrine must form the foundation of such Christology. Evangelical theologians critique what they perceive to be the unreserved acceptance of the opinions of modern historical criticism in the liberationist search for a biblical Christology and the historical Jesus.[46] Núñez argues:

---

[40] Núñez, *Liberation*, 209. See also Boff, *Jesus*, 43, 46.

[41] Padilla, "Cristología", 40.

[42] Cited by Padilla, "Christology", 19. See also Sobrino, *Christology*, 35. Sobrino writes, "We are hiding from real problems and serving the interests of ideology if we focus on the traditional theological problems of transubstantiation and the hypostatic union while issues such as underdevelopment and its implications go unexplored...", *Christology*, 34.

[43] Sobrino, *Christology*, 3.

[44] Sobrino, *Christology*, 9.

[45] See Sobrino, chapter 3 "Jesus in the Service of the Kingdom of God", *Christology*.

[46] For a brief discussion on the liberationist use of textual criticism in finding the historical Jesus see Núñez, *Liberation*, 210-214. Núñez is careful to discuss the hesitation shared by Edward Schillebeeckx, the avant-garde Catholic theologian, with regard to the

The basic problem of liberationist exegesis is found in the evidently indiscriminate use of historical-critical methods and, above all, in the lack of a high view of the revelation and inspiration of the Scriptures. Fundamentally the problem has to do with the authority of the written revelation of God.[47]

For the theology of liberation, the point of departure is not only the figure of Jesus who emerges through historical-critical studies of the New Testament; but also the Christ who emerges out of liberating historical praxis.[48] The evangelical critique of the precedence attributed to praxis has already been discussed (see section 4.3.1). As has been observed, this emphasis on historical praxis is fundamental to the theology of liberation. When this liberationist method is applied to Christology, the discussion moves from whether Christology is "from above" or "from below," and becomes a discussion of whether Christology is "from within" or "from without." Latin American evangelicals assert that, for liberationists, the *Sitz im Leben* of the interpreter, and the liberating historical praxis in which he or she is engaged, takes precedence over the written revelation of God. That is to say, theology developed in direct response to the contemporary context is considered to be as significant as, if not more significant than, the theology guarded by Christian tradition or theological understanding developed in response to the biblical witness. Such an approach is clear when Sobrino comments:

> Even after the church has formulated dogmatic statements about Christ, Christian communities are not excused from the task that the first Christian communities had to undertake. They, too, must contemplate and think about Christ in terms of their own situation and praxis...this Christology is meant to be historical Christology. Here I do not simply mean that it is worked out on the basis of present-day history...I mean that we must be historical in the very process of reflecting on Christ himself and analysing the content of Christology...If the end of Christology is to profess that Jesus is the Christ, its starting point is the affirmation that this Christ is the Jesus of history...[49]

Sobrino also acknowledges, at the time of writing, that the "second Enlightenment" of Marxist ideology influences his theology and subsequently his Christological thinking. As discussed in depth (section 4.3.3), evangelical theologians are critical of the liberationist ideological commitment which colours their Christology:

> Emphasis is placed on those Christological elements that serve to constitute a paradigm of liberation (e.g., the resurrection as utopia and the kingdom of God) or to highlight

---

possibility of discovering the historical Jesus through modern historical criticism. This is in an effort to show that evangelical theologians are not alone in their concerns and criticisms.

[47] Núñez, *Liberation*, 214.

[48] See Núñez, *Liberation*, 214-216; Padilla, "Cristología", 52.

[49] Sobrino, cited by Núñez, *Liberation*, 214. See Sobrino, *Christology*, xxi.

practical ways of understanding and realizing it (e.g., the socio-political activity of Jesus and the obligation to follow in his footsteps).[50]

It becomes clear that liberation Christology and evangelical Christology differ greatly. Liberation Christology responds to the surrounding social context, is moulded by the revolutionary ideology of the day, and is shaped by the struggle for political, economic, and social liberation. In response, Núñez warns:

> Inevitably, He is a changing Christ, subject to changes in the social context. His traits "which are most securely guaranteed" by modern biblical scholarship will have to become adjusted to each new situation. The point of departure for Christology will always have to be that offered at any given moment by theologians or ideologists of revolution…we must ask whether the Christ described to us by liberation theology is not actually another Christ, different to the One revealed in Scripture.[51]

The commitment of the theology of liberation to social and political involvement is also evident in liberation Christology. There is particular interest in the attitude of Christ to the political reality of his time. In his analysis of the liberationist approach, Kirk identifies three specific aspects which Gutiérrez, representative of liberation theologians, considers to be sufficient to deduce a Christological hermeneutic from the Gospels. Firstly, Gutiérrez discusses the relationship between Jesus and the Zealot movement. Secondly, he assesses the attitude of Jesus towards the religious and political leaders of the people. Thirdly, he examines the death of Jesus at the hands of Pilate.[52] The subsequent accusation of evangelical theologians with regard to liberation Christology, is that in its selectivity it does not take the wholeness of the gospel seriously. For evangelicals assert that in giving superior importance to the political implications of the life and death of Jesus, liberation Christology does so at the expense of the vital soteriological significance of the incarnation and the cross.[53]

In the light of this brief discussion on the Christological emphasis within the theology of liberation, the Latin American evangelical critique will be considered. Núñez is critical of three aspects, in particular. Firstly, he expresses concern regarding the notion that the early Christian community gradually came to confess Jesus as divine. Liberationists describe this knowledge of his divine nature to be a gradual "unfolding" in the consciousness of the church throughout time.[54] Secondly, Núñez confronts the liberationist interpretation of the life and earthly ministry of Jesus. For the interpretation is clearly influenced by the liberationist emphasis on the political implications of the life and ministry of Jesus; by the focus on the political changes brought about by the kingdom of God; and by the particular liberationist

---

[50] Sobrino, cited by Núñez, *Liberation*, 215. See Sobrino, *Christology*, 34.

[51] Núñez, *Liberation*, 216.

[52] For discussion on these aspects of the life and ministry of Jesus see Kirk, *Liberation*, 126-130.

[53] Escobar, "Search", 221.

[54] See Núñez, *Liberation*, 220-224. See also Padilla, "Cristología", 41-42.

understanding of violence and love.[55] Thirdly, as a consequence of the first two criticisms, Núñez rejects the liberationist understanding of the death of Jesus.[56]

Núñez considers there to be serious discrepancies between evangelical theology and liberation theology with regards to fundamental Christian doctrine. He asserts that not only does the theology of liberation question the manner in which the Christological creed was formulated by the post-apostolic church, but that it, in fact, questions the authenticity of portions of the New Testament. He maintains that the theology of liberation interprets biblical Christology in terms of theological evolution, which in the opinion of Núñez diminishes the significance of divine revelation.[57]

Núñez rejects the liberationist proposal of a "Christology of ascent" which suggests that Jesus of Nazareth slowly became the Son of God in the consciousness of the Christian community. He asserts that this "is more a Christology of human devising than of divine revelation."[58] Núñez opposes the idea that the understanding of the "pre-existent, eternal Word who came down from the Father to become a man in order to be the mediator between God and man" is simply a product of the theological development among the Christian community after the resurrection.[59]

Padilla, in his critical evaluation of the Christology evident in liberation thought, makes three observations.[60] Firstly, in the theology of liberation the humanity of Jesus is stressed and Christians are challenged to rediscover the social dimensions of the gospel as a result. Padilla acknowledges that Jesus Christ has often been reduced to an intellectual abstraction or a figure enshrined in ecclesiastical dogmas. The rediscovery of the historical Jesus, therefore, brings compassion, concern for the poor and oppressed, and commitment to the service of others right to the very heart of mission. Padilla cautions, however, that recognition of the deity of Jesus must balance the assertion of the humanity of Jesus. For without such a balance, as is evident in the work of Sobrino, Christian action is certain to be reduced to mere human effort. Padilla illustrates this by drawing attention to Sobrino's notion of the kingdom of God. "It is no mere coincidence that Sobrino should see the kingdom of God as a utopia to be fashioned by men rather than a gift to be received in faith."[61]

Secondly, Padilla acknowledges that liberation Christology rightly stresses the fact that the death of Jesus was the historical outcome of his life. Christians, consequently, are called to suffer for the cause of righteousness. An approach which

---

[55] See Núñez, *Liberation*, 224-229.

[56] See Núñez, *Liberation*, 229-235. See also Padilla, "Cristología", 43-44, 54-55.

[57] Núñez, *Liberation*, 235.

[58] Núñez, *Liberation*, 235.

[59] Núñez, *Liberation*, 234-235. See also Kirk, *Mission*, 45.

[60] See Padilla, "Christology", 39 – 41. In this article, Padilla is making observations on Two Thirds World Christology. While Padilla addresses Christological models from Asia and Africa, the focus of his discussion is the Christological work of Sobrino. Sobrino is considered representative of liberation thought, and for this reason it would appear justifiable to apply Padilla's observations to the theology of liberation at this juncture.

[61] Padilla, "Christology", 40.

considers the death of Jesus a result of his confrontation with the Jewish leaders recognises the political dimension of the life of Christians in the world, and the inevitability of suffering. Padilla considers the separation of the victory of the resurrection from the reality of the crucifixion to have led to a triumphalistic conception of mission in history. As a result, the church has often been more dedicated to her own preservation and interests than to anything else. Padilla warns, however, that the cross of Christ must not be reduced to a political death. If the death of Christ is reduced to a political execution alone, the central tenet of Protestant theology is lost. Protestants understand the death of Christ as the provision of atonement for sin, the basis for forgiveness, and the hope of justification.

Thirdly, liberation Christology emphasises the historical nature of the Christian life. In response, Christians are to be committed to the transformation of the world, for the sake of Jesus Christ. Padilla considers this emphasis on the practice of truth and on practice related to God's purpose of renewing creation to be a vital corrective to traditional Latin American Catholic Christology. Faith should not be limited to intellectual assent. Faith should not be limited to the search for individual inner peace. Similarly, the faith and the mission of the church cannot be limited to the salvation of souls.

Clearly, Latin American evangelicals acknowledge that liberation theologians have developed a Christology which sets out to be contextual. They have constructively engaged with the liberationist approach and in this critique have held to evangelical principles. They acknowledge that the development of a contextual Latin American evangelical Christology remains an unfinished task, to which they are committed.

7.4 The Search for a Latin American Evangelical Christology

Latin American evangelical theologians have sought to develop contextual theology which is distinct both from Catholic theology and, indeed, liberal Protestant theology.[62] Kirk notes:

> The new attempts to reflect christologically from within Latin America are far removed from…theoretical debate. The search for Christ is not undertaken with the desire to produce a Latin American Christology as such. The object is to regain an authentically liberating Christ in a situation where the popular images of Christ (as either vanquished or helpless, or celestial monarch and remote) are easily manipulated by conservative forces, fanatically opposed to any change in society's present balance of power. The task of Christological reflection in Latin America…is essentially hermeneutical: how

---

[62] See Samuel Escobar, "Evangelical Theology in Latin America: The Development of a Missiological Christology", *Missiology* XIX, no. 3 (1991): 315-332; Samuel Escobar, "Una cristología para la misión integral" in *El trino Dios y la misión integral*, Pedro Arana Quiroz, Samuel Escobar and C. René Padilla (Buenos Aires: Ediciones Kairós, 2003), 73-113, at 75.

should one read the New Testament from the perspective of a forlorn and suffering humanity?[63]

Latin American evangelicals seek a contextual theology, founded on a biblically informed Christology which is relevant to ministry and mission in Latin America.[64] For such Christology should influence not only the content of contextual evangelical theology but also the communication of the message. Costas expresses the relationship between the two:

> Theology and evangelization are two interrelated aspects of the life and mission of the Christian faith. Theology studies the faith; evangelization is the process by which it is communicated. Theology plumbs the depth of the Christian faith; evangelization enables the church to extend it to the ends of the earth and the depths of human life. Theology reflects critically on the church's practice of faith; evangelization keeps the faith from becoming the practice of an exclusive social group. Theology enables evangelization to transmit the faith with integrity by clarifying and organizing its content, analysing its context, and critically evaluating its communication. Evangelization enables theology to be an effective servant of faith by relating its message to the deepest spiritual needs of humankind. It is unfortunate that too often these two complementary ministries have been viewed as adversaries rather than partners.[65]

In their efforts to develop such theology and evangelization, Latin American evangelicals have found Christological concerns to be central.[66] For as Costas affirms: "The problem of Christology...affects the entire life and mission of the church, the ethical behaviour of Christians in the world and indeed the totality of our Christian faith."[67] As has already been discussed in this chapter (see section 7.2), the Western images of Christ imported into Latin America have been found wanting. They have proven to be ideologically distorted, culturally inappropriate, and insufficient as a foundation for the life and mission of the church which exists in a context of poverty and injustice.[68]

---

[63] Kirk, *Third*, 40.

[64] Escobar, "Search", 217.

[65] Costas, *Liberating*, 1.

[66] This concern has been shared by evangelical theologians from the Two Thirds World, as demonstrated at the Bangkok consultation on Christology, held from 20-25 March 1982. The statement of that consultation is available as "Hacia una cristología misionlogica en los Terceros Mundos", *Boletín Teológico* 8 (1982): 17-20. The conference findings are also available in English in Vinay Samuel and Chris Sugden, eds. *Sharing Jesus in the Two Thirds World* (Grand Rapids: Eerdmans, 1983), 409-412.

[67] Costas, "Proclaiming", 11.

[68] Padilla, "Christology", 18. See also the declaration of the Bangkok consultation, "Hacia", 18; for an overview of the Latin American evangelical understanding of Christology past and present see Rolando Gutiérrez Cortes, "Christology and Pastoral Action in Latin America" in *Sharing Jesus in the Two Thirds World*, eds. Vinay Samuel and Chris Sugden (Grand Rapids: Eerdmans, 1983), 87-114.

Many of us Latin American evangelicals are the heirs of an Anglo-Saxon Christology formulated in answer to Protestant liberalism, which questioned or openly denied the deity of Jesus Christ. Thus what was emphasized in evangelical conservative Christology was necessarily the deity of the Logos, without denying his humanity. We were presented with a divine-human Christ in the theological formula; but in practice He was far removed from the stage of this world, aloof to our social problems.[69]

Costas explains that while evangelical Protestantism stressed personal prayer life, reading the Bible and personal morality, it also had the tendency to be "a spirituality which isolates Christ from reality and interiorizes him in the individual domain of the private-self." This has proven to be "alienating and deadly for the Christian life and mission."[70]

The fundamental foundation of Latin American evangelical Christology is the belief that "the Gospels are essentially reliable historical records and that the portrait of Jesus that emerges from them provides an adequate basis for the life and the mission of the church today."[71]

If Christological reflection starts from the historical Jesus, then we have a real fundamental content to control our understanding of who Jesus is and was. Christ, as Sobrino states, is not abstract and impartial, but concrete and particular. His universal significance is measured by the transforming praxis of his own ministry. It follows too that, if the contours of this ministry cannot be recovered as historical fact, we have no real starting point for discovering how God acts in the world.[72]

The portrayal of Jesus in the Gospels, then, is a model for contemporary discipleship.[73] For, as Mackay rightly notes: "The manhood of Christ...has made little appeal to South American worshippers. Why? Because they have known no Christ save one whom they could patronize. An infant can be patronized; so can a suffering victim and a dead man; but the Christ of the Gospels cannot."[74] Latin American evangelicals consider the new emphasis on the humanity of Christ to be an attempt to redress the balance in an inherited evangelical Christology which "magnifies the deity of the Word incarnate at the expense of His humanity."[75] Costas succinctly expresses the significance of this fresh search:

Christians need to find Christ anew because, in the world in which we live, in this complex and confused "global village" of which Christians are a part, Christ's *real* identity has been hidden from the eyes of an overwhelming number of Christians...This

---

[69] Núñez, *Liberation*, 236.

[70] Costas, "Proclaiming", 9.

[71] Padilla, "Towards", 83. See Kirk, *Mission*, 40-44; Padilla, "Hacia", 19; Núñez, "Contexualización", 42-46; Escobar, "Cristología", 88.

[72] Kirk, *Third*, 41.

[73] Costas, *Liberating*, 49; Escobar, "Cristología", 76-78.

[74] Mackay, *Other*, 111.

[75] Núñez, *Liberation*, 236. See also Padilla, "Hacia", 19.

differentiation can be done only when we discover Christ's real identity in our local situations. Without such a discovery, it is possible neither to verify our knowledge of the biblical Christ nor communicate the gospel relevantly in an oppressed world. Since Christ is the heart of the gospel, it follows that effective evangelism is not possible where his liberating presence is not being experienced and his true identity is being distorted. In order to communicate him effectively to the world, we need to know experientially who he really is, where we may find him, and on what basis we can be related to him.[76]

Latin American evangelical theologians begin with the identity and the person of Jesus of Nazareth. Padilla presents the implications of his understanding of Jesus, constructed from the Gospels:

If the Christ of faith is the Jesus of history, then it is possible to speak of social ethics for Christian disciples who seek to fashion their lives on God's purpose of love and justice concretely revealed. If the risen and exalted Lord is Jesus of Nazareth, then it is possible to speak of a community that seeks to manifest the kingdom of God in history…The starting point for *Christian* social ethics is the fact that God revealed his purpose for human life in a unique man: Jesus of Nazareth…Because the Word became flesh, they [Christians] cannot but affirm history as the context in which God is fulfilling his redemptive will. The historicity of Jesus leaves no room for dualism in which the soul is separated from the body, or for a message exclusively concerned with salvation beyond death, or for a church that isolates itself from society to become a ghetto.[77]

Núñez identifies six aspects of the biblical portrayal of Jesus of Nazareth which he, and other Latin American evangelicals, consider vital for a contextual evangelical Christology.[78] Firstly, Jesus is approved by God and the miraculous works he performs testify to this.[79] The wonders and signs convey the power and compassion of God which have no limits. Secondly, Jesus is portrayed as the Christ crucified.[80] Naturally for Núñez, as an evangelical theologian, the cross is the distinctive characteristic of the ministry of Jesus.[81] The redemptive and salvific significance of the cross must be the foundation of evangelical Christology. "For evangelicals…it is clear that biblical Christology includes an unequivocal reference to the atoning work of Jesus Christ on the cross and the need of every person to respond to it. In this

---

[76] Costas, *Christ*, 15.

[77] Padilla, "Towards", 89-90. See also Costas, *Liberating*, 50-53; Padilla, "Hacia", 91-96; Núñez, *Desafíos*, 42, 43; Núñez, *Caminos*, 30-32, 54-58; Escobar, "Creer en Jesucristo" in *Cristianismo*, 20-22.

[78] Núñez, "Proclamación cristocéntrica" in *Desafíos*, 31-38.

[79] See Acts 2:22; John 10:37, 38.

[80] See Acts 2:23; Mark 10:45; 1 Corinthians 1:23.

[81] Samuel Escobar, "Hacia una filosofía bíblica de la educación", *Andamio* II (1996): 5-25, at 20; see also Samuel Escobar, *A Time for Mission: The Challenge for Global Christianity* (Leicester: IVP, 2003), 107.

respect the death of Christ is unique and no other death can ever equal it."[82] Escobar too, draws attention to four particular aspects of the cross which he considers influence holistic Christian mission. First, the cross clearly demonstrates the truth of the limitless love which God has for his creation and his creatures. Second, the cross is the central axis of the identity and vocation of Jesus: his identity as Redeemer and his vocation of service. Third, the cross demonstrates the redemptive aspect of the suffering of Jesus, in light of the witness of the Old and New Testaments.[83] Fourth, the death of Christ on the cross is exemplary for those who choose to follow him. These familiar notions regarding the cross of Christ emphasise afresh the reality of the cost of discipleship in contemporary Latin America.[84]

> The message of the cross is, first, a witness to Jesus' atoning death. That Jesus died on a cross is a fact of history, but that he died as an atonement for sin is a foundational claim of the gospel and a central fact of its communication...This is what the message of the cross is all about: life through suffering and death and hope beyond it. There is shame, to be sure, but shame, like suffering and death, is not and cannot be ultimate. Where there is life in all its fullness, there is hope, and where there is hope, there is certainty of love, because there is God...The proclamation of the cross is, therefore, the communication of liberating news – a message of life, of hope and love through faith in the one who suffered death and shame for all that all might live, look to the future with hope, and be assured of God's love, which surpasses all odds. We live accordingly, hoping and loving.[85]

Thirdly, Núñez asserts that Jesus is portrayed as the resurrected Christ.[86] The empty cross and the empty tomb reveal the power and the victory of God. Escobar too, reaffirms the fundamental significance of the incarnation, the death and the resurrection of Christ for contextual theology in Latin America. For not only is the resurrection evidence of the triumph of life over death, and the vindication of the victim on the cross, the resurrection is also confirmation that the kingdom of God is a new reality in the history of humanity. Furthermore, the resurrection is fundamental for the identity of the Christian and the realisation of mission. It is the resurrection which creates a firm sense of hope.[87]

Fourthly, Núñez emphasises the New Testament portrayal of Jesus as exalted.[88] The exaltation of Christ means the fulfilment of the promise of the Holy Spirit.[89] Fifthly, Núñez reexamines the significance of the New Testament declaration that

---

[82] Escobar, *Time*, 109. See also Costas, "The Message of the Cross: Life and Hope through Suffering and Death" in *Liberating*, 88-111.
[83] See Padilla, "Hacia", 98.
[84] Escobar, "Cristología", 97-102.
[85] Costas, *Liberating*, 89, 111.
[86] See Acts 2: 24-32.
[87] Escobar, "Cristología", 103-106; Padilla, "Hacia", 99.
[88] See Acts 2:32-36.
[89] See Escobar, "Cristología", 106-109.

Jesus Christ is Lord.[90] He contends that Christocentric proclamation of the gospel message is both an offer and a demand. It is the offer of the gift of grace. It is the demand for repentance and faith, evidenced by a life submitted to the authority and lordship of Christ. Sixthly, Núñez gives priority to the portrayal of Jesus Christ as Saviour.[91] While such an understanding of the portrayal of Christ in the New Testament is familiar, Latin American evangelicals seek to reapply these fundamental principles afresh to the Latin American context.[92] For they are convinced that a message which is centred on biblical Christology will be holistic and will bring authentic change in the lives of individuals, churches and local communities.[93] Kirk asserts:

> In spite of the difficulties...there has been a deep-rooted conviction throughout the history of the Christian community that following in the way of Jesus Christ (discipleship) is *the* test of missionary faithfulness...Though the problems of discovering and reapplying mission in the way of Christ may be complicated, the Christian community needs a standard by which to measure its own performance – a standard which is able to call in question its own policies, programmes and practices.[94]

In his contribution to the search for a biblical understanding of Jesus of Nazareth, Kirk traces the New Testament account of the life and ministry of Jesus in light of his baptism, his temptation, the controversies which he provoked and the conflict he entered into. Kirk also examines the attitude of Jesus towards tradition and the law; towards nationalism and kinship; towards the excluded; towards money, prestige and power; and also his attitude towards the temple.[95] As he concludes his reflection on the Gospel witness to Christ, Kirk maintains:

> The cleansing of the temple was the beginning of God's judgement on a people that had lost its way. The crucifixion was the end of God's judgement on all who believed that through his death and resurrection Jesus opened up a new era of salvation, a new order, a new concept of peoplehood, a liberation from the destructive forces of political corruption, economic oppression, nationalistic xenophobia, self-righteousness and trust in violence. Significantly, in keeping with Jesus' whole mission, the last word in the story is a call to the disciples to forgive: "Whenever you stand praying, forgive, if you have anything against anyone; so that your Father in heaven may also forgive you your trespasses" (Mark 11:25).[96]

---

[90] See Acts 2:34-36; Costas, *Integrity*, 16; Escobar, "Cristología", 109-113.

[91] See Acts 2:37-42.

[92] See Escobar, *Time*, 97-102.

[93] See also Escobar, "Espiritual", 134.

[94] Kirk, *Mission*, 39. See also Orlando E. Costas, *The Church and Its Mission: A Shattering Critique from the Third World*. (Wheaton: Tyndale House Publishers, 1974), 82.

[95] See Escobar, "Cristología", 93.

[96] Kirk, *Mission*, 52.

In his examination of the Gospel portrayal of Jesus of Nazareth, Padilla recognises the imbalance that dogmatic Christology has brought to the Christian faith. He acknowledges:

> The classic Christological formulas – the Nicene Creed and the Chalcedonian definition – systematized in metaphysical language the biblical data concerning Christ as fully God and fully man and as indivisibly one, but they lost sight of Jesus' concrete actions in history reported by the evangelists. The Christ of dogma replaced Jesus of Nazareth, who identified himself with the poor and oppressed.[97]

Padilla seeks to develop Christology in which there is no disjunction between the Jesus of history and the Christ of faith. He argues: "No Christology can claim biblical support if it does not take into account not only the New Testament passages related to the pre-existent and cosmic Christ but also the evidence that the Gospels provide concerning his life and ministry."[98] Biblical discipleship, therefore, seeks to live in the way of the earthly Jesus, with the understanding of the humanity of Jesus held in balance with the confession of Jesus as Lord.[99] He seeks to emphasise the significance of appreciating the humanity and the deity of Christ, held in balance. Padilla sets out to present a reading of the Gospels in which the relevance of the life and teaching of Christ for Christians today is evident. He asserts the importance and necessity of an understanding of the historical context in which Jesus lived and ministered.

Padilla asserts that a study of the Gospels exhibits a wide range of views among the contemporaries of Christ with regards to his person and identity. The ideas vary from the suggestion that Jesus is a troublemaker, a good man, a deceiver, an amazing miracle worker, a demon-possessed man, to the confession that he is the Christ.[100] Padilla claims:

> Jesus of Nazareth did intend to present to his contemporaries a coherent picture of himself – namely, that of God's Messiah who, in fulfilment of Old Testament prophecies, had come to inaugurate a new order in which God's rule of love and justice would be established in anticipation of the end. This new order would be made visible in the community of his own disciples, the firstfruits of a new humanity marked by love to God and neighbour as well as by renunciation of personal prestige, material wealth, and earthly power. His messianic role would be fulfilled in terms of the Isaianic Servant of the Lord who would take his people's sins in death upon himself and would win for them a favourable verdict from the Father and a righteous status before him. His mission would find its continuation in the mission of the church by the power of the Holy Spirit.[101]

---

[97] Padilla, "Towards", 81.

[98] Padilla, "Towards", 84.

[99] See also Costas, *Church*, 74-79.

[100] See Padilla, "Towards", 85.

[101] Padilla, "Towards", 86.

Having established the significant aspects of the person of Jesus of Nazareth for contextual Christology, Latin American evangelicals seek to discover the model for ministry demonstrated by Jesus in the Gospels.[102] For "in Christ's incarnation, crucifixion and resurrection is a pattern that shapes mission which is done in the name of Christ."[103] Escobar summarises the model for mission exhibited by Jesus to be a call to *conversion, compassion* and *confrontation*.[104] He examines the "creative contextual obedience" of Jesus and draws attention to five aspects of his ministry: a simple lifestyle, a holistic mission, the significance of the unity of the church for mission, the pattern of God's kingdom as a missiological paradigm, and the spiritual conflict he experienced.[105]

Escobar also examines the practical teaching example given by Jesus. He asserts that Christians can learn from this model of ministry as they seek to communicate the gospel.[106] To proclaim a gospel which is built around a firm Christological core, is to affirm that Jesus Christ is "the content as well as the model and the goal for the proclamation of the gospel."[107] It is to explore the significance of the eschatological and soteriological dimensions of the message centred on the person of Jesus Christ.[108] For "it is a message incarnated in Jesus of Nazareth. It celebrates his triumph over sin and death. It confirms his authority over this world. It announces a new order of life based on the Old Testament hope of a just, peaceful, and loving world. But it is also a call to action."[109] Latin American evangelicals recognise the need to translate the teaching, the model of ministry, and the life example given by Jesus into their respective life-situations. They argue that the rediscovery of aspects of the life and ministry of Jesus will lead to authentic contextual theology.[110]

Padilla too examines the features of the ministry of Jesus which he considers to be significant. These features contributed to the fact that people were puzzled by and suspicious of his ministry, and they also explain the anger directed towards Jesus by

---

[102] Escobar recalls the influence of John Stott's emphasis on the portrayal in John's Gospel of the incarnational example of Jesus as a model for contemporary mission, as early as 1969. Samuel Escobar, interview by author, 1 April 2004, video recording, Valencia.

[103] Escobar, *Time*, 106.

[104] Escobar, *Time*, 105-111; Kirk, *Mission*, 53; Costas, "The Evangelistic Legacy of Jesus" in *Liberating*, 49-70.

[105] Escobar, "Search", 220; Escobar, "Entender", 16; Núñez, "La nueva vida" in *Caminos*, 33-84. These characteristics of the ministry of Jesus are examined in Padilla, *Mission*, 129-141, 170-185.

[106] See Escobar, "Filosofía", 12-15.

[107] Padilla, Mission, 62. In the chapter entitled "The Evangelistic Legacy of Jesus: A Perspective from the Galilean Periphery" Costas also challenges Christians to "recover the prophetic, liberating, holistic, and global apostolic legacy in the tradition of Jesus, our Messiah and Lord, Saviour and Teacher." Costas, *Liberating*, 49-70, at 70.

[108] Escobar, "Evangelical", 325.

[109] Costas, *Church*, 71.

[110] Costas, *Integrity*, 24.

those in positions of privilege.[111] Padilla considers the following to be noteworthy:
the authority with which Jesus spoke; his claim to have the authority of a prophet;
the unique relationship he claimed to have with the Father; his involvement with
those people who were considered to be rejected by God; the manifestations of the
kingdom which he displayed in healing the sick, raising the dead, concern for the
poor and oppressed, preaching freedom for the captives, giving sight for the blind;
the promise of liberation; his concern and compassion to minister to the uneducated,
the ignorant and the disreputable; his rejection of empty religiosity and his attack on
religious oppression; his condemnation of wealth and finally his call to practise
kingdom economics.[112] Padilla affirms that Jesus took upon himself a prophetic role
in the tradition of the Old Testament prophets. It is clear that Jesus had become a
public figure and that his words and his actions were interpreted as an actual
political threat. Padilla also recognises that the Gospels evidence the political
implications of Jesus' death and that this aspect must be considered to do justice to
the reality of the crucifixion.[113]

It is significant to note that Padilla is not reticent about discussing the political
implications of the death of Christ.[114] Rather he upholds the claim that "the cross
was the most eloquent expression of Jesus' solidarity with sinners."[115] In his work,
Padilla broadens the significance of the cross, commenting that "Jesus' death was
not only God's atonement for sin but also his act of liberation from selfishness and
his norm for a lifestyle that asserts love and justice."[116] Padilla asserts that the Latin
American church needs to experience the cross as more than "the cultic figure of a
privatised faith."[117]

> [The church] needs to experience [the cross] as God's victory over the powers of
> darkness and therefore as the basis to challenge every dehumanising power, be it
> militarism or consumerism, statism or materialism, legalism or hedonism. It needs to
> experience it as God's call to affirm servanthood over against coercion, love over
> against violence. It will then be better able to proclaim it as the means to freedom for
> the oppressed and the oppressors, the rich and the poor.[118]

Holding in balance the soteriological and political understandings of the cross,
Padilla maintains the importance of the political aspect of the death of Jesus without
reducing Christ to a political figure alone. The cross of Christ and his resurrection
are pivotal for Latin American believers, if the disciples of Christ will take up his
cross, yet live in the power of his resurrection.

---

[111] See also Costas, *Liberating*, 57.
[112] For the full listing of the features of Jesus' ministry, see Padilla, "Towards", 87-89.
[113] See also Costas, Church, 242-246; Kirk, Liberation, 126-130.
[114] See also Escobar, *Time*, 109.
[115] Padilla, "Towards", 90.
[116] Padilla, "Towards", 90.
[117] See also Costas, "Proclaiming", 9.
[118] Padilla, "Towards", 90-91.

The power of the resurrection is the power for a new lifestyle patterned on Jesus. The same power that raised him from the dead is the power that transforms sinners into neighbours willing to act in love for others. Impelled by it, Christians are able to act in response to human need – not in order to bring in the kingdom but because the kingdom has already come in Jesus of Nazareth and is yet to come in all its fullness.[119]

Padilla maintains, therefore, that Christian disciples should be the community which seeks to manifest the kingdom of God in history, displaying love and justice concretely. He remarks:

To be sure, Jesus' example cannot simply be transposed to the modern world. The incarnation took place in a particular situation, and we live in another situation. The point here, however, is that because of the life and teaching of Jesus of Nazareth we are not free to understand Christian ethical conduct today as if his life were not an alternative – indeed, the only alternative – for us…"Jesus does not create a rigid model of action, but he does impel his disciples to creatively prolong the logic of his praxis in the different historical circumstances in which they are to proclaim, in word and deed, the gospel of the kingdom."[120]

The fundamental issue for Latin American evangelical theologians is the manner in which faith in Jesus is to be concretely and actively lived out. The reality of faith in the historical Jesus does not allow a message which separates the soul from the body, or a message which focuses on salvation beyond death, or a community of disciples, that is the church, which isolates itself from the rest of society.[121] "To contextualize the gospel is so to translate it that the Lordship of Christ is not an abstract principle or a mere doctrine but the determining factor of life in all its dimensions and the basic criterion in relation to which all the cultural values that form the very substance of human life are evaluated."[122] Similarly, Costas argues:

Evangelization is prophetic, and thus liberating, when it has a communal base, a basic, witnessing faith-community…The gospel seeks to set men and women free *from* all godless, dehumanizing, alienating, and oppressive forces *for* the service of God's kingdom of liberating love, justice, and peace, to enable them to live freely, obediently, and in solidarity for God and humankind…This can be achieved by forming faith communities… who will be transformed by the saving power of the gospel into a prophetic witnessing movement.[123]

Escobar recognises the significance of the search for "a Christology which will have as its focus the historical Jesus and provide a basis for Christian action in

---

[119] Padilla, "Towards", 91.
[120] Padilla, "Towards", 90. See also Padilla, *Mission*, 92; Justo L. Gonzalez, "Encarnación e historia" in *Fe cristiana y Latinoamérica hoy*, ed. C. René Padilla (Buenos Aires: Ediciones Certeza, 1974), 151-167.
[121] Escobar, "Filosofía", 17.
[122] Padilla, *Mission*, 93.
[123] Costas, *Liberating*, 62-63.

contemporary society."[124] He too appreciates that the context of Latin America demands rediscovery and reexposition of the concrete actions of Jesus. With this understanding, conclusions can be drawn regarding patterns for contemporary discipleship. Disciples are called both to know Christ and to participate in his mission. They are called to display compassion as a result of immersion among the multitudes. They are called to confront the power struggle and injustice. All these aspects constitute the "mission" of the church. These rediscoveries in the Gospels cause evangelicals to reflect on the application of such principles in Christian life and ministry. Evangelical theologians recognise that Christians living two thousand years after Christ may not be able to emulate the life of Jesus exactly. But they must learn to adapt his principles and his assertions for their specific historical circumstances and thus communicate his message by being willing to live out an alternative lifestyle to those around them, inspired by the life and ministry of Christ, empowered by his resurrection and motivated by the knowledge of his return. Kirk contends:

> The way of Jesus Christ has two obvious focal points: the first in his own life's work and the second in the conduct of his disciples. In the first case, we ask how Jesus carried out his vocation; in the second case, we ask how those who follow Jesus should shape their lives. This exploration is crucial if we wish to take seriously the most all-encompassing of the New Testament's texts on mission, "As the Father has sent me, so I send you" (John 20:21). We need to grapple particularly with the words "as" and "so": how exactly has Jesus been sent into the world? How does he send his disciples into the world?[125]

In 1947, Mackay wrote that the supreme religious task to be accomplished in Latin America is to strive to "reinterpret Jesus Christ to peoples who have never in any way regarded him as relevant to thought or life."[126] There is no doubt that Latin American evangelical theologians are rising to that challenge, and have committed themselves to developing a Christology which reinterprets Jesus Christ in a contextual and powerful way.

There are Western evangelical theologians who have come to recognise that "a balanced evangelical liberation theology, which takes into account all of the canonical data on Jesus is desperately needed."[127] The contribution to Christology from Latin American evangelicals, discussed in this chapter, is considered to be a hopeful pointer in the right direction. Latin American evangelicals would certainly agree with Craig Blomberg, when he notes:

---

[124] Escobar, "Search", 217.

[125] Kirk, *Mission*, 38. See also Escobar, "Cristología", 90-92.

[126] Cited by Padilla, "Towards", 83.

[127] Craig L. Blomberg, "'Your Faith Has Made You Whole': The Evangelical Liberation Theology of Jesus" in *Jesus of Nazareth: Lord and Christ, Essays on the Historical Jesus and New Testament Christology*, eds. Joel B. Green and Max Turner (Carlisle: Paternoster, 1994), 75-93, at 93.

While liberalism unjustifiably rejects the majority of the Gospel tradition as inauthentic, conservatism *de facto* ignores a substantial portion of Jesus' priorities in its practice. Evangelicals can supply a crucial orthodoxy; liberationists, a much needed orthopraxy. Together, to the extent that the sovereign Spirit of God makes possible in this age, they could transform the world in the name of Jesus, bringing to individuals, people, institutions, and cultures the faith which liberates, heals, eradicates poverty, and brings forgiveness of sins. Such faith can make women and men of all times and places whole. [128]

7.5 Conclusion

In this chapter, the search for a contextual Latin American evangelical Christology has been examined, in light of Christology proposed by the theology of liberation and the evangelical response to this proposal. An understanding of the images of Christ in popular Latin American culture has provided the backdrop for the development of a more holistic Christology founded on the biblical witness. The liberationist approach to Christology has been discussed briefly and the Latin American evangelical critique has been considered. The chief focus of this chapter, however, has been the search for a Latin American evangelical Christology. Latin American evangelical Christology "will be judged in time by whether it helps the church of the oppressed in general and its evangelical variant in particular to proclaim Jesus Christ more faithfully, to communicate his word more effectively, and to represent him more authentically in the Two Thirds World." [129]

It becomes clear that Latin American evangelical theologians provide a *via media* for Latin American Christology. It is a Christology which traces Christ as the fulfilment to the Old Testament Scriptures. It is a Christology informed by the New Testament witness to the historical Jesus. It is a Christology which places a balanced understanding of the humanity and the divinity of Jesus Christ at the heart of the gospel message. It is a Christology which is relevant and appropriate to the Latin American context. It is a Christology which prompts authentic, compassionate ministry within that context. It is a Christology which causes believers to live in the hope of Christ's return.

> We understand Christology to be what is *believed, confessed, taught, lived, said,* and *hoped* about Jesus Christ in the Old and New Testaments, the historical confessions of the church through the centuries, as well as the particular manifestations of this confession in different cultures and continents. What the church *believes* of Jesus Christ should be manifested in the intensity of its pastoral action. It is from this belief that the *confession of faith* is given…The *evangelical teaching* undertakes the design of Deuteronomy to love God above everything and the neighbour as oneself, besides getting involved in "all the things" that Jesus revealed as his father's will. But to

---

[128] Blomberg, "Faith", 93. Blomberg reflects further on these pertinent issues in Craig Blomberg, *Neither Poverty Nor Riches* (Leicester: Apollos, 1999), 111-146, 241-253.

[129] Costas, "Proclaiming", 15. See also Padilla, "Hacia", 20.

believe in Jesus Christ, to confess faith in him and teach his doctrine, implies to guarantee the mission of *life* which witnesses to this faith through redemptive service. All of this gives sense to the worship and praise offered to the Lordship of the Son until the *coming of the kingdom* for which the church in hope proclaims Maranatha![130]

It is clear that a holistic, biblical, evangelical Christology has serious implications for the life and ministry of the Christian church. In light of this examination of Latin American evangelical Christology, the focus of the following chapter, then, will be the search for a Latin American evangelical ecclesiology.

---

[130] Cortes, "Christology", 88.

CHAPTER 8

The Search for a Latin American Evangelical Ecclesiology

8.1 Introduction

The importance of the subject of ecclesiology for contextual theology in Latin America should not be underestimated. For the themes discussed in previous chapters of this thesis are doomed to ineffectuality if there is no community to enact them. Inevitably, elements of these familiar themes will be present here as the nature and mission of the church is considered.

It is no exaggeration to say that weak ecclesiology will lead to weak contextual theology.[1] Costas rightly contends:

> Every transforming action – praxis – needs a base. The base is the bottom, the infrastructure, the pivot, or the sector that guarantees the activating of an organism. It is the most specific reality of that organism. Without the base, reality is distorted, an edifice collapses, or a movement is paralysed...The base of evangelization is the congregation. As a community of love, faith, and hope, the congregation is God's instrument for the transmission of the gospel. Its life should be a continuous perpetual proclamation...the incarnation of love, faith, and hope, the reproduction of the good news of salvation in its social context...Evangelization is not a task that belongs to isolated believers. Rather, it is a mission that has been committed to the fellowship of faith.[2]

The purpose of this chapter, then, is to examine the search for a Latin American evangelical ecclesiology. In order to place the search for a thoroughly biblical, evangelical ecclesiology in context, it is necessary to focus on three ecclesiological proposals with which Latin American evangelical theologians have engaged during the past thirty years. First, I will begin by considering the ecclesiology proposed by the theology of liberation and the Latin American evangelical critique of such ecclesiology. Second, I will briefly discuss the evangelical response to the "new

---

[1] Padilla comments that "the gospel becomes relevant in the context of relationships...the local church then is the expression of the reality of God in the midst of people". C. René Padilla, interview with author, 13 June 2003, video recording, Buenos Aires.

[2] Costas, *Liberating*, 133. See also C. René Padilla, "Introducción: una eclesiología para la misión integral" in *La iglesia local como agente de transformación: una eclesiología para la misión integral*, eds. C. René Padilla and Tetsunao Yamamori (Buenos Aires: Ediciones Kairós, 2003), 13-45, at 45.

ecclesiology" proposed and practised by less radical Latin American Catholics. For it will become evident that this interaction contributed to the definition of evangelical ecclesiology, in light of the context shared by Catholic and Protestant theologians alike. Third, the evangelical critique of the ecclesiology proposed by the Church Growth movement will be considered. For the influence of the Church Growth school of thought was widespread in Latin America through the presence of a significant number of North American missionaries. Finally, in the light of the engagement and dialogue with these three proposals, the search for a Latin American evangelical ecclesiology will be examined.

8.2 The Latin American Evangelical Critique of Liberationist Ecclesiology

It would be fair to say that Núñez is the Latin American evangelical theologian who has engaged most directly with liberationist proposals regarding ecclesiology. Consequently, his critique will constitute the foundational argument here, dealing with three main issues.[3] First, the need for renovation within the church will be acknowledged. Second, the nature and mission of the contemporary church in the Latin American context and the subsequent responsibility of the church in that context will be examined. Third, the understanding of the church as the universal sacrament of salvation will be discussed.

At the Latin America Episcopal Council in Bogotá, Colombia, in 1973 it was stated that "...there are enormous voids and gaps in liberation theology...We are working with an implicit ecclesiology, but...one of the failures in some elaborations is precisely in [the] ecclesiological approach."[4] The fact that the theology of liberation proposed a transformation of society, which would not leave the institutional ecclesiological structures unscathed, obviously caused concern to those in authority in the Catholic Church. The first foundational issue of liberation ecclesiology is the recognition of the need for renovation and renewal, evident when Gutiérrez comments:

> Because the church has inherited its structures and its lifestyle from the past, it finds itself today somewhat out of step with the history which confronts it. But what is called for is not simply a renewal and adaptation of pastoral methods. It is rather a question of a new ecclesiastical consciousness and a redefinition of the task of the church in a world in which it is not only *present*, but of which it *forms a part* more than it

---

[3] This evangelical critique of liberationist ecclesiology can be followed in chapter 9 of Núñez, *Liberation*, 241-274. See also Emilio A. Núñez, "The Church in the Liberation Theology of Gustavo Gutiérrez: Description and Hermeneutical Analysis" in *Biblical Interpretation and the Church: Text and Context*, ed. D. A. Carson (Exeter: Paternoster Press, 1984), 166-194.

[4] Alfonso López Trujillo cited by Núñez, *Liberation*, 241.

suspected in the past. In this new consciousness and redefinition, intraecclesial problems take second place.[5]

While Núñez concurs with liberationists that the church, both Protestant and Catholic alike, is in need of renovation, he questions whether the "radical revision" proposed by the theology of liberation is based on biblical ecclesiology. Again, it is natural that as an evangelical theologian, Núñez reasserts the significance of biblical principles as the foundation for orthodox ecclesiology.

The second important issue for liberation ecclesiology is the nature and mission of the church in contemporary Latin America. The context raises specific questions for the church regarding her response to poverty, social injustice, political involvement, and violence. The main ecclesiological concern, therefore, is *"what it means to be a church* today in a revolutionary context, a context of extreme poverty and social injustice."[6] Gutiérrez illustrates this emphasis when he asserts:

> In Latin America the world in which the Christian community must live and celebrate its eschatological hope is the world of social revolution; the church's task must be defined in relation to this. Its fidelity to the gospel leaves it no alternative: the church must be the visible sign of the presence of the Lord within the aspiration for liberation and the struggle for a more human and just society. Only in this way will the message of love which the church bears be made credible and efficacious.[7]

Núñez recognises that "in the liberationist view the church is defined by what it does in fulfilment of its prophetic mission in the midst of the social whirlwind."[8] Therefore, in the scheme of liberation ecclesiology, the nature of the church and the mission of the church are inextricably linked. Gutiérrez and Boff, who can be considered representative of the theology of liberation, examine in depth the issues of the universality of the church and the unity of the church. Their contribution demonstrates that it is the focus on the praxis of the church which defines the nature of the church in liberation thought. As a result, "the church is not seen apart from its mission."[9] Gutiérrez emphasises that the purpose of the church is not a spiritual abstract ministry of salvation, in the eternal sense of "guaranteeing heaven." On the contrary:

> Salvation embraces all men and the whole man; the liberating action of Christ – made man in this history and not in a history marginal to the real life of man – is at the heart of the historical current of humanity; the struggle for a just society is in its own right very much a part of salvation history.[10]

---

[5] Gutiérrez, *Theology*, 143. Cited also by Núñez, *Liberation*, 242.

[6] Núñez, *Liberation*, 242.

[7] Gutiérrez, *Theology*, 148.

[8] Núñez, *Liberation*, 242.

[9] Núñez, *Liberation*, 254.

[10] Cited by Núñez, *Liberation*, 254.

With such an understanding of salvation, the class struggle and the definite siding with the poor against oppression, become the point of departure for the fulfilment of the liberationist mission of the church. Gutiérrez explains:

> In Latin America to be the church today means to take a clear position regarding both the present state of social injustice and the revolutionary process which is attempting to abolish that injustice and build a more human order. The first step is to recognise that in reality a stand has already been taken: the church is tied to the prevailing social system. In many places the church contributes to creating "a Christian order" and to giving a kind of sacred character to a situation which is not only alienating but is the worst kind of violence – a situation which pits the powerful against the weak.[11]

Drawing on the Old Testament Scriptures and the depiction of Yahweh as a God who displays a preference for the poor and defends them from those who oppress, liberationists call for the church to be "converted" to the poor. Indeed they call for the church to "become poor" in an effort to speak for the oppressed. For "only in solidarity with the exploited classes can we understand the gospel and make it understood."[12]

Concurring with the theology of liberation, Núñez expresses the conviction that the Old Testament clearly teaches the significance of social justice. He observes:

> No exegetical manipulation can silence the prophetic outcry for social justice. No hermeneutical escape is valid in order to say that that outcry, which is also a cry against the injustice that the poor were suffering, has no application for our time. If it does not have an application for us, why was it included in the Bible, seeing that "whatever was written in earlier times was written for our instruction"?[13]

Núñez also recognises that Christ identified, in a particular way, with the poor: the family he was born into, his lifestyle, his ministry and those he associated with. However, Núñez is careful to emphasise that Christ does not display partiality. Neither does he evidence class prejudice of any kind. Rather, Christ demonstrates that all human beings, whatever their status in society, are sinners in need of salvation.

> [Jesus] demonstrated [his impartiality] in the incarnation, identifying himself with the whole human race. He demonstrated it in His earthly ministry, breaking down racial, cultural, social, and especially religious barriers. He demonstrated it on the cross, where He died for all. He demonstrated it after the resurrection when He ordered His disciples to preach the gospel to every human being, in all nations, in all the world.[14]

---

[11] Cited by Núñez, *Liberation*, 255.
[12] Núñez, *Liberation*, 256.
[13] Núñez, *Liberation*, 256.
[14] Núñez, *Liberation*, 257.

Núñez is critical of the liberationist focus on the sin of the rich and the sinfulness of structures without reference to the existence of sin in the lives of poor individuals. While Núñez is careful to support the liberationist defence of the poor, and to affirm the validity of the liberationist critique of poverty, he balances this response with a caution against glorifying the poor. Núñez seeks an ecclesiology which maintains a biblical balance, both in the attitude towards the poor, and also in the attitude directed towards those of other social classes.

In light of the liberationist point of departure, prophetic denunciation is asserted as the obligation of the church in response to the context of social injustice. The church has serious decisions to make regarding the favoured position it may hold in the established order of social prestige. As a part of the oppressive situation, the church must begin the process of proclamation and transformation by modifying itself. After self-modification, Gutiérrez proposes three characteristics of prophetic denunciation, for which the church is responsible. The denunciation must be global and should renounce all dehumanising situations, including those to which the church has contributed in the past. The denunciation should be a radical critique of the present circumstances and accepted order. The denunciation should be active and orientated towards praxis. It is evident that these three aspects of prophetic denunciation stem from a revolutionary commitment which strives to undermine the prevailing social order and motivate new forces for social transformation.[15]

Núñez examines the liberationist assertion of the need for prophetic denunciation.[16] He observes that in the Bible there are two forms of denunciation displayed: the exposure of individual sin and social sins directly to those guilty of the sin, and the exposure of sin even when the accused is not present. While Núñez questions the accuracy of the term *denunciation*, he affirms the responsibility of the church to repudiate, to condemn, and to refuse participation in sin. Núñez also recognises the need to critique the suggestion made by some evangelicals that biblical prophets did not demand social or political transformation in their nation or in any other nation. Such evangelicals would consider the prophetic message to be a specific message, for a specific people in a covenant with Yahweh. Consequently, it is assumed that the message of the prophets cannot be used to denounce the sins of our society. Núñez counters this approach:

> There certainly is a great distance between the times of the prophets and ours. There is a great difference between the life context of those servants of God and ours today. It would not be proper to impose our cultural and social system upon the biblical world or to try to reproduce in our environment the political and religious situation of that far-away age. But Scriptures have been given to us because they include teachings and examples that we should follow in some way...It is very easy to try to avoid our social

---

[15] Núñez, *Liberation*, 259.
[16] See also Padilla, *Derechos*, 18-21.

responsibility by chaining the biblical message to the remote past, or limiting it to a future fulfilment, instead of applying it here and now.[17]

The Latin American context, the point of departure, and the biblical interpretation in the theology of liberation lead to the requirement that the church enters into the political arena in order to fulfil her mission. Liberating praxis has an inevitable political dimension. Gutiérrez asserts:

> Any claim to non-involvement in politics – a banner recently acquired by conservative sectors – is nothing but a subterfuge to keep things as they are...Every attempt to evade the struggle against alienation and the violence of the powerful and for a more just and more human world is the greatest infidelity to God. To know him is to work for justice. There is no other path to reach him.[18]

The theology of liberation does not allow for a "third way" open to the church. Liberationists categorically reject the notion of neutrality. The church either takes a stand against the established order in the struggle for the poor, or the church is on the side of the oppressor. The church is either active in support of the political left, or inactivity is interpreted as support for the political right. Faithfulness to God, for liberationists, is evident in affiliation with the political left and the struggle against the powerful.[19] Núñez counters the liberationist proposal that ideological commitment and subsequent political activity are evidence of faithful Christian witness. For such political struggle brings with it the issue of violence.

In Latin America, time and experience have proved that violence is an inevitable part of "liberating praxis." Núñez challenges the subjectivity of the liberationist attempt to distinguish between "sinful violence" and "non-sinful violence." Núñez is not attempting to justify the social injustice which leads to so much violence. Nevertheless, he maintains that the church must centre the discussion on "Christian violence" around the biblical perspective and the Gospel account of the life, ministry and death of Jesus. Núñez asserts the need to continually reexamine the controversial relationship between love, hatred, ethics and violence in liberating praxis.[20]

The theology of liberation firstly calls for the renovation of the church, and secondly presents an ecclesiology which is specific to the Latin American context. The third significant aspect of liberation ecclesiology is the liberationist understanding of the church as the universal sacrament of salvation. The church is not only a visible sign of sanctifying grace but confers that grace on those who believe in the teaching of the Catholic Church.[21] Gutiérrez interprets this notion of the church as a "universal sacrament of salvation" when he writes:

---

[17] Núñez, *Liberation*, 261.
[18] Cited by Núñez, *Liberation*, 265.
[19] Núñez, *Liberation*, 265.
[20] Núñez, *Liberation*, 267-272.
[21] Núñez, *Liberation*, 243.

As a sacramental community, the church should signify in its own internal structure the salvation whose fulfilment it announces. Its organization ought to serve this task. As a sign of the liberation of humankind and history, the church itself in its concrete existence ought to be a place of liberation. A sign should be clear and understandable. If we conceive of the church as a sacrament of the salvation of the world, then it has all the more obligation to manifest in its visible structures the message that it bears.[22]

Such liberation ecclesiology also asserts that the church must no longer regard itself as the exclusive locus of salvation. Rather the church should direct itself towards a new and radical service of people.[23] Núñez comments on this liberationist understanding:

In Gutiérrez's opinion...divine grace – whether accepted or rejected – is in all men. It is no longer possible to speak properly of a "profane world." There is no distinction between a profane world and a sacred world. Salvation therefore is also found outside the church. It is not just the Christian who is the temple of God; every man is. "The 'pro-fane', that which is located outside the temple, no longer exists." Consequently, we find God in our encounter with human beings, especially with the poor.[24]

That the profane and the sacred no longer exist in opposition is well illustrated when Gutiérrez argues:

Through the persons who explicitly accept his word, the Lord reveals the world to itself. He rescues it from anonymity and enables it to know the ultimate meaning of its historical future and the value of every human act. But by the same token the church must turn to the world, in which Christ and his Spirit are present and alive; the church must allow itself to be inhabited and evangelized by the world. It has been said for this reason that a theology of the church in the world should be complemented by a "theology of the world in the church."...This puts us on the track of a new way of conceiving the relationship between the historical church and the world. The church is not a non-world; it is humanity itself attentive to the word. It is the People of God which lives in history and is orientated toward the future promised by the Lord. It is, as Teilhard de Chardin said, the "reflectively Christified portion of the world." The church-world relationship thus should be seen not in spacial terms, but rather in dynamic and temporal ones.[25]

Boff too reflects on this fresh understanding of the mission of the church. He identifies three stages in liberation ecclesiology, beginning with mission and developing towards the notion of universality. In the first stage, "the church projected itself *from outside the world* as a *sacrament-instrument* necessary for salvation."[26] In the belief that the church had the monopoly on the truth, the effort

---

[22] Gutiérrez, *Theology*, 147.

[23] Núñez, *Liberation*, 244.

[24] Núñez, *Liberation*, 244.

[25] Gutiérrez, *Theology*, 147.

[26] Núñez, *Liberation*, 246.

was made to establish the ecclesiastical structure across the world. In the second stage, supported by Vatican II, "the church fulfils its mission from inside the world, as a sacrament-sign of universal salvation."[27] The church is evidence of both the grace it communicates, and the grace already present in the world.

> Its mission is not to mould everyone into its historical model but to defend and deepen that which is good and legitimate in all human manifestations…That's why this church can show itself flexible in cooperation with all movements which seek a truly human development and favour openness towards others and towards God…The great church, the grand church is made up of all those who anonymously live in the realization of truth and good in all human dimensions.[28]

In the third stage, Boff considers it necessary to "establish the bond between mission and universality within the sub-world, that is, the world of the poor, of the non-men, those who live in sub-human conditions due to social injustice."[29] Thus, by defending the cause of such people in society, the church becomes truly universal. Boff explains:

> The presence of the church and its evangelization assume in this way a political dimension in the struggle against the situation of dependence and oppression. In such a situation, to evangelise means to bring crisis and conflict to the creators of dependence and oppression.[30]

Núñez is critical of this liberationist understanding of the nature of the church. He finds a lack of biblical evidence for the liberationist notion of universality, and also considers such an understanding of universality to be in danger of universalism. That is to say, he perceives a dangerous tendency which begins from correctly seeing everyone as created and loved by God, and moves towards incorrectly seeing everyone as a follower or disciple of God. In light of New Testament teaching, Núñez regards the church as having been drawn out of the world and given to Christ. Thus, he argues that the church is in the world but does not belong to the world. The New Testament emphasises that the church has been sent to be the salt of the earth and the light of the world.[31] In contrast to the theologians of liberation, therefore, Núñez identifies a division between those who accept Christ and those

---

[27] Núñez, *Liberation*, 246.

[28] Cited by Núñez, *Liberation*, 246. Boff completed his specialist studies in Dogmatic Theology at the University of Munich under Karl Rahner. For a helpful discussion on the influence of Rahner in Boff's work, particularly the use and application of Rahner's concept of anonymous Christianity see Muskus, *Origins*, 125-140, at 137.

[29] Núñez, *Liberation*, 247.

[30] Cited by Núñez, *Liberation*, 247.

[31] John 17; Matthew 5:13-16; 1 Peter 2:9-10. See also Juan Carlos Ortiz, "Iglesia y sociedad" in *Fe cristiana y Latinoamérica hoy*, ed. C. René Padilla (Buenos Aires: Ediciones Certeza, 1974), 185-208, at 190-194.

who reject him.[32] For this reason, he considers the church to be "both a sign of saving grace and a sign of divine judgement upon the impenitent."[33]

Núñez also considers the liberationist notion of universality in the church to lead inevitably to a false concept of the unity of the church. Núñez exemplifies this concern in his critique of the three aspects of the New Testament term *koinonia*, that is communion or community, which Gutiérrez considers foundational to ecclesiology. First, Gutiérrez emphasises the New Testament church practice of the common ownership of possessions and sharing out of necessity. Second, Gutiérrez draws attention to the union of the faithful with Christ through the celebration of the Eucharist. Third, Gutiérrez stresses the significance of the union of Christians with the triune God; the Father, the Son and the Holy Spirit.[34]

Gutiérrez and the theologians of liberation relate these aspects of the unity of the church to the social reality and working for justice. The church must take the side of the oppressed in order to redress the imbalance of the unjust society in which the church exists. In this struggle against the causes of deep division among humanity, the church is an authentic sign of unity.[35] Núñez, however, describes this as a form of *secular ecumenism*. This secular ecumenism is evident as the Catholic Church opens the door for cooperation between non-Christian, Christian, and indeed anti-Christian movements in the struggle for the transformation of society. Núñez is critical that this liberationist struggle for unity does not reflect the biblical understanding of ecclesiology. Núñez asserts that thorough biblical exegesis displays that while there were distinct social classes in the early Christian community, Jesus and the apostles did not place an emphasis on class struggle or rebellion. Nor did they lead revolts. Núñez contends:

> Christianity was not destined to be just one more revolutionary movement among the many recorded in history. Its enormous potential for social changes has to be developed in other ways, by other means, not as the world and liberation theologians suggest. The message of the gospel contains powerful seeds of liberation; but they do not germinate in the way of the world, in soil fertilized by anti-human, or anti-Christian ideologies (whether of the left or of the right).[36]

Núñez traces the New Testament understanding of the unity of the church and concludes that it is a unity which is entered into explicitly. He also observes that the unity of the church, which Christ prays for, both includes and excludes. For it is dependent on whether a person receives or rejects the gospel. The unity experienced in the New Testament faith-community, therefore, is deep, spiritual and practical. Núñez explains that "Christian unity is much more than an ecclesiastical organisation – intraecclesiastical or interecclesiastical; it is much more than a social

---

[32] John 3:36, 14:6; Acts 14:12; 2 Thessalonians 1:3-10; 1 Timothy 2:5.

[33] Núñez, *Liberation*, 248.

[34] Núñez, *Liberation*, 248.

[35] Núñez, *Liberation*, 249.

[36] Núñez, *Liberation*, 251.

and political organisation."[37] Biblical Christian unity comes, not through human efforts for peace, but as a result of the person and work of the Son, sent by the Father, and through the powerful ministry of the Holy Spirit. While the church does not "create" the unity as such, Núñez emphasises that the church has a responsibility to keep the unity. He recognises that the deeply divided contemporary church is a "painful spectacle of a church that we ourselves have fragmented in practice."[38]

Despite the identification of the three ecclesiological issues of the renovation of the church, the relevance of the church, and the role of the church as the universal sacrament of salvation evident in the theology of liberation, Núñez considers that, as yet, there is no systematisation of liberation ecclesiology. It is necessary to glean information from across liberationist works to form an understanding of their teaching on the church. The foundational criticism Núñez has is the lack of reference made to the abundant New Testament material, which he considers would give a biblical base and a coherent structure to liberationist ecclesiology.[39] Liberationist method, as discussed in chapter four, is clearly employed in the liberationist approach to ecclesiology. For context, praxis and ideology are given utmost priority. Consequently, the New Testament understanding of the church and the world becomes ever more blurred in liberation thought.

Nevertheless, Núñez recognises the following positive aspects in the liberationist understanding of the church:

> The possibility of salvation outside the institutional, hierarchical church is underscored; clerical arrogance is put aside by recognising the church is the totality of the people of God; strong emphasis is given to the church as a community or fraternal body; it is recognised that in the past the church was allied with the powerful and became rich in the midst of a people steeped in poverty; there is a call for the profound renovation of the church; there is a demand for Christians to live a life of authentic love and total commitment to the service of one's neighbour…Their attitude moves us to ask whether we are not simply playing at being Christians, unwilling to leave our religious comfort in order to walk an extra mile for the sake of the gospel.[40]

Engagement with the ecclesiology proposed by liberation theology causes Latin American evangelical theologians to reevaluate the foundations of evangelical ecclesiological thought. It forces evangelicals to reflect on the theological, historical and cultural influences which have moulded their understanding of the church. It also prompts Latin American evangelical theologians to reexamine the biblical presentation of the church:

> It is evident that many of us Latin American evangelicals have been satisfied with repeating an ecclesiology formulated in other latitudes, in a cultural and social context

---

[37] Núñez, *Liberation*, 253.

[38] Núñez, *Liberation*, 253.

[39] See for example, Matthew 16:16-18; 1 Corinthians 12-14; Ephesians 1-4; Colossians 1; 1 Peter 2:1-10.

[40] Núñez, *Liberation*, 274.

very different from that of Latin America, in a time far from our own. It is now our turn to answer the challenge of liberation theology by producing an ecclesiology that is rooted in the Scriptures and responds to the particular needs of the church and the Latin American people.[41]

While there have been objections to the more radical liberationist assumptions, there is no doubt that the influence of liberation theology led to changes in the Catholic ecclesiastical structures and in the pastoral approach to ministry. What emerged in Latin America, particularly in the years following the Vatican II Council, is referred to as the "new ecclesiology."[42] This new ecclesiology is distinct from liberation ecclesiology, yet demonstrates the need for a reassessment of the life and the ministry of the Latin American Catholic Church. The propositions and practice of the new ecclesiology will be examined next, in order to place the search for a biblical Latin American evangelical ecclesiology in context.

8.3 The Challenge of the "New Ecclesiology"

In 1987, Padilla wrote an article observing the dramatic changes in the Latin American Catholic Church in the twenty years preceding his assessment.

> To be sure, the old church, sadly hampered by its heavy hierarchical structure, is still there, and one wonders whether all the changes will not in the end be neutralized by it. The fact remains, however, that a new church is taking shape in the womb of the old and that this may rightly be regarded as the most promising development within Roman Catholicism today.[43]

Padilla affirms that the origin of this grassroots movement may date back as early as the 1950s when groups of nuns and priests sought to experiment with new approaches in response to the challenge of the socio-economic situation, and indeed the challenge presented by Protestantism. Padilla explains that, at that time, evangelical Protestant churches were proving to be an attractive model for the common people:

> In line with the best evangelical congregational tradition, singing, praying and studying the Bible together, sharing problems and resources with one another, and making decisions and serving in a small community became essential aspects of the Christian experience of people who had previously known the body of Christ primarily as dogma

---

[41] Núñez, *Liberation*, 274.

[42] See C. René Padilla, "A New Ecclesiology in Latin America", *International Bulletin of Missionary Research* 11, no. 4 (1987): 156-164.

[43] Padilla, "Ecclesiology", 156.

– "the Mystical Body of Christ" – or as a hierarchical society in which they were passive members.[44]

Foundational to the new ecclesiology is the formation of *comunidades eclesiales de base* (grassroots ecclesial communities).[45] These are small groups of peasants and workers who meet together to read the Bible, to pray and to discuss issues relevant to their daily lives.[46] The "function is to articulate the communal experience of a growing number of Christians...who are rediscovering the meaning of the Christian faith for practical life in a context of oppression and poverty."[47] Padilla comments on the significant influence of these faith communities in the lives of poor Latin Americans:

> In the grassroots communities the rejects of society are discovering their own worth. They are learning that the evils of poverty and marginalization are not their God-given fate and that they have the power to change their situation through solidarity and mutual help, local initiatives, and a common struggle for justice. The power of oppression is thus broken and hope of a better future is born because the basis is laid for power to be exercised *from the bottom up*, not only in the church but also in the society.[48]

While there is no doubt that the base ecclesial communities represent potential for social activism, and that many of these communities came under the influence of liberation theology, they also represent a more conservative element within Catholicism seeking change at grassroots level. Escobar, for example, notes:

> Christian Base Communities have been hailed by the Roman Catholic bishops of Latin America as a cause for "joy and hope in the church." The bishops also said that such communities "embody the church's preferential love for the common people. In them their religiosity is expressed, valued and purified; and they are given a concrete opportunity to share in the task of the church and to work committedly for the transformation of the world."[49]

---

[44] Padilla, "Ecclesiology", 157. See also Escobar, "Five Hundred", 35; Padilla, "Actors", 86.

[45] It is important to note that the English translation "basic" or "base" is not an adequate translation of the term *de base*. In the phrase *communidades eclesiales de base*, the connotations implied are social, political, economic, cultural and theological aspects of those grassroot communities. *De base* refers to the large majority of lay people in the Latin American Roman Catholic Church who are poor, uneducated and powerless. See Padilla, "Ecclesiology", footnote 1, 163.

[46] Escobar "Grass Roots", 94-97.

[47] Padilla, "Ecclesiology", 156.

[48] Padilla, "Ecclesiology", 158. See also Escobar, "Conflict", 131; Escobar, "Espiritual", 123.

[49] Escobar, "Grass Roots", 95. See also Escobar, *Changing*, 72.

Escobar observes that the fact these communities are established at grassroot level, and the fact that they identify themselves as Christian communities, has led to controversy. For there are political implications evident in the collective feature of the communities, and yet the potential for radical action is held in balance by the relationship with the hierarchy and official teaching of the Catholic Church.[50]

Padilla identifies what he considers to be the three essential tenets of this new ecclesiology. It affirms that the church is of the poor and for the poor. It maintains a commitment to the priesthood of all believers.[51] It acknowledges the prophetic mission of the church, while it does not promote the radicalism of the liberationist approach.[52] It is evident, therefore, that such base ecclesial communities present a model of effective *social, ministerial,* and *missional* practice.

Firstly, base ecclesial communities present a *social* challenge. Padilla acknowledges that, like the members of the base ecclesial communities, the majority of Latin American Protestant Christians are poor and oppressed people. He observes, however, that the value system adhered to in Protestant churches can condition members to be more concerned about social respectability and influence than commitment to the gospel message. He comments: "Christianity is thus turned into a means to accommodate the *status quo,* the biblical message is domesticated, and the church becomes a fortress of conservative politics, oblivious of the needs of the poor and oppressed."[53] Padilla observes that such Protestant churches fear the kind of movement that gave them birth, or that revitalised their churches over the years. Evangelical churches, then, must face the social challenge presented by the base ecclesial communities to take the poor seriously and to be available to the marginalized in society.

Secondly, the grassroots ecclesial communities demonstrate a *ministerial* alternative for evangelical churches. Padilla maintains that the rediscovery of the missionary character of the whole evangelical church is needed. For in many cases, emphasis is placed on the ministry of the ordained, and as a result the ministry of the lay person is restricted.[54] He identifies the attitude within some evangelical churches that evangelization is not the responsibility of every believer, but rather the responsibility of the evangelist or those who communicate on radio or television. Padilla also recognises the challenge placed by base ecclesial communities in the approach taken to the Scriptures. For community members are encouraged to study

---

[50] Escobar, "Grass Roots", 96. Escobar illustrates this tension with a brief discussion on the circumstances of the base ecclesial communities in Nicaragua during the civil war.

[51] See also Kirk, *World*, 124-127; see also Padilla, "Toda la iglesia es misionera" in *Discipulado*, 86-89; Alberto Fernando Roldán, "El sacerdocio de todos los creyentes y la misión integral" in *La iglesia local como agente de transformación: una eclesiología para la misión integral,* eds. C. René Padilla and Tetsunao Yamamori (Buenos Aires: Ediciones Kairós, 2003), 103-132.

[52] Padilla, "Ecclesiology", 158.

[53] Padilla, "Ecclesiology", 162.

[54] See also C. René Padilla, "La iglesia: un pueblo sacerdote". TMs (photocopy), The Latin American Theological Fraternity, Buenos Aires, (n.d.), 1-20.

the Bible and discern the relationship between faith and life in their specific context. On the vocational level, Padilla considers the new ecclesiology to present a broader understanding of the concept of ministry. Service to God includes not only pastoral and teaching ministries but service through professions and trades in every area of human life. The variety of leadership, and the variety of contributions which are made by believers, has provoked wide discussion in evangelical circles.[55] The Latin American Theological Fraternity reflects on such a ministerial model in the final document of its consultation on *New Alternatives for Theological Education*:

> All members of the church need an integrated understanding of its mission and the motivation for actively participating in it. All have received gifts and ministries which they ought to discover and develop in service to God and to their neighbours. Every one needs theological education and the possibility of being involved in theological work. From this perspective, churches will complete their teaching task to the measure that, on their own, or in cooperation with others in the same area or city, they establish programs that help all their members to discover and exercise their gifts in the development of different ministries.[56]

Thirdly, Padilla recognises the *missional* example presented by the base ecclesial communities. The new ecclesiology is a reminder that the place to begin social transformation in response to the gospel message is within the local church. For the local community of faith is called to a prophetic mission. "The task...has to do with God's purpose to unify the human race and to restore his dominion in all dimensions of life and over the totality of creation."[57]

The new ecclesiology proposes to establish base ecclesial communities which are of the poor, from the poor and for the poor. There is no doubt that poor evangelical churches have also made a significant contribution in a similar context. Escobar reflects on such grassroot evangelical churches which are not connected to world communities, or denominational families; which have no access to funds or to the press; and which have no diplomatic ties.[58]

> The popular Protestant churches are popular movements in themselves. Their pastors and leaders do not have to identify with the poor; they are poor. They do not have a

---

[55] For further discussion on the biblical understanding of the priesthood of all believers and the discussion surrounding the issue during the Reformation and following the Vatican II Council see Padilla, "Pueblo"; C. René Padilla, "La misión cristiana en las Américas una perspectiva latinoamericana" in *Misión en el camino: ensayos en homenaje a Orlando Costas*, Samuel Escobar et al (Buenos Aires: Fraternidad Teológica Latinoamericana, 1992), 67-94, at 92; see also Jerjes Ruiz, "The Priesthood of All Believers" in *Faith born in the Struggle for Life*, ed. Dow Kirkpatrick (Grand Rapids: Eerdmans, 1988), 98-115. See also Emilio A. Núñez, "Hacia el liderato cristiano", *Apuntes Pastorales* 12, no. 3 (1995): 12-13.

[56] Cited by Padilla, "Ecclesiology", 163. For further discussion see C. René Padilla, ed, *Nuevas alternativas de educación teológica* (Buenos Aires: Nueva Creación, 1986).

[57] Padilla, "Ecclesiology", 163.

[58] See Escobar, *Time*, 17.

social agenda but an intense spiritual agenda, and it is through that agenda that they have been able to have a social impact. It could be said that these popular Protestant churches have become alternative societies that create a protective close world where people are accepted and become actors not on the basis of what gives them status but on the basis of values that come from their belief in the kingdom of God.[59]

In the search for a contextual Latin American ecclesiology, evangelical theologians, liberation theologians, and less radical Catholic theologians have all made significant contributions. In contrast, the third ecclesiological proposal to be considered in this chapter was developed outside the Latin American context. Nonetheless, it demanded a critical response. For missionaries and those influenced by the Church Growth theory sought to put such principles to work in Latin America.

8.4 The Latin American Evangelical Critique of Church Growth Theory

Latin American evangelical theologians have found it necessary to constructively critique the ecclesiology developed by the "Church Growth" school of thought.[60] In this way, Latin American evangelical theologians have dialogued and engaged with evangelical theologians internationally, particularly those from North America. This section does not set out to detail every aspect of the Church Growth movement, but rather seeks to highlight the specific critique which Latin American evangelicals make against the ecclesiology it proposes. Costas summarises the foundational criticism when he contends:

> There is a fundamental difference between the growth of the church and that of a business. The former is the result of the efficacious work of faith; the latter, of the efficiency of applied science, of technology. The growth of a business is the result of sound marketing analysis, planning, promotion, effective controls, and supervision. It is influenced, to be sure, by certain ethical criteria. Nevertheless, it operates on the basis of economic principles, not of ethical standards. That is, sound investment can produce sound profit, provided there are favourable conditions and an appropriate climate. But the church is something else. It is a community of faith. Its mission needs to be seen as the efficacious work of faith in the horizon of God's eschatological kingdom. It must be

---

[59] Escobar, "Grass Roots", 101. See also Escobar, "Conflict", 132.

[60] For an historical overview of the movement see Orlando E. Costas, "Origen y desarrollo del movimiento de crecimiento de la iglesia", *Misión* 8 (1984): 6-13; Orlando E. Costas, "Iglecrecimiento, el movimiento ecuménico y el 'evangelicalismo'", *Misión* 9 (1984): 56-60. For evangelical responses to Church Growth Theory see chapter 7 "An Appraisal of Church Growth Theory" in Costas, *Church*, 123-149; Samuel Escobar, "El crecimiento de la Iglesia en América Latina y la teoría de 'inglecrecimiento'", *Misión* 27 (1989): 15-19. For further discussion on the subject of church growth during this period, from a variety of viewpoints see Wilbert R. Shenk, ed., *Exploring Church Growth* (Grand Rapids: Eerdmans, 1983).

evaluated, therefore, not on the basis of its present institutional success, but on the basis of the future of God's kingdom.[61]

Padilla focuses on the unity of the church and the homogeneous unit principle proposed by Donald McGavran of the Church Growth movement. In light of the New Testament and the apostolic witness,[62] Padilla counters the principle and succinctly emphasises the Latin American evangelical position:

> Throughout the entire New Testament it is taken for granted that the oneness of the people of God is the oneness that transcends all outward distinctions. The idea is that with the coming of Jesus Christ all barriers that divide humankind have been broken down and a new humanity is now taking shape *in* and *through* the church. God's purpose in Jesus Christ includes the oneness of the human race, and that oneness becomes visible in the church.[63]

First, Padilla examines God's purpose of unity in Christ as it is presented in the New Testament. He asserts that the church is not an abstract illustration of unity but rather a new community in which the decisive factor is new life in Christ. In the light of Galatians 3:28,[64] Padilla argues:

> No justice is done to the text unless it is taken to mean that in Jesus Christ a new reality has come into being – a unity based on faith in him, in which membership is in no way dependent upon race, social status or sex. No mere "spiritual" unity, but a concrete community made up of Jews and Gentiles, slaves and free, men and women, all of them as equal members of the Christ solidarity.[65]

In contrast, McGavran defends the assertion that "men like to become Christians without crossing racial, linguistic or class boundaries."[66] Padilla demonstrates that this notion is not consistent with New Testament teaching. On the contrary, Padilla affirms that personal preference should not be an issue when one is incorporated into the new humanity under the Lordship of Christ. In the church, identity is found in Jesus Christ alone. Identity is not found in race, in culture, in sex or in class. Rather, the reconciliation between these groups within the community of faith is a clear reflection of the gospel:

---

[61] Costas, *Christ*, 53. See also Escobar, "Espiritual", 126; see also Kirk, "Kingdom", 1078-1080.

[62] C. René Padilla, "The Unity of the Church and the Homogenous Unit Principle" in *Exploring Church Growth*, ed. William R. Shenks (Grand Rapids: Eerdmans, 1983), 285-303, at 299-302.

[63] Padilla, *Mission*, 142. See also Escobar, "Crecimiento", 19.

[64] Galatians 3:28 reads "There is neither Jew nor Greek, slave nor free, male nor female, for you are all one in Christ Jesus."

[65] Padilla, *Mission*, 145. See also Núñez, *Caminos*, 58-63; Colossians 3:11-22, 4:11; Galatians 6:16; Philemon 16; 1 Corinthians 12:13.

[66] Cited by Padilla, *Mission*, 146.

Already, in anticipation of the end, a new humanity has been created in Jesus Christ, and those who are incorporated in him form a unity wherein all the divisions that separate people in the old humanity are done away with. The original unity of the human race is thus restored; God's purpose of unity in Jesus Christ is thus made historically visible.[67]

Kirk too concurs with Padilla that the crossing of racial, linguistic and class boundaries is a demonstration of the reconciliation possible within the community of faith. Once more, Kirk contends that this unity does not depend on personal preference but on a new understanding of what it means to be part of the family of the church.

The metaphors that the New Testament uses to describe the church – body, stones of a temple, family, race, people, priesthood – all emphasise the mutual dependence of each member upon all the others. Community implies both belonging and commitment to one another. Supremely it means accepting one another as those whom God himself has accepted because their hostility to him has been overcome in the death and resurrection of Jesus. All individual members of the community, however we may react to them on a personal level, have a unique relationship to us because we and they now belong equally to Christ.[68]

Second, Padilla examines the unity of the church in light of the apostolic practice presented in the New Testament.[69] There is no doubt that seeking to live in the light of God's purpose of unity in Christ caused difficulties for the early church. Padilla recognises that the breaking down of barriers between black and white, rich and poor, male and female is no easier today than the breaking down of barriers between Jew and Gentile, slave and free, male and female in the early church.[70] "Nevertheless, all the New Testament evidence points to an apostolic practice consistent with the aim of forming churches in which God's purpose would become a concrete reality."[71]

In response to the homogeneous principle proposed by the Church Growth movement, Padilla presents five conclusions which he considers to be biblical in their foundation. Firstly, in the early church the gospel was proclaimed to all people,

---

[67] Padilla, "Unity", 287. Padilla emphasises the significance of reconciliation for Latin America, across race boundaries, gender boundaries, and international boundaries as a reflection of the power of the gospel. C. René Padilla, interview by author, 13 June 2003, video recording, Buenos Aires.

[68] Kirk, *World*, 120. See Costas, "Crecimiento", 9.

[69] See Padilla, "Unity", 288-299 where the difficulties encountered in the church in Rome, the church in Corinth, the church in Syrian Antioch, the church in Jerusalem and the problems which arose during the mission to the Gentiles are examined.

[70] See for example Acts 6:1, 11:1-18, 13:1; Galatians 2:11-14; 1 Corinthians 8:7, 12:12-13; Romans 1:13.

[71] Padilla, *Mission*, 146. See also Escobar, "Vivir", 11.

without partiality.[72] Secondly, the breaking down of barriers was considered to be an essential aspect of the gospel message. Thirdly, the church grew across social barriers. Fourthly, the apostles did not consider the possibility of forming homogeneous church units despite difficulties encountered. Fifthly, the Christian community was to cross cultural barriers and such a community was a reflection of essential Christian teachings.[73] Latin American evangelical theologians, therefore, have strongly critiqued the segregationist principles permitted by the Church Growth movement. They have strongly voiced their assertion that the New Testament church is precisely the negation of such segregation.[74] For "discrimination…has absolutely no place among God's people."[75]

Latin American evangelical theologians have sought to base their critique of the Church Growth movement on a coherent and thoroughly biblical foundation. Escobar notes:

> Padilla especially has worked demonstrating that the hermeneutic procedure of the Church Growth movement coming from Pasadena bows before social sciences and pragmatism and accommodates Scripture to them rather than judging them by Scripture. In other words right in the middle of a very popular movement among Evangelicals we find the same hermeneutical procedure of Liberationist hermeneutics.[76]

In developing an evangelical ecclesiology, evangelical theologians have set out to counter the inconsistencies they perceive in Church Growth theory. In contrast, they seek to present what they understand to be a holistic and biblical concept of church growth.[77] Costas begins with the assertion that the church is God's creation: "It is not only the *product* of God's grace, but the very expression of divine love – a God-created and indwelt entity."[78] The church derives its nature from the Trinity and therefore can be described as the *body of Christ*, the *fellowship of the Holy Spirit* and the *covenant people of God*.[79] In light of this understanding Costas explains:

---

[72] See also Kirk, *World*, 121.

[73] See Padilla, *Mission*, 166-168.

[74] Escobar, "Crecimiento", 18: see also Samuel Escobar, "La responsabilidad social de la iglesia", *Iglesia y Misión* 74 (2000): 20-37, at 24.

[75] Kirk, *World*, 122.

[76] Escobar, Arana, Steuernagel and Zapata, "Critique", 61.

[77] See Emilio A. Núñez, "¿Cómo debe crecer la iglesia?", *Apuntes Pastorales* 10, no.2, (1992): 10-11; Orlando E. Costas, "A Wholistic Concept of Church Growth" in *Exploring Church Growth*, ed. Wilbert R. Shenk (Grand Rapids: Eerdmans, 1983), 95-107; Orlando E. Costas, "Dimensiones del crecimiento integral de la iglesia" in *La misión de la iglesia, una visión panorámica*, ed. Valdir Steuernagel (San José: Varitec, 1992), 109-122; see also chapter four "Mission as Integral Growth" in Costas, *Integrity*, 37-60.

[78] Costas, "Wholistic", 99.

[79] See also Núñez, "¿Cómo?", 11; Costas, "Dimensiones", 114-115; Costas, *Integrity*, 86-89; Orlando E. Costas, "Crecimiento integral y Palabra de Dios", *Misión* 2, no. 1 (1983): 6-13, at 9; Quiroz, "Misión", 9-72.

The church ought to grow in conformity with its divine nature. As the fellowship of the Spirit, it ought to grow in *holiness* and *communion*. As the body of Christ, it ought to grow in *apostolicity* and *unity*. As God's covenant people, it ought to grow in *fidelity* and *maturity*. Such an imperative proceeds from an indicative, namely, the fact that the church, understood theologically, is no historical accident or human creation, but rather the very expression of God and the firstfruits of his work. In other words, the church exists by the will and power of God.[80]

There should also be three theologically identifiable qualities of growth within the church. Firstly, growth in the *spirituality* of the church should be evident in the demonstration of faith which reflects the fruits of the Spirit; a joyful, vibrant, loving and hopeful community. Secondly, at an *incarnational* level, the church needs to experience growth "that bears a concrete (incarnate) witness to the commitment and comprehensive presence of Christ among the harassed and helpless multitudes of the world."[81] Thirdly, church growth must be assessed in regards to the *faithfulness* of the church, in the light of God's purpose and deeds revealed in the Scriptures and historically understood in the Christian tradition.[82]

A faith-filled church is a believing church because it actualises its faith in its *action*. Therefore it is always a trusting, enduring, and steadfast church; trusting in the power of the Holy Spirit to transform persons, families, clans, tribes and nations; steadfast in the promises of Christ to bless the witness of his people; enduring in the hope of God's coming kingdom...A faith-filled church is always a working church...It is always questioning and analyzing its missional performance in the light of God's word...[83]

In his model for holistic church growth, Costas applies these three qualities to the *numerical growth*, the *organic growth*, the *conceptual growth* and the *diaconal growth* of the church.[84] Through proclamation of the gospel and living faithfully in light of the gospel, new members should be incorporated into the fellowship of the church and as a consequence *numerical growth* is evident. Subsequent *organic growth* is the strengthening of relationships between the members of the community of faith.

The organic dimension has to do with culture and contextualization, Christian education and stewardship, *koinonia* and worship. It confronts the church with the need to be a culturally relevant (indigenous) community which forms and disciples its

---

[80] Costas, "Wholistic", 100. Escobar agrees that the concept of church growth presented in the New Testament is an integral one. Escobar observes "The use of the term *growth* in the New Testament has much more to do with holistic growth: growth in the sense of depth, maturity, grace, knowledge and love". Escobar, "Crecimiento", 15.

[81] Costas, "Wholistic", 101. See Costas, "Dimensiones", 117; Costas, *Christ*, 47; see also Padilla, "Eclesiología", 28-30.

[82] Costas, "Dimensiones", 115.

[83] Costas, *Christ*, 54. See also Cortes, "Christology", 102.

[84] Costas, "Dimensiones", 118. See also Núñez, *Desafíos*, 61-67.

members; manages well its time, talents and resources; promotes a warm fellowship between its members; and celebrates the faith in the language of the community where it is located, incorporating its symbols, creations, and values and identifying with its socio-historical situation.[85]

The church deepens its understanding of the faith, Scriptures, doctrine and the world,[86] leading to *conceptual growth* which enables the church to reflect critically, evaluate honestly and engage with internal and external assaults on the faith. The authenticity and credibility of the church is demonstrated in the love and the service it renders to the world, demonstrating *diaconal growth*. The church should participate in the life, conflicts, fears, and hopes of society and then is in a position to contribute to "the effective alleviation of human pain and the abrogation of the social conditions that keep people in poverty, powerlessness, and oppression."[87] This model enables researchers to comprehend church growth not only quantitatively but also qualitatively.[88] For evangelicals, the growth of the church should be a dynamic reality demonstrated by maturity, transformation, renovation and creativity.[89]

It becomes clear that the constructive criticism made of liberation ecclesiology, of the new ecclesiology within the Latin American Catholic church and of the Church Growth movement, has stimulated the development of a Latin American evangelical ecclesiology. For evangelical theologians have been motivated to pursue a more biblical and contextual approach to the subject.

8.5 The Search for a Latin American Evangelical Ecclesiology

As early as 1974, Costas published one of the first specific Latin American evangelical works on ecclesiology. *The Church and its Mission: A Shattering Critique from the Third World* was an influential contribution in its time. Costas intended his work to present a challenge for wholeness in missionary theory and practice. His work was an attempt to call the attention of the church in the North Atlantic to "the unity of the gospel and to the undichotomous character of the church's role as an instrument of God's mission."[90] He summarises his dual purpose:

---

[85] Costas, "Wholistic", 103. See also Escobar, "Responsabilidad", 22; Costas, "Crecimiento", 12. See C. René Padilla, "Viñetas de una iglesia sierva", *Iglesia y misión* 62 (1997): 6-11 for an account of the changing experience of a local church which sought to put these principles into action.

[86] See also Núñez, "¿Cómo?", 10-11.

[87] Costas, "Wholistic", 102. See also Núñez, "¿Cómo?", 11; Escobar, "Responsabilidad", 30-33.

[88] See also Núñez, *Desafíos*, 66-69.

[89] For a helpful discussion on lessons learned from the church growth of Chilean Protestantism and the involvement of the Chilean church in the state, see Costas, *Christ*, 48-54.

[90] Costas, *Church*, 10.

1. To provide a personal, evangelical, Latin American, holistic interpretation of the church as an instrument of God's mission to the world in the light of the witness of Scripture, the phenomenon of church growth, and the most outstanding tensions in the fulfilment of her responsibility. 2. To challenge Christians in the North Atlantic, particularly evangelicals, to a more integral and committed approach to the church's involvement in God's mission to the world.[91]

It is this holistic interpretation of the church as an instrument of God's mission to the world which will be the focus to begin with. In light of the witness of Scripture, four familiar aspects of the character of the church permeate evangelical ecclesiology: the church as the people of God;[92] the church as the body of Christ;[93] the church as the temple of the Holy Spirit;[94] and the church as an institution.[95] Costas reiterates the implications of this biblical understanding of ecclesiology:

The church...is a multitude of men and women from all walks of life, without distinction of race, nationality, economic and educational background. It is a community gathered from every tribe, tongue and nation. It is a people called out of darkness into God's marvellous light through the Holy Spirit, as a result of God's revealed and redeeming grace in Jesus Christ, to be God's own people, Christ's own body, and the temple of the Holy Spirit in the concrete situations of their everyday life.[96]

The church is the community of faith entrusted with the good news. It is not a community that isolates itself from the world, and protects its members from the influences of society. On the contrary:

The gospel has been committed to a community, is transmitted by that community, and demands a community experience. Without community there cannot be a living representation of the gospel. It is the community of believers that announces the kingdom of God as a reality, which proclaims a new order of life under the sovereign action of God, which relativizes all human authority...The witness has no meaning, however, if it is not backed by a community whose love is translated into works of mercy, a community whose faith is manifested in a commitment to social justice and whose hope is reflected in the struggle for a just peace.[97]

---

[91] Costas, *Church*, 16.

[92] See 1 Peter 2:9, 10, 5:10,11; Exodus 19:5; Isaiah 43:20, 61:6; Deuteronomy 7:7; Hebrews 13:13.

[93] See also Núñez, *Desafíos*, 63-67.

[94] For references to the church as the body of Christ and the temple of the Holy Spirit see 1 Corinthians 3:9-15, 6:15, 19; Ephesians 2:14-22, 4:16. See also Padilla, "Comunidad y misión" in *Discipulado*, 31-33.

[95] Costas, *Church*, 21-35. See also Orlando E. Costas, ed. *Hacia una teología de la evangelización* (Buenos Aires: La Aurora, 1973), 131-156.

[96] Costas, *Church*, 35.

[97] Costas, *Liberating*, 135. See also Núñez, *Caminos*, 109-123.

It has already been observed in this chapter that the liberationist understanding of the church as a "sacrament of salvation" led to concerns on the part of evangelical theologians. Costas expresses an evangelical understanding of the concept:

> To speak of the community of faith (or the congregation) as an evangelising base is to refer to the place where the gospel is manifested and lived in its most concrete reality. This is the starting point for the diffusion of the gospel in the world, the location where the good news becomes *communion*, is transformed into the *apostolate*, and gives *identity* to the new world promised in the gospel. The church is the sign by which the gospel is expressed and anticipated as a "sacrament of salvation" in the world...Leaving aside the density that such an expression may have in contemporary Roman Catholic theology, I hold that the ecclesial community, as people of God and as a communication base of the gospel, is the visible sign of salvation that God offers the world in the name of Christ by the Holy Spirit. As such, the church is the divine anticipation of that promise through the communal experience of forgiveness and the solidaristic commitment to justice and peace...The church is the gospel working in efficacious and transforming action for the salvation of the world.[98]

Having clearly established the importance of the witness of the local community of faith in society, through reflection on Scripture, five specific areas of ministry are identified. Such ministry is evidence of a holistic interpretation of the church and naturally evangelisation is considered foundational to each.

Firstly, the church has been called to *worship* God.[99] Such worship is displayed when the church celebrates and calls the world to honour and revere God. Such worship does not refer simply to the congregational gatherings but to the whole of the Christian life as an act of worship.[100]

> Christ's redemptive work is proclaimed in the celebration of baptism and the Eucharist. Through its formal worship the church becomes conscious of itself as an evangelistic community, proclaims corporately before the world the grace of the gospel, and offers thanks to God for the Spirit's power manifested in the daily witness of its members...to be faithful to its evangelistic cutting edge, worship has to be contextualised in the language and symbols of the celebrating community – without, of course, becoming so relative that it loses its theological depth and breadth.[101]

Secondly, the church is a *communion* created by God.[102] The fellowship experienced by the community, in the power of the Holy Spirit, foreshadows the reconciliation promised by the gospel. Costas notes:

---

[98] Costas, *Liberating*, 135. See also Padilla, "Cristiana", 90-91; Kirk, *World*, 122; Padilla, "La iglesia que queremos que crezca" in *Discipulado*, 96-98.

[99] See Costas, *Liberating*, 136-138. See also Costas, *Church*, 37-44; Costas, "Realidad", 36-40.

[100] See Romans 12:1-2, 15:16.

[101] Costas, *Liberating*, 138.

[102] See Costas, *Liberating*, 138-140.

The fellowship of the true followers of Christ is a sign of the promise and presence of the kingdom of God. It celebrates forgiveness and affirms solidarity. Through its communion the church declares before the world that in the gospel there is proclaimed a new order of life and a new mode of human existence. In *koinonia* the church bears witness to the fundamental unity that exists between God and the people of God, between the members of God's community and the Trinitarian community.[103]

Such communion is reflected in the community of faith by an attitude of openness to other members of the community. It is demonstrated in concrete acts and deeds. It is evident in the love exhibited one to the other.[104] Such communion gives credibility to the message proclaimed by the community of faith and demonstrates a model of life where barriers are overcome and divisions are denounced. Failure to live in communion is not only destructive to the proclamation of the gospel but, as Costas observes, it also "deprives society of a wholesome and constructive vision of a far better future and of an honest and sincere criticism of its fundamental problems."[105]

Thirdly, the community of believers is a *diaconate*, that is to say, "an agency at the service of humanity."[106] It is in this service to others that the church *incarnates* its message. Worship and communion are aspects of ministry which serve God, church members and the world. However, *diakonia* is a particular kind of service which is related to providing for the material necessities of those in need: the poor, the oppressed, the dispossessed, the thirsty, the hungry, widows, orphans, children, prisoners, strangers.[107] Costas contends:

> The church distinguishes itself from social and philanthropic agencies by the fact that it is motivated to serve by the love revealed in the gospel, proclaimed in mission, celebrated in worship, and experienced in communion. What the church does for social and material well-being of its members and the world is accomplished by the power of the Spirit of Christ. The church does not serve the world in order to have the opportunity to preach the gospel. Rather, its service is complete in itself, the proclaimed message of concrete deeds. *Diakonia* does not need any justification other than that of offering a gift of love for the sake of God's love.[108]

Fourthly, the church has a role as an *advocate for justice and peace*.[109] This is a ministry which reflects the prophetic tradition and the New Testament call for

---

[103] Costas, *Liberating*, 139. See also Padilla, "La iglesia y los grupos de *koinonia*" in *Discipulado*, 108-110.

[104] See Acts 2:1, 43, 44; John 13:35, 17:21.

[105] Costas, *Liberating*, 140.

[106] Costas, *Liberating*, 140-141. See Kirk, *World*, 119-120. See also chapter 9, "Mission as Transforming Service" in Escobar, *Time*, 142-154; see also chapter 10, "Siervos de Dios para el mañana" in Núñez, *Desafíos*, 133-139; Guerrero, "Líderes-siervos", 179-212.

[107] See Acts 6:1-2.

[108] Costas, *Liberating*, 140.

[109] Costas, *Liberating*, 141-143. See also Costas, *Church*, 44-47.

dikaioma, which Costas literally translates as "a just action."[110] The church announces the justice of God's kingdom and the good news of peace in the message of the gospel. It is the responsibility of the community to pray and work for a just peace. "The love that [the church] lives and expresses in its fellowship becomes enfleshed in solidarity with those who suffer, struggle, and look forward to a new world of *shalom*."[111] Such a call for justice and the pursuit of peace in the world testifies to God's love and is a faithful witness to that love. The ministry of justice and peace, like the ministry of service, enables the church to be a historical witness in the world and enables the church to become a contributor to the transformation of the world. When the church participates in the ministry of justice and peace, it presents the world with an alternative to a life of selfishness and power. It exhibits a new world order and it convinces believers that their discipleship cannot be superficial.[112]

Christian education is the fifth form of ministry for which the church has responsibility. This teaching ministry is the task of interpreting the faith, equipping the church for the practice of faith, and directing the church in effective communication of that faith. "It is through the ministry of Christian education that the church's content is taught, its practice is critically evaluated, its agents are equipped, and its base of support is encouraged."[113] Such Christian education should reflect the values of formation, information, and transformation. It should form character, abilities and thoughts. It should inform the mind, contemplation and praxis. It should transform values, individuals, institutions, and communities.

> The church finds its educational model *par excellence* in the teaching ministry of Jesus. To teach the faith is to do what Jesus did with his disciples – namely, to invite them to follow in his steps, enabling them to hear and understand God's word, equipping them to obey him in all things, and empowering them, by the Spirit, to communicate the gospel effectively.[114]

In practice, many churches have failed to communicate the gospel effectively. Costas identifies a significant reason for this to be the absence of a clear vision of the socio-historical context. It is vital, therefore, that holistic ministry is contextual. Drawing on two biblical models of ministry set "on the periphery" of their respective contexts, Costas asserts that in Latin America the gospel must be applied to the "base" or "margin" of society. For it is there that the most vulnerable, the most needy and indeed the "absentees of history" are to be found.[115]

Such contextual ministry must be grounded in a Trinitarian theology. Costas illustrates the significance of such a foundation when he comments:

---

[110] Isaiah 32:15-18; Psalm 72:1-4; 2 Corinthians 9:8-15; 1 John 3:10; Revelation 22:11.

[111] Costas, *Liberating*, 141.

[112] See Costas, *Church*, 54-57. See also Padilla, "Cristiana", 93.

[113] Costas, *Liberating*, 144.

[114] Costas, *Liberating*, 144.

[115] Costas, *Liberating*, 149.

It is to understand God as an eternal community of love, God as mission and unity who seeks and reconciles, sends and calls. The spirituality that proceeds from such an understanding is liberating and transforming…To be converted to Christ, therefore, will be to experience a change of mind, to reorient one's life in the direction of God's kingdom and its justice. To be justified by faith will be to appropriate the justice of God revealed in Christ, to be declared just before God and set free to do the works of justice. And sanctification will be understood as the process by which the Holy Spirit makes ever more efficacious the consecration of believers for the service of God's kingdom in history.[116]

Contextual ministry is also ministry in which the church bears witness to God's kingdom under the sign of the cross.[117] There is no place for ecclesiastical triumphalism. The message of the cross and commitment to the service of the kingdom produces "holistic growth, gratuitous but not superfluous, in which available energies are multiplied for the well-being of humanity and for the glorification of the God whose kingdom we await in faith and hope."[118]

Evangelical theologians are consistent in their assertion that the church, as a community of faith, must proclaim the message of the gospel not only in word, but also in deed. This is the responsibility of the church, in light of the teaching of Scripture, and in response to the specific Latin American context. The community of faith must present an alternative to their society.[119] "The principal and most powerful answer to the social and political needs of humanity, to humanity's search for freedom, justice and fulfilment, is given by Jesus in his own work and in the church."[120] In this respect, Escobar reflects on the biblical account of the distinctive witness of the early church. The early church demonstrated a new attitude with regard to money and property.[121] The early church also displayed an alternative understanding of power and the exercise of power.[122] The early church was a community in which social barriers and social prejudice were broken down, in the light of, and for the sake of the gospel.[123] The early church was prepared to suffer for justice and for good.[124] This is the biblical model of church and the New Testament model of ministry. Such a Christian community will inevitably have a "revolutionary effect which transforms society."[125]

---

[116] Costas, *Liberating*, 149.

[117] See also Padilla, "Eclesiología", 32-34.

[118] Costas, *Liberating*, 149. See also Costas, *Christ*, 45.

[119] Escobar, "Naturaleza", 75-101.

[120] Escobar, *Fe*, 186.

[121] Luke 22:23-31; Acts 2:43-45, 4:34, 20:35; James 2:14-16; 1 John 3:16,17.

[122] Luke 2:23-27; 2 Corinthians 10:8, 12:10-15; 1 Peter 5:1-3. See also Solano, "Iglesia", 49-61.

[123] Galatians 3:28; Colossians 3:11; Philemon 1:15-17.

[124] Matthew 5:10-12; Acts 7:51-60, 16:16-24; 1 Peter 3:13-18.

[125] Escobar, *Fe*, 186. See also Ortiz, "Iglesia", 194-208; Costas, "Crecimiento", 8-10.

Kirk presents the following characteristics of a church seeking to demonstrate the reality of the kingdom of God in a biblical and holistic manner.[126] The church will be a community where divisions and barriers will be broken down. The church will consciously practise forgiveness and strive for the restoration of relationships between members of the community of faith. The church will not retaliate in like manner when provoked in a violent or aggressive way. The church should be willing to share financial and material resources with others, whether those in need are part of the Christian community or not. For "the Scriptures certainly do not recognise any inalienable right of ownership for those who acknowledge that they belong to Christ."[127] The church will conduct all activities of any kind with absolute integrity. The church will be open and willingly expose itself to the suffering of others. Finally, the exercise of power within the community of faith will not dominate or oppress others.

> The key to this new way of being a community is the fullness of the love that Jesus offered as sheer grace. The main hindrance is fear (1 John 4:18-19). Fear divides, isolates, and creates hostility; it expresses distance and alienation. Love, on the other hand, integrates, brings people close to one another and eliminates every kind of suspicion and prejudice; it creates confidence, tolerance and communication; it gives dignity and value to people.[128]

The principles of ecclesiology proposed by Latin American evangelical theologians have become evident in evangelical churches across the continent, to the extent that the influence of such communities of faith in society has been noted by sociologists. David Martin, for example, observes:

> [The evangelical church] provides a new cell taken over from scarred and broken tissue. Above all it renews the innermost cell of the family and protects the woman from the ravages of male desertion and violence. A new faith is able to implant new disciplines, reorder priorities, counter corruption and destructive *machismo*, and reverse the indifferent and injurious hierarchies of the outside world. Within the enclosed haven of faith a fraternity can be instituted under firm leadership, which provides for release, for mutuality and warmth, and for the practice of new roles.[129]

While such observations are an encouragement to Latin American evangelical theologians, it is clear, nevertheless, that a thoroughly biblical evangelical ecclesiology remains vital for the growth and the maturity of churches in years to come. Míguez Bonino confronts Latin American Christians regarding the future of the church on their continent:

---

[126] Kirk, *World*, 122-123; Kirk, *Mission*, 33-37.
[127] Kirk, *World*, 123.
[128] Kirk, *World*, 123. See also Kirk, *Mission*, 28.
[129] Martin, *Tongues*, 284. See also Escobar, "Conflict", 134.

1. Will my church opt to accompany the growing marginalized and oppressed majorities in their religious and human quest? Or will it be satisfied with a "stable clientele" in the middle and high-middle sectors of society, with perhaps some "social service" to the poor on the side? 2. Will my church limit itself to entering the "religious market" with an offer of "salvation products" – health, inner peace, earthly prosperity, and a happy hereafter? Or will it be an invitation to the discipleship of a Lord who offers forgiveness, joy, peace, and eternal life, but who also demands prophetic courage, active solidarity, and a building of a different world? 3. Will my church offer closed communities of refuge or will it recruit for open communities of evangelising witness, solidarity and service? 4. How will my church define the centre of its message? By "reduction" – whether soteriological, ethical, pietistic, or social – or by the integrity of the wholeness of the biblical message? 5. Will my church give preference to the "success" of a narrow, self-concerned, and aggressive confessional or denominational militancy, or privilege the witness of a gospel that creates a spirit of cooperation and unity?[130]

Facing such pressing issues, Latin American evangelical theologians realise that a biblical ecclesiology will be founded on Christian hope for the future. This hope should lead to obedience. This obedience will be manifested in loving action. Such Christian praxis implies, therefore, that communities of faith will participate in liberating transformation. Escobar summarises the basis of Latin American evangelical ecclesiology succinctly:

> As a community of believers in Jesus Christ, the church performs various functions. It bears *testimony* just by being the church; the company of believers have *fellowship* and feel a sense of belonging; they express joyful gratitude to God in *worship*; they receive *teaching* on the Christian life; they provide *service* in meeting the needs of people both within and outside the church; and are *prophetic* in the denunciation of evil when God's kingdom is proclaimed…Sharing the good news, going to "the other" with the message of Jesus Christ, inviting others to Jesus' great banquet, gives focus and direction to all the other functions. Thus one can say that the church exists for mission and that a church which is only inward looking is not truly a church.[131]

Latin American evangelical theologians seek to present a holistic interpretation of the church as an instrument of God's mission to the world. They consistently present ecclesiology in light of the biblical witness, in a manner which clearly demonstrates the responsibility of the church to be faithful in her context, and in response to the phenomenon of church growth in Latin America. It would seem no exaggeration to say that they call evangelicals across the world to a more integral and committed understanding of the church's involvement in God's mission to the world.[132]

---

[130] Míguez Bonino, "Condition", 267. For an overview of the prosperity gospel influencing Latin American churches see Emilio A. Núñez, "El evangelio de la prosperidad", *Apuntes Pastorales* 11, no. 4 (1994): 33-35. See also Padilla, *Derechos*, 18.

[131] Escobar, *Time*, 11.

[132] Costas, *Church*, 16.

8.6 Conclusion

It has been demonstrated in this chapter, that fundamental to Latin American evangelical ecclesiology is the understanding that the church, as a community of faith, does not exist primarily for the benefit of its members. On the contrary, the community of faith exists to bear testimony to its faith in word and deed, in society and in the world.

The dramatic growth of this evangelical church in Latin America has been phenomenal in recent years. Evangelicals, therefore, must seek to ensure that their ecclesiology remains focused on the impact of the church in the world, for the world. For unless communities of faith are continually presented with this challenge, it is inevitable that numerous ghettos of evangelical believers will emerge, once more segregated from society. Evangelical theologians will need to actively guard against the criticism which may arise that an unnecessary dualism exists in their ecclesiological understanding of the church and the world.

For over thirty years, Latin American evangelical theologians have been committed to the search for contextual evangelical ecclesiology. In this chapter, the evangelical critique of three ecclesiological proposals has been outlined, namely, the critique of liberationist ecclesiology, the new ecclesiology within Catholicism and Church Growth ecclesiology. It would appear that Latin American evangelical theologians have made, and hold to five constructive ecclesiological propositions. First, ecclesiology needs to be thoroughly biblical. Second, the church is distinct from the world, and it needs to be entered into consciously. Third, the church should be understood in light of the biblical revelation of the triune God. Fourth, the church as the body of Christ should seek to reflect the diverse composition of society. Fifth, a contextual ecclesiology will focus on creating a worshipping community, which is integrally involved as servant, advocate and educator in the society in which it is found. "In other words, that the church would be a community centred on the word of God, made up of people fully committed to the triune God and pastored by people whose ministry is in keeping with the Son of Man, who did not come to be served, but to serve and give his life as a ransom for many."[133]

The ecclesiological principles established in this chapter are the foundation for the development of a Latin American evangelical missiology. The search for a biblical, holistic understanding of mission, relevant to the Latin American context will be examined presently in chapter nine.

---

[133] C. René Padilla, "Desafíos para la próxima década", *Apuntes Pastorales* 17, no. 2 (2000): 20-22.

CHAPTER 9

The Search for a Latin American
Evangelical Missiology

9.1 Introduction

In their commitment to structure a contextual theology, Latin American evangelical theologians are seeking to develop an effective, biblically based, holistic approach to Christian mission. The purpose of this chapter is to examine the development of Latin American evangelical thought on the subject of mission. First, Latin American evangelical missiology will be set in the context of the serious international evangelical dialogue which took place after 1970. It is evident that the defining interaction for Latin American evangelical theologians occurred within international evangelicalism. Second, in an attempt to focus specifically on Latin American evangelical missiology, the implications of mission as discipleship will be considered. The implications of discipleship for the mission of the church are foundational in Latin American evangelical theology. Third, for Latin American evangelicals, the communication of the gospel message should bring authentic change. For this reason, the understanding of mission as transformation will be considered. Fourth, because the transformational message of mission should engage directly with the local context of the community of faith, the relationship between mission and social responsibility will be examined. Fifth, in light of the international dialogue, and in light of mission as discipleship, transformation and social responsibility, Latin American evangelicals propose a biblical and thoroughly evangelical approach to be *misión integral*. It would be fair to say that *misión integral* is a concept particular to Latin American evangelical theology which is continually being refined. In this chapter, I have chosen not to translate the term *misión integral* as "holistic mission" or "integral mission" because the English translation may not convey all aspects understood by Latin American evangelical theologians when they employ the term. By leaving *misión integral* in the original Spanish, I hope to enable the reader to form a more precise understanding of the concept.

It will become evident in this chapter that Latin American evangelical missiology is a "two-pronged theological approach"[1] in which both critical theology and

---

[1] Samuel Escobar, "Mission Studies – Past, Present and Future", *Missiology: An International Review* XXXIV, no. 1, (1996): 3-29, at 20. See also Samuel Escobar, "Opresión y justicia", *Boletín Teológico* 42/43 (1991): 109-123, at 109.

missionary fervour are evident.[2] Firstly, it is a *critical task*, prepared to confront evangelical theologians, both within Latin America and at an international level. Secondly, it is a *constructive task* seeking to develop a theology of mission which expresses the dynamic missionary emphasis of Latin American evangelical churches.[3] It is "an effort to provide a solid biblical basis for new patterns of mission, evangelism, and discipleship in continuity with the best evangelical missionary tradition with its holistic commitment to spiritual and social transformation."[4] It will also become clear in this chapter that sharing the good news in Latin America is a *communitarian, contextual,* and *missiological* task.[5]

9.2 The International Evangelical Dialogue Regarding Mission

Early publications by members of the Latin American evangelical community demonstrate that missiology was of central concern, prior to and during the years of international discussion.[6] In the *critical task* of Latin American evangelical theology, they were prepared to challenge Western missiological presuppositions, critique the Western understanding of the biblical teaching on mission and present a vibrant evangelical alternative.[7]

9.2.1 The Latin American Evangelical Contribution at Lausanne

As has been discussed previously (see section 3.3), the years following the Second World War saw a crisis within the international evangelical community and the need to develop serious evangelical thought on many aspects of contextual theology was

---

[2] For a thorough contemporary theological exploration of the subject of mission see Kirk, *Mission*, 7-74; Escobar, *Changing*, 3-20, 111-130.

[3] Escobar, "Studies", 20.

[4] Escobar, "Studies", 20.

[5] See C. René Padilla, "Mensaje inaugural: todo el evangelio para todos los pueblos desde América Latina" in Congreso Latinoamericano de Evangelización (CLADE), III, 24 de agosto a 4 de septiembre de 1992, Quito: *Todo el Evangelio para todos los pueblos desde América Latina* (Quito: Fraternidad Teológica Latinoamericana, 1993), 6-11.

[6] See for example, C. René Padilla, "Lo de Dios y lo de César", *Certeza* 41 (1970): 2-3 in which Padilla discusses the Christian understanding of the relationship between the church and the state. See C. René Padilla, "Ser Prójimo", *Certeza* 69 (1978): 147-150 in which Padilla elaborates on the love of God and love for one's neighbour. See C. René Padilla, "Jesus y los pobres", *Certeza* 77 (1980): 151-156 for a discussion on the relationship between Jesus and the poor. *Certeza* is a journal addressed particularly to students. However, while it may not be an academic publication it is insightful to note the subjects under discussion are similar to those under discussion in the evangelical theological circles. Latin American evangelical theologians seek to present a challenge to all Latin American evangelical believers with regard to the mission and responsibility of the church. See also Escobar, "Social", 84-105; C. René Padilla "Proyecto para una ética social evangélica" in *Fe cristiana y Latinoamérica hoy*, ed. C. René Padilla (Buenos Aires: Ediciones Certeza, 1975), 209-214.

[7] See Kirk, *Theology*, 45-48.

acknowledged.[8] Latin American evangelical theologians demonstrated, at an early stage, an awareness of the serious nature of the relationship between faith, Christian mission and social responsibility. Escobar comments:

> I believe the life of the church is healthy only when there is this sense of mission. The health of the church is not measured mainly by her status in society, or her economic power, or the solidity and beauty of her creedal statements. It is measured by her commitment to mission and obedience to her missionary call... "A church which is not a 'church in mission' is no church at all."[9]

Latin American evangelicals consistently asserted that a biblical understanding of the mission of the church should include a relevant, contextual approach in which mission and social responsibility would go hand in hand.[10] In this respect, there is no doubt that the Lausanne Consultation of 1974 represents a turning point in the history of evangelical theology.[11]

The contribution made by the Latin American evangelical theologians to the consultation was stimulating, and at times controversial. Their presentations demonstrated commitment to both the *critical* and the *constructive* tasks which they considered necessary. It appears that "the Lausanne Covenant was a death blow to every attempt to reduce the mission of the church to the multiplication of Christians and churches through evangelism."[12]

At Lausanne, Costas affirmed the comprehensive reality which the gospel announces by focusing on the different structural dimensions of human life and the

---

[8] See chapter four "The Need for Historical Awareness" by Escobar in Samuel Escobar and John Driver, *Christian Mission and Social Justice* (Scottdale: Herald Press, 1978), 11-35. See Escobar, *Time*, 21-25, 142-154. See also chapter 3 "Latin America: Mission Land" and chapter 4 "Lessons from Missionary History" in Escobar, *Changing*, 23-44; Padilla gives a helpful historical perspective in "Fraternidad", 99-105.

[9] Samuel Escobar, *George Orwell's Nightmare and the Christian Mission Today* (Vrije Universiteit: Amsterdam, 1984), 3.

[10] For a helpful discussion on the history of the international evangelical debate and international evangelical responses to the challenge presented by Latin American evangelicals see Kirk, *World*, 14-23. See also Padilla, "Itinerario", 4-10.

[11] In his reflection on this period, Stott considers the contribution from Latin American theologians to have been significant. For not only did they reflect the concerns of other Two Thirds World theologians but they also resolutely challenged the presuppositions of Western evangelicalism. They were instrumental in raising the issues and in engaging internationally on the subjects. John Stott, interview with author, 20 September 2003, video recording, Blackpool.

[12] C. René Padilla, "Wheaton", 27. This article is a helpful overview of the development of a more holistic evangelical approach to mission during this period. It is also helpful in understanding the perspective of Two Thirds World theologians during the conferences. See also C. René Padilla and Chris Sugden, eds. *How Evangelicals Endorsed Social Responsibility* (Bramcote: Grove Books Limited, 1985), 4-17; Padilla and Sugden, *Texts*, 3.

responsibility of the church to take seriously not only the geographical spread of the gospel, but also the cultural and sociological impact of the gospel.

If the kingdom of God, which the gospel proclaims, is a new order of life characterized by the sovereign rule of God in Christ and his reconciling action in [sic] behalf of mankind, *if* this reality affects, as Scripture says, the personal present and future of the peoples of the earth as well as their collective present and future; *if* God's kingdom manifests itself both in the personal life of those who enter therein, through the regenerating power of the Holy Spirit, as well as in the structures of society and the dynamics of culture, through the leavening function of the gospel; *and if* in calling men and women to submit their lives to Christ, the King, it also addresses itself to their cultural ties and structural realities and calls them to repentance and obedience – *then* the communication of this message demands integrity. We need to recover in evangelism the biblical and dynamic fullness of the gospel so that those who are invited to come into the kingdom may have a clear perspective of what it is all about...to the end that evangelism be liberated from the tragedy which it has fallen into in many contemporary circles, namely, that of being a commercial, manipulative whitewash, and become, instead, a comprehensive enterprise where the gospel is shared in depth and out of the depth of man's needs and life situations, so that the knowledge of Christ may one day truly cover the earth as the waters cover the sea.[13]

Escobar addressed the issue of the human search for freedom, justice and fulfilment, emphasising the importance of communicating the good news of Christ in every sphere of life.

Part of the teaching is *how to live in the world as a Christian*: the ethics of the kingdom. Laymen then penetrate society by a *way of life* that is new in family relations, business, citizenship, and every area of daily life. Consequently, to mobilize the laymen is not only to teach them short summaries of the gospel, mini-sermons, and to send them to repeat these to their neighbours. It is also to teach them how to apply the teaching and example of Christ in their family life, in their business activities, in their social relationships, in their studies...[14]

Núñez sought to persuade evangelicals to confront the secularism which tries to sacralize the world and make the church mundane. Such confrontation displays the implications of the gospel for societal transformation:

It is necessary to recall that in the teaching of Christ there exists a ferment of deep social transformation. The principles which speak of human being, of the justice, mercy, peace, equality, liberty, and fraternity, did not fail to have repercussions on the conscience of our civilization over nearly two thousand years and, directly or indirectly, they have produced social changes for the benefit of humanity.[15]

---

[13] Costas, "In-depth", 211. See Costas, "Depth", 675-694.
[14] Escobar, "Evangelization", 324. See Escobar, "Kingdom", 27.
[15] Núñez, "Personal", 1065.

Núñez exhorted his listeners to recognise the validity of Romans 12:2 and John 2:12-17 and in response, to enter the social scene in order to demonstrate their experience of faith:

> It is hoped that this deliverance will show reality in the life of the redeemed. It is necessary to leave the servitude of sin and to live justly in the private experiences of every day and in all relationships either of family or society. We are called to live "as free, and not using our liberty for a cloak of maliciousness, but as the servants of God."[16]

While it would be unfair to stereotype contemporary evangelical believers as people committed only to the "saving of souls," Padilla expresses concern that, despite the challenges presented at Lausanne, when it comes to defining the importance of physical needs in relation to mission priorities the subject remains somewhat controversial. This tension still exists.[17] Nonetheless, there have been significant changes in the general evangelical understanding of the mission of the church and the social responsibility of Christians.[18]

9.2.2 The Latin American Evangelical Call for Holistic Mission since Lausanne

The renewal of this evangelical social conscience and understanding of holistic mission has been well documented in English writing. For this reason it is unnecessary to repeat such an overview given in Spanish.[19] Suffice it to say, that the significance of the contribution made by Two Thirds World theologians is unquestionable. The Consultation on the Church in Response to Human Need, held in Wheaton from June 20 – July 1 1983, marks what some would consider the completion of the process of shaping an evangelical social conscience.[20] Padilla, for example, observes:

> The document that emerged from it viewed *the whole of human life* as subject to the transforming power of God. In unequivocal terms it affirmed the inevitability of political involvement...It challenged individualism...It questioned private property as an absolute right...It also condemned the arms race...It pointed to the problem of

---

[16] Núñez, "Personal", 1067. See also Romans 6:11-13, 19-22; 1 Peter 2:16.

[17] See Stephen N. Williams, "Evangelicals and Eschatology: A Contentious Case" in *Interpreting the Bible: Historical and Theological Studies*, ed. A.N.S. Lane (Leicester: Apollos, 1997), 291-308, at 292.

[18] See for example Escobar, *Evangelio*, 115-127. Section II of this book is entitled "The response to Lausanne" in which Escobar details specific examples of practical developments in the evangelical approach to social concern.

[19] See for example, Padilla, "Evangelism", 27-33; Samuel Escobar, "Misión cristiana y transformación social" in Gregorio Rake, C. René Padilla and Tetsunao Yamamori, eds. *Servir con los pobres en América Latina* (Buenos Aires: Ediciones Kairós, 1997), 63-87.

[20] Padilla, "Evangelism", 31. See also Stephen N. Williams, "Looking Back", *Perichoresis* (forthcoming).

international injustice…and recognized the prophetic ministry of the church…By emphasizing that the kingdom of God is "both present and future, both societal and individual, both physical and spiritual," it laid a sound theological basis for the mission of the church, with no dichotomy between evangelism and social responsibility.[21]

Latin American evangelical theologians have consistently and persistently presented the Western evangelical community with the responsibility which they have been given as rich Christians in the world; the responsibility to communicate and testify to the powerful message of the gospel.[22] Costas asserts:

> The cry for justice and the promotion of peace are testimonies to God's love for the world. Both in the Hebrew Scriptures and in the New Testament God sends the people of faith to bear witness to his sovereign love, living for and advocating a new order of just peace. To live in the freedom of God's love is to struggle for, demand, and enjoy the blessing of being agents of justice and makers of peace. This implies nothing less than the protection of the right of every individual and every people to have access to the blessings of creation, to live in harmony with one another and the rest of creation. This right is protected when the church prays for, advocates and struggles for a project of "communal well-being where God's creation is governed justly," especially in situations where people live under the threat of death and extermination. In our time this implies what is called the Two Thirds World – Africa, Latin America, Asia and the islands of the Caribbean and the Pacific – as well as the impoverished, oppressed, and dispossessed minorities that live in the other one third of the world.[23]

In the three decades since Lausanne, and in the two decades since Wheaton, there is no doubt that Latin American evangelical theology contributed missiological lessons, not only in the critique of missionary practice presented by Latin American evangelical theologians but also from the impressive growth of popular Protestantism on the continent.[24] Escobar presents four observations in respect of this phenomenon.[25] First, flourishing Protestantism is a *religious movement*. Above all else, through the reading of the Scriptures and the teaching of pastors, members

---

[21] Padilla, "Evangelism", 31.

[22] Escobar comments "The existence of thriving churches in what used to be called the Third World confronts the old European or North American churches with a new set of questions and new ways of looking at God's word." Escobar, *Changing*, 128.

[23] Costas, *Liberating*, 142.

[24] Samuel Escobar, "Mission in Latin America: An Evangelical Perspective", *Missiology: An International Review* Vol. XX, no. 2 (1992): 241-253. See also C. René Padilla, "Hacia una evaluación teológica del ministerio integral" in *Servir con los pobres en América Latina*, eds. Gregorio Rake, C. René Padilla and Tetsunao Yamamori (Buenos Aires: Ediciones Kairós, 1997), 29-52 in which Padilla evaluates holistic ministry and the growth of the church. See also C. René Padilla, "El futuro del cristianismo en América Latina: perspectivas y desafíos misionológicos" in *Iglesia, ética y poder*, John H. Yoder, Lilia Solano and C. René Padilla (Buenos Aires: Ediciones Kairós, 1998), 62-87.

[25] See also Escobar, *Changing*, 92-96 where Escobar discusses five similar missiological lessons.

of such Protestant churches are searching for a religious experience of God. This experience of the powerful presence of the risen Christ confronts the supernatural darkness of existence and leads to the transformation of lives. Second, it is a *popular movement* that reaches the destitute, the marginalized, those who are denied a voice in society and those who are regarded as insignificant to the culture. Third, it is a *movement that mobilizes people for mission.* These communities of faith have a remarkable ability to mobilize all members of their churches. Escobar notes with interest that one Catholic observer "feels very strongly that this identification of the leaders with the people at the levels of ministry, liturgy, pastoral work, and teaching methods is very successful precisely at the points where Catholic priests are failing because of their elitist formation."[26] Fourth, popular Protestantism is a *movement that creates community.*[27] Despite criticism, observers of the popular Protestant movement recognise the religious and human warmth within the communities of faith, and the sense in which the experience of the riches of faith has implications for daily life.[28]

This growth of evangelical churches in Latin America, while not without problems, confronts the international evangelical community with the suggestion that Latin American evangelicals have been accurate in their call for holistic mission.[29] Padilla contends:

> In evangelical churches the possibility exists for "non persons" to know God as their Father and for the anonymous settlers of the poverty belts which encircle our cities to have a name. As a community located locally, but orientated globally, the church of the poor is a sign of the unity of all of humanity in the kingdom of God, but should exemplify this unity also at a political, economic and social level. If the gospel does not lead to obedience in the fields of politics, economics and society it is not the gospel of Jesus Christ, it is a gospel of a dualistic society which separates the sacred from the secular and which makes mission nothing more than a proselytising task.[30]

---

[26] Escobar, "Mission", 249.

[27] Samuel Escobar, "A Missiological Approach to Latin American Protestantism", *International Review of Mission* LXXXVII, no. 345 (1998): 161-173, at 171-172.

[28] Criticism has been directed towards the escapist eschatology, insensitivity to social problems, dualistic theology and the ostentatious displays of healing and spiritual gifts. See Escobar, "Mission", 250.

[29] See Samuel Escobar, "The Promise and Precariousness of Latin American Protestantism" in *Coming of Age: Protestantism in Contemporary Latin America*, ed. Daniel R. Miller (Lanham: University Press of America, 1993), 3-35. Escobar, for example, is careful to acknowledge the precariousness of young Latin American Protestantism and warns that all missiological reflection must be set within a firm theological framework, see Escobar, *Changing*, 58.

[30] C René Padilla, "Vigencia del Jubileo en el mundo actual (Levítico 25)", *Boletín Teológico* 63 (1996): 71-88, at 101. See also "Las iglesias locales y la misión mundial" in Padilla, *Discipulado*, 93-95. Costas concurs that mission is not an effort to proselytise and change the religious belief system, ideology or political allegiance of a person. Rather

The contribution made by Latin American evangelicals to the international dialogue has encouraged reflection on the evangelical understanding of the fullness of mission and the importance of partnership in mission.[31] There is no doubt that Western evangelicals have been motivated to reconsider their missiological presuppositions. Latin American theologians have been given the incentive to continue in their pursuit of an evangelical understanding of mission which demonstrates the biblical principles that they are convinced have been overshadowed in the past. Padilla remarks:

> The challenge facing the church in the field of development today is fundamentally the challenge of *human* development, in a context of justice. The need is for models of mission fully adapted to a situation characterized by a yawning chasm between rich and poor. The models of mission built on the affluence of the West condone this situation of injustice and condemn the indigenous churches to permanent dependence. In the long run, therefore, they are inimical to mission. The challenge both to Christians in the West and to Christians in the underdeveloped world is to create models of mission centred in a prophetic lifestyle, models that will point to Jesus Christ as the Lord over the totality of life, to the universality of the church, and to the interdependence of human beings in the world.[32]

Central to the Latin American evangelical understanding of mission presented to the international evangelical community, is the contention that faith should affect every aspect of the life of the believer, church and society. As is seen in this section, the integration of faith with life arises from an awareness of the structure of human life, the desires of human life, the need for social transformation in life, and the need for new life through evangelism. Despite this multifaceted analysis of the role of faith in the world, the Latin American evangelical contribution maintains as central the simple message: mission is discipleship. The Latin American evangelical understanding of the essence of mission as discipleship will be examined in the following section.

---

mission is "to share with others lovingly and respectfully the joyful news and liberating grace of the gospel...authentic evangelization refuses to be coercive and is always respectful of human dignity and freedom because it is an act of love." Costas, *Liberating*, 18.

[31] See chapter 10, "Sharing in Partnership" in Kirk, *Mission*, 184-204. See also Escobar, *Time*, 164-167.

[32] Padilla, *Mission*, 141.

9.3 Mission as Discipleship

9.3.1 The Latin American Evangelical Understanding of Discipleship

In the Latin American context it is vital to continually emphasise that Christians must be people who live lives distinct from society.[33] For Escobar, it is important to reiterate the familiar concept that Christians, as witnesses of the kingdom of God, must be a light in the darkness of the world. Confronting the emphasis on the theoretical, academic, or individualistic aspects of faith, he asserts: "Knowledge of God has to translate into a way of life. In the biblical language of the Old and the New Testament, the idea of 'walking' has to do with holiness, purity, obedience and ethics."[34] Thus, the new life of discipleship must be evident in a new attitude.[35] Balance, self-control, harmony, contentment, productivity, and fulfilment are the marks of joy in the life of a believer who lives in the knowledge of being created by God. In light of this truth, a believer should be one who delights in creation, who rests in the knowledge of being accepted, who enjoys a sense of purpose and fulfilment whatever circumstances life may bring.[36] Because life for Latin American communities has proven to be unstable and at times traumatic, the reapplication of such familiar biblical teaching on true discipleship is imperative. Kirk succinctly describes the essence of discipleship:

> Commitment to Jesus Christ is commitment to the one who preached, lived, suffered and rose again so that the kingdom might become a tangible reality in the world. Christian theology can only be done by those who, as disciples of this Jesus, are witnesses, agents and evidence of the kingdom – the central theme of God's drama.[37]

It is clear that Latin American evangelical theologians hold together the necessity of making a "decision of faith" with the understanding that one should become a disciple or follower of Christ as a result of that decision.[38] Jesus instructed his disciples to teach others all that he had taught them. An understanding of the totality of the content of the message of Jesus, therefore, is necessary for discipleship which leads to mission. For Jesus did not only preach the good news of the kingdom, but through his life and ministry of love and sacrifice presented the totality of the

---

[33] Samuel Escobar, "Luz y santidad", TMs (photocopy), paper presented at the CIEE Asamblea General in Duruelo, Colombia, 30 August - 8 September 1987, Latin American Theological Fraternity Archives, Buenos Aires, 1-17.

[34] Escobar, "Luz", 3.

[35] See for example chapter 13, "Cambio social y conversión" in Paredes, *Evangelio*, 169-181; Escobar, "Responsabilidad", 33.

[36] See Escobar, "Luz", 9-10. See also chapter 5 "Testimonio cristiano: palabra y acción" in Padilla, *Discipulado*, 28-31.

[37] Kirk, *Theology*, 42.

[38] See Emilio A. Núñez, "¿Qué es la misión de la Iglesia?", *Apuntes Pastorales* 11, no. 2 (1993): 18-20; Escobar, "Anabaptist", 82; Escobar, "Dynamism", 69, 81. See also Costas, *Liberating*, 112-130 where Costas discusses the call to conversion and the implications on the life of the believer.

principles of the kingdom in person. The reign of the kingdom is demonstrated by Jesus through love of enemies; in ethical behaviour; by doing good to those who hate; by pursuing peace; by healing the sick; in taking care of the poor and in struggling against the works of darkness. The life of Jesus is one of exemplifying action. He taught his disciples to pray; to proclaim the good news of the kingdom; to exclude no one; to identify with the poor without marginalizing the rich; to draw near to the sinner and the outcast; to speak against the powerful and to face the enemies of the kingdom of God with the word of God.[39] Naturally, Núñez also affirms that the significance of good works and discipleship is not limited to the example of Jesus, but permeates the entire New Testament teaching. He too emphasises the familiar implications of the fundamental principle of disciples being salt and light in their society and subsequently in the world.[40]

As one would expect, this presentation of discipleship is evident throughout the work of Latin American evangelical theologians.[41] It becomes clear that while this concept may be generally accepted within evangelical circles, evangelical theologians realise that the outworking of discipleship is lacking in their communities of faith. Consequently, Costas seeks to reiterate seven basic biblical principles of discipleship. First, a disciple follows Jesus in response to the invitation of Jesus. Following Christ, then, is a choice. Second, as a consequence of this choice, Christian discipleship implies a form of practical training which demands a complete change in lifestyle. Third, the choice to follow Christ and the willingness to live in a different manner is founded on personal relationship. Such a personal relationship with God should inevitably influence the relationships a believer has with other human beings. Fourth, to be permitted to follow Jesus is a gift of grace. Grace, then, should be the mark of every community of faith. Fifth, the disciple of Jesus is to show absolute commitment. Familiar as this may sound, in the political and social turmoil of Latin America, this principle, for many, has become a matter of life and death.[42] Sixth, the life of Christian discipleship is a life of close community with other believers. Once more, Costas counters the individualistic attitude evident in many evangelical churches. Seventh, to be a disciple of Jesus is permanent in the sense that the invitation to follow him is for life. Costas asserts: "To follow, to participate, to obey! These are the three fundamental signs of an authentic disciple, and we can adjudge, of faithful and true Christian mission."[43]

[39] See Núñez, "Misión", 19; Escobar, "Anabaptist", 84-88.

[40] See also Padilla, "Luz del mundo, sal de la tierra" in *Discipulado*, 41-43.

[41] Orlando E. Costas, "La misión como discipulado", *Boletín Teológico* 6 (1982): 45-59.

[42] See for example Samuel Escobar, "Transformation in Ayacucho: From Violence to Peace and Hope", *Transformation* 3, no. 1 (1986): 9-13; John Stam, "Christian Witness in Central America: A Radical Evangelical Perspective", *Transformation* 2, no.3 (1985): 14-17.

[43] Costas, "Discipulado", 58.

9.3.2 The Implications of Discipleship for Mission

In light of the evangelical understanding of discipleship, Padilla makes four observations regarding mission, based on the incarnation, the cross, the resurrection and the future hope. Firstly, the point of departure is the appreciation that God identified with humanity through Christ. Consequently, in mission, Christian disciples should seek to follow this "incarnational example" and identify with the rest of humanity in their context and situation.[44] While Latin American evangelicals recognise that the example of Jesus Christ is truly unique, they seek to learn from the manner in which Jesus ministered to others.[45] Contrary to other trends, at the time when Latin American evangelicals were first developing this understanding of mission, Padilla emphasises that it is not acceptable to consider the future salvation of the soul alone and as a result withdraw from society in anticipation of eschatological hope. "Christian *hope* is a hope that looks forward to the fulfilment of the universe but also takes a stand against injustice and death, hoping against hope."[46] Secondly, Christians must realise that the way of discipleship and consequently mission, is the way of the cross. That is to say, the way of suffering.[47]

> The Christian life is concretized from the standpoint of the cross. It is following Jesus to the cross, willing to experience God's abandonment on the cross through the experience of injustice in history, and willing to die in self-surrender with hopes of a new heaven and a new earth.[48]

Latin American evangelical theologians do not discuss suffering in the abstract. Rather, their reflection on the way of the cross is done with the integrity of those who are part of communities of faith that have actually experienced suffering. Thirdly, the resurrection of Christ reflects the power and freedom of God to create a new order and a new era. Christian mission, therefore, should be dynamised by new life in Christ, and characterised by love, service, and obedience.[49] Padilla considers the impact and so-called success of social action to be secondary to the demonstration such action makes of obedience and faithfulness to the command of God to love one's neighbour.[50] Fourthly, Christian mission focuses on the ultimate hope of a new creation. Naturally, Christians look back to what God has done in Christ, but also look forward to the final establishing of God's kingdom and the promise of a new creation.[51] Consequently, Christians are called to live in the shadow of the future:

---

[44] Escobar, "Responsabilidad", 23-30; Costas, *Christ*, 164; Padilla, *Mission*. 83, 90, 92.

[45] Escobar, "Evangelism", 320; Escobar, "Filosofía", 12-15; Escobar, "Formación", 69.

[46] Padilla, "Christology", 33.

[47] Escobar, "Responsabilidad", 30-32.

[48] Padilla, "Christology", 33-34.

[49] Escobar, "Responsabilidad", 33.

[50] See C. René Padilla, "Ser prójimo", *Iglesia y Misión* 74 (2000): 40-44.

[51] The evangelical understanding of the kingdom of God is discussed in more detail in chapter 6 of this book.

Christian conduct in society cannot be defined apart from an understanding of the action of God in Jesus Christ in order to fulfil his purpose to create a new humanity. A Christian approach to ethics is the gospel taken to its furthest consequences, the description of the lifestyle which points to what God has done and is doing through Jesus Christ...There is no place, however, for eschatological paralysis, passivity or conformism. The dilemma between an "otherworldly" attitude which does not give due attention to social responsibility and a "this worldly" attitude which reduces the church to an agency which promotes social and political action is a false dilemma. Biblical ethics (personal and social) arise from the simultaneous affirmation of the *already* and the *not yet* which condition the present.[52]

With such perspective, social action which is motivated by love of Christ, is not a way to redeem society, no more than good works are a way to justification before God. But social action is simply *the normal expression* of a disciple's new life in Christ. Escobar concurs with Padilla when he argues:

Political action and evangelism, social action and evangelism, service to the community and evangelism: these are signs of maturity and evidences of a new life. They are a symbol of death to the old life and an evidence of the new. Every cost in terms of sweat and blood, sacrifice, humiliation or persecution for the cause of right and justice will demonstrate that we are crucified with Christ, and not just experts on the doctrine of the crucifixion.[53]

Padilla presents five further biblical images of mission which are firmly rooted in the evangelical understanding of discipleship and the implications of this understanding for mission.[54] First, mission is presented as fishing for the kingdom.[55] It was vital for the disciples to recognise the needs of the multitude, to have a vision of Jesus Christ and consequently to engage in Christ's call to mission. Likewise the church today must have an encounter with Christ resulting in faithful discipleship which motivates mission to the multitudes in the world. Such mission is "God's way of pulling people out of the multitude into his kingdom, just as the fishers pull fish out of the sea."[56]

Second, mission is portrayed as compassion.[57] Indifference and apathy have no place in the life of a Christian disciple. In fact, such an attitude may be considered as a denial of faith in Christ. For "compassion is not mere pity; it is tenderness, a heartfelt sense of identification with those in need. It is a passionate, loving response leading to action on behalf of those who suffer, and thus presupposes personal

[52] C. René Padilla, *El evangelio hoy* (Buenos Aires: Certeza, 1975), 81, 92.

[53] Escobar, "Social", 100.

[54] C. René Padilla, "Misson is Compassion", *Missiology* 10, no. 3 (1982): 319-338.

[55] See Luke 5:1-11.

[56] Padilla, "Compassion", 322.

[57] See Matthew 9:35-38. See also Samuel Escobar, "The Global Scenario at the Turn of the Century" in *Global Missiology for the 21st Century*, ed. William D. Taylor (Grand Rapids: Baker Academic, 2000), 25-46, at 33.

contact with the needy."[58] Compassion, then, is the result of personal contact, prompted by social awareness and, as in the example of Jesus, translates into mission.

Third, mission is shown as feeding the multitude.[59] Jesus not only feeds the multitude but talks with them and discusses with his disciples. Every human need, therefore, is an opportunity for mission. "Mission is feeding the multitude, yet feeding it not only with bread *for* life but with the Bread *of* life. Christianity is not an ideology or a program. Its message concerns the whole of life, yet 'life is more than food and the body is more than clothes.'"[60]

Fourth, mission is displayed as confrontation.[61] In the New Testament, the mission of Jesus confronts the powers of death. Mission confronts such power with the truth, the justice, the righteousness and the authority of the crucified Messiah, who died and rose again to defeat such forces of power.

Fifth, mission is presented as suffering.[62] "There is no genuine Christian mission which is not marked by the cross. The inseparability of mission and suffering is taken for granted throughout the New Testament and clearly illustrated in Christ's mission to the multitudes."[63] Suffering was a mark of the messianic mission of Jesus and was the result of a struggle for power. Likewise, the suffering of Christ at the hands of Pilate was an indictment of human justice. Padilla asserts:

> Thus Christian mission and Christian discipleship are two sides of the same coin. Both derive their meaning from Jesus, the crucified Messiah, who even as Lord remains crucified. The Christian mission is the mission of those who have identified themselves with the Crucified and are willing to follow him to the cross.[64]

Evidently, for Latin American evangelical theologians the essence of mission is in discipleship, and in a life of obedience and service dedicated to following Jesus Christ. This has been seen in their commitment to incarnate the message of the gospel in the present, in anticipation of the future eschatological hope. Those who enter into discipleship do so in response to the good news of the gospel. The community of faith is responsible for sharing this good news. This good news is a message of transformation: transformation in the life of the individual,

---

[58] Padilla, "Compassion", 323. See also "The Valle de Bravo Affirmation" December 5-11, 1988, TMs (photocopy), Latin American Theological Fraternity Archives, Buenos Aires, 1-10.

[59] See John 6:1-71.

[60] Padilla, "Compassion", 330. See also Luke 12:23.

[61] See Luke 19:28-44; Padilla, "Estado", 32-33.

[62] See Matthew 27:11-26.

[63] Padilla, "Compassion", 334.

[64] Padilla, "Compassion", 338. The wording "who even as Lord remains crucified" is an unusual form of expression for an evangelical theologian. It is, nonetheless, a direct quotation from Padilla here in which he appears to be emphasising that while Jesus, as Lord, had the power to free himself from the cross, he did not, but remained on the cross.

transformation in the life of the faith community, and transformation of society as a result of the presence and actions of the disciple and the church.

9.4 Mission as Transformation

The two spheres of transformation through the power of the gospel which will be examined in this section, are the significance of the transformational message for the individual, and the importance of the transformational message for the mission and ministry of the community of faith.

Firstly, it is inevitable that evangelical theologians are convinced that mission begins with the transformation of an individual who responds positively to the gospel's call for repentance (see section 6.6).[65] Familiar as the call to repentance may be, Latin American evangelical theologians consider it necessary to reevaluate the biblical presentation of the concept, and reapply the implications of repentance directly to the Latin American context. For if repentance is demonstrated in the life of a follower of Christ through Christian ethics and concrete obedience, then this understanding of repentance is foundational to contextual theology, as evidenced in the discussion on the implications of discipleship on mission. Padilla contends:

> Where there is no concrete obedience there is no repentance, and without repentance there is no salvation...Salvation is man's return to God, but it is at the same time *also* man's return to his neighbour...It is not merely a subjective experience, it is a moral experience as well – an experience that affects his life...an experience that brings him out of himself and turns him towards his neighbour...Repentance is much more than a private affair between the individual and God. It is the complete reorientation of life in the world – among men – in response to the work of God in Jesus Christ...The gospel is not a call to social quietism. Its goal is not to take a man out of the world but to put him into it, no longer as a slave but as a son of God and a member of the body of Christ...If Jesus Christ is Lord, men must be confronted with his authority over the totality of life. Evangelism is not, and cannot be, a mere offer of benefits achieved by Jesus Christ. Christ's work is inseparable from his person; the Jesus who died for our sins is the Lord of the whole universe, and the announcement of forgiveness in his name is inseparable from the call to repentance, the call to turn from the "rulers of this world" to the Lord of glory.[66]

Transformation of the individual is demonstrated in this complete reorientation of life. Secondly, in becoming active members of the church, such transformed individuals contribute to the transformation of the community of faith. This is evident in the understanding the church has of her mission, in the human relationships within the church, and in the manner in which the church communicates the message of the gospel in society (see section 8.5).

First, it is vital that the understanding of the mission of the church in Latin America is transformed, in light of Scripture. The church must not seek to escape

---

[65] Padilla, *Mission*, 79-82.
[66] Padilla, *Mission*, 21.

reality and withdraw from the struggles of society in the name of "separation from the world."[67] The ministry of Jesus and the witness of the early church stand in direct contrast to such escapism.[68] For the New Testament demonstrates that ministries of preaching, teaching, healing and service engage with the contemporary world in anticipation of the world to come.

> [Jesus] does not take refuge in "religion" or "spiritual things," as if his kingdom had nothing to do with political and social life; rather he demythologizes the politics of man and presents himself as the Servant-King, the creator and model of a community that submits to him as Lord and commits itself to live as he lived.[69]

The salvation of individuals alone should not constitute the central concern of the church.[70] Padilla argues that "there is no place for statistics on 'how many souls die without Christ every minute' if they do not take into account how many of those who die are dying of hunger. There is no place for evangelism that passes by the man who was assaulted by thieves on the road from Jerusalem to Jericho and sees in him only a soul that must be saved."[71] For in contrast, "an unprejudiced reading of the Gospels shows us a Jesus who, in the midst of many political alternatives...personifies and proclaims a new alternative – the kingdom of God."[72] The distinctive aspect of the kingdom, proclaimed by Jesus, is sacrifice: "This service to the point of sacrifice belongs to the very essence of his mission. And this must be the distinctive sign of the community that acknowledges him as King."[73] Such sacrifice is not an "other-worldly" phenomenon but the outworking of the faith of the church here on earth. With similar implications for the mission of the church, Jesus confronts the power structures of his day by denouncing the ambition of the leaders to dominate.[74] In contrast he presents an alternative where love, service and dedication to others are foundational.

> [Jesus] presupposes a concept of salvation that includes the whole man and cannot be reduced to the simple forgiveness of sins and assurance of unending life with God in heaven. A comprehensive mission corresponds to a comprehensive view of salvation. Salvation is wholeness. Salvation is total humanization. Salvation is eternal life, the life of the kingdom of God, life that begins here and now (this is the meaning of the present

---

[67] See Padilla, *Mission*, 22.

[68] See also "The Evangelistic Ministry of Jesus" in Costas, *Liberating*, 49-70.

[69] Padilla, *Mission*, 23.

[70] See also Padilla, "Comunidad y misión" in *Discipulado*, 31-33.

[71] Padilla, *Mission*, 25. See also Escobar, "Responsabilidad", 32; Escobar, "Filosofía", 16-17.

[72] Padilla, *Mission*, 23. See also Escobar, "Kingdom", 29.

[73] Padilla, *Mission*, 23. See also the helpful collection of essays on the subject of the church as an agent of transformation in Padilla and Yamamori, *Iglesia*.

[74] See John H. Yoder, "Cristo y el poder" in *Iglesia, ética y poder*, John H. Yoder, Lilia Solano and C. René Padilla (Buenos Aires: Ediciones Kairós, 1998), 19-48. See also Kirk, *Theology*, 42.

tense of the verb "has eternal life" in the Gospel and the Epistles of John) and touches all aspects of man's being.[75]

Latin American evangelicals are careful to acknowledge, however, that the mission of the church cannot be reduced to a social, economic or political one. The church cannot be reduced to an organisation simply responsible for improvements in the human condition or in human circumstances. Nothing can replace the significance of spiritual regeneration in human beings, and so they "cannot accept the equation of salvation with the satisfaction of bodily needs, social amelioration, or political liberation."[76] Nevertheless, a more holistic understanding of the transformational mission of the church is consistently argued. Padilla, for example, contends:

> Here I first propose that repentance, conceived as a reorientation of one's whole personality, throws into relief the social dimension of the gospel, for it involves a turning from sin to God not only in the individual subjective consciousness but *in the world*. Without ethics, I say, there is no repentance. Am I slighting the personal aspect of evangelization, as I have been accused of doing? I don't think I am. What I am doing is recognizing that man is a social being and that there is no possibility for him to be converted to Christ and to grow as a Christian except as a social being. Man never turns to God as a sinner in the abstract, he always turns to God in a specific social situation.[77]

Second, it is clear that in light of Scripture, not only is the understanding of the mission of the church transformed, but also human relationships within the church should be transformed. The church is not a community which proclaims a message of reconciliation between individuals and God alone. Rather, a church in submission to the kingdom will seek reconciliation, not only between a human being and God but also between one human being and another. The expectation of the kingdom is that human relationships should be radically changed. Likewise, the relationship between humanity and the rest of creation should be renewed.[78]

> The aim of the gospel is to produce in us faith, but faith that works through love. Without the works of love there is no genuine faith. If it is true that we are not saved by works, it is also true that the faith that saves is the faith that works. As Luther put it, "Faith alone justifies, but faith is never alone." The indicative of the gospel and the imperative of Christian ethics may be distinguished but must never be separated.[79]

Latin American evangelical theologians seek to apply afresh the New Testament principles regarding human relationships to the life and ministry of the community of faith. Evangelical ecclesiology has already been discussed in detail in chapter

---

[75] Padilla, *Mission*, 22.
[76] Padilla, *Mission*, 41.
[77] Padilla, *Mission*, 37.
[78] Escobar, "Católicos", 74.
[79] Padilla, *Mission*, 39.

eight. Suffice it to say here, that in relation to the transformation of human relationships within the church, the community of faith should be generous and unselfish; it should be a community where racial, cultural, social and gender barriers are broken down; it should be committed to reconciliation between human beings; and it should resist the notions presented by the world. In sum, the church should be a community which presents a dramatic alternative to society, in response to the example of Jesus, and as a result of faithful discipleship.[80]

> The New Testament knows nothing of a gospel that makes a divorce between soteriology and ethics, between communion with God and communion with one's neighbour, between faith and works. The Cross is not only the negation of the validity of every human effort to gain God's favour by works of the law; it is *also* the demand for a new quality of life characterized by love – the opposite of an individualistic life centred on personal ambitions and indifferent to the needs of others. The significance of the Cross is both soteriological and ethical. This is so because Jesus not only created the indicative of the gospel ("By this we know love, that he laid down his life for us" – 1 John 3:16a) but also *simultaneously* provided the pattern for human life here and now ("And we ought to lay down our lives for the brethren" – 1 John 3:16b).[81]

The manner in which the church communicates the message of the gospel is the third aspect of transformation within the community of faith. A church which has a biblical understanding of mission, and a community of faith in which human relationships are under transformation will be aware that "it is easier to conform than to be transformed, and one can always find a theology to justify it."[82] Thus, the community of faith must continually assess whether the example being set in society is consistent with biblical ecclesiology and whether the good news is being communicated faithfully in word and deed.

The transformational message of the gospel proclaimed through mission and through the life of the church crosses all frontiers of geography, language, gender, culture, or society.[83] The gospel dignifies all culture and relativises every culture.[84] To cross these frontiers necessitates a return to the fundamental principles of mission evident in the New Testament; a revision of historical models of mission; an

---

[80] See Núñez, "Misión", 20; Costas, *Christ*, 69. For a helpful overview of the understanding of social transformation in the theology of liberation see José Míguez Bonino, "Love and Social Transformation in Liberation Theology" in *Love: The Foundation of Hope: the Theology of Jürgen Moltmann and Elisabeth Moltmann*, ed. Frederic B. Burnham, Charles S. McCoy and M. Douglas Meeks (New York: Harper and Row Publishers, 1988), 60-76.

[81] Padilla, *Mission*, 24. See also "The Message of the Cross" in Costas, *Liberating*, 88-111.

[82] Escobar, "Kingdom", 37. The original paper was presented to the Second Consultation of the Latin American Theological Fraternity in Lima, December 1972.

[83] Escobar, *Changing*, 6-7.

[84] See also chapter 8 "La comunicación transcultural del evangelio" in Paredes, *Evangelio*, 97-107.

appreciation of contemporary societies and cultures; and a disciplined spiritual maturity which is demonstrated in a balanced commitment to the practical outworking of faith.[85] The church must confront contemporary society with the reality of such a message.

> For it is only in the measure in which a church itself is the incarnation of God's purpose to put all things under the Lordship of Christ that it can denounce evils in society which are a denial of God's original purpose for man. There is an internal connection between the life of the church and its prophetic ministry, and between the prophetic ministry of the church and its evangelization. The church is called here and now to be what God intends the whole of society to be. In its prophetic ministry it lays open the evils that frustrate the purpose of God in society; in its evangelization it seeks to integrate men into that purpose of God the full realization of which is to take place in the kingdom to come. Consequently, wherever the church fails as a prophet it also fails as an evangelist.[86]

These ethical demands of the gospel are a heartfelt obedience in response to God, that is to say, an outward display of gratitude for the grace and mercy already received. It is the responsibility of the church to communicate the gospel as a community exhibiting the biblical principles of *reconciliation, personal authenticity, service* and *generosity*. Speaking on behalf of Latin American evangelicals, Padilla asserts with clarity: "Our greatest need is for a more biblical gospel and a more faithful church."[87]

A church seeking to communicate the transformational message in a holistic way will face conflict and confrontation. Despite this, Padilla calls for consistency and perseverance in the faithful witness of the Latin American church:

> Conflict is inevitable when the church takes the gospel seriously. It is just as true today in the consumer society as it was in the first century…What *is* important is that [man] be liberated from his slavery to the powers of destruction and integrated into the purpose of God to place all things under the Lordship of Jesus Christ, into the new creation which is made visible in the community that models its life on the Second Adam. When, in its desire to avoid the conflict, the church accommodates itself to the spirit of the age, it loses the prophetic dimension of its mission and becomes an agent of the *status quo*. The salt loses its savour.[88]

---

[85] Samuel Escobar, "Las nuevas fronteras de la misión" in Congreso Latinoamericano de Evangelización (CLADE), III, 24 de agosto a 4 de septiembre de 1992, Quito: *Todo el Evangelio para todos los pueblos desde América Latina* (Quito: Fraternidad Teológica Latinoamericana, 1993), 376-386.

[86] Padilla, *Mission*, 31. See also "The Prophetic Character of Evangelization" in Costas, *Liberating*, 33-48.

[87] Padilla, *Mission*, 41-44.

[88] Padilla, *Mission*, 60.

Once again, it seems that much of this missiological discussion centres on assertions generally accepted within evangelical circles. It would be fair to say that Latin American evangelical theologians are not concerned with novelty in theology but with integrity. If the Christian church believes it is to convey a transformational message, then the church must be willing to question the manner in which the message is being communicated if it is not leading to authentic change.

It is clear that the Latin American understanding of mission is based on the biblical consequences of faithful discipleship. The message of mission is one of personal, communal and societal transformation despite conflict which may ensue. It is this very issue of the place of social involvement in mission which has proven to be one of the most controversial topics in the history of evangelicalism. Despite controversy, Latin American evangelical theologians remain constant in their insistence that the biblical message of mission cannot be separated from the biblical teaching on social responsibility. This subject will be the focus of the following section.

9.5 Mission as Social Responsibility

The understanding of mission as discipleship, mission as transformation, and mission as social responsibility is expounded by Latin American evangelical theologians in their search for a missiology which is thoroughly biblical. The debate surrounding the relationship between the ministry of the word and the place of social responsibility in the mission of the church remains a subject of discussion within evangelicalism.[89] Padilla recognises the significance of a balanced understanding:

> The lack of appreciation of the broader dimensions of the gospel leads inevitably to a misunderstanding of the mission of the church. The result is an evangelism that regards the individual as a self-contained unit – a Robinson Crusoe to whom God's call is addressed as to one on an island – whose salvation takes place exclusively in terms of a relationship with God. It is not seen that the individual does not exist in isolation, and consequently that it is not possible to speak of salvation with no reference to the world of which he is part.[90]

In order to present the evangelical understanding of mission as social responsibility in Latin America, the following three aspects will be examined: *mission as social responsibility in light of the kingdom of God, mission as social responsibility in light of the Latin American context,* and *mission as social responsibility in the church.*

---

[89] For a helpful discussion on the relationship between evangelism and social responsibility which includes an overview of evangelical attitudes see Kirk, *World,* in particular chapters 5, 6 and 7; Escobar, "Responsabilidad", 21-22; Padilla, "Evangelism and Social Responsibility: From Wheaton '66 to Wheaton '83", *Transformation* 2, no.3 (1985): 27-33; Vinay Samuel and Christopher Sugden, eds. *The Church in Response to Human Need* (Grand Rapids: Eerdmans, 1987).

[90] Padilla, *Mission,* 1. See also Escobar, "Latin", 10-11.

9.5.1 Mission as Social Responsibility in Light of the Kingdom of God

Foundational to the Latin American understanding of mission as social responsibility is the biblical principle that "the church is clearly called to be a 'new society'…Here and now it is intended to reflect the values of the kingdom by the power of the Holy Spirit" (see section 6.7).[91] Representing the Latin American evangelical position, Padilla contends:

> It is true that "through the apostolic writings, Jesus and the apostles continue to speak"; it is equally true that through the church and its good works the kingdom becomes historically visible as a present reality. Good works are not, therefore, a mere addendum to mission; rather, they are an integral part of the present manifestation of the kingdom: they point back to the kingdom that has already come and forward to the kingdom that is yet to come. This does not mean, of course, that the good works – the signs of the kingdom – will necessarily persuade unbelievers of the truth of the gospel. Even the works that Jesus performed were sometimes rejected. Nor were his works alone rejected, some turned away from his words as well. We must, therefore, posit no interpretation of the Christian mission that leaves the impression that the verbal proclamation is "in itself persuasive to the unbelievers" while visible signs – good works – are not. Neither seeing nor hearing will always result in faith. Both word and deed point to the kingdom of God, but "no one can say 'Jesus is Lord' except by the Holy Spirit" (1 Corinthians 12:3).[92]

It becomes clear that, for Latin American evangelical theologians, evangelism and social responsibility cannot be understood apart from the fact that the kingdom of God in Jesus Christ has invaded history, and is both a present reality and a future hope. The kingdom of God evidences the release of the redemptive power of God in history. It is this power which brings good news to the poor, freedom to the prisoners, sight to the blind and liberation to the oppressed.[93] Such emphasis on the present reality and the future hope, held in balance, gives freedom to affirm both evangelism and social responsibility.

> As long as both evangelism and social responsibility are regarded as essential to mission, we need no rule of thumb to tell us which comes first and when. On the other hand, if they are not seen as essential, the effort to understand the relationship between them is a useless academic exercise. It would be as useless as the effort to understand the relationship between the right and left wings of a plane when one believes that the plane can fly with only one wing. And who can deny that the best way to understand the relationship between the two wings of a plane is by actually flying it rather than by merely theorizing about it?[94]

---

[91] Padilla, *Mission*, 192. See also Padilla, *Discipulado*, 37-40, 44-50.

[92] Padilla, *Mission*, 193. See also Escobar, "Formación", 70.

[93] Padilla, *Mission*, 197; Padilla, "Estado", 30-32.

[94] Padilla, *Mission*, 198.

It has been productive for Latin American evangelical theologians to consider missiological issues which are specifically relevant to the Latin American context. For only then have they been able to assess the manner in which the church should respond as an alternative community.

9.5.2 Mission as Social Responsibility in Light of the Latin American Context

Contextual theology by nature is specific theology, and Latin American evangelical theologians continue to reflect on a wide variety of issues in their commitment to attempt to cross all frontiers in Latin America with the message of good news. They are not reticent to discuss even the most controversial subjects with regard to mission and social responsibility.[95] Central to the debate, for Latin Americans, are the subjects of politics, urban mission, economics and poverty. It is necessary to briefly consider each here.

First, in the unstable political context of Latin America, evangelical reflection on social responsibility has inevitably led to discussion on the participation of Christians in politics.[96] In the past, evangelicals in Latin America came to be characterised by an apolitical attitude.[97] Padilla comments that the evangelical social engagement of contemporary times could not have been imagined in the post-Second World War era.

> The growth of Evangelicals has brought them to positions of power and responsibility as individuals and as communities. Unfortunately, because of their lack of theology of social realities and power, they have been tempted to become blind supporters of the government instead of critical co-operators. Constantinianism and the temptations of

---

[95] See for example, Emilio A. Núñez, "El SIDA llegó hasta nosotros", *Apuntes Pastorales* 10, no. 6 (1993): 46-48, in which Núñez reflects on the serious suffering caused by AIDS in society, the question of whether such illness is a judgement from God and the response of Christians to the crisis. See also Padilla, *Discipulado* for discussions on controversial issues such as violence, 170-177; human rights, 178-180; racism, 184-186; gender, 196-198; corruption, 212-218; tolerance, 199-201; and AIDS, 202-204.

[96] For early reflections on politics see Samuel Escobar, "Los evangélicos y la política", *Certeza* 8 (1967): 230-232; Samuel Escobar, "The Totalitarian Climate" in *One Race, One Gospel, One Task Volume II*, eds. C. Henry and W. Mooneyham (Minneapolis: World Congress on Evangelism, 1967), 288-290. For a helpful contemporary overview see the selection of essays in C. René Padilla, ed. *De la marginación al compromiso: Los evangélicos y la política en América Latina* (Buenos Aires: Fraternidad Teológica Latinoamericana, 1991); C. René Padilla, "Hacia una ética política evangélica", *Boletín Teológico* 44 (1991): 261-274; Emilio A. Núñez, "Dios y el gobierno humano." *Apuntes Pastorales* 11, no. 3 (1993): 30-33; Padilla, *Discipulado*, 135-144; Solano, "Iglesia", 49-61; Escobar, "Entender", 17; de Powell, "Participación", 233-248; Escobar, "¿Se revisa?", 8-11.

[97] For a discussion on the development of Latin American evangelical political involvement see C. René Padilla, "Latin American Evangelicals Enter the Public Square", *Transformation* 9, no. 3 (1995): 2-7; Padilla, "Actors", 82-88; Escobar, "Religious", 163-164; Escobar, "El poder", 168.

power and benefits should not be something that takes us by surprise, theologically unarmed.[98]

For this reason, the Latin American Theological Fraternity sought to respond to the need for evangelical theological reflection on political involvement during a consultation entitled "The Theology and Practice of Power" held in the Dominican Republic from 24 to 29 May, 1983.[99] The result of this consultation was the Jarabacoa Declaration.[100] While Padilla recognises the continuing need for discussion on evangelicals in politics, and indeed the serious negative influence which political involvement can have on evangelical believers, he affirms the hope that "the political awakening of evangelical Christians may point to the beginning of a new day" within a continent in crisis.[101]

> If the presence of evangelicals on the political scene proves anything…it is that…there are socioeconomic, political, and religious factors that at present force them to act on that scene. If in the past, when they were an insignificant religious minority, they could not avoid every kind of political involvement in a society whose life is strongly conditioned by institutional structures and relations, now, as a movement that is rapidly growing, they can avoid it even less. Under these circumstances, it is absolutely urgent that evangelicals face the political challenge with true Christian integrity on both the practical and theoretical levels.[102]

In the Latin American political context, it has also been imperative to reassert biblical principles in response to the reality which communities of faith face. Costas contends that the community of faith must affirm life and denounce violence in three ways.[103] Firstly, the church must defend the right of the poor to life, and must fight the socio-economic oppression and repression which continues to contribute to poverty. Secondly, the church must condemn torture and must champion fair legal procedures. Thirdly, the church must defend human freedom in relation to issues such as fair elections, and opposition to the arms race.

> The challenge to denounce this panorama of violence and to affirm life becomes unavoidable for Christians and churches in the Americas. The kingdom of which we are

---

[98] Escobar, Arana, Steuernagel and Zapata, "Critique", 62. See also Escobar, "Kingdom", 8-14; Escobar, "Elementos", 10-20; Escobar, "El poder", 176.

[99] The papers and proceedings of this conference can be found in Deiros, *Evangélicos*. See in particular, Sidney H. Rooy, "Relaciones de la iglesia con el poder político: modelo reformado", 41-72; Pablo Deiros, "Relaciones de la iglesia con el poder político: modelo bautista", 73-140; Padilla, "Estado"; Escobar, "Poder".

[100] This declaration was published in *Transformation* 2, no. 1 (1985): 23-28. See also Escobar, "Elementos", 17.

[101] Padilla, "Square", 7.

[102] Padilla, "Actors", 91.

[103] See C. René Padilla, "La violencia en el Nuevo Testamento", *Boletín Teológico* 39 (1990): 197-207.

a part and whose message we have been called to proclaim demands that we side with love, not with hate; with justice, not with inequality; with peace, not with aggression. Since this is the case, we have no alternative but to marshal our forces to denounce institutionalised violence, to affirm the right of the poor and oppressed to life, and to commit ourselves to programs that place the human being above the state and its institutions. To do anything different would be to turn coward and to deny our duties as firstfruits of God's new order of life.[104]

Second, evangelical theologians have come to recognise the significance of urban mission for the Latin American context.[105]

An analysis of the life and mission of the majority of evangelical churches in our great urban centres reveals a definite crisis with varied manifestations. The so-called "historical denominations" express a growing social awareness in their theoretical reflection about urban mission, but this concern is not manifest with equal intensity in practical terms. On the other hand, in our cities we continue to observe evangelistic models with an exclusive emphasis on mission as a proclamation centred in individual repentance and salvation. This emphasis not only reinforces the dehumanizing individualism of the large cities and ignores the dimension of community in the gospel of the kingdom of God…we affirm the urgent need of a constant renewal of the life and mission of the church. This renovation must come into being in the light of the word of God, in the ministerial example of Jesus Christ, and by the work of the Holy Spirit. Such a renovation ought to result in concrete transformations of our structures, styles and programs of urban mission.[106]

Globalisation and urbanisation have contributed to worsening economic conditions in Latin America.[107] Political instability, social unrest and environmental issues are particularly pertinent to churches seeking to demonstrate biblical ethics and social responsibility in urban regions.[108] The Valle de Bravo declaration formulated at the conference entitled, "Seeking the Peace of the City: a Consultation on Urban Mission" states:

---

[104] Costas, *Christ*, 96.

[105] See Samuel Escobar, "Las ciudades en la práctica misionera del apóstol Pablo: El caso de Filipos", *Misión* 31 (1990): 6-13; Orlando E. Costas, "La misión del pueblo de Dios en la ciudad", *Boletín Teológico* 7 (1982): 85-96. A consultation hosted by the Latin American Theological Fraternity on the subject of urban mission entitled "En busca de la paz de la ciudad: consulta misión urbana" was held in Valle de Bravo, Mexico from Dec. 5-11, 1988. "Afirmación de Valle de Bravo" can be found in *Boletín Teológico* 33. Available in English as the previously mentioned "The Valle de Bravo Affirmation".

[106] See "Valle", 1988, 4.

[107] See for example, chapter 15 "La contextualización del evangelio en un medio urbano globalizado" in Paredes, *Evangelio,* 195-210.

[108] See Samuel Escobar, "Formación del pueblo de Dios en los grandes urbes", *Boletín Teológico* 7 (1982): 37-84.

The church in the city is called to be a compassionate community, sensitive to pain and human tragedy, empathetic, and with a message of hope, since Christ, by his incarnation, death and resurrection, enables us to affirm life, in opposition to the death that surrounds us. The church is called to participate in solidarity with those who are without hope, and to serve them as an agent of peace. A compassionate church is called to seek out the multitudes who are abandoned and scattered, and to help them become a people of God who are united under the lordship of Jesus Christ, who are aware of their situation, and who have courage to undertake projects that fulfil God's purpose.[109]

Third, Latin American evangelical theologians have taken the subject of Christian economic responsibility seriously. They have presented biblical discussion which confronts Christian assumptions regarding money, stewardship, oppression, justice and the global economy.[110] Padilla, for example, recognises the desperate need for an ethical revolution with regard to global economics.[111] He opposes the suggestion that there is no alternative system which would function properly. He is critical of the current system which condemns millions to a life of poverty.[112] Padilla seeks to apply Old Testament principles to the contemporary economic situation in an exposition of Leviticus 25. Firstly, he identifies ecological integrity and liberation.[113] Such values highlight the vital stewardship of natural resources, and proper treatment of creation.[114] He also observes that the economy promoted in both the Old and New Testaments is what Padilla describes as "an economy of enough." That is to say, an economy where every person has sufficient and where every person is considered worthy of that dignity. There is no privileged minority. Secondly, Padilla recognises the significance of justice and peace in the society described in Leviticus

---

[109] "Valle", 1988, 7. See also Escobar, "Kingdom", 37.

[110] See the papers presented at the Latin American Theological Fraternity Consultation held in Quito during December 1990 on "Teología y vida" available in *Boletín Teológico* 42/43 (1991). For example, C. René Padilla, "Pobreza y mayordomía", 93-101; Samuel Escobar, "Autoritarismo y poder", 131-143; Escobar, "Opresión"; "Preguntas y respuestas" on subjects such as alternative economic models, the economy and theological reflection, the market economy and Christian faith and the crisis in Marxism and the collapse of socialism, 171-175. See also Padilla, "Vigencia", 71-88; H. Fernando Bullón, "El docente cristiano y las ciencias económicas y sociales en el proceso de transformación", 189-224; Marianne Scholte, "Reflexiones sobre la enseñanza de la economía desde un punto de vista cristiano", in Sidney H. Rooy, ed. Congreso Latinoamericano de Evangelización (CLADE), IV, Quito, Ecuador, 2 a 9 de septiembre de 2000: *Presencia cristiana en el mundo académico: el testimonio evangélico hacia el tercer milenio: palabra, espíritu y misión* (Buenos Aires: Ediciones Kairós, 2001), 225-242.

[111] See also Kirk, *World,* 64-66.

[112] See Padilla, "Vigencia", 71-88.

[113] Leviticus 25:1-12.

[114] See also papers presented on the consumer society and the stewardship of creation at CLADE IV in Fernando H. Bullón, Juliana Morillo and Sergio Membreño, eds. Congreso Latinoamericano de Evangelización (CLADE), IV, Quito, 2 a 9 de septiembre de 2000: *Sociedad de consumo y mayordomía de la creación: el testimonio evangélico hacia el tercer milenio: palabra, espítiru y misión.* (Buenos Aires: Ediciones Kairós, 2002).

25.[115] The economy presented is one where fair prices are paid, and where peace is promised. God demonstrates concern for the poor and their needs. It is the responsibility of the community of faith to reflect such an attitude. Thirdly, Padilla affirms that stewardship and solidarity with the poor are principles taught in the Bible.[116] Padilla considers the essence of the practice of Jubilee to be the firm conviction that all people are equal before God. It becomes evident that for Padilla, the ecological imbalance in the world and the socio-economic imbalance in the world are "two sides of the same coin."[117] Biblical ethics seek to restructure ecology, society and the economy with peace and justice as the foundation. The community of faith, therefore, is to present a prophetic vision of what is possible when the justice, peace and integrity of God are displayed in relation to creation and to humankind.

Fourth, in response to their context, Latin American evangelical theologians have sought to develop an evangelical understanding of poverty over many years.[118] The inextricable link between a theology of creation, a theology of stewardship, and a theology of love for one's neighbour is recognised as pertinent to the subject of poverty. While a systematized Latin American evangelical approach to poverty has yet to be produced, evangelicals are convinced of the significance of the subject. Costas, for example, observes:

> Their lives [the impoverished, oppressed and dispossessed] are worth little or nothing, caged in social systems and projects that have been designed and manufactured for a few, and imposed by local oligarchies and unscrupulous power-brokers operating in their own economic and political interests...these multitudes are not only sinners in need of the gospel but victims of sin. They challenge the people of God to bear witness to God's love by advocating, struggling for, and praying for their social well-being. "If the church would only say to the poor people of the world that they deserve to live, it would be making a powerful evangelistic pronouncement."[119]

The evangelical commitment to a simple lifestyle has constituted an important part of the evangelical response to poverty. Padilla, in particular, has sought to develop a biblical understanding of poverty which takes into consideration the life and ministry of Jesus, his call to discipleship, the example of the early church and

---

[115] Leviticus 25:13-23.

[116] Leviticus 25: 23-55.

[117] Padilla, "Vigencia", 86.

[118] Padilla, "Fraternidad", 110. For a brief overview of the evangelical contributions on the subject of poverty over the years see Padilla, "Pobreza", 93-101; see chapter 2 "The Gospel and the Poor" in Escobar and Driver, *Christian*, 36-56; Franklin Canelos, "Causas y orígenes de la pobreza en América Latina" in Congreso Latinoamericano de Evangelización (CLADE), IV, Quito, Ecuador, 2 a 9 de septiembre de 2000: *Misión integral y pobreza: el testimonio evangélico hacia el tercer milenio: palabra, espítiru y misión*, eds. C. René Padilla and Tetsunao Yamamori (Buenos Aires: Ediciones Kairós, 2001), 19-48; Kirk, *World*, 62-64; Kirk, *Mission*, chapter 7 entitled "Justice for the poor", 98-117.

[119] Costas, *Liberating*, 142. The Chilean theologian Pablo Richard is cited by Costas here.

the teaching of the apostles. Such Latin American reflections provide valuable insights to Western evangelicals whose experience of poverty does not compare to the reality experienced by theologians living in the Two Thirds World.[120]

Latin American evangelical theologians are developing their understanding of mission as social responsibility in light of the kingdom of God and in light of the Latin American context. They also focus on mission as social responsibility in the church. As Latin American evangelical ecclesiology is discussed in detail in the previous chapter, it will only be necessary to briefly overview the principles for social responsibility which are proposed.

9.5.3 Mission as Social Responsibility in the Church

In respect of mission as social responsibility, Costas identifies three foundational priorities for mission within the Latin American church.[121] Firstly, and most obviously, the community of faith must respond to the desperate need of those who have not had the opportunity to hear the good news of the kingdom of God. Secondly, the church should be enabled to reach those who are outside the frontiers of the gospel. The poor, the oppressed and the powerless form the majority of this group. For this reason, the church should become "incarnated in the struggles and thus help [the poor] articulate their fears and hopes, sharing their expectations and celebrating the gospel from within their concrete reality."[122] Thirdly, it is the responsibility of the church to include the promotion of human solidarity and Christian unity. For this will give credibility to the communication of the gospel across multiple frontiers of race, ideology, class, religion, denomination and gender.[123] The church, however, should not lose sight of the gospel message during involvement in societal struggles.

> A proclamation that does not hold forth the promises of the justice of the kingdom to the poor of the earth is a caricature of the gospel; but the Christian participation in the struggles for justice which does not point towards the promises of the kingdom also make a caricature of a Christian understanding of justice.[124]

Padilla identifies four key issues which he envisages will arise for a community of faith seeking the biblical integration of the mission of the church and social

---

[120] See "New Testament Perspectives on Simple Lifestyle" in Padilla, *Mission*, 170-185. See also the consultation document "An Evangelical Commitment to Simple Lifestyle, International (March 1980)" in Padilla and Sugden, *Texts*, 17-22; Padilla and Sugden, *Evangelicals*, 12-13.

[121] Orlando E. Costas, "The Mission of Ministry", *Missiology: An International Review* XIV, no. 4 (1986): 463-472.

[122] Costas, "Mission", 470.

[123] Padilla, "Prójimo", 42; Costas, *Christ*, 96-98.

[124] The World Council of Churches' Ecumenical Affirmation on Mission and Evangelism cited by Costas, "Mission", 470.

responsibility. Firstly, the church must decide how exactly it should be involved in justice and economics.[125] Believers are already involved in these aspects of society and therefore must make every effort to ensure that this involvement is faithful to the gospel.[126] Secondly, churches will have to coherently present social transformation as part of the evangelistic mandate. The kingdom of God manifests itself through the church present in the nations and political structures of humanity.[127] The mission of the church therefore cannot be separated from the life of the church and must be evident in its obedience in response to crucial issues such as social injustice and oppression, famine, war, racism, and illiteracy, to name a few.[128] Thirdly, evangelical churches must have a biblical understanding of the kingship of Jesus, in order to ensure they can appropriately respond to the assertion that Jesus was a political king. Padilla recognises that the biblical evidence witnesses to Jesus as the *Messiah*. Messiah is a political description for Christ came to bring everything under the rule of his government. However, this is not an earthly government. Rather, the community of faith is presented with a new model for human life, and the community is responsible for bringing both their personal lives and their corporate life into line with the ethics of God's kingdom. Fourthly, churches must be aware of the danger of moralism and legalism when the ethical dimension of faith is emphasised.

It is evident that Latin American evangelical theologians are committed to constructing effective contextual theology which will engender positive social responsibility. Escobar contends: "In order to comply with the social responsibility of the church, it is not necessary to abandon evangelization, nor is it necessary to adopt liberal or non-evangelical theology. It is simply a case of taking our beliefs to their final consequences."[129] Over the past three decades, as a result of such reflection, Latin American evangelicals have developed an understanding of *misión integral* which they believe is thoroughly biblical in its foundation and faithful to the principles of evangelical Christianity. *Misión integral*, therefore, will be the focus of the following discussion.

---

[125] See for example, Renato Espoz, "Los cristianos frente a la dependencia económica y la deuda externa", *Boletín Teológico* 39 (1990): 219-228; Titus Guenther Funk, "La dependencia económica y la deuda externa: un enfoque teológico", *Boletín Teológico* 39 (1990): 229-235; Pedro Arana Quiroz, "Reflexiones bíblicas y teológicas sobre la economía", *Textos para la Acción* 4, no. 6 (1996): 21-27.

[126] See for example Emilio A. Núñez, "El evangelio de la prosperidad", *Apuntes Pastorales* 11, no. 4 (1994): 33-35.

[127] For helpful reflection on the subject of the kingdom of God and the expression of kingdom principles see Kirk, *World*, 41-58.

[128] A helpful example of the Latin American evangelical response to such issues can be found in Samuel Escobar, "Migration: Avenue and Challenge to Mission", *Missiology: An International Review* XXXI, no. 1 (2003): 18-28.

[129] Escobar, "Responsabilidad", 36.

9.6 Misión Integral

The conference entitled "Iberianamerican Evangelical Mission: Word, Integrity and Leadership in the power of the Spirit" held in Villa Giardino in Córdoba from 27 to 30 October, 1999, reflects the significant development in the Latin American evangelical reflection on holistic mission.[130] It is the hope of the Fraternity that the term *misión integral* would convey the idea of doing justice to the biblical teaching with respect to the mission of the church. The need for balance of both theory and praxis in holistic mission is recognised. For such an understanding of mission is open to distortion and extremes.[131] In this section, *misión integral* will be discussed in relation to the purpose of God as revealed in Scripture, in relation to the understanding of humanity found in Scripture, and in relation to the New Testament witness of the ministry and mission of the early church.

First, *misión integral* is being developed in light of the purpose of God.[132] The primary focus of the purpose of God, as understood in biblical theology, is the redemption of the whole of creation.[133] This is indispensable, therefore, to a faithful evangelical understanding of the mission of the church.

> To speak of *misión integral* is to speak of mission orientated to the reconstruction of the person in every aspect of their life, as much in the spiritual as in the physical, as much in the physical as in the psychical, as much in the personal as in the social, as much in the private as in the public.[134]

Such an understanding of *misión integral* should create communities of faith who not only preach the love of God but evidence their confession of the Lordship of

---

[130] See Padilla, "Itinerario"; C. René Padilla, "Misión Integral", TMs (photocopy), Misión Evangélica Iberoamericana Conferencia "Palabra, Integridad, y Liderazgo en al poder del Espíritu", Córdoba, December 27 - 30, 1999, Latin American Theological Fraternity Archives, Buenos Aires, 1-5. For further details on the development of *misión integral* in Latin American evangelical thought see the papers presented at CLADE IV in September 2000 published in C. René Padilla and Tetsunao Yamamori, eds. Congreso Latinoamericano de Evangelización (CLADE), IV, Quito, Ecuador, 2 a 9 de septiembre de 2000: *Misión integral y pobreza: el testimonio evangélico hacia el tercer milenio: palabra, espíritu y misión* (Buenos Aires: Ediciones Kairós, 2001). See for example, Víctor Vaca, "Misión integral y transformación estructural desde América Latina", 49-72; Esteban Voth, "Bases bíblicas para la misión integral en contextos de pobreza", 73-124; Juan Pablo Ventura, "La cooperación entre iglesias en la misión integral", 239-250. See also C. René Padilla, "Hacia una definición de la misión integral" in *El proyecto de Dios y las necesidades humanas: más modelos de ministerio integral en América Latina,* eds. C. René Padilla and Tetsunao Yamamori (Buenos Aires: Ediciones Kairós, 2000), 19-34; Costas, *Christ,* 188-194.

[131] Padilla discusses two extreme positions and the need for balance in his article "Misión", 34-36.

[132] See also Pedro Arana Quiroz, "La misión de Dios y la nuestra" in Quiroz, Escobar Padilla, *Trino,* 9-72.

[133] Padilla, "Misión", 37. See also Padilla, *Discipulado,* 34.

[134] Padilla "Integral", 3.

Christ in every sphere of life.[135] These communities of faith demonstrate their discipleship in terms of their treatment of one another and in undertaking the good works which God has prepared in advance for them to do.[136]

Second, *misión integral* is being developed in relation to the biblical understanding of the human being as an inseparable unit of body, soul and spirit.[137] This is considered by Latin American evangelical theologians to be evident in both the Old and the New Testament Scriptures:

> From this perspective, *misión integral* is mission orientated towards the satisfaction of the basic necessities of a human being, including the need for God, but also the need for love, for food, for a roof over one's head, for a coat on one's back, for both physical and mental health, and for a sense of human dignity…to speak of *misión integral* is to speak of mission orientated towards the formation of people who demonstrate solidarity, who do not live for themselves but for others; people with the ability to receive and to give love; people who "hunger and thirst for justice" and who "work for peace."[138]

Padilla suggests that confusion regarding the place of holistic mission stems from a misunderstanding of the concept of the purpose of God and the nature of humanity. Such confusion leads to an understanding of God which limits God's purpose to eternal salvation of the soul rather than "the reconciliation of all things that are on earth and in the heavens above to himself."[139] Padilla affirms that not only does humanity need to be reconciled to God, but also needs to receive all that is necessary to live life to the fullness promised by God.[140]

> Mission only does justice to the biblical teaching and the concrete situation when it is holistic (*integral*). In other words, when mission crosses not only geographical frontiers but also cultural, racial, economic, social and political boundaries with the objective of transforming human life in all its dimensions, according to the purpose of God, and to empower humanity to enjoy the fullness of life which God wishes to give.[141]

Third, *misión integral* is being developed in response to the New Testament account of mission demonstrated by the early church. Escobar, in particular, draws on biblical lessons for a holistic, multifaceted understanding of mission. *Misión*

---

[135] See C. René Padilla, "Una eclesiología para la misión integral" in *La iglesia local como agente de transformación*, eds. C. René Padilla and Tetsunao Yamamori (Buenos Aires: Ediciones Kairós, 2003), 13-45.

[136] See Ephesians 2:10.

[137] Padilla, "Integral", 3; Padilla, "Misión", 37-38; see also James 2:15-17.

[138] Padilla, "Integral", 3-4. See Escobar, "Espiritual", 123. See also Matthew 5:6,9.

[139] See Colossians 1:20.

[140] See also chapter 3 "Economía y plenitud de vida" in Padilla, *Economía*, 53-72.

[141] Padilla, "Integral", 4. See also Padilla, "Misión", 38.

integral reflects the Christocentric nature of New Testament mission.[142] To pursue knowledge of Christ is the motivation of the life of every Christian. The life and death of Jesus influence the manner in which a Christian lives his or her life in the present. It is obvious then that Christ should be the central proclamation in holistic Christian mission. "In the early church, the Lordship of Christ was the *motivation* and *drive* that moved the church forward in her mission, and at the same time the *content* of the church's message."[143] The ministry of Jesus is a powerful example for contemporary Christians:

> Jesus did not understand his own mission and work apart from the divine initiative that is at work in the world. What we see in the travels of Jesus over the dusty roads of Palestine is God acting in the world in a unique and visible way. The word of God enters history, becomes history, and leaves its mark on history. Looking back from a twentieth-century perspective, we can grasp the impact of the presence of Jesus in the world. It is a transforming, healing, challenging, upsetting, prophetic presence that calls for radical change and delivers it. It is a presence registered by the witnesses in specific actions of approaching the poor, healing the sick, teaching the ignorant, and of kindness to children, openness to the outcast, forgiveness to the repentant, criticism of the powerful and corrupt – culminating in self-surrender for our salvation, and all of it in the power of the Spirit.[144]

The mission of the apostle Paul is also a model of ministry for *misión integral*.[145] Firstly, Paul's mission is rooted in his belief that God acts in history through human beings. Likewise, *misión integral* is motivated by such expectation. Secondly, there is a clear Pauline emphasis on the supremacy of Christ in mission. Paul clearly presents the centrality of Christ, the message of the cross and the power of the resurrection. Such an understanding of mission presents both the divine initiative

---

[142] Samuel Escobar, "Pablo y la misión a los gentiles" in *Bases bíblicas de la misión: perspectivas latinoamericanas*, ed. C. René Padilla (Buenos Aires: Nueva Creación, 1998), 307-350. This article studies the mission of Paul among the Gentiles and is helpful in understanding the development of Latin American missiology up to very recent times. See Samuel Escobar "Avancemos en la plenitud de la misión: un comentario latinoamericano sobre la misiología de San Pablo (Ro. 15:14-33)" in *Misión en el camino: ensayos en homenaje a Orlando E. Costas*, Samuel Escobar, Sidney Rooy, Valdir Steuernagel, C. René Padilla et al (Buenos Aires: Fraternidad Teologica Latinoamericana, 1992), 1-16; Padilla, "Eclesiología", 30-45; Escobar "Cristología", 73-113. See also "La búsqueda de una cristología misiológica en América Latina" in Escobar, *Misión*, 7-42. This is a revised and updated version of the paper previously written in English as Escobar, "Search".

[143] Escobar, "Return", 261. See also chapter 6 "Christ: God's best missionary" in Escobar, *Time*, 96-111.

[144] Escobar, *Changing*, 45. See also C. René Padilla, "La política de Jesús", *Certeza* 53 (1974): 152-155.

[145] See Samuel Escobar, "A Pauline Paradigm of Mission" in *The Good News of the Kingdom: Mission Theology for the Third Millenium*, eds. Charles Van Engen, Dean S. Gilliland and Paul Pierson (Maryknoll: Orbis Books, 1993), 56-66.

and also the demand for a human response.[146] Consequently, *misión integral* will communicate a message in which the cross of Christ demands a response of repentance and the resurrection of Christ motivates a vibrant life of faith. This leads to the third principle drawn from the New Testament, namely that *misión integral* is only possible in the power of the Holy Spirit.[147] Fourthly, Paul demonstrates a new way of looking at mission in the world. He was given the vision to take the gospel to the Gentiles. His vision was global. His vision was pioneering. His vision demanded life commitment. His vision was for the foundation of local churches which would also be teams of disciples committed to mission.[148] *Misión integral*, therefore, seeks to focus on such a vision. Fifthly, praxis and social teaching have a place in the mission of the apostle Paul, for example, the manner in which Paul was economically sustained, and the collection for the poor in Jerusalem. Seeking to ground the evangelical understanding of *misión integral* in such biblical evidence Escobar comments:

> The Pauline mission recognises the divine initiative and the sovereignty of Christ, it allows itself to be driven by Christ's example and the presence of the Holy Spirit, it has a global vision and a precise but flexible strategy, and includes a social praxis inseparable from the same nature of the gospel. For this reason it continues to inspire Christian mission in the twenty-first century.[149]

In the light of these three aspects of biblical teaching on mission, Latin American evangelical theologians have sought to clearly establish the following principles of *misión integral*.[150] *Misión integral* should seek to sustain life and meet the basic needs of human beings. *Misión integral* should insist on the equal distribution of goods and resources necessary for life.[151] *Misión integral* should advocate restorative justice which returns what has been taken from the weak, the poor and those who have been denied their rights in society.[152] *Misión integral* should demonstrate a commitment to the dignity of humanity and the inherent personal and social value of every human life.[153] *Misión integral* must strive for liberty but not

---

[146] See for example "Contextual Evangelization: a personal and social witness" in Costas, *Liberating*: 20-32 in which Costas discusses evangelization and the human situation, evangelization and the divine initiative and evangelization and praxis.

[147] See in particular C. René Padilla, "El Espíritu Santo y la misión integral de la iglesia" in Quiroz, Escobar and Padilla, *Trino*: 115-147. See also chapter 7 "The Holy Spirit and Christian Mission" in Escobar, *Time*, 112-127.

[148] Costas also emphasises mission as a ministry for the whole people of God, see Costas, *Liberating*, 86-87. See also Roldán, "Sacerdocio", 103-130; Padilla and Yamamori, *Proyecto*, 192.

[149] Escobar, "Pablo", 350. See also Escobar, *Time*, 27.

[150] Escobar, "Elementos", 19.

[151] See chapter 1 "La ética reformada y la mayordomía de los bienes materiales" in Padilla, *Economía*, 9-22.

[152] Padilla, *Derechos*, 21-22.

[153] Padilla, *Derechos*, 17; Escobar, "Entender", 17.

liberty which enables the strong to take advantage and oppress the weak.[154] *Misión integral* should encourage the participation of all human beings in society as members of that society and should promote mutual reciprocation between members of society. *Misión integral* should seek transformation which is appropriate to the local culture and transformation which preserves and cares for the natural environment of that local community.[155]

In summary, these principles of *misión integral* should facilitate the spiritual transformation of the individual and of the society in which that individual lives.[156] Latin American evangelical theologians continue to develop their understanding of *misión integral* which is founded on a biblical approach, which seeks to engender praxis and which persistently strives to mature in its ability to effectively communicate the good news of Jesus Christ.[157]

> True evangelization is integral: the whole gospel for the whole person and for all persons…We reject, therefore, all dichotomies, ancient and modern, which attempt to reduce the gospel to one dimension only or to fragment the human being created in the image and likeness of God. We do not accept it because it is insufficient…[158]

9.7 Conclusion

In this chapter, the search for a Latin American evangelical missiology has been examined. First, Latin American missiological reflection has been set in the context

---

[154] See Kirk, *Meaning*, 221 where Kirk comments "The Christian concern for freedom is expressed in searching for and discovering the right balance between liberty *from* arbitrary authority and liberty *for* non-oppressive structures. The authenticity of such structures is measured by their ability to enable people to become what God, revealed in Jesus Christ, created them to be."

[155] See for example, Nancy E. Bedford, "La teología de la misión integral y el discernimiento comunitario" in Padilla and Yamamori, *Iglesia*, 47-74; Padilla and Yamamori, *Proyecto*, 192. See also chapter 9 "Care of the Environment" in Kirk, *Mission*, 164-183; C. René Padilla, "La mayordomía de los bienes materiales: una exploración en la ética reformada", *Iglesia y Misión* 53 (1995): 6-11.

[156] See Escobar, "Opresión", 121-122. For several helpful examples of church models of *misión integral* see Section II "Modelos eclesiales de misión integral" in Padilla and Yamamori, *Iglesia*, 237-284. See also Padilla and Yamamori, *Proyecto*, 63-189; Rake, Padilla and Yamamori, *Servir*, 91-154.

[157] See for example the CLADE IV declaration which is available as "Testimonio evangélico hacia el tercer milenio: Palabra, Espíritu y Misión", *Iglesia y Misión* 74 (2000): 16-18. See also Samuel Escobar, "Viejos y nuevos caminos para la misión", *Boletín Teológico* 56 (1994): 275-280; Escobar, "Naturaleza", 75-101; Danilo Revilla, "De los principios a la práctica" in *El proyecto de Dios y las necesidades humanas*, eds. C. René Padilla and Tetsunao Yamamori (Buenos Aires: Ediciones Kairós, 2000), 131-142; Escobar, "Scenario", 26-27.

[158] Etchegoyen, "Theology", 163.

of the international evangelical dialogue regarding the subject of mission, in an effort to demonstrate the significance of the Latin American contribution. Second, it has been seen that the foundation of Latin American evangelical missiology is the understanding that mission flows from discipleship. Third, consequently, Latin American evangelicals consider the gospel, accepted by those who enter into discipleship, to be a transformational message. Fourth, therefore, it becomes clear that this transformational message affects not only the life of the individual disciple but should influence the community of faith, who in turn become agents of transformation in society. Mission and social responsibility are therefore inseparable. Finally, the Latin American evangelical reflection on the subject of Christian mission has developed into the concept known as *misión integral*. *Misión integral* is a biblical, contextual approach to mission which seeks to inspire Christians to dedicate themselves to the expression of their faith in every sphere of their existence, as they seek to extend the kingdom of God.

> When passive conformity, disguised as realism or else spiritualised, tells us that it isn't worth trying to change the world, we can respond that by the mere fact of being faithful to Christ, we are already changing it, that we are living our social and political action, like our whole lives, in the light of the kingdom: And this hope does not fail us, because God has filled our hearts with His love by means of the Holy Spirit whom he has sent us.[159]

---

[159] Escobar, "Kingdom", 38. Padilla too emphasises that the biblical understanding of the church as leaven, as light and as salt are simple images which do not assume global changes but which imply that Christians living faithfully to the gospel will influence their local communities. C. René Padilla, interview by author, 13 June 2003, video recording, Buenos Aires.

Conclusion

This study has sought to provide a systematic presentation of liberation themes in Latin American evangelical theology. Within the context in which the theology of liberation flourished, Latin American evangelical theologians are seeking to structure an alternative contextual theology which explicates and demonstrates the liberation possible through the gospel of Christ. In the introduction, the twofold purpose of this work was identified. Firstly, this book sought to set Latin American evangelical theology in historical and cultural context. A greater awareness of the historical and cultural context has brought greater understanding of the theological project which Latin American evangelical theologians have undertaken. Secondly, this book sought to present Latin American evangelical theology in a systematic and coherent manner. It is hoped, therefore, that this presentation of liberation themes has demonstrated both the consistency of the evangelical approach and the continuing development of contextual evangelical theology in Latin America. It is acknowledged that much of what Latin American evangelicals contribute is not original. For familiar patterns of evangelical thought are clearly demonstrated. The readiness to question, reassess and reapply traditional concepts, however, is less familiar. The simplicity of a theological contribution which places authentic ministry to those in need before academic acclaim is, similarly, less familiar. The courage to confront long held presuppositions and to pursue biblical theology which will speak into desperate circumstances with power and hope, likewise, is less familiar. This theology stands in direct contrast to the ambiguous, uncertain and unstable Latin American context for which it is being developed.

It has been argued that Latin American evangelical theology is not simply a form of reactionary theology. While there is no doubt that Latin American evangelical theology directly engaged with the theology of liberation, it would be an inaccurate portrayal and a misunderstanding of the essence of Latin American evangelical theology to limit it to such engagement.[1] Likewise, it would be an underestimation of Latin American evangelical theology to claim that it has developed only in light of its critique of international evangelical theology, and its subsequent interaction with international evangelical theologians.

This study seeks to demonstrate that not only is Latin American evangelical theology capable of engaging with other theological positions, but it is also capable of developing authentic, contextual theology. Such contextual theology is in direct response to the context and culture in which Latin American evangelical theologians live, and the context and culture in which evangelical communities of faith seek to

---

[1] Escobar asserts clearly the fact that Latin American evangelical theologians were reflecting on issues pertinent to the Latin American context in the decade before the theology of liberation flourished. By the time evangelical theologians engaged with liberationists they had already established firm foundations in their own theological approach. Samuel Escobar, interview with author, 1 April 2004, video recording, Valencia.

minister. In the development of such theology, however, contextual principles have been employed which make this Latin American evangelical theology hold relevance for those reflecting and ministering within alternative contexts.

In this conclusion, I will firstly submit an overview of the present work in order to bring into sharper focus the implications of each chapter for liberation themes in evangelical perspective. Secondly, I will submit four observations regarding the Latin American evangelical theology examined here.

First, a brief synopsis will be submitted. In chapter two, the historical background of the Latin American continent, as understood by Latin American evangelicals, was explored. It is evident that the sensitivity which Latin American evangelical theologians demonstrate in their historical awareness of the continent enables them to understand the structures of society, the evolution of national identity, and the practice of religion evident in contemporary Latin America. It is also demonstrated that an understanding of the engagement with liberation theology is a vital aspect of Latin American evangelical theology. The presentation of the immediate context of the theology of liberation demonstrated the readiness of evangelical theologians both to confront the movement and also to structure a coherent alternative.

In order for any movement to critique its context and contest theological proposals made within that context, it must evidence self-awareness. Thus, chapter three considered the historical context and the immediate context of Latin American evangelicalism. It has been demonstrated that Latin American evangelical theologians have not blindly followed "evangelical tradition" from the West. Rather, they strive to construct indigenous evangelical theology in which the emphasis is placed decisively on a life of personal discipleship to Christ, on dedication to contextual biblical theology and on commitment to sharing the good news of Jesus Christ with others. Arising from the historical development of Latin American Protestantism, it has been established that the Latin American Theological Fraternity was founded on the desire to promote relevant evangelical theology which had been absent in the past. The initiative taken by the Fraternity has been influential in the progress of Latin American evangelical theology.

As explained at the outset, this is not a study or critique of the theology of liberation. It has been constructive, however, to approach Latin American evangelical theology with reference to the theology of liberation. For in this engagement, the methodological awareness of the Latin American evangelical contribution is more clearly defined and the fundamental evangelical principles are actively employed. Whilst both evangelicals and liberationists search for liberation (which may be perceived in theologically distinct terms), each adopts a different methodology. The focus of chapter four, therefore, was the distinguishing feature of Latin American contextual theology, namely its proposed theological method. While evangelical theologians affirm the liberationist search for relevant and appropriate methodology, the evangelical critique of liberation method centres on the evangelical perception that Scripture appears to occupy an inferior position within liberationist methodology. Evangelicals propose a distinctive method which is based on the divine initiative, founded on biblical authority, expressed through the community of faith, developed in light of the context, and committed to sharing the gospel with others.

The evangelical critique of liberationist methodology is rooted in the evangelical commitment to the sufficiency of Scripture. Chapter five, therefore, focused on the search for a contextual Latin American evangelical hermeneutic. Latin American evangelical theologians clearly evidence biblical awareness in their work. They consistently affirm the centrality of the Scriptures, rightly contending that the authoritative nature of the Scriptures allows for an authoritative interpretation and application of Scripture to the life, ministry and mission of the church. Under the guidance of the Holy Spirit, each new historical context calls for new dialogue between Scripture and that context. The gospel will take shape within historical reality as the community of faith displays the word of God in action. In this way, the gospel and the situation remain mutually engaged. The proposed Latin American evangelical hermeneutic suffers from the weakness perceived in evangelical hermeneutics in general, that is to say, the Latin American evangelical hermeneutic is built upon contentious issues. For example, the belief inherent in evangelicalism that God is revealed in the Scriptures and is revealed supremely in Christ, and that this Christ alone is the way to the Father. However, Latin American evangelical theologians are conscious of such presuppositions and clearly contend that they are writing as evangelicals, for the evangelical community. Furthermore, they would contend that their methodology is not only orthodox but provokes orthopraxis.

The criticism could be raised that Latin American evangelical theologians, like liberationists, can impose their own methodological presuppositions on the text. It remains pertinent to ask how evangelical theologians will ensure that the hermeneutical circulation which they propose does not, in fact, give authority to the context over and above Scripture. As the text and the context are "mutually engaged", Latin American evangelical theologians must consistently demonstrate self-criticism and self-awareness. Not only must "cultural conditioning" within international evangelicalism, or "ideological conditioning" within liberationist readings of Scripture be recognised but Latin American evangelical theologians must also guard against the dominance of culture, context, and potential selectivity in their own interpretation. Strategies must be in place to continually challenge Latin American evangelical presuppositions, to motivate a broad understanding of hermeneutical developments and biblical scholarship, and to ensure this is disseminated to the community of faith. It is also recognised that the Reader Response approach to Scripture, encouraged within base ecclesial communities and by liberationists, is sometimes present in Latin American evangelical communities. The need for vigilance, therefore, is necessary to safeguard the authority of Scripture in practice, not only in principle. The Latin American evangelical commitment to Scriptural authority and to thoroughly evangelical contextual interpretation must be sustained. It is also important that contemporary hermeneutical method is not determined by past debates. Rather, Latin American evangelical theologians must continue to promote biblical interpretation which clearly speaks into the contemporary situation with the power demonstrated in their past contributions.

An understanding of the general themes presented in chapter six is important for a balanced appreciation of Latin American evangelical theology. The Latin American evangelical reflection on biblical anthropology demonstrates an appreciation of the origin, the nature, the dignity, and the creativity of *humanity*. This reflection leads to the realisation that in many human societies true humanity is lacking. As a result, a coherent presentation of the biblical doctrine of *sin* is essential. For the evangelical understanding of sin is central to the evangelical understanding of *liberation*. In their biblical concept of liberation, evangelical theologians ground the present possibilities of liberation in light of the liberation promised in the future. Consequently, communities of faith live in hope which enables people to bear testimony to the purpose of God, as creatures made in the image of God.

The theme of *salvation* then, is inextricably linked to the understanding of humanity, sin, and liberation. Latin American evangelical theologians seek to present a biblical understanding of efficacious salvation that holds in tension salvation of the soul and the body, salvation of the individual and society, and salvation of humanity and the whole of creation. The evangelical understanding of salvation is distinctive in that it is based on the call to *conversion*, communicating a new beginning, a new attitude, a new life-commitment, a new membership of the community of faith and a new hope for the future.

The final general theme dealt with in chapter six was the *kingdom of God*. For theologians of liberation and Latin American evangelical theologians alike, the doctrine of the kingdom of God has been particularly powerful in the development of contextual theology. Latin American evangelicals assert that active adherence to the principles demonstrated in the biblical portrayal of God's kingdom will inevitably present a dramatic alternative to the Latin American reality: ethically, critically, apologetically and eschatologically.

Latin American evangelicals recognise that these general themes form a firm foundation on which to structure a contextual approach to evangelical Christology, ecclesiology and missiology. The theological reflection on the person and work of Jesus Christ in Latin American evangelical theology employs the method and the hermeneutical approach previously discussed. Without an understanding of the general themes in contextual theology, the reflection on the person and work of Jesus Christ would be incomplete. Likewise, an appreciation of Latin American history and culture, as examined in chapters two and three, is also pertinent to the Christological search. In chapter seven, it was shown that Latin American evangelical theologians are seeking to structure Christology which is biblically informed; which presents a balanced understanding of the humanity and the divinity of Christ; which is relevant to the contemporary Latin American context; which motivates compassionate ministry within that context; and which causes believers to live in the hope of Christ's return.

The biblical and holistic Christology being developed by Latin American evangelical theologians has serious implications for the life and ministry of the church. The principles established in respect of contextual method, contextual hermeneutics and contextual Christology should be evident in the practice of the church. For without a community of faith willing to enact the principles discussed in the previous chapters, any attempt to develop active contextual theology will fail. Chapter eight, therefore, focused on the search for a Latin American evangelical ecclesiology. This ecclesiology continues to stand in contrast to the traditional sacramental and institutionalised understanding of the church evident within Latin American Catholicism. As a result of the interaction with the three ecclesiological proposals identified, and the remaining conviction of the need for a contextual ecclesiology, Latin American evangelical theologians continue their search for a more biblical, more holistic understanding of what it means to be the church.

As was noted in chapter eight, the criticism may be raised by some that Latin American evangelical theologians demonstrate an unnecessary dualism in their understanding of the church and the world. It may be that in their attempt to identify who is part of the community of faith, they have undermined the doctrine of the sovereignty of God who is both the Lord of the church and the Lord of the world. The role of the Holy Spirit in the world may be devalued as a consequence of such emphasis. Evidently, Latin American evangelical theologians contend that the community of faith should impact the society in which it exists. However, some may perceive that this adversarial position, in which the church stands apart from society, may lean towards a dualism in which the church is placed always in opposition to the world, rather than becoming a church in and for the world. Latin American evangelical theologians must continue to be aware of a theological conservatism which in practice may draw evangelicals away from the world, as the church seeks to be utterly distinct and model a counter community. Latin American evangelical theologians must seek to continually clarify their ecclesiological position to ensure that their assertions are not misunderstood in this regard.

Despite this criticism, a community of faith prepared to explore Scripture in order to structure a biblical understanding of the general themes discussed in this thesis, and a community of faith which sets out to follow the New Testament example of Christ and the early church, will be a community of faith which appreciates that there is a mission to fulfil. That is to say, such a community of faith will realise there is a purpose for their existence, a purpose beyond their own needs.

Chapter nine, therefore, examined the search for a Latin American evangelical understanding of mission. The subject of mission was the final chapter of this thesis for two reasons. Firstly, to a large extent, the evangelical understanding of mission is the logical outcome of the evangelical perspective on the liberation themes. It is imperative to appreciate the evangelical perspective on these themes in order to accurately present the background, the context and the significance of the Latin American evangelical proposal known as *misión integral*. Secondly, it would seem fair to say that the missiological discussion emanating from Latin America, encapsulated in the *misión integral* concept, is the most significant contribution which Latin American evangelicals have made internationally.

While a clear understanding of *misión integral* has been established, it is a concept which is continually being structured in relation to the purpose of God as revealed in Scripture, in light of the biblical understanding of humanity and in response to the witness of the ministry and mission of the early church in the New Testament. Practical principles of *misión integral* are being developed, in the hope that such principles might facilitate the spiritual transformation of individuals and as a consequence, the transformation of the society in which that individual lives. *Misión integral* is an understanding of mission founded on the Scriptures. It is an understanding of mission which seeks to engender praxis. It is an understanding of mission which is committed to seeking the effective communication of the gospel message of Christ in word and deed.

The work of five key evangelical theologians (Orlando E. Costas, Samuel Escobar, J. Andrew Kirk, Emilio A. Núñez and C. René Padilla) has been outlined in an attempt to present a historical account of liberation themes in Latin American evangelical theology. My purpose has not been to provide a critical analysis of these themes but rather to provide a systematisation of this evangelical thought. It is hoped that Latin American evangelical theology has been portrayed as vibrant, biblical, coherent, wholeheartedly evangelical, and sensitively contextual.

Second, in light of the previous chapters and the preceding synopsis, it is possible to present some concluding remarks. It is clear that these five evangelical theologians are seeking to structure specific contextual theology. Consequently, there is weakness in a critique directed towards their theology from a position which is far removed from the Latin American reality. There is also weakness in a critique which does not recognise that these theologians openly acknowledge that they are writing within a well defined evangelical framework. It is also important to take cognisance of the fact that the liberation themes identified here constitute one particular approach to Latin American evangelical theology. Any constructive analysis of Latin American evangelical theology would also need to take into consideration the work of theologians who have not been discussed in this book, and similarly, the subjects dealt with in Latin American evangelical theology which have not been included here. Any reflections on Latin American evangelical theology, therefore, are presented here in the knowledge that they are made by an observer who has had little experience of the reality of life in Latin America. They are also reflections made by an author who finds herself largely persuaded by these evangelical theologians. Affirming such provisos and acknowledging my own reticence, I will nonetheless submit four observations in relation to the Latin American evangelical contribution in the past and the necessity of future contributions.

Firstly, wide dissemination of this evangelical thought has not been achieved. It is acknowledged that particular circumstances have contributed to this difficulty: for example, the economic instability of Latin America and the lack of available technology continue to present complications for the publication and distribution of material; the financial circumstances of evangelical believers continue to make the possibility of purchasing resources or undertaking training difficult; the lack of educational opportunities for the vast number of evangelical pastors and believers continues to make communication of this theological contribution limited. In addition, there is evidence of a lack of creative communication of evangelical thought.[2] Evangelicals must face the challenge of making their theological reflection more accessible through strategic forms of dissemination at two levels.

At one level, Latin American evangelical theologians must seek to make their work accessible to local evangelical communities of faith.[3] Strategic development of resources, text books and educational ministries will be essential if evangelical theology is to influence the life and ministry of evangelical churches in Latin America. This dissemination is also imperative if evangelical theological reflection is to continue to develop and mature.[4]

At another level, Latin American evangelical theologians must seek to make their theological reflection accessible to the international evangelical community. It is evident that in the early years of the Theological Fraternity, publications were made not only in Spanish but also in English.[5] In more recent years, however, it would appear that many key publications are not translated from Spanish.[6] The engagement in the past with the international evangelical community has proved fruitful and has demonstrated the potential influence Latin American theologians can have through such dialogue. For example, as shown in this work, Latin American evangelical theologians have clearly established principles for *misión integral*. Such reflection would be of significant insight to the continuing development of missiology within the Western evangelical community. It would confront, once again, the presuppositions and imbalance of some contemporary Western evangelical

---

[2] While journal articles, magazine articles, consultation papers and books have been published on Latin American evangelical theology, I did not locate many examples of Bible study notes, short pamphlets, thematic booklets, text books or radio broadcasts, for example, which may be possible forms of wider communication.

[3] For example, I encountered several evangelical communities of faith in North West Argentina who continue to struggle against the segregationalist proposals of the Church Growth movement. Articles and material referred to in chapter eight of this thesis would be insightful, constructive and encouraging for such believers, if this work was more accessible to them.

[4] The ministry of the Kairós Foundation is one example of a more strategic and creative approach, particularly in the fields of training, publishing, library resources, and publications on the internet.

[5] Escobar recognises that the Fraternity have not published sufficiently in English to communicate effectively with the international evangelical community. He suggests that a more aggressive approach is needed in the future. Samuel Escobar, interview by author, 1 April 2004, video recording, Valencia.

[6] Samuel Escobar has had several books translated and published in English in recent years, including *Changing Tides* and *A Time for Mission*. (To avoid confusion, it is important to note that *Changing Tides*, not *A Time for Mission* is, in fact, a translation and development of the text published in Spanish as *Tiempo de misión*.) The papers and documents from the CLADE IV Consultation in 2000, however, are not published in English. Similarly, the most recent publications which focus on specific aspects of *misión integral* are not available in English. It would seem that such work would be a valuable contribution to theological reflection within the international evangelical community.

discussion. It could, at the same time, strengthen and encourage those struggling to minister elsewhere within the context of the Two Thirds World.

Secondly, Latin American evangelical theologians underestimated the significance of their contribution in the past and therefore failed to systematise their work.[7] Escobar and Padilla both consider *Bases bíblicas de misión: perspectivas latinoamericanas* (Biblical foundations of mission: Latin American perspectives)[8] to be the closest example of a first systematic presentation of Latin American evangelical missiology. It would seem that the international evangelical community would benefit from a translation of this work. Similarly, it would appear that the Latin American evangelical contribution could be strengthened through the publication of other systematic presentations of the Latin American evangelical perspective on hermeneutics, Christology, ecclesiology, and ethics for example.[9]

Thirdly, the strength of the past can become the weakness of the present. That is to say, as Latin American societies change, Latin American evangelical theologians will need to be willing to respond to new subjects within familiar contexts. Continual contemporary reflection will be necessary on cultural and historical issues (see chapter two), on global issues (see chapter three), on theological issues (see chapters four, five and seven), on political and economic issues (see chapters six and nine) and on ecclesiological issues (see chapter eight).[10]

In respect of Latin American cultural issues, there has been some failure to structure evangelical theology on the role of women within the family, the church and society, for example. The historical Latin American culture of *machismo* (male chauvinism) remains dominant, and as a result, a biblical approach to issues of sexuality and sexual ethics will also need to be more clearly defined.

In regard to global issues, Latin American evangelical theologians will find it necessary to provide a Christian response to globalisation. It will be important to explicate the significant implications this exposure to the world will have for the life and ministry of believers and for the mission of the church.

---

[7] This was confirmed in discussion with René Padilla during a visit to the Kairós Foundation in Buenos Aires (13-16 June, 2003) where I was given access to articles produced by the Theological Fraternity over many years. Unfortunately, these articles and papers are not systematically archived. Therefore, locating specific papers and articles is not a straightforward task.

[8] C. René Padilla, ed. *Bases bíblicas de la misión: perspectivas latinoamericanas* (Buenos Aires: Nueva Creación, 1998.)

[9] Certainly a contribution has been made on these subjects, as the bibliography of this thesis clearly demonstrates. However, a more systematic presentation of available material, or a structured selection of essays, for example would be helpful. Again, if such work was to be made available in English, the value and accessibility of this contribution would be more widespread within the international evangelical community.

[10] These reflections are made in light of the personal interviews undertaken. C. René Padilla, interview by author, 13 June 2003, video recording, Buenos Aires; José Míguez Bonino, interview by author, 17 June 2003, video recording, Buenos Aires; Samuel Escobar, interview by author, 1 April 2004, video recording, Valencia.

The pressing theological issue within contemporary Latin America appears to be the doctrine of the Holy Spirit. There is evidence that, despite the tremendous growth of Latin American Pentecostalism, evangelical theologians have failed to provide a coherent pneumatology. Evangelical theologians, therefore, will need to construct a clear, biblical and cogent understanding of the person and work of the Holy Spirit. Not only that, but serious theological reflection will need to be promoted and sustained within the Pentecostal stream of evangelical churches. The dramatic numerical growth in evangelical churches, the influence of international denominations and, in particular, the founding of *mega churches* contribute to the complexity of the current ecclesiological reality in Latin America. It is evident that evangelical reflection on ecclesiology will also need to be continually refined and consistently reapplied to the context in the future.[11]

It could be argued that in recent decades Latin American evangelicals have become involved in politics and have avoided involvement in politics with equal fervour. For some who have chosen involvement, this has led to encounters with corruption, human rights abuses, and unethical behaviour.[12] Evangelical theologians, therefore, must face the challenge of coherently presenting Christians with biblical principles for contemporary political situations. It will be imperative that evangelicals continue to reflect on contemporary social and political engagement, thus enabling Christians to make wise decisions in regard to the actual practical outworking of such engagement. As Latin American evangelical theologians have structured criticism of other contextual responses in the past, they must sustain the ability to be self-critical regarding forms of political and social involvement manifested in the present. Contemporary evangelical theologians, therefore, must pursue relevant, biblical responses in order to guide a new generation of believers through the ethical dilemmas which will arise from within a context which continues to be unstable and volatile.

In contrast to those who have chosen to be politically active, there are those who continue to be reticent about such involvement. Such reticence is, to some extent, understandable when involvement may necessitate cooperation with those who are hostile to Christianity (for example, Marxists). Latin American evangelical

---

[11] See Samuel Escobar, "Evangelicals in Latin America", *Evangelical Missions Quarterly* (July 2003): 286-297, at 291.

[12] For example, Efrain Rios Montt, a charismatic evangelical, came to power in Guatemala after a military coup. He encountered difficulties in pursuing his political career after accusations of genocide among indigenous groups during military operations against guerilla factions. Serrano Elías, another charismatic evangelical who rose to power in Guatemala after elections, resigned under pressure, due to the serious corruption which was discovered in his regime. In Peru, several evangelical politicians in Congress failed to make any significant contribution which would be viewed as consistent with evangelical conviction. However, in contrast, several members of traditional churches elected to office, such as José Míguez Bonino in Argentina, Pedro Arana Quiroz in Peru and Jaime Ortiz in Colombia, made significant contributions, shaped by evangelical conviction, to legislation and debate. See Escobar, "Evangelicals", 293.

theologians will need to reflect further on the influence that evangelical communities can have within society, and prepare church leaders and local believers for constructive political interaction with others in business, in commerce, in government, in education, in community projects, and in struggles where working alongside non-believers may be necessary for the good and welfare of all.

In relation to the contemporary economic circumstances of believers, there is a need for the presentation of a viable, biblical alternative to the materialism which is becoming ever more evident in the Latin American context. This has also been compounded by the proliferation of churches which preach and teach a "prosperity gospel." It is important, therefore, that Latin American evangelical theologians structure a biblical understanding of personal property and wealth, which is both relevant and applicable.[13]

Fourthly, the strength of Latin American evangelical theology has come from its relatively recent introduction to the continent. It brought a different voice, a fresh approach and a new concept of Christian community. In time, however, this strength will be drained by the apathy which often develops in second and third generations of believers. These younger members of the community have not had to take a stand for religious freedom as previous evangelical generations had to. Similarly, they have not had to struggle to establish an evangelical identity. Rather, they will grow up within an evangelical subculture where belonging depends more on certain behaviour and adherence to social regulations than to personal conviction. Latin American evangelical theologians have critiqued the cultural Christianity of the West in previous decades. They will have to respond to the evolution of such a culture on the Latin American continent. Already there are signs of a potential decline in church growth as a result of disillusioned young people abandoning communities of faith.[14] Discernment will be needed if Latin American evangelicalism is to succeed where the Western church has failed.

In conclusion, despite some weaknesses in the past and the need for contemporary theological reflection in the future, it is my contention that Latin American evangelical theology merits careful study. It is theology seeking to learn from the history and culture of the Latin American continent. It is theology being written with the integrity of those who are seeking a thoroughly biblical response to the reality of life. It is theology seeking to speak with relevance to a context which has echoed with imposed and insufficient theology in the past. It is theology seeking to be founded on a biblical understanding of humanity, and the sinfulness of humanity. It is theology seeking salvation and liberation for humanity in light of the biblical image of the kingdom of God. It is theology willing to seriously examine what it means to be church in a context of poverty, social injustice and oppression. It is theology seeking to reassess and renew missiological presuppositions and principles in light of Scripture, of history, and of the Latin American context. It is

---

[13] Padilla reflects on the subject in C. René Padilla, "Misión y prosperidad", *Textos para la Acción* 4, no. 6 (1996): (no page numbers given).

[14] Escobar, "Evangelicals", 288.

theology affirming personal discipleship which leads to membership of the community of faith and active witness to others. It is theology struggling for true liberation. It is theology calling each of us to do likewise.

Bibliography

Alves, Rubem. "Injusticia y rebelión." *Cristianismo y Sociedad* 6 (1964): 40-53.

Alves, Rubem. *Religion: ¿opio o instrumento de liberación?* Montevideo: Tierra Nueva, 1970.

Alves, Rubem. "The Protestant Principle and Its Denial." In *Faith Born in the Struggle for Life*, ed. Dow Kirkpatrick, 213-228. Grand Rapids: Eerdmans, 1988.

Arana Quiroz, Pedro. "La revelación de Dios y la teología en Latinoamérica." In *El debate contemporáneo sobre la Biblia*, ed. Pedro Savage, 37-78. Barcelona: Ediciones Evangélicas Europeas, 1972.

Arana Quiroz, Pedro. "Reflexiones bíblicas y teológicas sobre la economía." *Textos para la Acción* 4, no. 6 (1996): 21-27.

Arana Quiroz, Pedro. "La misión de Dios y la nuestra." In *El trino Dios y la misión integral*, Pedro Arana Quiroz, Samuel Escobar and C. René Padilla, 9-72. Buenos Aires: Ediciones Kairós, 2003.

Arana Quiroz, Pedro, ed. *Teología en el camino: documentos presentados en los últimos veinte años por diferentes comunidades cristianas de América Latina*. Lima: Ediciones Presencia, 1987.

Arana Quiroz, Pedro, Samuel Escobar and C. René Padilla. *El trino Dios y la misión integral*. Buenos Aires: Ediciones Kairós, 2003.

Archiniegas, Germán. *Latin America: A Cultural History*. Translated by Joan MacLean. New York: Alfred A. Knopf, 1972.

Arguedas, Alcides. *Pueblo Enfermo*. La Paz: Librería Editorial Juventud, 1982.

Arias, Esther and Mortimer Arias. *The Cry of My People*. New York: Friendship Press, 1980.

Armerding, Carl E., ed. *Evangelicals and Liberation*. USA: Presbyterian and Reformed Publishing Company, 1977.

Armesto, Felipe Fernández. *Columbus*. Oxford: Oxford University Press, 1991.

Assmann, Hugo. *Theology of a Nomad Church*. Translated by Paul Byrnes. Maryknoll: Orbis Books, 1975.

Atiencia, Jorge, Samuel Escobar and John Stott. *Así leo la Biblia: cómo se forman maestros de la palabra*. Barcelona, Buenos Aires and La Paz: Certeza Unida, 1999.

Baker, David. "Interpreting Texts in the Context of the Whole Bible." *Themelios* 5, no. 2 (1980): 21-25.

Barro, Antônio C. "The Identity of Protestantism in Latin America." In *Emerging Voices in Global Theology*, ed. William A. Dyrness, 229-252. Grand Rapids: Zondervan, 1994.

Barja, César. *Libros y autores contemporáneos*. New York: Las Américas, 1964.

Barreto César, Ely Eser. "A Reading of the Bible, Beginning with the Poor of Latin America." In *Faith Born in the Struggle for Life*, ed. Dow Kirkpatrick, 38-51. Grand Rapids: Eerdmans, 1988.

Bartholomew, Craig, Robin Parry and Andrew West, eds. *The Futures of Evangelicalism*. Leicester: IVP, 2003.

Baum, Gregory. "Community and Identity." In *The Future of Liberation Theology: Essays in Honor of Gustavo Gutiérrez*, eds. Marc H. Ellis and Otto Maduro, 102-112. Maryknoll: Orbis Books, 1989.

Bebbington, David. *Evangelicalism in Modern Britain: A History from the 1730s to the 1980s*. London: Unwin Hyman, 1989.

Bedford, Nancy E. "La teología de la misión integral y el discernimiento comunitario." In *La iglesia local como agente de transformación: una eclesiología para la misión integral*, eds. C. René Padilla and Tetsunao Yamamori, 47-74. Buenos Aires: Ediciones Kairós, 2003.

Berger, Peter and Michael Novak. *Speaking to the Third World: Essays on Democracy and Development*. Washington DC: American Enterprise Institute for Public Policy Research, 1985.

Bevans, Stephen. *Models of Contextual Theology*. Maryknoll: Orbis Books, 1992.

Blomberg, Craig L. " 'Your Faith Has Made You Whole': The Evangelical Liberation Theology of Jesus." In *Jesus of Nazareth: Lord and Christ, Essays on the Historical Jesus and New Testament (istology*, eds. Joel B. Green and Max Turner, 75-93. Carlisle: Paternoster, 1994.

Blomberg, Craig L. *Neither Poverty Nor Riches*. Leicester: Apollos, 1999.

Boff, Leonardo. *Jesucristo el liberador*. Rio de Janeiro: Editora Vozes, 1972.

Boff, Leonardo. *Teología desde el cautiverio*. Bogotá: Indo- American Press Service, 1975.

Boff, Leonardo. *Jesus Christ, Liberator*. Translated by Patrick Hughes. Maryknoll: Orbis Books, 1979.

Boff, Leonardo. "The Originality of the Theology of Liberation." In *The Future of Liberation Theology: Essays in Honor of Gustavo Gutiérrez*, eds. Marc H Ellis and Otto Maduro, 38-48. Maryknoll: Orbis Books, 1989.

Boff, Leonardo, and Clodovis Boff. *Liberation Theology: From Confrontation to Dialogue*. San Fransisco: Harper and Row Publishers, 1986.

Bradford Burns, E. *Latin America: A Concise Interpretative History*, 4th ed. Englewood Cliffs: Prentice-Hall, 1986.

Breneman, Mervin. "El uso del Antiguo Testamento en el Nuevo Testamento. In *Hacia una hermenéutica evangélica Tomo II*, C. René Padilla, Mervin Breneman, Sidney H. Rooy, B. Melano Couch, Eugene Nida, Elsa R. Powell and Samuel Escobar, 1-5. Buenos Aires: Ediciones Kairós, 1977.

Breneman, Mervin, ed. *Liberación, Éxodo y Biblia*. Miami: Editorial Caribe, 1975.

Brown, Colin. *Christianity and Western Thought: A History of Philosophers, Ideas and Movements Vol I*. Downers Grove: IVP, 1990.

Bullón, H. Fernando. "El docente cristiano y las ciencias económicas y sociales en el proceso de transformación." In Congreso Latinoamericano de Evangelización (CLADE), IV, Quito, Ecuador, 2 a 9 de septiembre de 2000:

Presencia cristiana en el mundo académico: el testimonio evangélico hacia el tercer milenio: palabra, espíritu y misión, ed. Sidney H. Rooy, 189-224. Buenos Aires: Ediciones Kairós, 2001.

Bullón, H. Fernando, Juliana Morillo and Sergio Membreño, eds. Congreso Latinoamericano de Evangelización (CLADE), IV, Quito, 2 a 9 de septiembre de 2000: *Sociedad de consumo y mayordomía de la creación: el testimonio evangélico hacia el tercer milenio: palabra, espíritu y misión.* Buenos Aires: Ediciones Kairós, 2002.

Calienes, Raúl Fernández. "Bibliography of the writings of Orlando E. Costas." *Missiology: An International Review* XVII, no. 1 (1989): 87-105.

Canelos, Franklin. "Las instituciones financieras y comerciales internacionales y el derecho al desarrollo." *Boletín Teológico* 37 (1990): 31-37.

Canelos, Franklin. "Causas y orígenes de la pobreza en América Latina." In Congreso Latinoamericano de Evangelización (CLADE), IV, Quito, Ecuador, 2 a 9 de septiembre de 2000: *Misión integral y pobreza: el testimonio evangélico hacia el tercer milenio: palabra, espíritu y misión.* eds. C. René Padilla and Tetsunao Yamamori, 19-48. Buenos Aires: Ediciones Kairós, 2001.

Camargo López, Jesús. "La dependencia económica de América Latina: un enfoque evangélico." *Boletín Teológico* 37 (1990): 7-30.

Cardenal, Ernesto. *El evangelio de Solentiname.* Salamanca: Sígueme, 1975.

Carmona, Harold Segura. *Hacia una espiritualidad evangélica comprometida.* Buenos Aires: Ediciones Kairós, 2002.

Carson, D.A. "Hermeneutics: A brief assessment of some recent trends." *Themelios* 5, no. 2 (1980): 12-20.

Cetina, Edesio Sanchez. *¿Qué es la Biblia? Respuestas desde las ciencias bíblicas.* Buenos Aires: Ediciones Kairós, 2003.

Chang-Rodríguez, Eugenio. *Latinoamérica: su civilación y su cultura.* Boston: Heinle Publishers, 1991.

Chasteen, John Charles. *Born in Blood and Fire.* New York: W.W. Norton and Company, 2001.

Clarke, P.B. and A. Linzey, eds. *The Dictionary of Ethics, Theology and Society.* London: Routledge, 1996.

Collier, Simon, Thomas E. Skidmore and Harold Blakemore, eds. *The Cambridge Encyclopedia of Latin America and the Caribbean.* Cambridge: Cambridge University Press, 1992.

Comblin, José. *Called for Freedom: The Changing Context of Liberation Theology.* Translated by Philip Berryman. Maryknoll: Orbis Books, 1998.

Compton, Roberto. *La teología de la liberación. Una guía introductoria.* El Paso: Casa Bautista de Publicaciones, 1984.

Cortes, Rolando Gutiérrez. "Christology and Pastoral Action in Latin America." In *Sharing Jesus in the Two Thirds World*, eds. Vinay Samuel and Chris Sugden, 87-114. Grand Rapids: Eerdmans, 1983.

Costas, Orlando E. *La iglesia y su misión evangelizadora*. Buenos Aires: La Aurora, 1971.

Costas, Orlando E. *Comunicación por medio de la predicación*. Miami: Editorial Caribe, 1973.

Costas, Orlando E. "El culto como índice de la realidad que vive la iglesia." *Vida y Pensamiento* 1, no. 1 (1973): 13-18.

Costas, Orlando E. *The Church and Its Mission: A Shattering Critique from the Third World*. Wheaton: Tyndale House Publishers, 1974.

Costas, Orlando E. "La realidad de la iglesia evangélica latinoamericana." In *Fe cristiana y Latinoamérica hoy*, ed. C. René Padilla, 34-65. Buenos Aires: Ediciones Certeza, 1974.

Costas, Orlando E. "Depth in Evangelism – An Interpretation of 'In-Depth Evangelism' Around the World." In *Let the Earth Hear His Voice*, ed. J.D. Douglas, 675-694. Minneapolis: World Wide Publications, 1975.

Costas, Orlando E. "In-depth evangelism in Latin America." In *Let the Earth Hear His Voice*, ed. J. D. Douglas, 211- 212. Minneapolis: World Wide Publications, 1975.

Costas, Orlando E. *El protestantismo en América Latina hoy: ensayos del camino*. Costa Rica: Publicaciones INDEF, 1975.

Costas, Orlando E. *Theology of the Crossroads in Contemporary Latin America: Missiology in Mainline Protestantism 1969-1974*. Amsterdam: Rodopi, 1976.

Costas, Orlando E. *The USA: a Missionfield for Third World Christians?* Louisville: Southern Baptist Theological Seminary, 1977.

Costas, Orlando E. *Compromiso y misión: una reflexión sobre la misión de la iglesia*. Miami: Editorial Caribe, 1979.

Costas, Orlando E. *The Integrity of Mission: the Inner Life and Outreach of the Church*. New York: Harper and Row, 1979.

Costas, Orlando E. "Conversion as a Complex Experience – A Personal Case Study." In *Down to Earth*, eds. J.R.W. Stott and R. Coote, 240-262. Grand Rapids: Eerdmans, 1980.

Costas, Orlando E. "Pecado y salvación en América Latina." In Congreso Latinoamericano de Evangelización (CLADE), II, noviembre de 1979, Quito: *América Latina y la evangelización en los años 80*, eds. Pedro Savage and Rolando Gutiérrez, 271-287. Mexico: Fraternidad Teológica Latinoamericana, 1980.

Costas, Orlando E. *Christ Outside the Gate*. Maryknoll: Orbis Books, 1982.

Costas, Orlando E. "La misión como discipulado." *Boletín Teológico* 6 (1982): 45-59.

Costas, Orlando E. "La misión del pueblo de Dios en la ciudad." *Boletín Teológico* 7 (1982): 85-96.

Costas, Orlando E. "Proclamando a Cristo en los Terceros Mundos." *Boletín Teológico* 8 (1982): 1-15.

Costas, Orlando E. "Crecimiento integral y Palabra de Dios." *Misión* 2, no. 1 (1983): 6-13.

Costas, Orlando E. "Proclaiming Christ in the Two Thirds World." In *Sharing Jesus in the Two Thirds World*, eds. Vinay Samuel and Chris Sugden, 3-15. Grand Rapids: Eerdmans, 1983.

Costas, Orlando E. "A Wholistic Concept of Church Growth." In *Exploring Church Growth*, ed. William R. Shenk, 95-107. Grand Rapids: Eerdmans, 1983.

Costas, Orlando E. "Origen y desarrollo del movimiento de crecimiento de la iglesia." *Misión* 8 (1984): 6-13.

Costas, Orlando E. "Iglecrecimiento, el movimiento ecuménico y el 'evangelicalismo'." *Misión* 9 (1984): 56-60.

Costas, Orlando E. "Teológo en la encrucijada." In *Hacia una teología evangélica latinoamericana*, ed. C. René Padilla, 13-36. San José: Editorial Caribe, 1984.

Costas, Orlando E. *Evangelización contextual: fundamentos teológicos y pastorales*. San José: Ediciones Sebila, 1986.

Costas, Orlando E. "Evangelical Theology in the Two Thirds World." In *Conflict and Context: Hermeneutics in the Americas*, eds. Mark Lau Branson and C. René Padilla, 311-323. Grand Rapids: Eerdmans, 1986.

Costas, Orlando E. "The Mission of Ministry." *Missiology: An International Review* XIV, no. 4 (1986): 463-472.

Costas, Orlando E. "La vida en el Espíritu." *Boletín Teológico* 21-22 (1986): 105-112.

Costas, Orlando E. "Sobrevivencia, esperanza y liberación en la iglesia hispana de Estados Unidos: estudio de un caso." *Vida y Pensamiento* 17, no. 1/2 (1987): 101-109.

Costas, Orlando E. "La teología evangélica en el mundo de los dos tercios." *Boletín Teológico* 28 (1987): 201-229.

Costas, Orlando E. *Liberating News*. Grand Rapids: Eerdmans, 1989.

Costas, Orlando E. "Dimensiones del crecimiento integral de la iglesia." In *La misión de la iglesia, una visión panorámica*, ed. Valdir Steuernagel, 109-122. San José: Varitec, 1992.

Costas, Orlando E, ed. *Hacia una teología de la evangelización*. Buenos Aires: La Aurora, 1973.

Costas, Orlando E, ed. *Predicación evangélica y teología hispana*. Miami: Editorial Caribe, 1982.

Croatto, J. Severino. *Liberación y libertad. Pautas hermenéuticas*. Buenos Aires: Mundo Nuevo, 1973.

Croatto, J. Severino. *Los Pobres: encuentro y compromiso*. Buenos Aires: Editorial La Aurora, 1978.

Croatto, J. Severino. *Exodus, A Hermeneutic of Freedom*. Translated by Salvator Attanasio. Maryknoll: Orbis Books, 1981.

Croatto, J. Severino. *Hermenéutica bíblica*. Buenos Aires: La Aurora, 1984.

Cross, F.L. and E.A. Livingstone, eds. *The Oxford Dictionary of the Christian Church*. Oxford: Oxford University Press, 1997.

Deiros, Pablo A. "Relaciones de la iglesia con el poder político: modelo bautista." In *Los evangélicos y el poder político en América Latina*, ed. Pablo A. Deiros, 73-140. Grand Rapids: Nueva Creación, 1986.

Deiros, Pablo A. "Protestant Fundamentalism in Latin America." In *Fundamentalism Observed*, eds. Martin E. Marty and R. Scott Appleby, 142-196. Chicago: The University of Chicago Press, 1991.

Deiros, Pablo A, ed. *Los evangélicos y el poder político en América Latina*. Buenos Aires: Nueva Creación, 1986.

Denton, Charles F. "La mentalidad protestante: un enfoque sociológico." In *Fe cristiana y Latinoamerica hoy*, ed. C. René Padilla, 67-79. Buenos Aires: Ediciones Certeza, 1974.

de Powell, Elsa Romanenghi. "Participación de los evangélicos en la política latinoamericana: una crónica." *Boletín Teológico* 40 (1991): 233-248.

de Santa Ana, Julio. "Through the Third World Towards One World." *Exchange* 19, no. 3 (1990): 217-235.

de Unamuno, Miguel. "El Cristo Yacente de Santa Clara (Iglesia de la Cruz) de Palencia." In *El concepto contemporáneo de España*, eds. Angel del Rio and M.J. Benardete, 130. Buenos Aires: Editorial Losada, 1946.

de Villiers, Pieter, ed. *Liberation Theology and the Bible*. Pretoria: University of South Africa, 1987.

Dixon, David and Richard Dixon. "Culturas e identidades populares y el surgimiento de los evangélicos en América Latina." *Cristianismo y Sociedad* XXX/4, no. 114 (n.d.): 61-71.

Dockery, David S. *The Challenge of Postmodernism: An Evangelical Engagement*. Grand Rapids: Baker Books, 1995.

Domínguez, Enrique. "The Great Commission." *NACLA Report on the Americas* 18, no.1 (1984): 12-22.

Douglas, J.D., ed. *Let the Earth Hear His Voice*. Minneapolis: World WidePublications, 1975.

Douglas, J.D., ed. *The Encyclopaedia of Religious Knowledge*, 2d ed. Michigan:Baker Book House, 1991.

Dozer, Donald Marquand. *Latin America: An Interpretative History*, Revised ed. Tempe: Center for Latin American Studies, Arizona State University, 1979.

Dunn, James D.G. *Word Biblical Commentary: Romans 1-8*. Texas: Word Books, 1988.

Dussel, Enrique. *History and the Theology of Liberation: A Latin American Perspective*. Translated by John Drury. Maryknoll: Orbis Books, 1976.

Dussel, Enrique. *A History of the Church in Latin America: Colonialisation to Liberation*. Translated by Alan Neely. Grand Rapids: Eerdmans, 1981.

Dyrness, William A., ed. *Emerging Voices in Global Theology*. Grand Rapids: Zondervan, 1994.

Ellis, M.H. and Otto Maduro, eds. *The Future of Liberation Theology: Essays in Honor of Gustavo Gutiérrez*. Maryknoll: Orbis Books, 1989.

Ellis, M.H. and Otto Maduro, eds. *Expanding the View: Gustavo Gutiérrez and the Future of Liberation Theology*. Maryknoll: Orbis Books, 1990.

Erickson, Millard J. *The Evangelical Left: Encountering Postconservative Evangelical Theology*. Grand Rapids: Baker Books, 1997.

Escobar, Samuel. *Diálogo entre Cristo y Marx*. Lima: Publicaciones AGEUP, 1967.

Escobar, Samuel. "Los evangélicos y la política." *Certeza* 8 (1967): 230-232.

Escobar, Samuel. "The Totalitarian Climate." In *One Race, One Gospel, One Task Volume II*, eds. C. Henry and W. Mooneyham, 288-290. Minneapolis: World Congress on Evangelism, 1967.

Escobar, Samuel. "El Cristo de Iberoamérica." In *¿Quién es Cristo hoy?*, Samuel Escobar, C. René Padilla and Edwin M. Yamauchi, 9-23. Buenos Aires: Ediciones Certeza, 1970.

Escobar, Samuel. "Responsabilidad social de la iglesia." In *Acción en Cristo para un continente en crisis*, ed. Samuel Escobar, 32-39. San José: Editorial Caribe, 1970.

Escobar, Samuel. "La revolución de Jesús: dos versiones." *Certeza* 44 (1971): 99-103.

Escobar, Samuel. *Decadencia de la religión*. Buenos Aires: Ediciones Certeza, 1972.

Escobar, Samuel. "The Social Impact of the Gospel." In *Is Revolution Change?*, ed. B. Griffiths, 84-105. London: IVP, 1972.

Escobar, Samuel. "Una teología evangélica para Iberoamérica." In *El debate contemporáneo sobre la Biblia*, ed. Pedro Savage, 17-36. Barcelona: Ediciones Evangélicos Europeas, 1972.

Escobar, Samuel. "La situación latinoamericana". In *Fe cristiana y Latinoamérica hoy*, ed. C. René Padilla, 13-34. Buenos Aires: Ediciones Certeza, 1974.

Escobar, Samuel. "Evangelization and Man's Search for Freedom, Justice and Fulfilment." In *Let the Earth Hear His Voice*, ed. J. D. Douglas, 319-326. Minneapolis: World Wide Publications, 1975.

Escobar, Samuel. "El reino de Dios, la escatología y la ética social y política en América Latina." In *El reino de Dios y América Latina*, ed. C. René Padilla, 127-156. El Paso: Casa Bautista de Publicaciones, 1975.

Escobar, Samuel. "The Kingdom of God, Eschatology and Social and Political Ethics in Latin America." *Theological Fraternity Bulletin* 1 (1975): 1-42.

Escobar, Samuel. "The Return of Christ." In *The New Face of Evangelicalism*, ed. C. René Padilla, 255-264. Downers Grove: IVP, 1976.

Escobar, Samuel. "Hacia una hermenéutica evangélica." In *Hacia una hermenéutica evangélica Tomo II*, C. René Padilla, Mervin Breneman, Sidney H. Rooy, B. Melano Couch, Eugene Nida, Elsa R. Powell and Samuel Escobar, 1-7. Buenos Aires: Ediciones Kairós, 1977.

Escobar, Samuel. *Hacia una perspectiva cristiana de la historia*. Buenos Aires: Ediciones Kairós, 1977.

Escobar, Samuel. "Identidad, misión y futuro del protestantismo latinoamericano." *Boletín Teológico* 3/4 (1977): 1-38.

Escobar, Samuel. *Irrupción juvenil*. Miami: Editorial Caribe, 1977.

Escobar, Samuel. "Vivir el evangelio." *Certeza* 65 (1977): 11-13.

Escobar, Samuel. *La chispa y la llama*. Buenos Aires: Ediciones Certeza, 1978.

Escobar, Samuel. "Identity, Mission and Future of Latin American Protestantism." *Theological Fraternity Bulletin* 1 and 2 (1978): 1-28.

Escobar, Samuel. "The Need for Historical Awareness." In *Christian Mission and Social Justice*, Samuel Escobar and John Driver, 11-35. Scottdale: Herald Press, 1978.

Escobar, Samuel. "Esperanza y desesperanza en la crisis continental." In Congreso Latinoamericano de Evangelización (CLADE), II, noviembre de 1979, Quito: *América Latina y la evangelización en los años 80*, eds. Pedro Savage and Rolando Gutiérrez, 318-335. Mexico: Fraternidad Teológica Latinoamericana, 1980.

Escobar, Samuel. "Formación del pueblo de Dios en los grandes urbes." *Boletín Teológico* 7 (1982): 37-84.

Escobar, Samuel. "¿Qué significa ser evangélico hoy?" *Mision* 1, no. 1 (1982): 15-18, 35-39.

Escobar, Samuel. *El estudiante evangélico*. Lima: Ediciones Certeza, 1983.

Escobar, Samuel. *George Orwell's Nightmare and the Christian Mission Today*. Vrije Universiteit: Amsterdam, 1984.

Escobar, Samuel. "Heredero de la reforma radical." In *Hacia una teología evangélica latinoamericana*, ed. C. René Padilla, 51-72. San José: Editorial Caribe, 1984.

Escobar, Samuel. "El problema ecuménico en América Latina." *Misión* 14 (1985): 78-81.

Escobar, Samuel. *God's Word in a Young World*. London: Scripture Union International Council, 1985.

Escobar, Samuel. "Our Hermeneutic Task Today." In *Conflict and Context: Hermeneutics in the Americas*, eds. C. René Padilla and Mark Lau Branson, 3-8. Grand Rapids: Eerdmans, 1986.

Escobar, Samuel. "El poder y las ideologías en América Latina." In *Los evangélicos y el poder político*, ed. Pablo A. Deiros, 141-180. Buenos Aires: Nueva Creación, 1986.

Escobar, Samuel. "Transformation in Ayacucho: From Violence to Peace and Hope." *Transformation* 3, no. 1 (1986): 9-13.

Escobar, Samuel. *La fe evangélica y las teologías de la liberación*. El Paso: Casa Bautista de Publicaciones, 1987.

Escobar, Samuel. "The Hermeneutical Task in Global Economics." *Transformation* 4, no. 3/4 (1987): 7-11.

Escobar, Samuel. "Missions and Renewal in Latin American Catholicism." *Missiology: An International Review* 15:2 (1987): 33-46.

Escobar, Samuel. *Evangelio y realidad social*. El Paso: Casa Bautista de Publicaciones, 1988.

Escobar, Samuel. "El crecimiento de la iglesia en América Latina y la teoría de 'iglecrecimiento'." *Misión* 27 (March 1989): 15-19.

Escobar, Samuel. "El espíritu de Lausana 1974 en América Latina." *Misión* 29 (1989): 110-113.

Escobar, Samuel. "In Memory of Orlando E. Costas (1942-1987)." *Missiology: An International Review* XVII, no. 1 (1989): 85-86.

Escobar, Samuel. "Lausana II y el peregrinaje de la misiología evangélica." *Boletín Teológico* 36 (1989): 321-333.

Escobar, Samuel. *Liberation Themes in Reformational Perspective*. Sioux Center: Dordt College Press, 1989.

Escobar, Samuel. "Las ciudades en la práctica misionera del apóstol Pablo: el caso de Filipos." *Misión* 31 (1990): 6-13.

Escobar, Samuel. "The Role of Translation in Developing Indigenous Theologies – a Latin American View." In *Bible Translation and the Spread of the Church: the Last Two Hundred Years*, ed. Philip C. Stine, 81-94. Leiden, The Netherlands: E. J. Brill, 1990.

Escobar, Samuel. "Autoritarismo y poder." *Boletín Teológico* 42/43 (1991): 131-143.

Escobar, Samuel. "Catholicism and National Identity in Latin America." *Transformation* 8, no. 3 (1991): 22-30.

Escobar, Samuel. "Evangelical Theology in Latin America: The Development of a Missiological Christology." *Missiology* XIX, no. 3 (1991): 315-332.

Escobar, Samuel. "A Movement Divided: Three Approaches to World Evangelisation Stand in Tension with One Another." *Transformation* 8, no. 4 (1991): 7-13.

Escobar, Samuel. "Opresión y justicia." *Boletín Teológico* 42/43 (1991): 109-123.

Escobar, Samuel. "Avancemos en la plenitud de la misión: un comentario latinoamericano sobre la misiología de San Pablo (Ro. 15:14-33)." In *Misión en el camino: ensayos en homenaje a Orlando E. Costas*, eds. Samuel Escobar, Sidney Rooy, Valdir Steuernagel, C. René Padilla, 1-16. Buenos Aires: Fraternidad Teológica Latinoamericana, 1992.

Escobar, Samuel. "The Legacy of John Alexander Mackay." *International Bulletin of Missionary Research* 16, no.3 (1992): 116-122.

Escobar, Samuel. "Mission in Latin America: An Evangelical Perspective." *Missiology: An International Review* XX, no. 2 (1992): 241-253.

Escobar, Samuel. "La misión en América Latina: interpretación sociopolítica desde una perspectiva evangélica." In *La misión de la iglesia: una vision panorámica*, ed. Valdir R. Steuernagel, 237-264. San José: Visión Mundial, 1992.

Escobar, Samuel. "¿Se revisa la nueva leyenda negra?" *Cuadernos de Reforma* suplemento 1992: 1-20.

Escobar, Samuel. "Las nuevas fronteras de la misión." In Congreso Latinoamericano de Evangelización (CLADE), III, 24 de agosto a 4 de septiembre de 1992, Quito: *Todo el Evangelio para todos los pueblos desde América Latina*, 376-386. Quito: Fraternidad Teológica Latinoamericana, 1993.

Escobar, Samuel. "A Pauline Paradigm of Mission." In *The Good News of the Kingdom: Mission Theology for the Third Millenium*, eds. Charles Van Engen, Dean S. Gilliland and Paul Pierson, 56-66. Maryknoll: Orbis Books, 1993.

Escobar, Samuel. *Paulo Freire: una pedagogía latinoamericana.* Mexico: Casa Unida de Publicaciones – Editorial Kyrios, 1993.

Escobar, Samuel. "The Promise and Precariousness of Latin American Protestantism." In *Coming of Age: Protestantism in Contemporary Latin America*, ed. Daniel R. Miller, 3-35. Lanham: University Press of America, 1993.

Escobar, Samuel. "The Whole Gospel for the Whole World from Latin America." *Transformation* 10, no. 1 (1993): 30-32.

Escobar, Samuel. "Beyond Liberation Theology: A Review Article." *Themelios* 19, no. 3 (1994): 15-17.

Escobar, Samuel. "Católicos y evangélicos en América Latina frente al desafío misionero del siglo veintiuno." *Kairós* 14/15 (January –December 1994): 63-80.

Escobar, Samuel. "The Church in Latin America after Five Hundred Years: An Evangelical Missiological Perspective." In *New Face of the Church in Latin America*, ed. Guillermo Cook, 21-37. Maryknoll: Orbis Books, 1994.

Escobar, Samuel. "Conflict of Interpretations of Popular Protestantism." In *New Face of the Church in Latin America*, ed. Guillermo Cook, 112-134. Maryknoll: Orbis Books, 1994.

Escobar, Samuel. "La presencia protestante en América Latina." In *Historía y misión: revisión de perspectivas*, Samuel Escobar, Estuardo McIntosh, and Juan Inocencio, 7-56. Lima: Ediciones Presencia, 1994.

Escobar, Samuel. "The Search for a Missiological Christology in Latin America." In *Emerging Voices in Global Theology*, ed. William A. Dyrness, 199-227. Grand Rapids: Zondervan, 1994.

Escobar, Samuel. "Viejos y nuevos caminos para la misión." *Boletín Teológico* 56 (1994): 275- 280.

Escobar, Samuel. "La fundación de la Fraternidad Teológica Latinoamericana: Breve ensayo histórico." *Boletín Teológico* 59/60 (1995): 7- 33.

Escobar, Samuel. "Latin America." In *Toward the Twenty-first Century in Christian Mission*, eds. James M. Phillips and Robert T. Coote, 125-138. Grand Rapids: Eerdmans, 1993, Reprint, Grand Rapids: Eerdmans, 1995.

Escobar, Samuel. "Hacia una filosofía bíblica de la educación." *Andamio* II (1996): 5-25.

Escobar, Samuel. "Mission Studies – Past, Present and Future." *Missiology: An International Review* XXXIV, no. 1 (1996): 3-29.

Escobar, Samuel. "La misión cristiana y el poder espiritual: una perspectivamisiológica." In *Poder y misión. Debate sobre la guerra espiritual en América Latina*, Edward Rommen, Robert Priest, Thomas Campbell, Bradford Mullen, Charles Kraft, Patrick Johnstone, Juan Kessler,Alberto Barrientos and Samuel Escobar, 110-137. San José: Asociación Instituto Internacional de Evangelización a Fondo, 1997.

Escobar, Samuel. "Misión cristiana y transformación social. " In *Servir con los pobres en América Latina*, eds. Gregorio Rake, C. René Padilla and Tetsunao Yamamori, 63- 87. Buenos Aires: Ediciones Kairós, 1997.

Escobar, Samuel. "Religious and Social Change at the Grass Roots in Latin America." *The Annals of the American Academy of Political and Social Science* 554 (1997): 81-103.

Escobar, Samuel. *Sola Escritura: La Biblia en la misión de la iglesia*. Madrid: Sociedad Bíblica, 1997.

Escobar, Samuel. *De la misión a la teología*. Buenos Aires: Ediciones Kairós, 1998.

Escobar, Samuel. "Pablo y la misión a los gentiles." In *Bases bíblicas de la misión: perspectivas latinoamericanas*, ed. C. René Padilla, 307-350. Buenos Aires: Nueva Creación, 1998.

Escobar, Samuel. "A Missiological Approach to Latin American Protestantism." *International Review of Mission* LXXXVII /345 (1998): 161-173.

Escobar, Samuel. "The Two-Party System and the Missionary Enterprise." In *Re-forming the Center: American Protestantism, 1900 to the Present*, eds. Douglas Jacobsen and William Vance Trollinger, Jr., 341-360. Grand Rapids: Eerdmans, 1998.

Escobar, Samuel. "Formación bíblico-teológica del misionero transcultural." *Kairós* 24 (January-June 1999): 61-70.

Escobar, Samuel. "Missionary Dynamism in Search of Missiological Discernment." *Evangelical Review of Theology* XXIII, no. 1 (1999): 69-91.

Escobar, Samuel. *Tiempo de misión: América Latina y la misión cristiana hoy*. Colombia: Ediciones Clara – Semilla, 1999.

Escobar, Samuel. "Entender a la América Latina en el nuevo milenio." *Apuntes Pastorales* 17, no. 2 (2000): 12-18.

Escobar, Samuel. "Elementos para una evaluación de la experiencia política deevangélicos." *Textos para la Acción* 8, no.13 (2000): 9-22.

Escobar, Samuel. "The Global Scenario at the Turn of the Century." In *Global Missiology for the 21st Century*, ed. William D. Taylor, 25-46. Grand Rapids: Baker Academic, 2000.

Escobar, Samuel. "La responsabilidad social de la iglesia." *Iglesia y Misión* 74 (2000): 20-37.

Escobar, Samuel. "Latin America and Anabaptist Theology." In *Engaging Anabaptism: Conversations with a Radical Tradition*, ed. John D. Roth, 75-88. Scottdale: Herald Press, 2001.

Escobar, Samuel. *Changing Tides: Latin America and World Mission Today.* Maryknoll: Orbis Books, 2002.

Escobar, Samuel. "Religious Transitions and Civil Society in Latin America." In *Local Ownership, Global Change. Will Civil Society Save the World?*, eds. Roland Hoksbergen and Lowell M. Ewert, 162-182. Monrovia: World Vision, 2002.

Escobar, Samuel. "Aprender a vivir y a escribir." In *La Aventura de Escribir: testimonio de catorce escritores cristianos*, ed. Adriana Powell, 217-229. Lima: Ediciones Puma, 2003.

Escobar, Samuel. "Una cristología para la misión integral." In *El trino Dios y la misión integral*, Pedro Arana Quiroz, Samuel Escobar and C. René Padilla, 73-113. Buenos Aires: Ediciones Kairós, 2003.

Escobar, Samuel. "Evangelicals in Latin America." *Evangelical Missions Quarterly* (July 2003): 286-297.

Escobar, Samuel. "Migration: Avenue and Challenge to Mission." *Missiology: An International Review* Vol. XXXI, no. 1 (2003): 18-27.

Escobar, Samuel. "La naturaleza comunitaria de la iglesia." In *La iglesia local como agente de transformación: una eclesiología para la misión integral*, eds. C. René Padilla and Tetsunao Yamamori, 75-101. Buenos Aires: Ediciones Kairós, 2003.

Escobar, Samuel. *A Time for Mission: the Challenge for Global Christianity.* Leicester: IVP, 2003.

Escobar, Samuel. *Cristianismo Esencial.* Lima: Sociedad Bíblica Peruana, n.d.

Escobar, Samuel ed. *Acción en Cristo para un continente en crisis.* San José: Editorial Caribe, 1970.

Escobar, Samuel, C. René Padilla and Edwin M. Yamauchi. *¿Quién es Cristo hoy?* Buenos Aires: Ediciones Certeza, 1970.

Escobar, Samuel, and John Driver. *Christian Mission and Social Justice.* Pennsylvania: Herald Press, 1978.

Escobar, Samuel and Kwame Bediako, *The Gospel and Contemporary Ideologies and Cultures.* n.p.: NFES Publication, 1979.

Escobar, Samuel, Pedro Arana Quiroz, Valdir Steuernagel and Rodrigo Zapata, "A Latin American Critique of a Latin American Theology." *Evangelical Review of Theology* 7, no. 1 (1983): 48-62.

Escobar, Samuel, Sidney Rooy, Valdir Steuernagel, C. René Padilla, Guillermo Cook, Beatriz Melano Couch, Edesio Sanchez Cetina and Daniel Schipani. *Misión en el camino: ensayos en homenaje a Orlando E. Costas.* Buenos Aires: Fraternidad Teológica Latinoamericana, 1992.

Escobar, Samuel, Estuardo McIntosh, and Juan Inocencio. *Historia y misión: revisión de perspectivas.* Lima: Ediciones Presencia, 1994.

Espoz, Renato. "Los cristianos frente a la dependencia económica y la deuda externa." *Boletín Teológico* 39 (1990): 219-228.

Etchegoyen, Aldo. "Theology of Sin and Structures of Oppression." In *Faith Born in the Struggle for Life*, ed. Dow Kirkpatrick, 156-166. Grand Rapids: Eerdmans, 1988.

Ewell, W. A., ed. *The Evangelical Dictionary of Theology*. Carlisle, Paternoster Press, 1984.

Ferm, D.W. *Third World Liberation Theologies: An Introductory Survey.* Maryknoll: Orbis Books, 1986.

Fernández, Dagoberto Ramírez. "The Judgement of God on the Mulitnationals: Revelation 18." In *Subversive Scriptures: Revolutionary Readings of the Christian Bible in Latin America*, ed. Leif E. Vaage, 75-100. Valley Forge:Trinity Press International, 1997.

Freire, Paulo. "Conscientizing as a Way of Liberating (1970)." In *Liberation Theology: A Documentary History*, ed. Alfred T. Hennelly, 5-13. Maryknoll: Orbis Books, 1990.

Funk, Titus Guenther. "La dependencia económica y la deuda externa: un enfoque teológico." *Boletín Teológico* 39 (1990): 229-235.

Galeano, Eduardo. *Open Veins of Latin America*. Translated by Cedric Belfrage. New York: Monthly Review Press, 1973.

Gibellini, Rosino, ed. *Frontiers of Theology in Latin America*. Translated by John Drury. London: SCM, 1980.

Goldsmith, Martin. "Contextualization of Theology." *Themelios* 9, no.1 (1983): 18-23.

Gonzalez, Justo L. "Encarnación e historia." In *Fe cristiana y latinoamérica hoy*, ed. C. René Padilla, 151-167. Buenos Aires: Ediciones Certeza, 1974.

Gonzalez, Justo L. *Mañana: Christian Theology from a Hispanic Perspective.* Nashville: Abingdon Press, 1990.

Goodpasture, H. McKennie. *Cross and Sword*. Maryknoll: Orbis Books, 1989.

Gottwald, Norman, ed. *The Bible and Liberation: Political and Social Hermeneutics*. Maryknoll: Orbis Books, 1983.

Griffiths, B., ed. *Is Revolution Change?* London: IVP, 1972.

Grudem, Wayne. *Systematic Theology: An Introduction to Biblical Doctrine.* Leicester: IVP, 1994.

Guerreo, Alberto. "Líderes-siervos: facilitadores de la misión integral." In *La iglesia local como agente de transformación: una eclesiología para la misión integral*, eds. C. René Padilla and Tetsunao Yamamori, 179-212. Buenos Aires: Ediciones Kairós, 2003.

Gutiérrez, Gustavo. *The Power of the Poor in History*. Translated by Robert R. Barr. Maryknoll: Orbis Books, 1983.

Gutiérrez, Gustavo. *A Theology of Liberation*, 2nd ed. Translated by Sister Caridad Inda and John Eagleson. Maryknoll: Orbis Books, 1988.

Gutiérrez, Tomás J. "De Panamá a Quito: los congresos evangélicos en América Latina. Iglesia, misión e identidad (1916-1992)." *Boletín Teológico* 59/60 (1995): 34-65.

Gutiérrez, Tomás J., ed. *Protestantismo y cultura*. Quito: Consejo Latinoamericano de Iglesias, 1994.

Hanks, Thomas, D. *God so loved the Third World*. Maryknoll: Orbis Books, 1983.

Harrison, Lawrence E. *Underdevelopment is a State of Mind: The Latin American Case*. Boston: Harvard University and University Press of America, 1985.

Hastings, A., A. Mason and H. Pyper, eds. *The Oxford Companion to Christian Thought*. Oxford, Oxford University Press, 2000.

Hennelly, Alfred T. *Liberation Theology: A Documentary History*. Maryknoll, Orbis Books, 1990.

Henry, C. and W. Mooneyham. *One Race, One Gospel, One Task Vol II*. Minneapolis: World Congress on Evangelism, 1967.

Hicks, Peter. *Evangelicals and Truth*. Leicester: Apollos, 1998.

Hong, Sik, Edgardo Moffatt, Daniel Tomasini and Nancy Bedford. *Etica y religiosidad en tiempos posmodernos*. Buenos Aires: Ediciones Kairós, 2001.

Hundley, Raymond C. *Radical Liberation Theology: An Evangelical Response*. Wilmore: Bristol Books, 1987.

Hunter, James Davison. *Evangelicalism: The Coming Generation*. London: The University of Chicago Press, 1987.

Huntington, Deborah. "God's Saving Plan." *NACLA Report on the Americas* 18 no.1 (1984): 23-33.

Kay, Cristóbal. "Estructuralismo y teoría de la dependencia en el períodoneoliberal: Una perspectiva latinoamericana." *Nueva Sociedad* 158 (1998): 100-119.

Keen, Benjamin. *A History of Latin America*, 4th ed. Boston: Houghton Mifflin Company, 1992.

Keen, Benjamin. *The History of Latin America: Volume II Independence to the Present*. Boston: Houghton Mifflin Company, 1996.

Kirk, Andrew J. "La Biblia y su hermenéutica en relación con la teología protestante en América Latina." In *El debate contemporáneo sobre la Biblia*, ed. Pedro Savage, 115-214. Barcelona: Ediciones Evangélicas Europeas, 1972.

Kirk, Andrew J. *Jesucristo revolucionario*. Buenos Aires: La Aurora, 1974.

Kirk, Andrew J. "The Kingdom of God and the Church in Contemporary Protestantism and Catholicism." In *Let the Earth Hear His Voice*, ed. J.D. Douglas, 1071-1080. Minneapolis: World Wide Publications, 1975.

Kirk, Andrew J. *Así confesamos la fe cristiana*. Buenos Aires: La Aurora, 1976.

Kirk, Andrew J. "The Meaning of Man in the Debate between Christianity and Marxism." *Themelios* 1, no. 2 (1976): 41-49.

Kirk, Andrew J. "The Meaning of Man in the Debate between Christianity and Marxism Part 2." *Themelios* 1, no. 3 (1976): 85-93.

Kirk, Andrew J. "Algunas pautas para una definición de la perspectiva evangélica." In *Hacia una hermenéutica evangélica Tomo III*, J. Andrew Kirk, Samuel Escobar, Toribio Martínez, and Mervin Breneman, 1-11. Buenos Aires: Ediciones Kairós, 1977.

Kirk, Andrew J. "Exegesis técnica y anuncio de la fe." In *Hacia una hermenéutica evangélica Tomo III*, J. Andrew Kirk, Samuel Escobar, Toribio Martínez, and Mervin Breneman, 11-19. Buenos Aires: Kairos, 1977.

Kirk, Andrew J. *Hombre marxista y hombre cristiano*. Barcelona: Ediciones Evangélicas Europeas, 1977.

Kirk, Andrew J. *Liberation Theology: An Evangelical View from the Third World*. Basingstoke: Marshall, Morgan and Scott, 1979.

Kirk, Andrew J. *Theology Encounters Revolution*. Leicester: IVP, 1980.

Kirk, Andrew J. *The Good News of the Kingdom Coming*. Downers Grove: IVP, 1983

Kirk, Andrew J. *A New World Coming*. Basingstoke: Marshalls, Morgan and Scott, 1983.

Kirk, Andrew J. *Theology and the Third World Church*. Downers Grove: IVP, 1983.

Kirk, Andrew J. "Race, Class, Caste and the Bible." *Themelios* 10, no. 2 (1985): 4-14.

Kirk, Andrew J. *God's Word for a Complex World: Discovering How the Bible Speaks Today*. Basingstoke: Marshall, Morgan and Scott, 1987.

Kirk, Andrew J. *Loosing the Chains*. London: Hodder and Stoughton, 1992.

Kirk, Andrew J. *The Mission of Theology and Theology as Mission*. Leominster: Trinity Press International, 1997.

Kirk, Andrew J. *The Meaning of Freedom: A Study of Secular, Muslim and Christian Views*. Carlisle: Paternoster Press, 1998.

Kirk, Andrew J. *What is Mission? Theological Explorations*. London: Darton, Longman and Todd Ltd, 1999.

Kirk, J. Andrew, Samuel Escobar, Toribio Martínez, and Mervin Breneman. *Hacia una hermenéutica evangélica Tomo III*. Buenos Aires: Ediciones Kairós, 1977.

Kirkpatrick, Dow, ed. *Faith Born in the Struggle for Life*. Grand Rapids: Eerdmans, 1988.

Lambert, Jacques. *Latin America: Social Structures and Political Institutions*. Translated by Helen Katel. Berkeley: University of California, 1971.

López, Jesús Camargo. "La dependencia económica de América Latina: Un enfoque evangélico." *Boletín Teológico* 37 (1990): 7-30.

Mackay, John A. *The Other Spanish Christ*. London: SCM, 1932. Reprint, Eugene: Wipf and Stock Publishers, 2001.

Mackay, John A. *That Other America*. New York: Friendship Press, 1935.

Maduro, Otto and Marc H. Ellis. *The Future of Liberation Theology: Essays in Honor of Gustavo Gutiérrez*. Maryknoll: Orbis Books, 1989.

Makower, Katharine. *Don't cry for me*. London: Hodder and Stoughton, 1989.

Marshall, I. Howard. "How do we interpret the Bible today?" *Themelios* 5, no. 2 (1980): 4-12.

Martin, David. *Tongues of Fire: The Explosion of Protestantism in Latin America*. Oxford: Basil and Blackwell, 1990.

Martin, David. "Evangelicals and Economic Culture in Latin America: An Interim Comment on Research in Progress." *Social Compass* 39, no. 1 (1992): 9-14.

Martin, David. *Forbidden Revolutions*. London: SPCK, 1996.

Martin, David. "Iglesia popular: El resurgimiento evangélico global y sus consecuencias políticas." *Textos para la Acción* 8, no. 13 (2000): 23-38.

McBrien, R.P., ed. *The Harper Collins Encyclopaedia of Catholicism*. New York: Harper Collins, 1995.

McCleod, D. *The Person of Christ*. Leicester: IVP, 1998.

McGovern, Arthur F. *Liberation Theology and Its Critics*. Maryknoll: Orbis Books, 1989.

McGrath, Alister. "Evangelical Theological Method: The State of the Art." In *Evangelical Futures*, ed. John G. Stackhouse, 15-37. Grand Rapids: Baker Books, 2000.

McGrath, Alister, ed. *The Blackwell Encyclopaedia of Modern Christian Thought* Oxford: Blackwell, 1993.

McKnight, Scott. "Matthew, Gospel of." In *Dictionary of Jesus and the Gospels*, eds. Joel B. Green and Scott McKnight, 526-541. Downers Grove and Leicester: IVP, 1992.

Miranda, José Porfirio. *Marx and the Bible: A Critique of the Philosophy of Oppression*. Translated by John Eagleson. Maryknoll: Orbis Books, 1974.

Míguez Bonino, José. "Escritura y traición: un antiguo problema en una nueva perspectiva." *Cuadernos Teológicos* 9 (June 1960): 94-107.

Míguez Bonino, José. "Implicaciones del Segundo Concilio Vaticano para la vida religiosa de nuestros tiempos, particularmente en América Latina." In *Los Protestantes y el Segundo Concilio Vaticano: Consulta sobre las actuales relaciones y actitudes entre evangélicos y católicos romanos*, ed. Federcio J. Huegel, 88-95. Mexico: Casa Unida de Publicaciones, 1964.

Míguez Bonino, José. *Concilio abierto: una interpretación protestante del Concilio Vaticano II*. Buenos Aires: La Aurora, 1967.

Míguez Bonino, José. "El nuevo catolicismo." In *Fe cristiana y Latinoamérica hoy*, ed. C. René Padilla, 83-118. Buenos Aires: Ediciones Certeza, 1974.

Míguez Bonino, José. *Doing Theology in a Revolutionary Situation*. Philadelphia: Fortress Press, 1975.

Míguez Bonino, José. "El reino de Dios y la historia." In *El reino de Dios y América Latina*, ed. C. René Padilla, 75-95. El Paso: Casa Bautista de Publicaciones, 1975.

Míguez Bonino, José. *La fe en busca de la eficacia*. Salamanca: Sígueme, 1977.

Míguez Bonino, José. *Toward a Christian Political Ethics*. London: SCM Press, 1983.

Míguez Bonino, José. "Love and Social Transformation in Liberation Theology." In *Love: the Foundation of Hope: the Theology of Jürgen Moltmann and Elisabeth Moltmann*, eds. Frederic B. Burnham, Charles S. McCoy and M. Douglas Meeks, 60-76. New York: Harper and Row Publishers, 1988.

Míguez Bonino, José. "On Discipleship, Justice and Power." In *Freedom and Discipleship*, ed. Daniel Schipani, 131-138. Maryknoll: Orbis Books, 1989.

Míguez Bonino, José. "The Condition and Prospects of Christianity in Latin America." In *New Face of the Church in Latin America*, ed. Guillermo Cook, 259-267. Maryknoll: Orbis Books, 1994.

Míguez Bonino, José. *Faces of Latin American Protestantism*. Translated by Eugene L. Stockwell. Grand Rapids: Eerdmans, 1997.

Míguez Bonino, José. "La teología evangélica y los evangélicos." *Boletín Teológico* 65 (1997): 7-15.

Míguez Bonino, José. *Poder del evangelio y poder político*. Buenos Aires: Ediciones Kairós, 1999.

Míguez Bonino, José, ed. *Faces of Jesus: Latin American Christologies*. Translated by Robert R. Barr. Maryknoll: Orbis Books, 1984.

Míguez Bonino, José, Juan Sepúlveda and Rigoberto Gálvez, eds. Congreso Latinoamericano de Evangelización (CLADE), IV, Quito, 2 a 9 de septiembre de 2000: *Unidad y diversidad del protestantismo latinoamericano: el testimonio evangélico hacia el tercer milenio: palabra, espíritu y misión* Buenos Aires: Ediciones Kairós, 2002.

Miranda, Jose Porfirio. *El Ser y el Mesías*. Salamanca: Sígueme, 1973.

Miranda, Jose Porfirio. *Being and the Messiah*. Translated by John Eagleson. Maryknoll: Orbis Books, 1974.

Miranda, Jose Porfirio. *Communism in the Bible*. Maryknoll, Orbis Books, 1982.

Moltmann, Jürgen. "An Open Letter to José Míguez Bonino (March 29, 1976)." In *Liberation Theology: A Documentary History*, ed. Alfred T. Hennelly, 195-204. Maryknoll: Orbis Books, 1990.

Moo, Douglas. *The Epistle to the Romans*. Grand Rapids: Eerdmans, 1996.

Moreau, A.S., ed. *The Evangelical Dictionary of World Missions*. Carlisle: Paternoster Press, 2000.

Morison, Samuel E. *Admiral of the Ocean Sea – A Life of Christopher Columbus*. Boston: Little, Brown and Company, 1942.

Muskus, Eddy José. *The Origins and Early Development of Liberation Theology in Latin America*. Carlisle: Paternoster Press, 2002.

Myers, Bryant L. *Walking with the Poor*. Maryknoll: Orbis Books, 1999.

Nash, Ronald H., ed. *On Liberation Theology*. Michigan: Mott Media, 1984.

Nicholls, Bruce, ed. *In Word and Deed*. Exeter: Paternoster Press, 1985.

Nickoloff, James, ed. *Gustavo Gutiérrez: Essential Writings*. London: SCM, 1996.

Novak, Michael. *The Spirit of Democratic Capitalism*. New York: American Enterprise Institute/Simon and Schuster, 1982.

Novak, Michael, ed. *Liberation South, Liberation North*. Washington DC: American Enterprise Institute for Public Policy Research, 1981.

Núñez, C. Emilio Antonio. "Posición de la iglesia frente al 'aggiornamento'." In *Acción en Cristo para un continente en crisis*, ed. Samuel Escobar, 39-44. San José: Editorial Caribe, 1970.

Núñez, C. Emilio Antonio. "¡Aquí España!" *Boletín Teológico* 8 (1974): 1-5.

Núñez, C. Emilio Antonio. "Salvación personal y eterna y liberación humana." *Boletín Teológico* 10 (1974): 7-18.

Núñez, C. Emilio Antonio. *Caminos de renovación*. Grand Rapids: Outreach Publications, 1975.

Núñez, C. Emilio Antonio. "La naturaleza del reino de Dios." In *El reino de Dios y América Latina*, ed. C. René Padilla, 17-36. El Paso: Casa Bautista de Publicaciones, 1975.

Núñez, C. Emilio Antonio. "Personal and Eternal Salvation and Human Redemption." In *Let the Earth Hear his Voice*, ed. J.D. Douglas, 1060-1070. Minneapolis: World Wide Publications, 1975.

Núñez, C. Emilio Antonio. *Constantes en la esperanza: primera carta al los tesalonicenses*. Guatemala: Tema Publicaciones, 1976.

Núñez, C. Emilio Antonio. "La influencia del protestantismo." *Boletín Teológico* 2 (1978): 1-15.

Núñez, C. Emilio Antonio. *El Cristo de Hispanoamérica*. Mexico: Ediciones las Americas, 1979.

Núñez, C. Emilio Antonio. "Herederos de la Reforma." In Congreso Latinoamericano de Evangelización (CLADE), II, noviembre de 1979, Quito: *América Latina y la evangelización en los años 80*, eds. Pedro Savage and Rolando Gutiérrez, 163-170. Mexico: Fraternidad Teológica Latinoamericana, 1980.

Núñez, C. Emilio Antonio. "The Church in the Liberation Theology of Gustavo Gutiérrez: Description and Hermeneutical Analysis." In *Biblical Interpretation and the Church: Text and Context*, ed. D. A. Carson, 166-194. Exeter: Paternoster Press, 1984.

Núñez, C. Emilio Antonio. "Dios y el ser humano." *Boletín Teológico* 16 (1984): 15-27.

Núñez, C. Emilio Antonio. "Testigo de un nuevo amanecer." In *Hacia una teología evangélica latinoamericana*, ed. C. René Padilla, 101-112. San José: Editorial Caribe, 1984.

Núñez, C. Emilio Antonio. *Liberation Theology*. Chicago: Moody Press, 1985.

Núñez, C. Emilio Antonio. "Los 'cristos' de nuestras tierras." *Apuntes Pastorales* 8, no. 6 (1991): 6-13.

Núñez, C. Emilio Antonio. "Panorama teológico de la América Latina." *Apuntes Pastorales* 9, no. 2 (1991): 35-37.

Núñez, C. Emilio Antonio. "¿Cómo debe crecer la iglesia?" *Apuntes Pastorales* 10, no. 2 (1992): 10-11.

Núñez, C. Emilio Antonio. "Los evangélicos y la nueva cristología." *Apuntes Pastorales* 10, no. 1 (1992): 14-16.

Núñez, C. Emilio Antonio. "Mi credo." *Apuntes Pastorales* 9, no. 5 (1992): 24-25.

Núñez, C. Emilio Antonio. "¿Vendrá Cristo en el año 2000?" *Apuntes Pastorales* 9, no. 6 (1992): 28-29.

Núñez, C. Emilio Antonio. "Dios y el gobierno humano." *Apuntes Pastorales* 11, no. 3 (1993): 30-33.

Núñez, C. Emilio Antonio. "La palabra de evangelio." *Apuntes Pastorales* 10, no. 5 (1993): 14-16.

Núñez, C. Emilio Antonio. "¿Qué es la misión de la iglesia?" *Apuntes Pastorales* 11, no. 2 (1993): 18-20.

Núñez, C. Emilio Antonio. "Que prediques la Palabra." *Apuntes Pastorales* 10, no. 4 (1993): 30-32.

Núñez, C. Emilio Antonio. "El SIDA llegó hasta nosotros." *Apuntes Pastorales* 10, no. 6 (1993): 46-48.

Núñez, C. Emilio Antonio. "El evangelio de la prosperidad." *Apuntes Pastorales* 11, no. 4 (1994): 33-35.

Núñez, C. Emilio Antonio. "Hacia el liderato cristiano." *Apuntes Pastorales* 12, no. 3 (1995): 12-13.

Núñez, C. Emilio Antonio. *Teología y misión: perspectivas desde América Latina.* San José: Visión Mundial Internacional, 1996.

Núñez, C. Emilio Antonio. *Desafíos Pastorales.* Grand Rapids: Editorial Portavoz, 1998.

Núñez, C. Emilio Antonio. "Mi afición a las letras." In *La Aventura de Escribir: testimonio de catorce escritores cristianos*, ed. Adriana Powell, 121-136. Lima: Ediciones Puma, 2003.

Núñez, C. Emilio Antonio. *Conciencia e identidad evangélica y la renovación católica.* Guatemala: Grupo Evangélico Universitario, n.d.

Núñez, C. Emilio Antonio and William David Taylor. *Crisis and Hope in LatinAmerica: An Evangelical Perspective*, Revised ed. Pasadena: William Carey Library, 1996.

Ortiz, Juan Carlos. "Iglesia y Sociedad." In *Fe cristiana y latinoamérica hoy*, ed. C. René Padilla, 185-208. Buenos Aires: Ediciones Certeza, 1974.

Ortiz, Israel. "El quehacer teológico de Emilio A. Núñez." In *Teología y misión: perspectivas desde América Latina*, Emilio A. Núñez, 11-40. San José: Visión Mundial Internacional, 1996.

Packer, James. "Hermeneutics and Biblical Authority." *Themelios* 1, no. 1 (1978): 3-12.

Padilla, C. René. " El propósito de la Biblia." *Certeza* 10 (1962): 95.

Padilla, C. René. "Lo de Dios y lo de César." *Certeza* 41 (1970): 2-3.

Padilla, C. René. "Mensaje bíblico y revolución." *Certeza* 39 (1970): 200.

Padilla, C. René. "La Biblia hoy." *Certeza* 42 (1971): 56-59.

Padilla, C. René. "La autoridad de la Biblia en la teología latinoamericana." In *El debate contemporáneo sobre la Biblia*, ed. Pedro Savage, 121-154. Barcelona: Ediciones Evangélicas Europeas, 1972.

Padilla, C. René. "Revolution and Revelation." In *Is Revolution Change?*, ed. Brian Griffiths, 70-83. London: IVP, 1972.

Padilla, C. René. "Iglesia y Sociedad en América Latina." In *Fe cristiana y Latinoamérica hoy*, ed. C. René Padilla, 119-147. Buenos Aires: Ediciones Certeza, 1974.

Padilla, C. René. "La política de Jesús." *Certeza* 53 (1974): 152-155.

Padilla, C. René. "Proyecto para una ética social evangélica." In *Fe cristiana y Latinoamérica hoy*, ed. C. René Padilla, 209-214. Buenos Aires: Ediciones Certeza, 1974.

Padilla, C. René. *El evangelio hoy*. Buenos Aires: Certeza, 1975.

Padilla, C. René. "El reino de Dios y la iglesia." In *El reino de Dios y América Latina*, ed. C. René Padilla, 43-68. El Paso: Casa Bautista de Publicaciones, 1975.

Padilla, C. René. "El círculo hermenéutico." In *Hacia una hermenéutica evangélica Tomo II*, C. René Padilla, Mervin Breneman, Sidney H. Rooy, B. Melano Couch, Eugene Nida, Elsa R. Powell and Samuel Escobar, 1-4. Buenos Aires: Ediciones Kairós, 1977.

Padilla, C. René. "God's Word and Man's Myths." *Themelios* 3, no. 1 (1977): 3-9.

Padilla, C. René. "El lugar de la revelación en la epistemología." In *Hacia una hermenéutica evangélica Tomo II*, C. René Padilla, Mervin Breneman, Sidney H. Rooy, B. Melano Couch, Eugene Nida, Elsa R. Powell and Samuel Escobar, 1-2. Buenos Aires: Ediciones Kairós, 1977.

Padilla, C. René. "Ser prójimo." *Certeza* 69 (1978): 147-150.

Padilla, C. René. "Hermeneutics and Culture – A Theological Perspective." In *Down to Earth: Studies in Christianity and Culture*, eds. John R. W. Stott and Robert Coote, 63-87. Grand Rapids: Eerdmans, 1980.

Padilla, C. René. "Jesús y los pobres." *Certeza* 77 (1980): 151-156.

Padilla, C. René. "The Interpreted Word: Reflections on Contextual Hermeneutics." *Themelios* 7, no. 1 (1981): 18-23.

Padilla, C. René. "Cristología y misión en los dos-terceros mundos." *Boletín Teológico* 8 (1982): 39-60.

Padilla, C. René. "Mission is Compassion." *Missiology: An International Review* 10, no. 3 (1982): 319-338.

Padilla, C. René. "Una nueva manera de hacer teología." *Misión* 1, no. 1 (1982): 20-23.

Padilla, C. René. "La teología de la liberación: una evaluación crítica." *Misión* 1, no. 2 (1982), 16-21.

Padilla, C. René. "Biblical Foundations: A Latin American Study." *Evangelical Review of Theology* 7, no. 1 (1983): 79-88.

Padilla, C. René. "Christology and Mission in the Two Thirds World." In *Sharing Jesus in the Two Thirds World*, eds. Vinay Samuel and Chris Sugden, 17-47. Grand Rapids: Eerdmans, 1983.

Padilla, C. René. "La Fraternidad Teológica Latinoamericana: una evaluación crítica." *Misión* 7 (1983): 28-30.

Padilla, C. René. "The Unity of the Church and the Homogenous Unit Principle." In *Exploring Church Growth*, ed. William R. Shenk, 285-303. Grand Rapids: Eerdmans, 1983.

Padilla, C. René. "El uso de la Biblia en el púlpito." *Misión* 7 (1983): 21-23.

Padilla, C. René. "La Fraternidad Teológica Latinoamericana en tela de juicio." *Misión* 9 (1984): 62-64.

Padilla, C. René. "Justicia y paz." *Misión* 11 (1984): 140-143.

Padilla, C. René. "La Palabra de Dios y las Palabras Humanas." *Pensamiento Cristiano* 100 (1984): 31-32.

Padilla, C. René. "Siervo de la Palabra." In *Hacia una teología evangélica latinoamericana*, ed. C. René Padilla, 113-120. San José: Editorial Caribe, 1984.

Padilla, C. René. "Cuatro tesis de Leonardo Boff sobre la iglesia." *Mision* 14 (1985): 94- 96.

Padilla, C. René. "Evangelism and Social Responsibility: From Wheaton '66 to Wheaton '83." *Transformation* 2, no. 3 (1985): 27-33.

Padilla, C. René. "Evangelismo y la responsabilidad social: de Wheaton '66 a Wheaton '83." *Misión* (Sept 1985): 82-90.

Padilla, C. René. *Mission Between the Times*. Grand Rapids: Eerdmans, 1985.

Padilla, C. René. "Nuevas Alternativas de educación teológica." *Boletín Teológico* 19 (1985): 4-20.

Padilla, C. René. "Por qué Leonardo Boff ha sido silenciado." *Cuadernos de Teología* Año VI, no. 4 (1985): 107-112.

Padilla, C. René. "El reino de Dios y la historia en la teología Latinoamericana." *Cuadernos de Teología* 7, no. 1 (1985): 5-12.

Padilla, C. René. "El estado desde una perspectiva bíblica." In *Los evangélicos y el poder político en América Latina*, ed. Pablo A. Deiros, 23-40. Buenos Aires: Nueva Creación, 1986.

Padilla, C. René. "La nueva eclesiología en América Latina." *Boletín Teológico* 24 (1986): 201-229.

Padilla, C. René. "Towards a Contextual Christology from Latin America." In *Conflict and Context: Hermeneutics in the Americas*, eds. Mark Lau Branson and C. René Padilla, 81-91. Grand Rapids: Eerdmans, 1986.

Padilla, C. René. "A New Ecclesiology in Latin America." *International Bulletin of Missionary Research* 11, no.4 (1987): 156-164.

Padilla, C. René. "Hacia una cristología evangélica contextual." *Boletín Teológico* 30 (1988): 87-101.

Padilla, C. René. "Liberation Theology: An Appraisal." In *Freedom and Discipleship*, ed. Daniel S. Schipani, 34-51. Maryknoll: Orbis Books, 1989.

Padilla, C. René. "La misión en la década de los años noventa." *Boletín Teológico* 34 (1989): 159-166.

Padilla, C. René. *La palabra interpretada: reflexiones sobre hermenéutica contextual.* Lima: Asociación de Grupos Evangélicos, 1989.

Padilla, C. René. "La violencia en el Nuevo Testamento." *Boletín Teológico* 39 (1990): 197-207.

Padilla, C. René. "Hacia una ética política evangélica." *Boletín Teológico* 44 (1991): 261-274.

Padilla, C. René. "Pobreza y mayordomía." *Boletín Teológico* 42/43 (1991): 93-101.

Padilla, C. René. *Los derechos humanos y el reino de Dios.* Lima: Concilio Nacional Evangelico de Peru – PROMIES: 1992.

Padilla, C. René. "La misión cristiana en las Américas: una perspectiva latinoamericana." In *Misión en el camino: Ensayos en homenaje a Orlando E. Costas.* Samuel Escobar, Sidney Rooy, Valdir Steuernagel, C. René Padilla, Guillermo Cook, Beatriz Melano Couch, Edesio Sanchez Cetina and Daniel Schipani, 67-94. Buenos Aires: Fraternidad Teológica Latinoamericana, 1992.

Padilla, C. René. "Mensaje inaugural: Todo el evangelio para todos los pueblosdesde América Latina." In Congreso Latinoamericano de Evangelización (CLADE), III, 24 de agosto a 4 de septiembre de 1992, Quito: *Todo el Evangelio para todos los pueblos desde América Latina,* 6-11. Quito: Fraternidad Teológica Latinoamericana, 1993.

Padilla, C. René. *Discipulado, compromiso y misión.* San José: Vision Mundial, 1994.

Padilla, C. René. "New Actors on the Political Scene." In *New Face of the Church in Latin America,* ed. Guillermo Cook, 82-95. Maryknoll: Orbis Books, 1994.

Padilla, C. René. "La Fraternidad Teológica Latinoamericana y la responsabilidad social de la iglesia." *Boletín Teológico* 59/60 (1995): 98-114.

Padilla, C. René. "Latin American Evangelicals Enter the Public Square." *Transformation* 9, no. 3 (1995): 2-7.

Padilla, C. René. "La mayordomía de los bienes materiales: una exploración en la ética reformada." *Iglesia y Misión* 53 (1995): 6-11.

Padilla, C. René. "Pentecostés y la iglesia." *Encuentro y Fe* 35 (1995): 10-13.

Padilla, C. René. "Kairós: Formar al pueblo de Dios para la misión integral." *Orientación Cristiana* (October-December, 1996): 1-2.

Padilla, C. René. "Misión y prosperidad." *Textos para la Acción* 4, no. 6 (1996): (no page numbers given).

Padilla, C. René. "Vigencia del Jubileo en el mundo actual (Levítico 25)." *Boletín Teológico* 63 (1996): 71-88.

Padilla, C. René. *Discipulado y misión: compromiso con el reino de Dios.* Buenos Aires: Ediciones Kairós, 1997.

Padilla, C. René. "Hacia una evaluación teológica del ministerio integral." In *Servir con los pobres en América Latina*, eds. Gregorio Rake, C. René Padilla and Tetsunao Yamamori, 29-52. Buenos Aires: Ediciones Kairós, 1997.

Padilla, C. René. "Viñetas de una iglesia sierva." *Iglesia y misión* 62 (1997): 6-11.

Padilla, C. René. "El futuro del cristianismo en América Latina: perspectivas y desafíos misionológicos." In *Iglesia, ética y poder*, John H. Yoder, Lilia Solano and C. René Padilla, 62-87. Buenos Aires: Ediciones Kairós, 1998.

Padilla, C. René. "Desafíos para la próxima década." *Apuntes Pastorales* 17, no. 2 (2000): 20-22.

Padilla, C. René. "Hacia una definición de la misión integral." In *El Proyecto de Dios y las necesidades humanas: más modelos de ministerio integral en América Latina,* eds. C. René Padilla and Tetsunao Yamamori, 19-34. Buenos Aires: Ediciones Kairós, 2000.

Padilla, C. René. "Itinerario de la misión integral: de CLADE I a CLADE IV." *Iglesia y Misión* 74 (2000): 4-15.

Padilla, C. René. "Misión integral y evangelización." *Iglesia y Misión* 71/72 (2000): 34-39.

Padilla, C. René. "Ser prójimo." *Iglesia y misión* 74 (2000): 40-44.

Padilla, C. René. *Economía humana y economía del reino de Dios.* Buenos Aires: Ediciones Kairós, 2002.

Padilla, C. René. "El Espíritu Santo y la misión integral de la iglesia." In *El trino Dios y la misión integral*, Pedro Arana Quiroz, Samuel Escobar and C. René Padilla, 115-147. Buenos Aires: Ediciones Kairós, 2003.

Padilla, C. René. "Una eclesiología para la misión integral." In *La iglesia local como agente de transformación: una eclesiología para la misión integral,* eds. C. René Padilla and Tetsunao Yamamori, 13-45. Buenos Aires: Ediciones Kairós, 2003.

Padilla, C. René. "Un largo aprendizaje." In *La Aventura de Escribir: testimonio de catorce escritores cristianos*, ed. Adriana Powell, 139-148. Lima: Ediciones Puma, 2003.

Padilla, C. René, ed. *Fe cristiana y Latinoamérica hoy.* Buenos Aires: Ediciones Certeza, 1974.

Padilla, C. René, ed. *El reino de dios y América Latina.* El Paso: Casa Bautista de Publicaciones, 1975.

Padilla, C. René, ed. *The New Face of Evangelicalism.* Downers Grove: IVP, 1976.

Padilla, C. René, ed. *Hacia una teología evangélica latinoamericana.* San José: Editorial Caribe, 1984.

Padilla, C. René, ed. *Nuevas alternativas de educación teológica.* Buenos Aires: Nueva Creación, 1986.

Padilla, C. René, ed. *New Alternatives in Theological Education*. Oxford: Regnum Books, 1988.

Padilla, C. René, ed. *De la marginación al compromiso: los evangélicos y la política en América Latina*. Buenos Aires: Fraternidad Teológica Latinoamericana, 1991.

Padilla, C. René, ed. *Bases bíblicas de la misión: perspectivas latinoamericanas*. Buenos Aires: Nueva Creación, 1998.

Padilla, C. René, Mervin Breneman, Sidney H. Rooy, B. Melano Couch, Eugene Nida, Elsa R. Powell and Samuel Escobar. *Hacia una hermenéutica evangélica Tomo II*. Buenos Aires: Ediciones Kairós, 1977.

Padilla, C. René and Carmen de Perez. *Hacer el amor en todo lo que hace: como se cultivan relaciones conyugales permanentes*. Colombia: Fraternidad Teológica Latinoamericana: 1996.

Padilla, C. René and Chris Sugden, eds. *Texts on evangelical social ethics, 1974-1983*. Nottingham: Grove Books Limited, 1985.

Padilla, C. René and Chris Sugden, eds. *How Evangelicals Endorsed Social Responsibility*. Bramcote: Grove Books Limited, 1985.

Padilla, C. René and Mark L. Branson, eds. *Conflict and Context: Hermeneutics in the Americas*. Grand Rapids: Eerdmans, 1986.

Padilla, C. René and Tetsunao Yamamori, eds. *El Proyecto de Dios y las necesidades humanas*. Buenos Aires: Ediciones Kairós, 2000.

Padilla, C. René and Tetsunao Yamamori, eds. Congreso Latinoamericano de Evangelización (CLADE), IV, Quito, Ecuador, 2 a 9 de septiembre de 2000: *Misión integral y pobreza: el testimonio evangélico hacia el tercer milenio: palabra, espíritu y misión*. Buenos Aires: Ediciones Kairós, 2001.

Padilla, C. René and Tetsunao Yamamori, eds. *La iglesia local como agente de transformación: una eclesiología para la misión integral*. Buenos Aires: Ediciones Kairós, 2003.

Padilla, Washington, ed. *Hacia una transformación integral*. Buenos Aires: Fraterniad Teológica Latinoamericana, 1988.

Pagán, Luis N. Rivera. "Toward a Theology of Peace: Critical Notes on the Biblical Hermeneutic of Latin American Theology of Liberation." In *Faith Born in the Struggle for Life*, ed. Dow Kirkpatrick, 52-75. Grand Rapids: Eerdmans, 1988.

Paredes, Tito. *El evangelio: un tesoro en vasijas de barro*. Buenos Aires: Ediciones Kairós, 2000.

Pendle, George. *A History of Latin America*. Middlesex: Penguin Books, 1963.

Perez, Pablo, Emilio A. Núñez, Sidney Rooy, Mervin Breneman and Elsa R. de Powell. "Mesa redonda sobre la conversión." *Misión* 12 (March 1985): 12-18.

Perry, John. "Dissolving the Inerrancy Debate: How Modern Philosophy Shaped the Evangelical View of Scripture." *Journal for Christian Theological Research* [http://apu.edu/ctrf...] 6:3 (2001): 1-17.

Piedra, Arturo, Sidney Rooy and H. Fernando Bullón. *¿Hacia dónde va el protestantismo?* *Herencia y prospectivas en América Latina*. Buenos Aires: Ediciones Kairós, 2003.

Pixley, Jorge. *Hacia una fe evangélica latinoamericana: una perspectiva bautista*. San Jose: Departamento Ecuménico de Investigacioines, 1988.

Powell, Adriana, ed. *La aventura de escribir: testimonio de catorce escritores cristianos*. Lima: Ediciones Puma, 2003.

Rake Gregorio, C. René Padilla and Tetsunao Yamamori, eds. *Servir con lospobres en América Latina: modelos de ministerio integral*. Buenos Aires: Ediciones Kairós, 1997.

Revilla, Danilo. "De los principios a la práctica." In *El proyecto de Dios y las necesidades humanas*, eds. C. René Padilla and Tetsunao Yamamori, 131-142. Buenos Aires, Ediciones Kairós, 2000.

Roldán, Alberto Fernando. *Escatología: una visión integral desde América Latina*. Buenos Aires: Ediciones Kairós, 2002.

Roldán, Alberto Fernando. "El sacerdocio de todos los creyentes y la misiónintegral." In *La iglesia como agente de transformación: una eclesiología para la misión integral*, eds. C. René Padilla and Tetsuano Yamamori, 103-130. Buenos Aires: Ediciones Kairós, 2003.

Rooy, Sidney H. "Un modelo histórico hermenéutico." In *Hacia unahermenéutica evangélica Tomo II*, C. René Padilla, Mervin Breneman, Sidney H. Rooy, B. Melano Couch, Eugene Nida, Elsa R. Powell and Samuel Escobar, 1-17. Buenos Aires: Kairós, 1977.

Rooy, Sidney H. "Relaciones de la iglesia con el poder político: modelo reformado." In *Los evangélicos y el poder político en América Latina*, ed. Pablo Alberto Deiros, 41-72. Grand Rapids: Nueva Creación, 1986.

Rooy, Sidney H. *Misión y encuentro de culturas*. Buenos Aires: Ediciones Kairós, 2001.

Rooy, Sidney H., ed. Congreso Latinoamericano de Evangelización (CLADE), IV, Quito, Ecuador, 2 a 9 de septiembre de 2000: *Presencia cristiana en el mundo académico : el testimonio evangélico hacia el tercer milenio: palabra, espíritu y misión*. Buenos Aires: Ediciones Kairós, 2001.

Rowland, Christopher, ed. *The Cambridge Companion to Liberation Theology*. Cambridge: Cambridge University Press, 1999.

Ruiz, Jerjes. "The Priesthood of All Believers." In *Faith Born in the Struggle for Life*, ed. Dow Kirkpatrick, 98-115. Grand Rapids: Eerdmans, 1988.

Samuel, Vinay and Chris Sugden, eds. *Sharing Jesus in the Two Thirds World*. Grand Rapids: Eerdmans, 1983.

Samuel, Vinay and Chris Sugden, eds. *The Church in Response to Human Need*. Grand Rapids: Eerdmans, 1987.

Savage, Pedro, ed. *El debate contemporáneo sobre la Biblia*. Barcelona: Ediciones Evangélicas Europeas, 1972.

Savage, Pedro and Rolando Gutiérrez, eds. Congreso Latinoamericano de Evangelización (CLADE), II, noviembre de 1979, Quito: *América Latina y la evangelización en los años 80.* Mexico: Fraternidad Teológica Latinoamericana, 1980.

Schipani, Daniel. *Freedom and Discipleship.* Maryknoll: Orbis Books, 1989.

Scholte, Marianne. "Reflexiones sobre la enseñanza de la economía desde un punto de vista cristiano." In Congreso Latinoamericano de Evangelización (CLADE), IV, Quito, Ecuador, 2 a 9 de septiembre de 2000: *Presenciacristiana en el mundo académico: el testimonio evangélico hacia el tercer milenio: palabra, espíritu y misión,* ed. Sidney H. Rooy, 225-242. Buenos Aires: Ediciones Kairós, 2001.

Scott, Luis and Titus Guenther. *Del sur al norte: aportes teológicos desde la periferia.* Buenos Aires: Ediciones Kairós, 2003.

Segundo, Juan Luis. *The Liberation of Theology,* 6th ed. Translated by John Drury. Maryknoll: Orbis Books, 1991.

Sépulveda, Juan. "Pentecostal Theology in the Context of the Struggle for Life." In *Faith Born in the Struggle for Life,* ed. Dow Kirkpatrick, 298-318. Grand Rapids: Eerdmans, 1988.

Shenk, Wilbert, ed. *Exploring Church Growth.* Grand Rapids: Eerdmans, 1983.

Sherlock, Charles. *The Doctrine of Humanity.* Leicester: IVP, 1996.

Sider, Ronald J. *Lifestyle in the Eighties: An Evangelical Commitment to a Simple Lifestyle.* Philadelphia: The Westminster Press, 1982.

Sigmund, Paul. *Liberation Theology at the Crossroads. Democracy or Revolution?* New York: Oxford University Press, 1990.

Smith, Christian. *The Emergence of Liberation Theology, Radical Religion and Social Movement Today.* Chicago: University of Chicago Press, 1991.

Sobrino, Jon. *Cristología desde América Latina: esbozo a partir del seguimiento del Jesús histórico.* México: Centro de Reflexión Teológica, 1976.

Sobrino, Jon. *Christology at the Crossroads: A Latin American Approach.* Translated by John Drury. London: SCM. 1978.

Sobrino, Jon, and Ignacio Ellacuria, eds. *Systematic Theology: Perspectives from Liberation Theology.* London: SCM Press, 1996.

Solano, Lilia. "Iglesia, ética y poder." In *Iglesia, ética y poder,* eds. John H. Yoder, Lilia Solano and C. René Padilla, 49-61. Buenos Aires: Ediciones Kairós, 1998.

Stackhouse, John G. "Evangelical Theology should be Evangelical." In *Evangelical Futures: A Conversation on Theological Method,* ed. John G. Stackhouse, 39-58. Vancouver: Regent College Publishing, 2000.

Stackhouse, John G., ed. *Evangelical Futures.* Vancouver: Regent College Publishing, 2000.

Stam, John. "Christian Witness in Central America: A Radical Evangelical Perspective." *Transformation* 2, no.3 (1985): 14-17.

Stoll, David. *Is Latin America Turning Protestant? The Politics of Evangelical Growth.* Oxford: University of California Press, 1990.

Stoll, David and Virginia Garrard-Burnett, eds. *Rethinking Protestantism in Latin America.* Philadelphia: Temple University Press, 1993.

Stott, J.R.W. and R. Coote, eds. *Gospel and Culture*. Pasadena: William Carey Library, 1979.

Stott, J.R.W. and R. Coote, eds. *Down to Earth: Studies in Christianity and Culture*. Grand Rapids: Eerdmans, 1980.

Stuart, Gene S. and George E. Stuart. *Lost Kingdoms of the Maya*. National Geographical Society, 1993.

Tidball, Derek J. *Who are the Evangelicals?* London: Marshall Pickering, 1994.

Tinker, Melvin. *Evangelical Concerns*. Great Britain: Mentor, 2001.

Tinker, Melvin, ed. *Restoring the Vision: Anglican Evangelicals Speak Out*. Eastbourne: MARC, 1990.

Vaage, Leif. E., ed. *Subversive Scriptures: Revolutionary Readings of the Christian Bible in Latin America*. Valley Forge: Trinity Press International, 1997.

Vaca, Víctor. "Misión integral y transformación estructural desde América Latina." In Congreso Latinoamericano de Evangelización (CLADE), IV, Quito, Ecuador, 2 a 9 de septiembre de 2000: *Misión integral y pobreza: el testimonio evangélico hacia el tercer milenio: palabra, espíritu y misión*, eds. C. René Padilla and Tetsunao Yamamori, 49-72. Buenos Aires: Ediciones Kairós, 2001.

Vallier, Ivan. *Catolicismo, control social y modernización en América Latina*. Buenos Aires: Amorrortu Editores, 1971.

Ventura, Juan Pablo. "La cooperación entre iglesias en la misión integral." In Congreso Latinoamericano de Evangelización (CLADE), IV, Quito, Ecuador, 2 a 9 de septiembre de 2000: *Misión integral y pobreza: el testimonio evangélico hacia el tercer milenio: palabra, espíritu y misión*. eds. C. René Padilla and Tetsunao Yamamori, 239-250. Buenos Aires: Ediciones Kairós, 2001.

Volf, Miroslav. "Doing and Interpreting: an Examination of the Relationships Between Theory and Practice in Latin American Liberation Theology." *Themelios* 8, no.3 (1983): 11-19.

Voth, Esteban. "Bases bíblicas para la misión integral en contextos de pobreza."In Congreso Latinoamericano de Evangelización (CLADE), IV, Quito, Ecuador, 2 a 9 de septiembre de 2000: *Misión integral y pobreza: eltestimonio evangélico hacia el tercer milenio: palabra, espíritu y misión*, eds. C. René Padilla and Tetsunao Yamamori, 73-124. Buenos Aires: Ediciones Kairós, 2001.

Ward, Keith. *Religion and Human Nature*. Oxford: Clarendon Press, 1998.

Williams, Stephen, N. "Evangelicals and Eschatology: A Contentious Case." In *Interpreting the Bible: Historical and Theological Studies*, ed. A.N.S. Lane 291-308. Leicester: Apollos, 1997.

Williams, Stephen, N. "Looking Back." *Perichoresis* (forthcoming).

Wright, Chris and Chris Green, eds. *Fanning the Flame: Bible, Cross and Mission*. Grand Rapids: Zondervan, 2003.

Yates, Timothy. *Christian Misson in the Twentieth Century.* Cambridge: Cambridge University Press, 1994.

Yoder, John H. "La expectativa mesiánica del reino y su carácter central para una adecuada hermenéutica contemporánea." In *El reino de Dios y América Latina*, ed. C. René Padilla, 103-120. El Paso: Casa Bautista de Publicaciones, 1975.

Yoder, John H. "Cristo y el poder." In *Iglesia, ética y poder*, John J. Yoder, Lilia Solano and C. René Padilla, 19-48. Buenos Aires: Ediciones Kairós, 1998.

Yoder, John H, Lilia Solano and C. René Padilla. *Iglesia, ética y poder.* Buenos Aires: Ediciones Kairós, 1998.

Young, Howard T. *The Victorious Expression: a Study of Four Contemporary Spanish Poets: Miguel de Unamuno, Antonio Machado, Juan Ramón Juménez, Federico García Lorca.* Madison: University of Wisconsin Press, 1964.

Yuasa, Key. "The Image of Christ in Latin American Indian Popular Religiosity." In *Sharing Jesus in the Two Thirds World*, eds. Vinay Samuel and Chris Sugden, 61-85. Grand Rapids: Eerdmans, 1983.

Other Sources Consulted

Avila, Mariano. "Latin American Reality and Hermeneutics in the *Fraternidad Teológica Latinoamericana.*" Ph.D. diss., Westminster Theological Seminary, 1996.

Coy, Terrell Frank. "Incarnation and the Kingdom of God: The Political Theologies of Orlando Costas, C. René Padilla and Samuel Escobar." Ph. D. diss., Southwestern Baptist Theological Seminary, 1999.

Elliot, Daniel C. "Theology and Mission from Latin America: The Latin American Theological Fraternity." Masters diss., Wheaton College Graduate School, 1992.

Escobar, Samuel. "Fostering Indigenous Authorship." TMs (photocopy). Paper presented at Evangelical Literature in the Latin World Consultation, Pinebrook, Pennsylvania, June 23-27, 1975, Latin American Theological Fraternity Archives, Buenos Aires, 1-30.

Escobar, Samuel. "Luz y santidad." TMs (photocopy). Paper presented at the CIEE Asamblea General in Duruelo, Colombia, 30 August - 8 September 1987, Latin American Theological Fraternity Archives, Buenos Aires, 1-17.

Escobar, Samuel. "Paulo Freire: otra pedagogía política." Ph.D. diss., Universidad Complutense de Madrid, 1990.

Escobar, Samuel. "Faith and Hope for the Future: Towards a Vital Evangelical Theology for the 21st Century." TMs (photocopy). Paper presented at the Theological Commission of the World Evangelical Fellowship, London Bible College, April 9-14, 1996, Latin American Theological Fraternity Archives, Buenos Aires, 1-34.

Escobar, Samuel. "Theology Back to the Mission Frontier." Convocation Address at McMaster Divinity College Hamilton, Ontario, May 13, 1997.

Escobar, Samuel. *Latin America: Mission Field and Mission Base.* Livingston Memorial Lecture 1998, Belfast Bible College, Belfast.

Escobar, Samuel. Interview by author, 1 April 2004, Valencia. Video recording.

Kirk, J. Andrew. Interview by author, 25 September 2003, Lechlade. Video Recording.

Míguez Bonino, José. Interview by author, 17 June 2003, Buenos Aires. Video Recording.

Núñez, Emilio A. "La Iglesia Católica Romana y las Escrituras." TMs (photocopy). Latin American Theological Fraternity Archives, Buenos Aires, 1-40.

Padilla, C. René. "La iglesia: un pueblo sacerdote." TMs (photocopy). Latin American Theological Fraternity Archives, Buenos Aires, (n.d.), 1-20.

Padilla, C. René. "The New Face of Religion in Latin America and the Caribbean." TMs (photocopy). The Latin American Theological Fraternity Archives, Buenos Aires, (n.d.), 1-10.

Padilla, C. René. "Misión Integral" TMs (photocopy). Misión Evangélica
Iberoamericana Conferencia "Palabra, Integridad, y Liderazgo en al poder del
Espíritu", Córdoba, December 27 – 30, 1999, Latin American Theological
Fraternity Archives, Buenos Aires, 1-5.

Padilla, C. René. Interview by author, 13 June 2003, Buenos Aires. Video
Recording.

Phillips, Steven. "The Use of Scripture in Liberation Theologies." Ph.D.
diss.,Ann Arbor: University Microfilms International, 1980.

Smith, Anthony Christopher. "The Essentials of Missiology from the
Evangelical Perspective of the 'Fraternidad Teológica Latinoamericana'." Ph.
D. diss., Southern Baptist Theological Seminary, 1983.

Steuernagel, Valdir Raul. "The Theology of Mission in its Relation to Social
Responsibility within the Lausanne Movement." Ph.D. diss., The Faculty of
the Lutheran School of Theology at Chicago, 1988.

Stott, John R. W. Interview by author, 20 September 2003, Blackpool. Video
Recording.

Weishein, Jorge Daniel. "La dialéctica de la obediencia. La tematización del
cambio social en el discurso teológico protestante de José Míguez Bonino
entre 1954-1984." Ph.D. diss., ISEDET, 2000. *América hoy*. Montevideo:
ISAL, 1966.

Congreso Latinoamericano de Evangelización (CLADE), III, 24 de agosto a 4 de
septiembre de 1992, Quito: *Todo el evangelio para todos los pueblos desde
América Latina*. Quito: Fraternidad Teológica Latinoamericana, 1993.

Congreso Latinoamericano de Evangelización (CLADE), IV, Quito, Ecuador, 2
a 9 de septiembre de 2000: *Palabra, espíritu y misión: el testimonio
evangélico hacia el tercer milenio: documentos*. Buenos Aires: Ediciones
Kairós, 2001.

Congreso Latinoamericano de Evangelización (CLADE), IV, Quito, Ecuador, 2
a 9 de septiembre de 2000: *Palabra, espíritu y misión: el testimonio
evangélico hacia el tercer milenio: La relación hombre-mujer en perspectiva
cristiana*. Buenos Aires: Ediciones Kairós , 2002.

*Cristo, la esperanza para América Latina: Confederación Evangélica
Latinoamericana (CELA II, Lima, 1961)*. Buenos Aires: Conferencia
Evangélica Latinamericana del Rio de la Plata, 1962.

"Cronología de actividades de la Fraternidad Teológica Latinoamericana."
Boletín Teológico 59-60 (1995): 26-33.

*El cristianismo evangélico en la América Latina: informes y resoluciones de la
Primera Conferencia Evangélica Latinoamericana*. Buenos Aires: La
Aurora, 1949.

"El comité de traducción bíblica de la Nueva Versión Internacional." *Iglesia y
Misión* 65 (July – September 1998): no page numbers given.

Fundación Kairós: una comunidad al servicio del reino de Dios y su justicia
(Buenos Aires: Ediciones Kairós, 2002).

"Hacia una cristología misionlógica en los Terceros Mundos." *Boletín Teológico* 8 (1982): 17-20.

Hacia una teología indígena. Lima: Fraternidad Teológica Latinoamericana, n.d.

"The Jarabacoa Declaration." *Transformation* 2, no.1 (1985): 23-28.

"Testimonio evangélico hacia el tercer milenio: palabra, espíritu y misión." *Iglesia y Misión* 74 (2000): 16-18.

"The Valle de Bravo Affirmation" December 5-11, 1988, TMs (photocopy). Latin American Theological Fraternity Archives, Buenos Aires, 1-10.

General Index

Paternoster Biblical Monographs

(All titles uniform with this volume)
Dates in bold are of projected publication

Joseph Abraham
Eve: Accused or Acquitted?
A Reconsideration of Feminist Readings of the Creation Narrative Texts in Genesis 1–3
Two contrary views dominate contemporary feminist biblical scholarship. One finds in the Bible an unequivocal equality between the sexes from the very creation of humanity, whilst the other sees the biblical text as irredeemably patriarchal and androcentric. Dr Abraham enters into dialogue with both camps as well as introducing his own method of approach. An invaluable tool for any one who is interested in this contemporary debate.
2002 / 0-85364-971-5 / xxiv + 272pp

Octavian D. Baban
Mimesis and Luke's on the Road Encounters in Luke-Acts
Luke's Theology of the Way and its Literary Representation
The book argues on theological and literary (mimetic) grounds that Luke's on-the-road encounters, especially those belonging to the post-Easter period, are part of his complex theology of the Way. Jesus' teaching and that of the apostles is presented by Luke as a challenging answer to the Hellenistic reader's thirst for adventure, good literature, and existential paradigms.
2005 */ 1-84227-253-5 / approx. 374pp*

Paul Barker
The Triumph of Grace in Deuteronomy
This book is a textual and theological analysis of the interaction between the sin and faithlessness of Israel and the grace of Yahweh in response, looking especially at Deuteronomy chapters 1–3, 8–10 and 29–30. The author argues that the grace of Yahweh is determinative for the ongoing relationship between Yahweh and Israel and that Deuteronomy anticipates and fully expects Israel to be faithless.
2004 / 1-84227-226-8 / xxii + 270pp

Jonathan F. Bayes
The Weakness of the Law
God's Law and the Christian in New Testament Perspective
A study of the four New Testament books which refer to the law as weak (Acts, Romans, Galatians, Hebrews) leads to a defence of the third use in the Reformed debate about the law in the life of the believer.
2000 / 0-85364-957-X / xii + 244pp

Mark Bonnington
The Antioch Episode of Galatians 2:11-14 in Historical and Cultural Context
The Galatians 2 'incident' in Antioch over table-fellowship suggests significant disagreement between the leading apostles. This book analyses the background to the disagreement by locating the incident within the dynamics of social interaction between Jews and Gentiles. It proposes a new way of understanding the relationship between the individuals and issues involved.

2005 / 1-84227-050-8 / approx. 350pp

David Bostock
A Portrayal of Trust
The Theme of Faith in the Hezekiah Narratives
This study provides detailed and sensitive readings of the Hezekiah narratives (2 Kings 18–20 and Isaiah 36–39) from a theological perspective. It concentrates on the theme of faith, using narrative criticism as its methodology. Attention is paid especially to setting, plot, point of view and characterization within the narratives. A largely positive portrayal of Hezekiah emerges that underlines the importance and relevance of scripture.

2005 / 1-84227-314-0 / approx. 300pp

Mark Bredin
Jesus, Revolutionary of Peace
A Non-violent Christology in the Book of Revelation
This book aims to demonstrate that the figure of Jesus in the Book of Revelation can best be understood as an active non-violent revolutionary.

2003 / 1-84227-153-9 / xviii + 262pp

Robinson Butarbutar
Paul and Conflict Resolution
An Exegetical Study of Paul's Apostolic Paradigm in 1 Corinthians 9
The author sees the apostolic paradigm in 1 Corinthians 9 as part of Paul's unified arguments in 1 Corinthians 8–10 in which he seeks to mediate in the dispute over the issue of food offered to idols. The book also sees its relevance for dispute-resolution today, taking the conflict within the author's church as an example.

2006 / 1-84227-315-9 / approx. 280pp

Daniel J-S Chae
Paul as Apostle to the Gentiles
*His Apostolic Self-awareness and its Influence on the Soteriological Argument
in Romans*
Opposing 'the post-Holocaust interpretation of Romans', Daniel Chae com-
petently demonstrates that Paul argues for the equality of Jew and Gentile in
Romans. Chae's fresh exegetical interpretation is academically outstanding and
spiritually encouraging.
1997 / 0-85364-829-8 / xiv + 378pp

Luke L. Cheung
The Genre, Composition and Hermeneutics of the Epistle of James
The present work examines the employment of the wisdom genre with a certain
compositional structure and the interpretation of the law through the Jesus
tradition of the double love command by the author of the Epistle of James to
serve his purpose in promoting perfection and warning against doubleness
among the eschatologically renewed people of God in the Diaspora.
2003 / 1-84227-062-1 / xvi + 372pp

Youngmo Cho
Spirit and Kingdom in the Writings of Luke and Paul
The relationship between Spirit and Kingdom is a relatively unexplored area in
Lukan and Pauline studies. This book offers a fresh perspective of two biblical
writers on the subject. It explores the difference between Luke's and Paul's
understanding of the Spirit by examining the specific question of the
relationship of the concept of the Spirit to the concept of the Kingdom of God in
each writer.
***2005** / 1-84227-316-7 / approx. 270pp*

Andrew C. Clark
Parallel Lives
The Relation of Paul to the Apostles in the Lucan Perspective
This study of the Peter-Paul parallels in Acts argues that their purpose was to
emphasize the themes of continuity in salvation history and the unity of the
Jewish and Gentile missions. New light is shed on Luke's literary techniques,
partly through a comparison with Plutarch.
2001 / 1-84227-035-4 / xviii + 386pp

Andrew D. Clarke
Secular and Christian Leadership in Corinth
A Socio-Historical and Exegetical Study of 1 Corinthians 1–6
This volume is an investigation into the leadership structures and dynamics of first-century Roman Corinth. These are compared with the practice of leadership in the Corinthian Christian community which are reflected in 1 Corinthians 1–6, and contrasted with Paul's own principles of Christian leadership.
2005 / 1-84227-229-2 / 200pp

Stephen Finamore
God, Order and Chaos
René Girard and the Apocalypse
Readers are often disturbed by the images of destruction in the book of Revelation and unsure why they are unleashed after the exaltation of Jesus. This book examines past approaches to these texts and uses René Girard's theories to revive some old ideas and propose some new ones.
2005 / 1-84227-197-0 / approx. 344pp

David G. Firth
Surrendering Retribution in the Psalms
Responses to Violence in the Individual Complaints
In *Surrendering Retribution in the Psalms*, David Firth examines the ways in which the book of Psalms inculcates a model response to violence through the repetition of standard patterns of prayer. Rather than seeking justification for retributive violence, Psalms encourages not only a surrender of the right of retribution to Yahweh, but also sets limits on the retribution that can be sought in imprecations. Arising initially from the author's experience in South Africa, the possibilities of this model to a particular context of violence is then briefly explored.
2005 / 1-84227-337-X / xviii + 154pp

Scott J. Hafemann
Suffering and Ministry in the Spirit
Paul's Defence of His Ministry in II Corinthians 2:14–3:3
Shedding new light on the way Paul defended his apostleship, the author offers a careful, detailed study of 2 Corinthians 2:14–3:3 linked with other key passages throughout 1 and 2 Corinthians. Demonstrating the unity and coherence of Paul's argument in this passage, the author shows that Paul's suffering served as the vehicle for revealing God's power and glory through the Spirit.
2000 / 0-85364-967-7 / xiv + 262pp

Scott J. Hafemann
Paul, Moses and the History of Israel
The Letter/Spirit Contrast and the Argument from Scripture in 2 Corinthians 3
An exegetical study of the call of Moses, the second giving of the Law (Exodus
32–34), the new covenant, and the prophetic understanding of the history of
Israel in 2 Corinthians 3. Hafemann's work demonstrates Paul's contextual use
of the Old Testament and the essential unity between the Law and the Gospel
within the context of the distinctive ministries of Moses and Paul.
2005 / 1-84227-317-5 / xii + 498pp

Douglas S. McComiskey
Lukan Theology in the Light of the Gospel's Literary Structure
Luke's Gospel was purposefully written with theology embedded in its patterned
literary structure. A critical analysis of this cyclical structure provides new
windows into Luke's interpretation of the individual pericopes comprising the
Gospel and illuminates several of his theological interests.
2004 / 1-84227-148-2 / xviii + 388pp

Stephen Motyer
Your Father the Devil?
A New Approach to John and 'The Jews'
Who are 'the Jews' in John's Gospel? Defending John against the charge of
antisemitism, Motyer argues that, far from demonising the Jews, the Gospel
seeks to present Jesus as 'Good News for Jews' in a late first century setting.
1997 / 0-85364-832-8 / xiv + 260pp

Esther Ng
Reconstructing Christian Origins?
The Feminist Theology of Elizabeth Schüssler Fiorenza: An Evaluation
In a detailed evaluation, the author challenges Elizabeth Schüssler Fiorenza's
reconstruction of early Christian origins and her underlying presuppositions. The
author also presents her own views on women's roles both then and now.
2002 / 1-84227-055-9 / xxiv + 468pp

Robin Parry
Old Testament Story and Christian Ethics
The Rape of Dinah as a Case Study

What is the role of story in ethics and, more particularly, what is the role of Old Testament story in Christian ethics? This book, drawing on the work of contemporary philosophers, argues that narrative is crucial in the ethical shaping of people and, drawing on the work of contemporary Old Testament scholars, that story plays a key role in Old Testament ethics. Parry then argues that when situated in canonical context Old Testament stories can be reappropriated by Christian readers in their own ethical formation. The shocking story of the rape of Dinah and the massacre of the Shechemites provides a fascinating case study for exploring the parameters within which Christian ethical appropriations of Old Testament stories can live.

2004 / 1-84227-210-1 / xx + 350pp

Ian Paul
Power to See the World Anew
The Value of Paul Ricoeur's Hermeneutic of Metaphor in Interpreting the Symbolism of Revelation 12 and 13

This book is a study of the hermeneutics of metaphor of Paul Ricoeur, one of the most important writers on hermeneutics and metaphor of the last century. It sets out the key points of his theory, important criticisms of his work, and how his approach, modified in the light of these criticisms, offers a methodological framework for reading apocalyptic texts.

2006 / 1-84227-056-7 / approx. 350pp

Robert L. Plummer
Paul's Understanding of the Church's Mission
Did the Apostle Paul Expect the Early Christian Communities to Evangelize?

This book engages in a careful study of Paul's letters to determine if the apostle expected the communities to which he wrote to engage in missionary activity. It helpfully summarizes the discussion on this debated issue, judiciously handling contested texts, and provides a way forward in addressing this critical question. While admitting that Paul rarely explicitly commands the communities he founded to evangelize, Plummer amasses significant incidental data to provide a convincing case that Paul did indeed expect his churches to engage in mission activity. Throughout the study, Plummer progressively builds a theological basis for the church's mission that is both distinctively Pauline and compelling.

2006 / 1-84227-333-7 / approx. 324pp

David Powys
'Hell': A Hard Look at a Hard Question
The Fate of the Unrighteous in New Testament Thought
This comprehensive treatment seeks to unlock the original meaning of terms and
phrases long thought to support the traditional doctrine of hell. It concludes that
there is an alternative—one which is more biblical, and which can positively
revive the rationale for Christian mission.
1997 / 0-85364-831-X / xxii + 478pp

Sorin Sabou
Between Horror and Hope
Paul's Metaphorical Language of Death in Romans 6.1-11
This book argues that Paul's metaphorical language of death in Romans 6.1-11
conveys two aspects: horror and hope. The 'horror' aspect is conveyed by the
'crucifixion' language, and the 'hope' aspect by 'burial' language. The life of
the Christian believer is understood, as relationship with sin is concerned ('death
to sin'), between these two realities: horror and hope.
2005 / 1-84227-322-1 / approx. 224pp

Rosalind Selby
The Comical Doctrine
The Epistemology of New Testament Hermeneutics
This book argues that the gospel breaks through postmodernity's critique of
truth and the referential possibilities of textuality with its gift of grace. With a
rigorous, philosophical challenge to modernist and postmodernist assumptions,
Selby offers an alternative epistemology to all who would still read with faith
and with academic credibility.
2005 / 1-84227-212-8 / approx. 350pp

Kiwoong Son
Zion Symbolism in Hebrews
Hebrews 12.18-24 as a Hermeneutical Key to the Epistle
This book challenges the general tendency of understanding the Epistle to the
Hebrews against a Hellenistic background and suggests that the Epistle should
be understood in the light of the Jewish apocalyptic tradition. The author
especially argues for the importance of the theological symbolism of Sinai and
Zion (Heb. 12:18-24) as it provides the Epistle's theological background as well
as the rhetorical basis of the superiority motif of Jesus throughout the Epistle.
2005 / 1-84227-368-X / approx. 280pp

Kevin Walton
Thou Traveller Unknown
The Presence and Absence of God in the Jacob Narrative
The author offers a fresh reading of the story of Jacob in the book of Genesis
through the paradox of divine presence and absence. The work also seeks to
make a contribution to Pentateuchal studies by bringing together a close reading
of the final text with historical critical insights, doing justice to the text's
historical depth, final form and canonical status.
2003 / 1-84227-059-1 / xvi + 238pp

George M. Wieland
The Significance of Salvation
A Study of Salvation Language in the Pastoral Epistles
The language and ideas of salvation pervade the three Pastoral Epistles. This
study offers a close examination of their soteriological statements. In all three
letters the idea of salvation is found to play a vital paraenetic role, but each also
exhibits distinctive soteriological emphases. The results challenge common
assumptions about the Pastoral Epistles as a corpus.
2005 / 1-84227-257-8 / approx. 324pp

Alistair Wilson
When Will These Things Happen?
A Study of Jesus as Judge in Matthew 21–25
This study seeks to allow Matthew's carefully constructed presentation of Jesus
to be given full weight in the modern evaluation of Jesus' eschatology. Careful
analysis of the text of Matthew 21–25 reveals Jesus to be standing firmly in the
Jewish prophetic and wisdom traditions as he proclaims and enacts imminent
judgement on the Jewish authorities then boldly claims the central role in the
final and universal judgement.
2004 / 1-84227-146-6 / xxii + 272pp

Lindsay Wilson
Joseph Wise and Otherwise
The Intersection of Covenant and Wisdom in Genesis 37–50
This book offers a careful literary reading of Genesis 37–50 that argues that the
Joseph story contains both strong covenant themes and many wisdom-like
elements. The connections between the two helps to explore how covenant and
wisdom might intersect in an integrated biblical theology.
2004 / 1-84227-140-7 / xvi + 340pp

Stephen I. Wright
The Voice of Jesus
Studies in the Interpretation of Six Gospel Parables
This literary study considers how the 'voice' of Jesus has been heard in different periods of parable interpretation, and how the categories of figure and trope may help us towards a sensitive reading of the parables today.
2000 / 0-85364-975-8 / xiv + 280pp

Paternoster
9 Holdom Avenue,
Bletchley,
Milton Keynes MK1 1QR,
United Kingdom
Web: www.authenticmedia.co.uk/paternoster

Paternoster Theological Monographs
(All titles uniform with this volume)
Dates in bold are of projected publication

Emil Bartos
Deification in Eastern Orthodox Theology
An Evaluation and Critique of the Theology of Dumitru Staniloae
Bartos studies a fundamental yet neglected aspect of Orthodox theology: deification. By examining the doctrines of anthropology, christology, soteriology and ecclesiology as they relate to deification, he provides an important contribution to contemporary dialogue between Eastern and Western theologians.
1999 / 0-85364-956-1 / xii + 370pp

Graham Buxton
The Trinity, Creation and Pastoral Ministry
Imaging the Perichoretic God
In this book the author proposes a three-way conversation between theology, science and pastoral ministry. His approach draws on a Trinitarian understanding of God as a relational being of love, whose life 'spills over' into all created reality, human and non-human. By locating human meaning and purpose within God's 'creation-community' this book offers the possibility of a transforming engagement between those in pastoral ministry and the scientific community.
2005 */ 1-84227-369-8 / approx. 380 pp*

Iain D. Campbell
Fixing the Indemnity
The Life and Work of George Adam Smith
When Old Testament scholar George Adam Smith (1856–1942) delivered the Lyman Beecher lectures at Yale University in 1899, he confidently declared that 'modern criticism has won its war against traditional theories. It only remains to fix the amount of the indemnity.' In this biography, Iain D. Campbell assesses Smith's critical approach to the Old Testament and evaluates its consequences, showing that Smith's life and work still raises questions about the relationship between biblical scholarship and evangelical faith.
2004 / 1-84227-228-4 / xx + 256pp

Tim Chester
Mission and the Coming of God
Eschatology, the Trinity and Mission in the Theology of Jürgen Moltmann
This book explores the theology and missiology of the influential contemporary theologian, Jürgen Moltmann. It highlights the important contribution Moltmann has made while offering a critique of his thought from an evangelical perspective. In so doing, it touches on pertinent issues for evangelical missiology. The conclusion takes Calvin as a starting point, proposing 'an eschatology of the cross' which offers a critique of the over-realised eschatologies in liberation theology and certain forms of evangelicalism.
2006 / 1-84227-320-5 / approx. 224pp

Sylvia Wilkey Collinson
Making Disciples
The Significance of Jesus' Educational Strategy for Today's Church
This study examines the biblical practice of discipling, formulates a definition, and makes comparisons with modern models of education. A recommendation is made for greater attention to its practice today.
2004 / 1-84227-116-4 / xiv + 278pp

Darrell Cosden
A Theology of Work
Work and the New Creation
Through dialogue with Moltmann, Pope John Paul II and others, this book develops a genitive 'theology of work', presenting a theological definition of work and a model for a theological ethics of work that shows work's nature, value and meaning now and eschatologically. Work is shown to be a transformative activity consisting of three dynamically inter-related dimensions: the instrumental, relational and ontological.
2005 / 1-84227-332-9 / xvi + 208pp

Stephen M. Dunning
The Crisis and the Quest
A Kierkegaardian Reading of Charles Williams
Employing Kierkegaardian categories and analysis, this study investigates both the central crisis in Charles Williams's authorship between hermetism and Christianity (Kierkegaard's Religions A and B), and the quest to resolve this crisis, a quest that ultimately presses the bounds of orthodoxy.
2000 / 0-85364-985-5 / xxiv + 254pp

Keith Ferdinando
The Triumph of Christ in African Perspective
A Study of Demonology and Redemption in the African Context
The book explores the implications of the gospel for traditional African fears of occult aggression. It analyses such traditional approaches to suffering and biblical responses to fears of demonic evil, concluding with an evaluation of African beliefs from the perspective of the gospel.
1999 / 0-85364-830-1 / xviii + 450pp

Andrew Goddard
Living the Word, Resisting the World
The Life and Thought of Jacques Ellul
This work offers a definitive study of both the life and thought of the French Reformed thinker Jacques Ellul (1912-1994). It will prove an indispensable resource for those interested in this influential theologian and sociologist and for Christian ethics and political thought generally.
2002 / 1-84227-053-2 / xxiv + 378pp

David Hilborn
The Words of our Lips
Language-Use in Free Church Worship
Studies of liturgical language have tended to focus on the written canons of Roman Catholic and Anglican communities. By contrast, David Hilborn analyses the more extemporary approach of English Nonconformity. Drawing on recent developments in linguistic pragmatics, he explores similarities and differences between 'fixed' and 'free' worship, and argues for the interdependence of each.
2006 */ 0-85364-977-4 / approx. 350pp*

Roger Hitching
The Church and Deaf People
A Study of Identity, Communication and Relationships with Special Reference to the Ecclesiology of Jürgen Moltmann
In *The Church and Deaf People* Roger Hitching sensitively examines the history and present experience of deaf people and finds similarities between aspects of sign language and Moltmann's theological method that 'open up' new ways of understanding theological concepts.
2003 / 1-84227-222-5 / xxii + 236pp

John G. Kelly
One God, One People
The Differentiated Unity of the People of God in the Theology of
Jürgen Moltmann
The author expounds and critiques Moltmann's doctrine of God and highlights
the systematic connections between it and Moltmann's influential discussion of
Israel. He then proposes a fresh approach to Jewish–Christian relations building
on Moltmann's work using insights from Habermas and Rawls.
2005 / 0-85346-969-3 / approx. 350pp

Mark F.W. Lovatt
Confronting the Will-to-Power
A Reconsideration of the Theology of Reinhold Niebuhr
Confronting the Will-to-Power is an analysis of the theology of Reinhold
Niebuhr, arguing that his work is an attempt to identify, and provide a practical
theological answer to, the existence and nature of human evil.
2001 / 1-84227-054-0 / xviii + 216pp

Neil B. MacDonald
Karl Barth and the Strange New World within the Bible
Barth, Wittgenstein, and the Metadilemmas of the Enlightenment
Barth's discovery of the strange new world within the Bible is examined in the
context of Kant, Hume, Overbeck, and, most importantly, Wittgenstein.
MacDonald covers some fundamental issues in theology today: epistemology,
the final form of the text and biblical truth-claims.
2000 / 0-85364-970-7 / xxvi + 374pp

Keith A. Mascord
Alvin Plantinga and Christian Apologetics
This book draws together the contributions of the philosopher Alvin Plantinga to
the major contemporary challenges to Christian belief, highlighting in particular
his ground-breaking work in epistemology and the problem of evil. Plantinga's
theory that both theistic and Christian belief is warrantedly basic is explored and
critiqued, and an assessment offered as to the significance of his work for
apologetic theory and practice.
2005 / 1-84227-256-X / approx. 304pp

Gillian McCulloch
The Deconstruction of Dualism in Theology
With Reference to Ecofeminist Theology and New Age Spirituality
This book challenges eco-theological anti-dualism in Christian theology, arguing that dualism has a twofold function in Christian religious discourse. Firstly, it enables us to express the discontinuities and divisions that are part of the process of reality. Secondly, dualistic language allows us to express the mysteries of divine transcendence/immanence and the survival of the soul without collapsing into monism and materialism, both of which are problematic for Christian epistemology.
2002 / 1-84227-044-3 / xii + 282pp

Leslie McCurdy
Attributes and Atonement
The Holy Love of God in the Theology of P.T. Forsyth
Attributes and Atonement is an intriguing full-length study of P.T. Forsyth's doctrine of the cross as it relates particularly to God's holy love. It includes an unparalleled bibliography of both primary and secondary material relating to Forsyth.
1999 / 0-85364-833-6 / xiv + 328pp

Nozomu Miyahira
Towards a Theology of the Concord of God
A Japanese Perspective on the Trinity
This book introduces a new Japanese theology and a unique Trinitarian formula based on the Japanese intellectual climate: three betweennesses and one concord. It also presents a new interpretation of the Trinity, a co-subordinationism, which is in line with orthodox Trinitarianism; each single person of the Trinity is eternally and equally subordinate (or serviceable) to the other persons, so that they retain the mutual dynamic equality.
2000 / 0-85364-863-8 / xiv + 256pp

Eddy José Muskus
The Origins and Early Development of Liberation Theology in Latin America
With Particular Reference to Gustavo Gutiérrez
This work challenges the fundamental premise of Liberation Theology, 'opting for the poor', and its claim that Christ is found in them. It also argues that Liberation Theology emerged as a direct result of the failure of the Roman Catholic Church in Latin America.
2002 / 0-85364-974-X / xiv + 296pp

Jim Purves
The Triune God and the Charismatic Movement
A Critical Appraisal from a Scottish Perspective
All emotion and no theology? Or a fundamental challenge to reappraise and
realign our trinitarian theology in the light of Christian experience? This study
of charismatic renewal as it found expression within Scotland at the end of the
twentieth century evaluates the use of Patristic, Reformed and contemporary
models of the Trinity in explaining the workings of the Holy Spirit.
2004 / 1-84227-321-3 / xxiv + 246pp

Anna Robbins
Methods in the Madness
Diversity in Twentieth-Century Christian Social Ethics
The author compares the ethical methods of Walter Rauschenbusch, Reinhold
Niebuhr and others. She argues that unless Christians are clear about the ways
that theology and philosophy are expressed practically they may lose the ability
to discuss social ethics across contexts, let alone reach effective agreements.
2004 / 1-84227-211-X / xx + 294pp

Ed Rybarczyk
Beyond Salvation
Eastern Orthodoxy and Classical Pentecostalism on Becoming Like Christ
At first glance eastern Orthodoxy and classical Pentecostalism seem quite
distinct. This ground-breaking study shows they share much in common,
especially as it concerns the experiential elements of following Christ. Both
traditions assert that authentic Christianity transcends the wooden categories of
modernism.
2004 / 1-84227-144-X / xii + 356pp

Signe Sandsmark
Is World View Neutral Education Possible and Desirable?
A Christian Response to Liberal Arguments
(Published jointly with The Stapleford Centre)
This book discusses reasons for belief in world view neutrality, and argues that
'neutral' education will have a hidden, but strong world view influence. It
discusses the place for Christian education in the common school.
2000 / 0-85364-973-1 / xiv + 182pp

Hazel Sherman
Reading Zechariah
The Allegorical Tradition of Biblical Interpretation through the Commentary of
Didymus the Blind and Theodore of Mopsuestia
A close reading of the commentary on Zechariah by Didymus the Blind
alongside that of Theodore of Mopsuestia suggests that popular categorising of
Antiochene and Alexandrian biblical exegesis as 'historical' or 'allegorical' is
inadequate and misleading.
2005 / 1-84227-213-6 / approx. 280pp

Andrew Sloane
On Being a Christian in the Academy
Nicholas Wolterstorff and the Practice of Christian Scholarship
An exposition and critical appraisal of Nicholas Wolterstorff's epistemology in
the light of the philosophy of science, and an application of his thought to the
practice of Christian scholarship.
2003 / 1-84227-058-3 / xvi + 274pp

Damon W.K. So
Jesus' Revelation of His Father
A Narrative-Conceptual Study of the Trinity with Special Reference to
Karl Barth
This book explores the trinitarian dynamics in the context of Jesus' revelation of
his Father in his earthly ministry with references to key passages in Matthew's
Gospel. It develops from the exegeses of these passages a non-linear concept of
revelation which links Jesus' communion with his Father to his revelatory words
and actions through a nuanced understanding of the Holy Spirit, with references
to K. Barth, G.W.H. Lampe, J.D.G. Dunn and E. Irving.
2005 / 1-84227-323-X / approx. 380pp

Daniel Strange
The Possibility of Salvation Among the Unevangelised
An Analysis of Inclusivism in Recent Evangelical Theology
For evangelical theologians the 'fate of the unevangelised' impinges upon
fundamental tenets of evangelical identity. The position known as 'inclusivism',
defined by the belief that the unevangelised can be ontologically saved by Christ
whilst being epistemologically unaware of him, has been defended most
vigorously by the Canadian evangelical Clark H. Pinnock. Through a detailed
analysis and critique of Pinnock's work, this book examines a cluster of issues
surrounding the unevangelised and its implications for christology, soteriology
and the doctrine of revelation.
2002 / 1-84227-047-8 / xviii + 362pp

Scott Swain
God According to the Gospel
Biblical Narrative and the Identity of God in the Theology of Robert W. Jenson
Robert W. Jenson is one of the leading voices in contemporary Trinitarian theology. His boldest contribution in this area concerns his use of biblical narrative both to ground and explicate the Christian doctrine of God. *God According to the Gospel* critically examines Jenson's proposal and suggests an alternative way of reading the biblical portrayal of the triune God.
2006 / 1-84227-258-6 / approx. 180pp

Justyn Terry
The Justifying Judgement of God
A Reassessment of the Place of Judgement in the Saving Work of Christ
The argument of this book is that judgement, understood as the whole process of bringing justice, is the primary metaphor of atonement, with others, such as victory, redemption and sacrifice, subordinate to it. Judgement also provides the proper context for understanding penal substitution and the call to repentance, baptism, eucharist and holiness.
2005 / 1-84227-370-1 / approx. 274 pp

Graham Tomlin
The Power of the Cross
Theology and the Death of Christ in Paul, Luther and Pascal
This book explores the theology of the cross in St Paul, Luther and Pascal. It offers new perspectives on the theology of each, and some implications for the nature of power, apologetics, theology and church life in a postmodern context.
1999 / 0-85364-984-7 / xiv + 344pp

Adonis Vidu
Postliberal Theological Method
A Critical Study
The postliberal theology of Hans Frei, George Lindbeck, Ronald Thiemann, John Milbank and others is one of the more influential contemporary options. This book focuses on several aspects pertaining to its theological method, specifically its understanding of background, hermeneutics, epistemic justification, ontology, the nature of doctrine and, finally, Christological method.
2005 / 1-84227-395-7 / approx. 324pp

Graham J. Watts
Revelation and the Spirit
A Comparative Study of the Relationship between the Doctrine of Revelation
and Pneumatology in the Theology of Eberhard Jüngel and of
Wolfhart Pannenberg
The relationship between revelation and pneumatology is relatively unexplored. This approach offers a fresh angle on two important twentieth century theologians and raises pneumatological questions which are theologically crucial and relevant to mission in a postmodern culture.

2005 / 1-84227-104-0 / xxii + 232pp

Nigel G. Wright
Disavowing Constantine
Mission, Church and the Social Order in the Theologies of John Howard Yoder
and Jürgen Moltmann
This book is a timely restatement of a radical theology of church and state in the Anabaptist and Baptist tradition. Dr Wright constructs his argument in dialogue and debate with Yoder and Moltmann, major contributors to a free church perspective.

2000 / 0-85364-978-2 / xvi + 252pp

Paternoster:
thinking faith

Paternoster
9 Holdom Avenue,
Bletchley,
Milton Keynes MK1 1QR,
United Kingdom
Web: www.authenticmedia.co.uk/paternoster

July 2005